Death and Bereavement

Death and Bereavement

The psychological, religious and cultural interfaces

Second Edition

Dewi Rees MD FRCGP

Formerly Medical Director,
St Mary's Hospice, Birmingham,
and Senior Clinical Lecturer,
University of Birmingham

W

WHURR PUBLISHERS
LONDON AND PHILADELPHIA

© 2001 Dewi Rees by arrangement with Mark Paterson
First edition published 1997
Whurr Publishers Ltd
19b Compton Terrace, London N1 2UN, England and
325 Chestnut Street, Philadelphia PA 19106, USA

Reprinted 2001 and 2005

British Library Cataloguing in Publication Data
A catalogue record for this book is available from the
British Library.

ISBN 1 86156 223 3

Printed and bound in the UK by Athenaeum Press Ltd,
Gateshead, Tyne and Wear

Contents

Foreword

In my long public life nothing has held greater challenge for me than having to deal with families who have a loved one suffering from terminal illness, or who are immersed in grief following bereavement. It is a truism that the more we love, the greater is our suffering at a time of bereavement.

However strong our faith in life after death may be, the sense of loss that accompanies bereavement is something deeply personal: no one can bear it for us.

When I served as a Minister in the Welsh Office I had the shattering experience of being the government's representative during the cruel Aberfan tragedy when a school was smothered by a coal waste tip sliding down the mountainside. Over a hundred children died. I shall never forget stepping over the bodies of little boys and girls as rescuers dragged them from under the sludge.

I visited every home that had suffered sudden bereavement, and the concentrated agony of weeping families has left a scar on me for the rest of my life.

I am fortunate that I am fortified by a faith in the Risen Lord Jesus that has given me an inner peace when, in my own illnesses, death has apparently been close at hand.

In this sensitive book Dr Dewi Rees tackles, head on, the psychological, religious, and cultural issues involved for all who deal with suffering and anxious families.

Dr Rees has long years of experience as a practising doctor of medicine. His scholarship, his Christian faith, and his caring nature, all combine to make this book a source of inspired guidance for all of us who try to care for families and for individuals confronted with the crisis of bereavement.

George Tonypandy
Speaker of the House of Commons, 1976–1983

Preface to the first edition

When Aldous Huxley wrote that 'One of the most extraordinary and gratuitous pieces of twentieth century vanity is that nobody knew anything about psychology before the days of Freud', it is possible that he was being deliberately provocative.[1] But there is more than an element of truth in the statement, and this is most apparent in our ideas about death and bereavement. We have, during the past century, greatly enlarged our understanding of the way people respond to the inner crises that are induced by the death of a loved one but we tend not to consider it within its wider social and cultural contexts. Nor do we pay much attention to the particular insights provided by the religious traditions of the world, even though death, and people's response to it, is central to religious teachings.

Readers now have a wide choice of books that deal with death and bereavement. These range from textbooks on bereavement counselling to simple works written for children. They all tend, however, to be specialized both in terms of content and targeted reader, whether this be nurse, counsellor or bereaved parent.

This book is intended to be innovative in the following ways. First, it sets out to be comprehensive by presenting the psychology of death and bereavement in a single volume and by doing so in depth. Second, these subjects are placed within the cultural contexts of the major world religions and their associated mourning and funeral customs. Third, it includes certain aspects of death, such as deathbed visions and near-death experiences, which are the concern of parapsychologists and which are not normally included in books dealing with the psychology of death or bereavement. Fourth, and most importantly, it has a central theme – the significance that people ascribe to death, both within their religious teachings and beyond it, and why this should be so.

The book is not written for a particular specialist group but for the educated reader, who has an interest in, or professional involvement with, bereavement and death, and in the significance that can be ascribed to the latter. It contains a large number of case histories based on my own practice as a general practitioner, hospice doctor and university lecturer, and I have, of course, tried to ensure that no living person can be identified. I have also tried to make the book as interesting and readable as possible.

Many people have helped in the writing of this book, most especially my wife and it would not have been completed without her help. Professor Moelwyn Merchant – author, sculptor, priest and professor of English, has shown a continued interest in its development and has provided ideas that are included in the final chapter. Lord Tonypandy wrote a most moving foreword, and one obviously based on his own experiences. Although he was best known as an outstanding Speaker of the House of Commons he achieved eminence in other fields – in education, in government, as a Methodist lay-preacher and in his work for Cancer Relief. I am most grateful to them, and to the many people I have not named, for their help with this book.

Dewi Rees

Preface to the second edition

A new edition gives the author a chance to correct any minor errors and to update the contents of his book. This has been done. More importantly, three new chapters have been included in this second edition of *Death and Bereavement*. Also the chapters entitled 'Reactions to Bereavement' and 'Suicide' have been largely rewritten: they are now presented as four chapters 'Bereavement: the basics' – 'Bereavement: medical and social issues' – 'Suicide' – and 'Euthanasia and assisted suicide'. This has allowed for a wider and more detailed survey of these issues.

With hindsight, it seems strange that a book dealing with death in its widest context says nothing about the scientific and legal perspectives of the subject. This omission has been rectified in a new opening chapter 'What is death?' Another new chapter looks at the psychological insights provided by William Shakespeare. Aldous Huxley provided its justification when he wrote "One of the most extraordinary and gratuitous pieces of twentieth century vanity, is that nobody knew anything about psychology before the days of Freud." The truth of this statement is reflected in Shakespeare's plays and sonnets, which Freud rated highly and studied carefully. This chapter provides a literary counterpoint to the more prosaic writings of modern psychologists. The third new chapter is entitled 'New religions and new sects'. This deals with the beliefs and customs of minority groups – the Bahá'ís, Jehovah's Witnesses, Mormons, Quakers, Spiritualists and Seventh-day Adventists, people with their own deeply held views on death and bereavement from which many of us can perhaps gain new insights.

A common assessment given in reviews of the first edition is that the book is 'accessible', even 'highly accessible'. I find this pleasing because one of my stated aims was to make the book interesting and readable, and this seems to have been achieved. I sometimes tell my friends that the best way to read *Death and Bereavement* is to start with those chapters that catch the eye, and not to read it sequentially from beginning to end. This method works well, as each chapter – while forming part of a coherent whole – is an entity in itself. I am mindful of Jung's advice that the best way to read a Buddhist manuscript is to start at the end, where the most important statements are to be found, and I think this applies to other non-fictional writings as well.

Finally, I would like to record again my gratitude for the support given by two old friends, now deceased, Viscount Tonypandy and Professor Merchant. In particular, I would like to dedicate the chapter on Shakespeare to that ebullient Shakespearean scholar, Professor Moelwyn Merchant, who thought it had merit.

Dewi Rees
January 2001

Chapter 1
What is Death?

Shake off this drowsy sleep, death's counterfeit
and look on death itself.

Macbeth

Philosophers may debate the significance of life and death, but scientific criteria are needed to distinguish between them. The most useful biological descriptions of life are those that stress function, with death being described usually as the irreversible loss of function. This applies whether death is considered in terms of molecular biology, physiology or genetic potential. At its most basic level, life is the state characterized by metabolism — the chemical changes in the living cell by which energy is provided for vital processes. Death is the cessation of metabolic processes.[1]

In complex organisms such as man, these metabolic processes do not cease to function simultaneously, they cease at different moments in different tissues. Consequently, scientists see death as a process and not as a sharply delineated event. This is in contrast to the common view of death, which looks upon dying as a process and death as the final event. Putrefaction of the corpse is the most certain indicator that a person has died, but practical considerations require that the death of a human being should be ascertained before this occurs. This means that exact criteria have to be established for determining death and these criteria have to be acceptable to doctors, the judiciary and the public at large.

The Point of No Return

When someone is dying, that person's condition deteriorates until he or she reaches 'a point of no return', which is death itself. The method used for determining this point of no return varies between

1

different cultures. Some may be content with the observation that breathing has stopped. Others will want to substantiate this observation by noting that the heart has stopped beating. Surgeons, who transplant organs from the dead to a living person, rely on criteria that establish the presence of brainstem death. Whatever method is used, an agreed standard for determining the death of an individual is essential. It is necessary for three reasons. First, it is important for the deceased that their death should be clearly established before they are buried or cremated. Second, the relatives need to be sure that the person is really dead before they can accept the loss and arrange for the disposal of the corpse. Third, this knowledge is of importance to other interested parties: these include the registrar of deaths, lawyers, the police and anyone who might benefit from the deceased's possessions, including someone waiting for a heart or kidney transplant.

Although death usually implies the dissolution of the whole body, it may affect just part of it leaving the rest viable. The irreversible loss of function, or death, of part of the body is referred to as 'localized death'. It may occur at the cellular level, as when a red blood corpuscle disintegrates, or in a more complex part of the body as in the case of a gangrenous limb. Neither the disintegrated red blood corpuscle nor the gangrenous limb can regain their ability to function normally. Both have passed their point of no return and are functionally dead.

Cell Death

The cell is the simplest living structure. It may exist as an independent entity, such as a bacillus, or like a white blood corpuscle as part of a more complex system. The microbiologist in particular is interested in cell death but it has theoretical and practical significance in other disciplines. A cell dies either from an external cause or because the death was programmed from within the cell itself. External causes of cell death include excessive heat (hyperthermia), lack of oxygen (anoxia), immunological attack and exposure to various toxins. The onset of cell death can be postponed by cooling and hastened by heating. Most tissues die when they are subjected to temperatures exceeding 45°C. The irreversible effect of heat can be observed whenever a fresh, shelled egg is dropped into hot water and poached. When this is done the protein coagulates, new protein can no longer be synthesized and all biological functions cease.

Anoxia is a common cause of cell death. The ability of cells to withstand oxygen deprivation, and still remain viable, depends on the organs of which they are a part. A satisfactory skin graft can be obtained from a corpse 24 hours after the heart has stopped beating. A bone graft can be taken 48 hours and a viable arterial graft 72 hours after cessation of heart beat. The phylogenetically younger parts of the central nervous system have a greater oxygen need than those that developed at an earlier stage of evolution. The oxygen need and susceptibility to death from anoxia is therefore greater in the upper brain – the cerebrum – than in the brainstem and spinal cord. When the brain experiences anoxia as a result of cardio-respiratory arrest, death of the upper brain precedes death of the brainstem. Consequently if the brainstem has died, the upper brain must also be dead. This fact enables brainstem death to be taken as the ultimate point of no return and an absolute criterion for death in man.

Programmed Cell Death

Programmed cell death is not caused by any external agent. It occurs because each cell seems to be designed to destroy itself at some phase of its life. The result is that the cell disintegrates instead of continuing to multiply as in normal growth. Programmed cell death has an important role in the development of the embryo and it is essential if a complex organ is to reach its final, normal form. In the human embryo, waves of genetically determined cell death are needed for the proper development of organs, for example, for the formation of the convolutions that increase the surface area of the brain. Until the fourth month of embryonic life, the surface of the human brain is smooth. Thereafter, local depressions become apparent and these extend over the surface to form grooves or sulci. The change is effected by a programme of localized cell death occurring at precise moments during the embryo's development. A similar process is necessary for the formation of the digits.

In animals, programmed cell death is responsible for the meta-morphoses that affect tadpoles and caterpillars. It may also explain why some species, such as salmon and spiders, die within a predictable time after mating or reproduction.[2] Programmed cell death has been observed in some cells of untreated cancer and in normally involuting tissues such as the thymus gland. It may also have a role in the process of ageing, with cells being designed to die after a certain number of mitotic divisions.

Brainstem Death

The diagnosis of death is usually determined by the cessation of heart beat and respiration for at least five minutes. These simple criteria were adequate until the 1940s when the introduction of positive pressure ventilation into anaesthetic practice enabled people to be kept alive when normal respiration had been halted by disease or drugs. Various consequences accompanied this advance in anaesthetic practice. Surgeons were able to operate within the thorax with increasing ease and develop the techniques necessary for complex operations on the heart and lungs; and people with severe brain damage, who would otherwise have died from respiratory arrest, could be kept alive indefinitely, albeit in a vegetative state. A wider aspect of positive pressure ventilation was the introduction, in the 1960s, of mouth-to-mouth respiration for resuscitating people whose lives were threatened as a result of drowning and cardiac arrest. This technique has resulted in the apparently dead being restored to life in unprecedented numbers.

All of these developments had important legal, ethical and social implications; they also made the diagnosis of death less certain than formerly. Society was again confronted with a problem mentioned by Pliny the Elder 2000 years ago: 'that so uncertain are men's judgements that they cannot determine even death itself.' The lack of consensus on this point in the 1960s led to review by expert committees in the USA and in the UK, and new guidelines were formulated. The clinical criteria for determining brainstem death, agreed by these experts, have been accepted by doctors and most legislatures, throughout the world. The most important result is that doctors, relatives and lawyers now know when it is morally and legally proper to stop artificial respiration in a severely brain damaged individual. This knowledge also enables surgeons to remove functioning organs from corpses for transplantation into people who would probably die if a replacement heart, kidney or other vital organ were not provided.

Brainstem death has been described as a physiological decapitation caused by anoxia. It is the ultimate point of no return for the individual. Its diagnosis is not technically difficult and it is usually made on purely clinical grounds. Most countries insist that the relevant examinations are made by physicians of appropriate seniority. In the UK, two doctors must agree on the diagnosis of brainstem death before stopping artificial respiration and one of these must be the consultant in charge of the case. The possibility of death is not

considered until at least six hours after the onset of coma, or if this
was caused by cardiac arrest 24 hours after the circulation has been
restored. The tests are usually repeated at least once to exclude
observer error. Body temperature must first be recorded and it
should not be less than 35 °C when the tests are carried out. The
clinical criteria that enable a diagnosis of brainstem death to be
made are given at the end of this chapter.

Organ Transplants

The diagnosis of brainstem death makes it ethically and legally
permissible to stop the mechanical ventilation of a comatose patient.
It does not automatically mean that an organ can be removed for
transplantation into another person. The authority for such an
action usually depends on decisions taken by the deceased's relatives.
The legal requirements for consent to remove organs differ between
countries. In France, transplant organs are routinely removed from a
suitable cadaver unless the family clearly withholds its consent. The
reverse situation applies in the UK, where organs can be removed
only with the prior written consent of the relatives.

No payment may be made for an organ that is to be transplanted
in the UK, and this includes the giving of blood by a live donor.
Different ethical considerations apply in other countries. In India,
impoverished people are paid to donate their organs and more than
2,000 kidneys, usually from living donors, are sold each year. In
China, where capital punishment is still widely enforced and many
people are executed each year, organs are commonly removed from
the bodies of these criminals without the consent or knowledge of the
relatives. Execution is usually effected by a single revolver shot to the
back of the head. If an organ is needed and a suitable one is available, this is removed in an ambulance at the site of execution and
transferred to the transplant hospital. The Chinese consider this to
be ethically correct. In their opinion, the crimes for which people
have been sentenced to death are rendered less blameworthy if the
criminals have helped other people in this way. Many of these organs
are sold to expatriate Chinese who travel to the People's Republic of
China for the operations.[3] There is a similar approach in Taiwan
where transplant organs have been regularly removed from executed
criminals since October 1990.[4]

The Japanese were unexpectedly reluctant to use the diagnosis of
brainstem death and transplant organs from the dead to the living.
Their attitude was affected by an incident in 1962, when Japan's first

heart transplant was performed. The heart was taken from a student who had drowned and given to an 18-year-old boy who died 81 days later. After the death it was suggested that the donor had not been properly diagnosed as dead by the surgical transplant team. The leading surgeon was charged with murder although the case was later dropped. For many years afterwards the removal of organs from people diagnosed as brainstem dead was not acceptable in Japan.[5] The situation changed only in 1992 when, after a prolonged enquiry, a special commission recommended that a diagnosis of brainstem death should be accepted to increase the number of potential organ donors, and this recommendation was approved by the government.

Ethical Considerations

In Denmark the acceptance of brainstem death as a criterion was delayed until 1991. There the issue was largely a philosophical one. Which was ethically more important: people's concept of death or its scientific diagnosis? If the concept of death was of primary importance, then it was argued that the cessation of heartbeat should remain the criterion of death for two interrelated reasons. First, because it is a traditionally recognized sign of death that is understood and accepted by most people. Second, because family and friends are less likely to have difficulty in accepting that a loved one has died if they know that the heart had stopped beating.

This viewpoint was advanced by the Danish Council of Ethics, but was eventually rejected by the Danish Parliament, and a diagnosis of death that is based only on brainstem criteria is now legally acceptable in Denmark. Paradoxically, if the proposal put forward by the Council of Ethics had been accepted, organs could still have been removed for transplantation even when the person was only brain dead, provided the relatives gave their consent. The Danish Council of Ethics reached this conclusion in the following way. It accepted that brain death is the point of no return that enables organs to be removed, but considered for ethical and cultural reasons that cessation of heart beat is a more final indication of death itself.[6] This may seem to be a casuistic nicety but it indicates the type of philosophical problems that arise in discussions on death.

Conclusion

It is now generally accepted that brainstem death signifies that a human life has ended. In clinical practice decisions concerning life support regimes and organ transplants are thereby simplified. Though certain legal and medical problems are solved by the acceptance of brainstem death, the latter does not provide answers to the fundamental questions, what is death, what is its significance and what conditions should be provided for the dying and their relatives? As the Danish Council of Ethics insisted, there is an important difference between the concept and the criterion of death. The latter merely establishes the fact of death, people's concept of death includes the significance they ascribe to it.

Medical science may define the moment of death but it is not competent to assess the ethical aspect of death in all its religious, moral and human complexity. The criterion of death has been clearly defined and is generally accepted but a concept of death that includes an understanding of its meaning for the individual and society as a whole has not yet been so clearly determined. One of the obstacles to a unified understanding of the significance of death is the lack of agreement on whether human life ceases abruptly at the moment of death, or whether having passed through the 'gateway of death' it continues in some different mode, perhaps indefinitely.

The brainstem criteria are not of necessity in conflict with traditional religious and ethical views on what constitutes death, as was suggested by the Danish Council of Ethics. Most religious traditions hold that the two invariable attributes of death are the loss of the breath of life and the departure of the soul from the body – the soul being recognized as a conscious soul. If a medical interpretation of these attributes is allowed, we may say that the loss of the breath of life is irreversible apnoea – the complete cessation of respiration and that the departure of the soul from the body is the irreversible loss of consciousness.[7] Irreversible apnoea and irreversible loss of consciousness are both essential elements of the diagnosis of brainstem death.

Criteria for Brainstem Death

The diagnosis must be made by two doctors of appropriate seniority. One must be the consultant in charge of the patient. Neither doctor should be a member of any surgical transplant team that may wish to use an organ removed from the patient. The tests should be repeated at least once to exclude observer error. The temperature of the body should first be recorded and it should not be less than 35 °C. Before considering a diagnosis of brainstem death, all the following criteria must coexist.

1. The patient is deeply comatose, and the coma is not due to drugs, primary hypothermia or metabolic or endocrine disturbance.
2. The patient is being maintained on a ventilator because spontaneous respiration had previously been inadequate or had ceased altogether.
3. There is no doubt that the patient's condition is due to irremediable, severe brain damage.

The following criteria are used to prove brainstem death, with all the criteria needing to be present.

1. Fixed pupils that do not respond to sharp changes in light.
2. No corneal reflex.
3. Absent ventriculo-ocular reflexes. These are absent when no eye movement occurs after the slow injection of 20 ml ice cold water into each ear.
4. No motor response to deep pain.
5. No gag response to tracheal suction.
6. No respiratory movement occurring when mechanical ventilation is stopped long enough to ensure that the arterial carbon dioxide tension rises above the threshold for stimulating respiration; that is the PCO_2 should be greater than 6.6 kPa after the administration of 5% CO_2 in oxygen through the ventilator.

Chapter 2
Western Attitudes
to Death

But that the dread of something after death,
The undiscovered country from whose bourne
No traveller returns, puzzles the will
And makes us rather bear those ills we have
Than fly to others that we know not of?

Hamlet

Introduction

The subject of death has always troubled the human imagination, and men and women have conjured up many images of what might lie beyond it. Its uncertain outcome continues to cause problems for the individual psyche today, and this was highlighted in two brief discussions I had quite recently. The first took place in a prison where a young offender spoke of his fear of death and in particular of burning in hell. He mentioned this fear after another young inmate had slashed his wrists in an unsuccessful attempt to commit suicide.

The next day I had a short chat with an elderly American in Coventry Cathedral, where I help as a voluntary guide. Perhaps it was the ambience of the building that encouraged him to talk of his religious scepticism and of the inadequate religious faith displayed by some clergy. Anyway, he chose to illustrate the latter point by saying how a clergyman friend, after recovering from a coronary thrombosis, had told him that he had almost died and was lucky to be still alive. He found this latter remark somewhat typical of his clergy acquaintances but inconsistent with their role as Christian ministers and professional advocates of a belief in a loving and merciful god, and of eternal bliss in the hereafter.

Death is one of the great mysteries of life and it is not surprising if people's attitude towards it is diverse and ambiguous. The significance people ascribe to it ranges within two main polarities of belief.

At one end of the spectrum is the concept that death is the end of life, and apart from dust and ashes nothing exists of the individual person thereafter. This is a minority viewpoint but one with a long tradition among free thinkers. It was the view held by the Sophists and Epicureans in Ancient Greece, and by Indian philosophers in medieval times, and is a main tenet of secular humanism in our own era. Sigmund Freud, the founder of modern psychology, held firmly to this belief, and when he could no longer tolerate the pain and burden of life gladly accepted the terminal relief provided by his friend and physician, Dr Max Schur.[1]

The opposing view is held by those who believe that people have a spiritual as well as a physical dimension to their lives. This has been the traditional belief of most peoples in all continents – ranging from the North America of the Sioux Indian and Eskimo, across the veld of the African Bushman to the lands of the Japanese samurai and Chinese peasant – though communist regimes have provided an important exception to this general finding. It is the viewpoint that was favoured by Carl Jung and is most clearly expressed in the teachings of the world religions, whether they are of Eastern or Western origin.

Religious teachings are relevant to a book dealing with the psychology of death and bereavement for four reasons. First, they are important formulators of popular opinion. Second, the underlying beliefs are so widely held that any discussion on the subject of death would be incomplete without considering them closely. Third, although based on ancient traditions and teachings they have an intrinsic dynamism that enables them to be modified in line with current human needs. Fourth, present psychological theories and beliefs have not evolved in a conceptual vacuum. They have been developed on a substratum of ideas that can be traced back over hundreds and thousands of years. It is important therefore that we should have some understanding of the religious beliefs of people and how these arose and evolved. We shall start with the beliefs held by the Ancient Egyptians.

Ancient Egypt

The Ancient Egyptians believed in many gods but the god they loved best was Osiris, the God of the Dead. Legend states that Osiris, originally a fertility god, was murdered by his brother Set, who then cut up the corpse and scattered the pieces across the world. Isis, the wife and sister of Osiris, recovered the pieces, reunited the body and revivified it with wind from her wings. After his resurrection Osiris became the God of the Dead and the prototype of the saviour-god, who by his death and resurrection enables his devotees to attain immortality after death. Ceremonies connected with the celebration of Osiris's suffering, death and resurrection were enacted in Egypt for at least 5,000 years, and the cult of Osiris continued to flourish in the Roman Empire until all non-Christian religions were suppressed by the Emperor Theodosius in the fourth century AD. The old saviour-god, Osiris, was then replaced by the new saviour-god, Christ.

The Ancient Egyptians had a complex concept of the nature of man, and records show that they considered that a person had nine constituent parts. Apart from the physical body (*khat*), soul (*khu*) and spiritual body (*sahu*), they recognized the existence of the shadow (*kaibit*), double (*ka*), name (*ren*), heart (*ab*), heart soul (*ba*) and power (*sekhem*). It would be unwise to dismiss these ideas as being just primitive or irrational. They are evidence of an attempt to explain the nature of man in a way that resembles that used by Freud and Jung when they introduced such terms as the ego, id, unconscious, anima and shadow, for different aspects of the human psyche.

The Ancient Egyptians were the first people known to have held the belief that people's conduct in life determines their destiny after death. Their acceptance of this belief is considered to have been a landmark in the history of ethics. The judgement of the dead took place soon after death. The judge was Osiris supported by his *paut* or company, and the deceased was supported by the prayers of the living and the appropriate funeral rites.

The trial had two distinct features. First, the soul made a solemn declaration of its innocence; this declaration was then tested by weighing and inspecting the *ab*, or heart. There was no confession of sins but only a firm declaration of innocence. Among the protestations of innocence recorded in *The Book of the Dead*, we find souls declaring that they had not ill-treated servants, not inflicted pain, not caused any person to go hungry or to weep, not thought scornfully of God, and not defrauded the temples of their oblations. The truth of such declarations was tested by weighing the heart, the seat of the conscience, against a feather, the symbol of right and wrong. If the soul was vindicated it entered the domain of Osiris, where it became a god and enjoyed all the comforts and amenities it could have desired on Earth. The fate of the soul condemned at the judgement was quick and irreversible. It was immediately devoured by the Eater of the Dead, and ceased to exist.[2]

Zoroastrianism

When the Jewish people were exiled to Babylon in the sixth century
BC, Zoroastrianism was the state religion of the then mighty Persian
empire. It now has only about 150,000 adherents, mainly among the
Parsee community in India, but many of the fundamental beliefs of
Jews, Christians and Muslims can be traced to early Jewish contacts
with this once powerful religion.

Zoroastrianism is both a monotheistic and a dualistic religion,
recognizing a Supreme Creator and also a fundamental conflict
between good and evil. According to Zoroastrian mythology, at the
creation of the universe God gave freedom of choice to all spiritual
beings, including his two sons, Spenta Mainyu and Angra Mainyu.
Spenta Mainyu chose goodness and dwelt in Heaven, whereas
Angra Mainyu, who later became the prototype of the Devil, chose
falsehood and evil, and made his abode in Hell. According to this
doctrine each person also chooses to base his or her life on good or
evil and will be judged accordingly, eventually being consigned to
Heaven or Hell.

Zoroastrianism taught that the soul was judged immediately after
death. The judgement took place at the Chinvat Bridge which
stretched from the centre of the universe to paradise. At its distant
end the bridge narrowed to the width of a razor's edge. If the life had
been predominantly good, the soul was led across the bridge by a
beautiful maiden. If the life had been otherwise the soul was led by
an old hag, and as the soul approached the razor's edge it fell into the
fires of Hell which burnt in the chasm beneath the bridge. The bliss
enjoyed in Heaven and the torments endured in Hell were not
considered to be eternal. Eventually there would be a new age or
millennium, when creation would be rehabilitated. This would be
inaugurated by the appearance of a *Sayoshyant* (Saviour), who would
be the son of a virgin. At his appearance the bodies of the dead
would be reunited with their souls and, thus resurrected, everyone
would be plunged into a sea of molten metal to purge away their sins.
The whole human race would then enter into a paradisal state and
rejoice for ever. The outlook for the Devil and the angels who
supported him was less bright. They would be confined to Hell,
where they would be totally annihilated or made powerless for ever.[3]

Some of these Zoroastrian ideas are clearly reflected in the beliefs
of Jews, Christians and Muslims. It is probable that the Jews derived
from this source their beliefs in a new era, which would begin with
the appearance of a Messiah, and in the resurrection of the dead,[4]

though it took some centuries for this last belief to become generally accepted by Judaism. Zoroastrianism provided the first clear concepts of Hell, the Devil, a final judgement at the end of time and the physical resurrection of the dead. All four concepts became part of Christian and Islamic belief. Judaism never accepted the idea of Hell as a place of eternal torment but belief in the physical resurrection of the dead, when the Messiah would inaugurate the new millennium, eventually became an important Jewish doctrine.

Judaism

Jewish teaching has always maintained that because no man or woman can know the nature of life after death, speculation on the form it takes is pointless and this is therefore actively discouraged. There is however a quite definite belief in life after death,[5] a belief that developed its philosophic structure over many centuries and probably arose during the Jewish exile in Babylon. In the early recorded history of the Jews, death is mainly regarded in a naturalistic way, as the dissolution of the body and the end of life. When Yahweh made his covenant with the Jewish people, it was a covenant for this life on earth, not for some future immortal state.

Yahweh did not promise Abraham personal immortality, only that he would have many descendants. His covenant with Moses and the Israelites made no mention of eternal bliss in heaven, it was altogether more earthly and pragmatic. Israel was to be dedicated to Yahweh alone, to serve him as a holy nation, and they would be his chosen people. It is in line with this covenant that the Jews have retained their strong intent to survive as a nation, and look forward to a Messianic era, when all nations will recognize the special status and calling of Israel.[6] They expect this new era to be marked by the return of the Jewish people to Palestine, the rebuilding of the temple in Jerusalem, and the restoration of the Davidic dynasty in the person of the Messiah. Not surprisingly the establishment of the State of Israel in 1948 and its repossession of Jerusalem in 1967 are seen, by some Jews, as indicative of the near approach of this long awaited new era. Orthodox Jews also believe that this momentous occasion will be marked by the physical resurrection of the dead.

The earliest intimation in Jewish history of a belief in life after death is the mention of *Sheol*, where the dead were said to retain a shadowy existence. They could be contacted by mediums but this practice was frowned upon because it was contrary to the Jewish tradition of relying on Yahweh alone. Jewish antipathy to any dealings with the dead spirits was demonstrated by the first king of Israel, Saul. He rooted out all mediums from his kingdom and when later he was distressed and sought their help, he could find only one remaining, the Witch of Endor.[7]

The early Israelites regarded the living person as a union of body and soul (*nephesh*). At death this unity was shattered, the body disintegrating and the soul maintaining a shadowy existence in *Sheol*. It was many centuries before the present belief arose that after death the soul ascends to *Olam Ha'ba* (The World to Come) where, after spending one year in purgatory, it enters paradise.[6] This sojourn in paradise is however only a transient state because in the Messianic era, at the final resurrection of the dead, the unity of the soul and body will be restored.

Belief in the resurrection of the dead seems to have arisen during the exile in Babylon, when the Jews were exposed to the influence of Zoroastrianism. The emergence of this belief was based on the Jew's sense of the justice of God. They felt that God's justice was such that he was bound to reward the increasing number of Jews who were martyred for keeping the faith. They expected that this reward would be a physical resurrection in the Messianic era, when the martyrs would be able to witness the military and political triumph of the Jewish people throughout the world. Their resurrection would be a temporary affair only for, after a period of new earthly life, the martyrs would die again. Subsequently the idea of a physical resurrection was extended to include all the Jewish people. It was always seen more as a communal than an individual event. The emphasis was on the resurrection of the Jewish people as a race, not on the personal survival of the individual.[8]

This belief in the resurrection of the dead was not at first accepted by all Jews, and it was a long-standing source of controversy between the two main Jewish sects, the Pharisees and the Sadducees. The Pharisees were the more radical sect. They were the new thinkers who supported the idea of resurrection, whilst the Sadducees, who held the key positions in the temple, had a more conservative and sceptical outlook. The Sadducees rejected the resurrection theory on the principle that there was no warrant for it in the written Mosaic law. The issue was not resolved until after the destruction of the temple in 70 AD, when the idea became part of orthodox Jewish belief.

Although the resurrection of the body has been a belief of the Jews since Pharisaic times and rabbinical literature has insisted on it as essential doctrine, it has again become a controversial issue.

Modern liberal Jews find this dogma most unacceptable though orthodox Jews still hold it and the *Authorized Daily Prayer Book* declares: 'I believe with perfect faith that there will be a resurrection of the dead at the time when it shall please the Creator, blessed be his name, and exalted be the remembrance of him for ever and ever.'[9] Liberal Jews have deleted all reference to the resurrection of the dead from their *Reform Prayer Book* and replaced it with the less contentious phrase 'life eternal'. Some modern Jewish theologians consider it unnecessary to have any views on this subject.

In summary we may say that Judaism places its greatest emphasis on personal conduct in this life and the survival of the Jewish people. It has developed a belief in an immortal soul but speculation about the subsequent life of the soul in the 'World to Come' is discouraged. It rejects the Zoroastrian concept of Hell, which became an important part of Christian and Islamic doctrine. Orthodox Jews believe that in the Messianic era there will be a general resurrection, when the souls and bodies of the dead will be reunited. This dogma is not acceptable to Liberal or secular Jews, but it is in line with the traditional doctrines of Christianity and Islam, and provided the original base for those doctrines.

Christianity

Christianity is the major world religion with over one billion members and an increasing number of adherents. The significance it ascribes to death is therefore of considerable social and psychological importance. Its teachings, though based on the Bible and tradition, are not rigid formulations but have evolved according to the needs of each generation. One such change may be cited here. Whilst the practice of cremation is forbidden by Islam and Orthodox Jewry, and was forbidden by the Roman Catholic Church until 1963, it is now generally accepted by Christians and widely practised for the disposal of corpses. This acceptance of cremation supports the view that Christians no longer expect the physical resurrection of the dead so often portrayed by medieval artists, and that the afterlife is increasingly seen as solely a spiritual mode of existence.

Whilst Judaism is reluctant to speculate about the significance of death, Christianity proclaims it as an essential element of its teaching. Christianity was founded on the life, crucifixion and resurrection of Jesus, a Jew from Nazareth, and his reappearance after death was crucial to the development of the Christian religion. By itself the crucifixion of Jesus would have had little significance and would have affected only those people who were closely associated with him. The astounding revelation for the Apostles was their meeting with the risen and living Jesus, not as a spirit but as a person whom they could touch, speak to and share a meal with. The 'good news' proclaimed by the Apostles was thus centred on the resurrection of the dead and the atonement of sin through the death of Christ. He was the Messiah whom the Jews had expectantly awaited. He was the new saviour-god.

Christianity arose as a heretical sect of Judaism, and many of its early beliefs and practices were based on Jewish traditions. The development of a Christian theology was mainly the work of St Paul, who was, as he called himself, a 'Pharisee of the Pharisees'. As such, Paul would have held the Pharisaical belief that a person was complete only as a composite unit of body and soul; and that this unity, broken at death, would be restored with the resurrection of the dead in the Messianic era. This resurrection would be of the physical body reunited with the *nephesh* or soul, and not just of some insubstantial spiritual body. A parallel idea is to be found nowadays in the teachings of the Jehovah's Witnesses who, whilst denying the existence of a soul, believe in the ultimate resurrection of the 'elect' in their physical bodies.

The conversion experience that Paul had whilst travelling to Damascus included two distinct elements – he was blinded by a great light and heard the voice of the dead Jesus.[10] The latter may be discounted as an auditory hallucination, and the blindness as a transient hysterical reponse to a highly emotive experience, and other explanations have also been advanced; but whatever interpretation one gives to the event, it was a decisive moment in the development of the religious beliefs and attitude to death of billions of people over the next 2,000 years. Also, it seems likely that it caused Paul to reassess his own understanding of the afterlife in an attempt to make it more intelligible to himself and other people. He enlarged the Jewish idea that a person is essentially a union of body and soul by drawing a distinction between the 'natural body', which dies and is buried, and the 'spiritual body' which is resurrected. In doing this he seems, perhaps unwittingly, to have taken on board the Egyptian idea that a person has a physical body (*khat*), soul (*khu*) and a spiritual body (*sahu*).

The concept of a resurrected spiritual body which Paul now offered the church was inconsistent with Jewish tradition and probably also caused some controversy among the early Christians, but eventually a compromise solution seems to have been reached. The soul was considered to be the essential self and immortal, with a pre-existent spiritual body in heaven which would replace the physical body after death.[11] But belief in the resurrection of the physical body was also retained as part of Christian doctrine and seems to have been particularly prominent during the Middle Ages. This belief was reinforced in 1950 by the papal Bull, *Munificentissimus Deus*, on the Assumption of the Virgin Mary, which emphasized her incorruptibility, and expressly stated the coexistence of her earthly body with her soul in heaven. This doctrine resembles Islamic teaching on the death of Christ, as the *Qur'ān* states that Jesus was not crucified or killed by the Jews, but that 'Allah raised him up unto Himself'. Most Muslims believe that the relevant verses in the *Qur'ān* mean that Jesus did not die a physical death but was taken up to Allah and still lives in his body in heaven.[12]

The central tenets of the Christian faith are summarized in the Apostles' and Nicene Creeds, which were formulated over 1,500 years ago. They include statements on the divinity of Christ and the resurrection of the dead. The nature of this resurrection is still disputed; in the past it seems to have been understood in both a physical and spiritual sense, but the present consensus seems to be that it should be viewed in a spiritual sense only and that, to use Paul's words: 'This is how it will be when the dead are raised to life ... When buried it is a physical body; when raised it will be a spiritual body.'[13] Christianity also replaced the Jewish idea of resurrection, as being a community event in which the Jewish people would be vindicated as a race, into one concerned specifically with the destiny of individuals. It also established a doctrine of two judgements, an immediate 'particular judgement' of the soul after death before it entered purgatory, and the 'general judgement' of the risen dead on the Last Day. The doctrine of purgatory was rejected by the Protestant churches 400 years ago though it remains an essential belief in the Roman Catholic church.

Islam

Just as Christians believe that the coming of Christ has superseded the prophecy of Moses, Muslims believe that Islam has superseded all other religions and that Muhammad is the last and greatest of the prophets. There is however an interesting difference of emphasis. Christianity sees itself as a direct descendant of Judaism, and acknowledges its historical relationship with and indebtedness to the Jewish people. The Muslims do not accept such an evolutionary dependence. They consider that the revelation given to Muhammad came directly from God, and that consequently the *Qur'ān* is divine thought and divine law incarnated in words.[14] As a consequence they reject any suggestion that their religion may have developed from Jewish, Christian or Zoroastrian sources. Nevertheless, their eschatology (doctrine of 'last things') is remarkably similar to that of the Christian and Zoroastrian religions.

The five main Articles of Faith of Islam are belief in God, in his Angels, in Revelation, in the Prophets and in the Hereafter. The Hereafter is a composite term which includes the Last Day, Resurrection, *Barzahk*, Judgement, Paradise and Hell. *Barzahk* is the name given to the state of suspension experienced by the soul in the period between death and the Final Day of Judgement,[15] and appears to be similar in concept to the Catholic doctrine of purgatory and the Jewish idea of *Olam Ha'ba* (the World to Come).

There is a general belief within Islam in the doctrine of two judgements, though this is not explicitly stated in the *Qur'ān*. According to this belief souls are judged immediately after death by the angels Munkar and Nakīr, and are then consigned either to torment or ease. On the Last Day the souls will be reunited with their bodies, the dead will come out of their graves, and everyone will be judged by Allah, the King of the Last Judgement. Those who merit suffering will be consigned to Hell, but the faithful will enjoy the bliss of Paradise. Some notable Muslim philosophers, such as Avicenna and Averroes,[16] have suggested less orthodox interpretations of these doctrines, but their ideas have made little impact on the fundamental Islamic belief in the physical resurrection of the dead, or the physical nature of the rewards and punishments that will be provided in Heaven and Hell. Not surprisingly Muslims, like the Orthodox Jews, do not permit cremation of the corpse.

Secular Humanism

So far, this chapter has dealt with the impact that Western religious ideas have had on our understanding of death. But there is an important minority group who do not subscribe to any religious doctrine or belief. In fact, they consider such beliefs to be not just misguided but sometimes harmful to the wellbeing of the human race. They find, for instance, that religious teachings on death and eternity influence the debate on legalizing euthanasia, and that this option of an easy premeditated death – the equivalent at the end of life to the birth of a child by Caesarean section, is blocked by unsubstantiated teachings that were formulated thousands of years ago.

Secular humanists' approach to life and death is logical and objective. They concentrate on issues that are directly relevant to people's present needs and are not concerned with the possibility of a life after death. In fact, they hold that such an idea is wish-fulfilling nonsense as it cannot be proved by any objective evidence. Similarly they reject the universal belief in a god or gods, and consider the claims of religion to be based on historical records of such dubiety that no one would accept them as trustworthy if they claimed to be accounts of recent events.

Although secular humanism has become more influential in the past century, it is not just a modern viewpoint but part of a long-standing minority tradition that can trace its origins back to the fifth century BC. The first humanist is said to have been the Greek philosopher Protagoras (c.480–410 BC) who established the itinerant group of professional teachers known as the Sophists. His followers were renowned for their skill in debate, their scepticism and the emphasis they placed on achieving material success in life. Their key axiom and belief was that 'man is the measure of all things'. In other words there is no ideal or standard for mankind that is outside human purposes, and all ethical values are derived solely from human experiences and understanding. This principle, which is central to humanist philosophy, is considered by humanists to be the main difference between religious faith and their own beliefs.

Although secular humanism is said to have its origins in Ancient Greece, a materialistic philosophy existed in India during medieval times. These Indian philosophers rejected the religious doctrines of karma and reincarnation, and condemned religious teachers as frauds.[17] A similar attitude was discernible in some followers of the Chinese sage Confucius, but it is to Ancient Greece that Western humanists naturally trace their root beliefs. They have a high regard for the Greek teacher, Epicurus (c.341–270 BC) possibly because he was more concerned with the art of living than with death. He taught that death is simply the end of life, and epitaphs on the graves of his followers were often inscribed with the words, *I was not – I have been – I am not – I do not mind.*[18]

Secular humanism is a positive, human-centred philosophy that is concerned only with life in this world. Its followers are agnostics or atheists who have made a positive commitment to make the best possible use of life, both from self-interest and to help other people. As a simple definition of their philosophy one may say that they are Epicurean materialists, and that they are also utilitarian empiricists. They see themselves as Epicurean in the emphasis they place on the art of living, and materialists in that they have no belief in a soul, or spirits, or gods, or of any conscious experience that is separate from the body. They are empiricists in their approach to knowledge. They believe that all knowledge is dependent upon observations made by the physical senses alone, and are suspicious of any ideas that claim to be true but which cannot be verified by normal sensory perception. In their moral and ethical outlook they are utilitarian, believing that society should aim for the greatest happiness of the greatest number of people, and that an action is morally right or wrong according to whether it increases or decreases human happiness. Humanists see the living body as a wonderful machine that eventually ceases to function. They believe that when a person dies there can be no further existence for that individual, nor can there be any contact between the living and the dead.

Secular Funerals

Humanists recognize that the disposal of the corpse is a moment of great psychological importance for close relatives and friends. They also realize that the religious ceremony that usually accompanies a cremation or interment is not a legal requirement, and that in an increasingly secular society there is a place for non-religious funerals. Consequently, there is a discernible trend among secular humanists for humanists to officiate at, and devise, their own funeral ceremonies. There is no set rule for such funerals but they almost invariably take place at crematoria. Sample ceremonies are available for those people who have been asked to conduct a secular funeral and are uncertain how this may best be done. This lack of expertise is becoming less acceptable as secular funerals become more popular, and humanists are now insisting on training and licensing all their celebrants.[19]

The first requirement for the conductor of a secular funeral is to visit and support the family and then make the necessary arrangements with the funeral director. These may include the removal, or covering, of any religious symbols at the crematorium which the participants, because of their atheist beliefs, might consider offensive. The ceremony, which will probably include the music and songs enjoyed by the deceased, is likely to be in five parts. It will begin with a few opening words of welcome, followed by some thoughts on life and death which may be based on appropriate readings from poetry or great works of literature. The core of the ceremony is the tribute to the dead person. The coffin is then committed to the furnace. The ceremony ends with a few closing words, in which friends are thanked for their attendance and encouraged to continue their lives strengthened by the memories of their dead friend.[18]

Eco-friendly Funerals

Funerals with biodegradable coffins are popular with people who are concerned about the environment, as they are less wasteful of energy than cremation. There is also an increasing trend – particularly among pagans, for woodland funerals, a form of disposal that has an obvious appeal for anyone who likes the idea of having a funeral in a rural setting away from the functionalism of the crematorium. Both local authorities and private firms are setting aside sites for woodland funerals with the intention that they should be maintained as nature reserves. The Carlisle Woodland Burial Service in Cumbria is perhaps typical of such enterprises. Gravestones are forbidden but a metal plate is buried a few inches below the surface of the earth to enable specific graves to be identified: the authority maintains a plan of the whole area to facilitate such identification. Oak trees are planted above each grave to enhance the woodland aspect of the site.[20] This type of burial may seem ideal but I have reservations about them, especially when the weather is bad and the mourners get tired and cold at the graveside. Such exposure is a hazard to the living whilst they are paying their respects to the dead. I became acutely aware of this danger when I was a general practitioner in rural Wales and was summoned to three funerals where mourners had dropped down dead at open graves on exposed Welsh hillsides.

Chapter 3
Reincarnation and Rebirth

All the world's a stage
And all the men and women merely players;
They have their exits and their entrances;
And one man in his time plays many parts,

As You Like It

Introduction

The Indian subcontinent has been a most fertile environment for the development of new religions and different attitudes to death. Four great religions – Hinduism, Buddhism, Jainism and Sikhism all originated in India and, although they all teach a doctrine of reincarnation or rebirth, each has developed its own eschatology and practices.

Reincarnation may seem to be a very ancient idea but it was first formulated probably less than 3,000 years ago. Moreover, as we shall see when considering the African approach to reincarnation, it is open to various interpretations. The origin of the theory is not known but the underlying principle is not entirely new to Western philosophers as it was taught in classical Greece by Pythagoras (c.582–507 BC), by the Christian theologian Origen (c.185–254 AD), by Jewish Cabbalists and the Cathars in medieval Europe.[1]

The Indian doctrine of reincarnation affirms that each individual experiences a succession of births and deaths throughout many lifetimes and in countless bodies. People are born, acquire knowledge and experience, die and then repeat the cycle until the soul reaches its final goal, released from the cycle of rebirth and *karma*. The doctrine of *karma* is inseparable from the Indian understanding of reincarnation. It is based on the concept that the good and bad deeds of former lives have a formative and continued influence on the pattern and events of one's present life. A corollary of this doctrine is that all life whether supernatural, human, animal, insect or, with some sects, even plant, is governed by the law of *karma*.

In contrast to the Indian viewpoint, Western religions teach that man is a special creation, possessing an immortal soul that is denied to animals. Inherent in Western thought is the supposition that life is a gift of God, and that life on earth is extremely important as it is a preparatory stage to life eternal. The Indian religions view the situation differently from the Western traditions. Human life is not seen as God's greatest gift to man but as a curse inherent in the nature of things. Reincarnation is seen not as a desirable process but as the supreme evil. Man is enmeshed by his *karma*; it is matter, the body as such, which is the persistent drag on the soul and from which the soul longs to be separated.

The longing for non-existence or escape into the uncertainties of death, is not unknown in the West. 'I will say nothing', wrote Goethe in 1824, 'against the course of my life. But at the bottom it has been nothing but pain and burden, and I can affirm that during my whole 75 years, I have not had four weeks of genuine wellbeing. It is but the perpetual rolling of a rock that must be raised up for ever.' Similarly, when the Electress Dowager said to Martin Luther: 'Doctor, I wish you may live forty years to come', he replied 'Madam, rather than live forty years more, I would give up my chance of Paradise. I am utterly weary of life. I pray the Lord will come forthwith and carry me hence.'[2]

Hindus, like the Buddhists and Sikhs, ascribe little importance to the corpse even though they consider the funeral rites to be important. They look upon the body as a transitory garment, which the soul discards at death and replaces with a new physical body at rebirth. The disposal of the dead is seen simply as a sanitary procedure, which ensures that a rapidly putrefying body is disposed of as quickly and expeditiously as possible. This is achieved most effectively by cremation, and cremation soon after death is the customary method of disposal in India.

Supporting the bereaved and helping to dispose of the corpse are community events in the Indian subcontinent. All friends and relatives are expected to visit the family and attend the funeral, though they do so in roles that are predetermined by their sex and kinship. The leading role is undertaken by the senior male member of the family, for in the Eastern rites of death there is no equality of the sexes. The funeral rites of parents, for instance, can only be properly carried out by a son. Parents who have no sons cannot expect a happy afterlife. They are likely to languish in Hell or become dissatisfied ghosts.

Hinduism

Hinduism is the oldest of the Indian religions, it is rooted in Indian history and has no identifiable founder. It is a complex and ancient religion, which has been likened to the trunk of a tree with many branches.[3] The branches of the tree are the great variety of customs, gods, artistic forms, rituals, philosophies and forms of worship within Hinduism. It contains many primitive aspects alongside highly developed philosophical systems. Within Hinduism there is a primitive animism that inhabits every tree and hill with spirits, and a system of yoga providing the four main paths for God-realization or *moksha* (release from the material world and the cycle of births and deaths). In seeking *moksha*, a Hindu may practice *Karma Yoga* (the way of service), *Bhakti Yoga* (the path of devotion), *Raja Yoga* (intellectual insight), or *Jnana Yoga* (the path of spiritual insight).[4] The last method is particularly recommended for people in the last two stages (*ashramas*) of life, when they can gradually renounce the world and proceed towards the goal of *moksha* in the hope that this may be attained in their present incarnation.

Hindu social and spiritual systems are based on the premise that there are four castes (*varnas*) and four main stages in life (*ashramas*), the last stage being a preparation for death. The origin of the caste system is described in the *Hymn of the Primeval Man*, in the last book of the *Rig Veda* (c.900 BC).[5] In this hymn, it is said that at the beginning of time a great primeval power (*purusha*) was killed as a sacrifice by lesser gods. He miraculously survived his death and dismemberment, and from the various parts of his body created the different features of the universe including the four castes of society – priests (*Brahmins*), warriors (*kshatatriyas*), artisans (*vaishyas*) and labourers (*shudras*). Within these four main castes, there are now hundreds of sub-castes with the untouchables forming the lowest of all groups. A similar distinction exists between the sexes. Women are definitely considered to be inferior to men by traditionally minded Hindus.

The first recorded reference to reincarnation occurs in the *Upanishads* (c.800 BC) where it is described as something which had been previously unknown to the Brahmin priests. In later centuries it became the subject of much philosophical discussion and eventually the belief arose that even if one went to Heaven, one might die there.

Then it was suggested that the gods also die, only to be replaced by new gods, and that all beings are reborn over and over again in an endless cycle.

Thoughtful people began to question the value of a place in Heaven if it was but one phase in the endless cycle of birth, life and death. Some of these questioners became ascetics, living in isolated places and pondering the significance of life, death and the universe. Among these were Gautama Buddha the founder of Buddhism, and Mahāvira the founder of Jainism. Other ascetics maintained their links with Hinduism and their teachings are recorded in the later texts of the *Upanishads* (c.600 BC). These texts stress one chief theme, the unity of the individual soul (*atman*) with the one impersonal and absolute World-Soul (*Brahman*) which pervades and underlies the cosmos. This doctrine emphasizes the unity of all things in the one Absolute Being (*Brahman*) and that each creature contains in its soul (*atman*) part of the divine nature. Thus whilst *Brahman* is god transcendent, the *atman* is god immanent, that is the god existing in oneself.[6]

Hindus believe that each person consists of many parts; there is the physical body, the intellect, thoughts, emotions, the *atman* and an inner subtle self called the *jeevatma*. The *atman* is indestructible and unchangeable, but all the other parts are in a state of constant transformation. This transformation is most apparent at death, when the physical body disintegrates and only the *jeevatma* remains of the transformable parts. The *jeevatma* is the personality or ego, and during each incarnation its character is modified by the experiences it undergoes. The *jeevatma* must continue to seek reincarnation until it learns to distinguish between reality (*Brahman*) and *samsara*, the illusory physical world.[7] This can only occur when a person becomes fully conscious of his *atman* and realizes that it is none other than God within himself. The way of liberation is now open; it is achieved by the *jeevatma* discarding all notions of a finite self and merging with the *atman*, and thus with *Brahman*. When this is achieved the immediate experience may be described, perhaps inadequately, as a mystical union with God, or the attainment of *nirvana*.

Preparing for death

Hindus consider it important to have a 'good death' and to feel free from all their sins before they die. This requires spiritual preparation together with a voluntary and peaceful acceptance of death. People nearing the ends of their lives will undertake long journeys to the sacred cities – Benares, Gaya and Haridwar, on the banks of the Ganges – so that they can wash away their sins in the river or die in its waters. The banks of the Ganges at Benares are considered to be as sacred as the river itself and terminally ill people living nearby will leave their homes and live in huts on the river banks until they die.[8]

Atonement ceremonies are held in the homes of the many people who cannot make the pilgrimage to the Ganges. Brahmin priests are invited to the house and the invalid makes a confession of sins in their presence, and prays for forgiveness. Gifts are given to the priests and they choose a representative who is willing to accept all the dying person's sins, except such major offences as murder and adultery. Having accepted the burden of guilt, the Brahmin then departs to take a purificatory bath, which will wash away the sins.[9] Before he leaves, the Brahmin may tie a thread around the wrist of the invalid to indicate that a blessing has been given. This should not be removed after death; and similarly the sacred thread worn by Hindu men around the right shoulder, and the nuptial thread worn by women around their necks, should be left undisturbed. Thus purified by the waters of the Ganges or by the atonement ceremonies, devout Hindus will wish to die lying on the floor close to mother Earth, with the name of God on their lips and in their heart.

Hindu funeral customs

All Hindu scriptures teach that only men are competent to perform the funeral rites, and that these rites are essential for the wellbeing of the soul. This belief permeates the Hindu attitude to death and provides one of the main reasons for Hindus preferring to have sons rather than daughters. The importance of having a male descendant is apparent in the Sanskrit word for son (*putra*) which means 'he who delivers one from *Put* or Hell'.[10] Hindus believe that, within the laws of *karma*, the ultimate fate of the soul is dependent upon immediate cremation and the performance of the correct funereal rituals. These rituals vary with the caste of the deceased and the area in which they lived. Family practices are not always known to Hindus living outside India, and a suitable priest may not be available. Consequently some of the important ceremonies for dead emigrants are now performed by proxy in India, without the immediate mourners being present.

After death the corpse is washed, perfumed, dressed in normal clothes, garlanded with flowers and, in Western countries, placed in a coffin. Cremation is customary though small children and aesthetics are often buried. Hindus do not usually use coffins. Instead the corpse is carried in a linen wrap on a bamboo stretcher to the cremation ground. The funeral procession is led by the eldest son, or if there is no son by the chief mourner. A widow does not normally accompany her husband's cortège, but stays at home with the women who are likely to wail and lament, sometimes with the aid of professional mourners. At the cremation ground the shroud is cut and the body placed on a pyre. This is set alight by the chief mourner, at the head of the corpse if it is male and near the feet if the deceased is a woman. Those present will ensure that the skull bursts while the body burns, for according to Hindu belief the soul is entrapped in the skull at death and cannot escape if the skull remains intact. If necessary the skull is broken by a blow with a cudgel. After leaving the cremation ground the mourners have a purificatory bath and then return home.

On the third day after cremation, a 'bone gathering' ceremony is held. Close relatives assemble at the remains of the funeral pyre where a priest conducts a short ceremony of prayers and sprinkles holy water on the ashes. He then places the burnt bones in a vase and presents them to the son or nearest male relative of the deceased. If it is at all possible, relatives will take the bones to the Ganges or some other sacred spot for disposal. This is done in the hope that the act will facilitate the deceased's entry into a heavenly realm before their next earthly incarnation. If the bones – or when disposal has been in a modern crematorium, the ashes – cannot be taken to a sacred place, they are thrown into the nearest river or stream because every stream is believed to be mystically connected to the Ganges, the mother of all waters.

Hindu mourning customs

A family is considered to be unclean for 10 days after bereavement and during this time they are secluded from society, and various other prohibitions are observed. Adult members of the family usually fast on the first day, and they may not shave, eat sweet food or offer food to guests. Daily ceremonies are performed to ensure that the disembodied soul of the dead person acquires a new spiritual body with which it may be clothed during its next phase of life.

Each day of mourning has its special ceremony, which is conducted in the deceased's home. If performed correctly, the soul gets a head on the first day, a neck on the second, then a heart, a back on day four, and a navel on day five. The sexual organs are formed on the sixth day, the thighs on the seventh, knees on the eighth day, and finally hands and feet on the next two days. If the ceremonies are not carried out properly, the body is not properly formed and the individual wanders in space as a deformed spirit.

Once the deceased have acquired their spiritual bodies, they must be fed before they can travel to the celestial abodes where they will live until their next earthly incarnation. This food is provided by the *Shraddha* ceremony, one of the most important and expensive of the many Hindu rites. Basically, it involves a dialogue that takes place beside the Ganges, represented symbolically by a bowl of water, between the priest, the head of the family and the soul of the departed, and during this ceremony rice and milk are given to the deceased spirit. The *Shraddha* ceremony is usually repeated each year but the later ceremonies are simpler and less costly, and poor families may undertake these rites without the help of a priest. After the *Shraddha* ceremony is completed, the priest lights the sacred fire in the house and prays for the peace of the departed soul. Family mourning then ceases except for the spouse and sons, who observe a 12-month mourning period.

Sikhs

The most recent of the major religions to originate in the Indian subcontinent is Sikhism. It arose in the Punjab during the fifteenth century AD when there was considerable tension in the area between Muslims and Hindus. The religion was founded by Guru Nānak, a Hindu of the warrior caste and an itinerant poet and hymn writer. He is said to have received a call from God whilst bathing in a stream, and that his first words afterwards were 'There is no Hindu, there is no Muslim.' The keynote of his message was the brother-hood of Hindus and Muslims in the sight of God.

Sikhism had nine gurus or leaders after Nānak, the last being Gobind Singh (1666-1708 AD) who, in order to preserve the Sikh community from being annihilated by their enemies, transformed a relatively peaceful community into a nation of redoubtable warriors. Since the death of Gobind Singh the Sikhs have recognized only one guru, the *Guru Granth Sahib*, their sacred scriptures. These scriptures and the Sikh community itself are now the ultimate spiritual author-ity of the Sikh religion.

Sikhism is a religion without a priesthood. It may be looked upon as a synthesis that incorporates the monotheism of Islam with Hindu metaphysics. Its essential tenets include a belief in one God, equality between men and women, the importance of service, and a belief in *karma* and reincarnation. Sikhism has a more positive attitude to life on earth than the other Indian religions. Whilst accepting the idea of *karma*, the Sikh does not see this world as a place created for suffering but as the 'abode of the True One, a garden of flowers where life is ever in bloom'.[11] He considers that each life is pure in its origin and remains essentially pure throughout its existence. God is a 'God of Grace' and he did not create men and women to punish them for their sins but that they may return enriched, after transitory incarnations on earth, to the source from which they came. During these incarnations individuals acquire merit by their behaviour, by service to others and devotion to God. In this way each person is eventually released from the wheel of life and restored to his or her place in heaven.

Sikh funeral customs

Cremation is customary among the Sikhs; the ashes are scattered on running water, the river Sutlej in the Punjab being the most favoured site. But the Sikh attitude to the disposal of the corpse was clearly formulated by Guru Nānak. He said, 'whether you burn the dead body in sandalwood or throw it on the filth is immaterial', for the soul has already discarded its now useless body and seeks a new incarnation.

When a Sikh dies the people utter the words of praise: *Wahiguru, Wahiguru* (Wonderful Lord, Wonderful Lord). The body is washed, clothed, wrapped in a shroud and placed in a coffin. Most importantly in death, as in life, a man continues to wear the five Ks or symbols of Sikhism. These are the *kais, kangha, kaccha, kara* and *kirpan*, the uncut hair, the comb, undershorts, steel bangle and dagger.

Friends and relatives consider it a sacred duty to visit the bereaved family and accompany the body to the place of cremation. Before the funeral procession begins, the body may be viewed by those present and there may be expressions of grief with tears and lamentations. Whilst such a public display of grief is understood and accepted, it is not encouraged as the Gurus spoke against excessive lamentations at funerals. On its way to the crematorium the body is taken to the Sikh temple (*gurdwara*) where prayers are said by initiated elders. At the crematorium, the body is consigned to the furnace by the eldest son and a verse from the evening hymn, the *kirlan sophila*, is chanted whilst the body is consumed by the fire. Then the mourners wash and return to the *gurdwara* for more prayers and readings from the scriptures, before accompanying the family back to their home.

Sikh mourning ceremonies

On the day immediately after the death, friends provide the family with food; but in the subsequent 10–13 days of mourning the family provides all the food for its numerous visitors and does so in the name of the deceased. During this period of mourning, there is an *akhand path*, a complete public reading of the *Guru Granth Sahib*, the Sikh Holy Scriptures. This is done either in the *gurdwara* or in a part of the deceased's house that has been converted into a temple. In the latter instance, a room is cleared of all furniture and hangings, and these are replaced by a covered dais (*manji*) surmounted by a canopy (*palki*). Cushions are placed on the dais and the *Guru Granth Sahib* is set on the cushions. In this way the room is converted into a temple.

People entering the room do so shoeless with their heads covered by a turban, veil or clean cloth. On entering they kneel before the *Guru Granth Sahib*, place money at the base of the dais as a contribution to the communal food and the poor, and then sit on the floor to hear the elders read from the holy scriptures. This complete reading of the holy book is undertaken by a succession of readers, men and women, some of whom understand what they read and others who do not. The readings are frequently not understood by the listeners. There are modern language translations of the scriptures but public readings of the *Guru Granth Sahib* are usually taken from the antiquated *Gurmukhi* script in which it was originally written, and many Sikhs are not proficient in this language. Despite this lack of comprehension, all the family and friends will attempt to be present for at least part of the *akhand path*.

Everyone attends the final reading on the last day of mourning, an occasion which is known as the *bhog* ceremony. This is followed by a distribution of *karah parshad*, the Sikh holy food, a mixture of flour, honey and milk blessed with the prayers of Guru Gobind Singh. If the deceased was the head of the family, a turban is now placed on the head of the eldest son to indicate that he has become the senior member of the family. Finally, the family provides all those present with a *langar*, a community meal. The dais, canopy and the *Guru Granth Sahib* are now removed from the room, which reverts to its secular status, but a lamp may be kept alight for some weeks in memory of the deceased.

Buddhism

A belief in reincarnation seems implicit in Buddhism, but the Buddhist philosophy does not speak of reincarnation but of rebirth. The distinction is subtle; the doctrine of reincarnation involves the concept of a self or soul, and Buddhism rejects such an idea as a non-reality (*Annattā*) or illusion. For Buddhists, rebirth means the continuous change in consciousness that people experience every succeeding moment. These changes are mainly subliminal and pass unnoticed by people involved in the normal activities of daily life, but they are perceived by those who practise the systematic meditations taught by the Buddhists. For the Buddhist every moment involves the death and rebirth of consciousness. Rebirth is not just the start of a new physical incarnation as in Hinduism; it occurs throughout life, as well as during the particular change in consciousness that is associated with physical death.

Buddhists say that in the moments immediately preceding death everyone experiences a *Kamma Nimmitta* in which they recollect, in part or completely, their past life, and in which they may have a vision of their future life. At the moment of death, the mind drops into the *bvanga* state. This is a neutral phase like sleep, in which there is conscious activity but no awareness. According to different authorities this phase may last for any period from a few hours to 40 days. There is then a reawakening into one of the six realms which Buddhists say exist in the universe. They call these places the Realm of Hell, the Hungry Ghost Realm, the Animal Realm, the Human Realm, the Realm of the Jealous Gods and the Realm of the Gods.

A precise description of the after-death state, and of the six realms, is given in the Buddhist text, the *Bardol Thötröl* or *Tibetan Book of the Dead*. It maps out these realms and gives clear instructions to the deceased on how to cope with each new experience. This forthrightness differs markedly from the uncertainty in the West about the nature of the after-life and after-death experiences. It is not, however, just a book of instruction for the dead; it is also an important psychological treatise for the living. It helps to prepare those who read it for the psychological pitfalls that life offers, and at the moment of death it tells them the steps they should take for a better rebirth or even a final liberation into the state of *nirvāna*.

In Buddhism every moment is a moment of death and rebirth, and the conscious mind is considered to be in a state of flux moving rapidly from one state to the other and experiencing something of the nature of the six realms. Chögyan Trungpa says that the six realms should be seen as present psychological realities, and the after-death state as an extension of people's present attitudes to life. The Realm of Hell is a highly emotional state in which the emotions are either fiery hot or icy cold. In the hot Hell a person is inflamed with anger or fear. In the icy cold Hell this anger is suppressed and becomes a bitter indignation, which is often reinforced by a pride that refuses to communicate with other people. The Hungry Ghosts of the second realm continually seek new possessions and are never satisfied with the things they have. The third or Animal Realm is characterized by a well-organized and mechanical life style, in which individuals are easily upset by the unpredictable. Inhabitants of this realm lack a sense of humour and a sense of proportion and, like animals, cannot laugh or smile. The Human Realm is the arena where a passion for exploration and enjoyment are much in evidence; it is the realm of research and development but it is also a state in which people are liable to resent the achievements of others. The Realm of the Jealous Gods is the realm of intrigue and relationships. Here keen intelligence holds sway but it is tinged with envy, the main occupation being the weaving of plots and the manipulation of other people. The sixth state is the Realm of the Gods, which is the realm of pride, where the individual becomes absorbed by his own sense of achievement and importance.[12] None of these states is portrayed as being particularly desirable. Buddhism instead teaches a doctrine of liberation from *karma* into the state of *nirvāna*. This state cannot be easily defined but it has been achieved already by the Enlightened One, the Buddha, and the way to enlightenment and liberation is open to all.

Buddhist rites of passage

Most Buddhists believe that consciousness remains in the body for eight to 12 hours after death and that it is possible to speak meaningfully to the deceased during this period. As a consequence of this belief, some Buddhists maintain that the body should not be touched during the immediate post-death period. Some say that the vibrancy of life leaving the body can be felt for some hours after death if a hand is placed near the crown of the head.[13] Also, that after the death of a great spiritual teacher the continued presence of his or her soul is indicated by a persistent warmth over the heart.[14]

It is very important for the dying to have the most elevated thoughts at the moment of death, as this will determine the nature of their next incarnation. According to the Dalai Lama, a person dies with either a virtuous, a non-virtuous or a neutral mind, and the aim should be to strive for the first. To achieve this the dying person should contemplate a virtuous object – such as the Three Jewels of Buddhism or the love of Christ – thereby engendering a mind of faith. Or a person might cultivate equanimity, becoming free from desire and hatred towards any sentient being. This can be done through one's own efforts or through the urging of others. The Dalai Lama also points out that the presence of many relatives and friends around the deathbed constitutes two hazards for the dying. The first is that some of them by their nervousness, may irritate the dying person and make him or her feel angry. The second is that the overt grief of relatives may arouse an intense desire in the patient to remain with them. Buddhists consider it very important for the dying to be free of desire and hatred, as it is dangerous to die in such a frame of mind.[15]

A Buddhist monk should be present immediately before death, or as soon after it as possible. If more than one monk is able to attend, then it is customary for an even number of monks to visit. Following a death, monks of the *Theravāda* sect (Thai and Ceylonese Buddhists) will chant passages from the *Abhidhamma*, a complex treatise on the psychology of Buddhism. The listeners, including the dead person, may not fully understand the meaning of the verses but it is a strong reminder to them, and to the deceased, that he or she is dead. In the *Māhāyana* (Tibetan) tradition, the readings may be taken from other texts such as the *Tibetan Book of the Dead*.

Buddhist funeral rites

Buddhist burial and mourning customs depend to a large extent on the country where the deceased lived and therefore on local customs. Thai Buddhists cremate their dead, Chinese Buddhists bury them, whilst Burmese Buddhists may first bury the body and then later disinter it and cremate it. In Tibet, the corpse may be buried, cremated, embalmed, just left in an isolated place, or an 'air burial' may be chosen. The latter involves throwing the body over a cliff, a procedure that is said to be quite a tourist attraction for the Chinese. The disposal of the dead is undertaken by a special group of Tibetans, possibly akin to Western grave diggers. The flesh of the exposed corpses is eaten by wild carnivores. When the bones are clean they are collected and pounded to a powder, which is then scattered across the earth.

The time between death and the disposal of the body varies greatly in Buddhist countries. Disposal may take place immediately or be postponed for many months, as in Burma, where the body may be first buried, then exhumed, and some months later cremated with elaborate rituals. If the body is to be cremated, it is usually placed in an open coffin or on a bier, and the monks followed by lay people then process past the body for a final viewing, for to look and meditate on death is a basic requisite for Buddhists. The monks may cense the body with incense before the pyre is lit, and at the very last moment the corpse is turned on to its side by a kinsman. The reason for this is simple. When the fire ignites, the gases within the corpse explode and this causes the body to move. This movement can be disturbing for the mourners but is reduced if the body is laid on its side. When cool the ashes are collected and scattered, or buried in the ground where a tree may be planted later as a symbol of rebirth.

Jainism

Jainism is a small but influential Indian sect with about 1,500,000 adherents. Founded by Māhavira (c.599–527 BC) a contemporary of Buddha, it recognizes no deity but holds to the traditional Indian beliefs in *karma* and reincarnation. It combines an atheistic philosophy with a very pessimistic view of the universe, and an ascetic system of moral and spiritual training. It is a monastic religion with a supporting lay community, the lay people visiting the monks for spiritual training, or receiving Jain monks and nuns in their homes for instruction.

The ethical code of the Jain is based on sympathy and compassion towards all forms of life. No other religion has carried the doctrine of non-violence to such extremes. Jains consider it more serious to injure the higher forms of life than to harm lesser creatures, but even the maltreatment of fire and water damages the soul and must be avoided as far as possible. Jains are totally vegetarian and the occupations they can undertake are strictly limited. They cannot be farmers, for ploughing the earth will injure the animal life as well as the earth itself. They cannot work with metal or wood, because these materials experience pain if beaten or sawn. The safest profession for them is trade, and many Jains are successful in business.

Jainism sees the soul (*jiva*) as enmeshed in matter. Salvation is attained only by freeing the soul from matter, so that the former may rise by its natural lightness to the top of the universe (*lokakasa*), where it will enjoy self-sufficient bliss for eternity. Jains who seek to escape the wheel of life must subject themselves to rigorous hardships to get rid of the *karma* they have acquired. No other method is effective in eliminating *karma*. The *karma* accruing from good deeds is dissipated almost immediately conferring few benefits on the individual. On the other hand, selfish, careless or cruel actions produce much heavy *karma*, which is not easily eliminated. One effective way of achieving salvation for the spiritually prepared Jain is *sallekhana*, or fasting to death.[16] Pious laity, as well as nuns and monks, sometimes terminate their lives in this way, hoping thereby to be freed from matter so that they may rise to the heights of *lokakasa*.

Despite its austerity Jainism has its joyful festivals. The major festival is *Paryushan* which, although a serious occasion, is also associated with much chanting, singing and cheerful noise. *Paruyshan* lasts for eight days and concludes with each person asking forgiveness from everyone else for the wrongs they have deliberately or unknowingly committed. Among the traditional teachings is the *Shanti Shanti* prayer, which is a prayer of thankfulness for everything to everyone, and for peace throughout the universe for all souls. The Jain is also taught that 'you should not cry after the dead have died, because otherwise you stop the dead from rising'. However, it is becoming increasingly difficult for young Jains to understand their own religion. Their vernacular is Gujerati, but many of the mantras are in the ancient Maghadhi language, which they do not understand. The Sikhs have a similar problem, but the problem is particularly serious for young Jains living abroad as leading monks have been reluctant to travel outside India to support the overseas communities.

Chapter 4
The Cult of the
Ancestors

A ministering angel shall my sister be.

Hamlet

Japanese Religions

The spiritual traditions of Japan are complex and diverse. Shinto is the indigenous religion, but for over 1,500 years the religious scene has been enriched by the presence of Buddhism, Confucianism and Taoism, and more recently of Christianity. There are, also, the new religions (the *Shinkō Shūkyō*), now one of the most dynamic forces in Japan. These are essentially lay organizations with easy conditions of entry, and often a large number of adherents. Some were founded at the beginning of the nineteenth century but the number has increased rapidly during the past 50 years, and there are now over 200 such religions in Japan. The founder is often a lay person who felt impelled to establish a new religion by divine revelation.[1]

Despite the vigour and the capacity for growth shown by the new religions, and the special status of Shinto, Buddhism is probably the predominant religion in Japan. There has always been a friendly relationship between Buddhism and Shinto and it is quite natural for a Japanese house to have a shrine for the Shinto gods (a *kamidana*) and a *Butsudan*, or Buddha altar. When the Japanese marry, they often have the union blessed by a Shinto ceremony but if funeral rites are needed they seek the help of Buddhist monks. Within this varie-gated pattern the most consistent element in all Japanese religions, and one that transcends sectarian lines, is the deep-seated regard the people have for their ancestors. This is most evident in non-Christian circles where the dead are referred to as *kami* or *hotoko*, which are the respective Shinto and Buddhist terms for divine beings.[2]

Shinto

Shinto is the word used in English-speaking countries for the Japanese term *Kami-no-Michi*, the way of the gods or *kami*. Its origin can be traced to the myths of ancient times, but it possesses no canon of sacred scriptures, nor does it possess a rigid set of doctrines. Consequently it is not easy to depict the essential nature of Shinto. It is best seen as an animistic religion that reflects the importance to the Japanese of perfection, cleanliness and of harmony with nature and the world of the spirits. Perhaps the most obvious feature of Shinto ritual is the emphasis given to purification from pollution. An inherent need to feel pure may be a reason for the infrequency with which Shinto priests conduct funeral ceremonies and why they are content to leave funeral rites, usually cremations, to the Buddhist monks.

According to Japanese mythology there are three elements in the universe – man, nature and the *kami*. The word *kami* is usually translated into English as god or spirit, but the Japanese do not regard the *kami* just as divine inhabitants of a heavenly realm. Many of the *kami* are ancestors who remain close to the world of earthly and human life. Others inhabit sacred places in the mountains, rivers, rocks and seas. There are also tutelary *kami* who are integrated into the life of a particular clan. The *kami* reside in many different spheres, in heaven (*Takamanohara*) and the underworld (*Yomi*), but many live in *Nakatsuni* (the middle land) the earth. The heavenly *kami* are the most important but those of *Nakatsuni* take a greater interest in human and clan affairs. They can be contacted at the shrines and their help is often sought by prayers and offerings.

The *kami* are aware of what happens on earth and are tolerant of people's foibles. They understand human sexuality and realize that human nature is essentially innocent, even though people may behave in ways that are unworthy of them. Death however is an evil that must be accepted realistically. It is inevitable and irreversible, and can be heart-breaking for everyone involved, including the *kami*. After death there is no judgement and no consignment to Heaven or Hell. The spirits of the dead merely move into a land that is no longer pure. It is a place of decay and corruption, where they are finally released from all physical limitations and again become part of the universal life force.[3] However, although death is irreversible it does not necessarily entail an immediate and complete separation from one's earthly family. Just as heaven and the underworld are close to the middle land, so the dead remain close to the living.

Shinto rituals provide the dead with a means of escape from total disintegration. Through the festivals (*matsuri*) for the deceased, the dead are enabled to escape from the impure world of death. Their spirits are purified by these ceremonies and enabled to grow into exalted beings, who retain their individuality and eventually become part of the world of *kami*.[4] Having been rescued and exalted by these special ceremonies, the ancestors are able to watch over their descendants from their spiritual realm and assist them with blessings and guidance. In return the family continues to venerate the ancestors, providing them with offerings at the family shrine and seeking their help by means of prayers and gifts. This practice is not confined to those who follow the way of Shinto, it is also common among Japanese who belong to other religious faiths.

Tamishii, the souls

The souls, *tamishii*, are said to be capable of assuming various forms after death and may choose to appear as ghosts, as bright lights or even as monsters. The souls of people who died a violent death are considered to be particularly restless, and potentially dangerous to the living unless they are placated by food and purification. This belief accounts for the many roadside shrines found at accident black spots in Japan.

When a person dies, appeasement of the soul is considered to be a sacred duty for the family. The act of appeasement is called *chinkon*, which means an inner act of meditation. It is particularly important that *chinkon* is observed during the 49 days that the soul of the dead person is believed to linger in the house. Thereafter the soul is free to depart. Provided the correct rites have been performed the *tamishii* becomes a *kami* after 33 years, and then reaches the stage of complete happiness. An ancestral *kami* is therefore a soul, or more accurately a person's higher self, which has been saved from disintegration by the offerings and rituals of the living. These enable it to grow into an exalted being capable of seeking beyond the self, and beyond the human, for what is ultimately divine.

Shinto funeral rites

A Shinto funeral is held only for Shinto priests, for important Shinto devotees and for the Emperor and his family. The ritual used at these *sosai* is characterized by the simplicity and aesthetic beauty invariably present in Shinto ceremonies. The ritual begins in the home where the corpse has been washed, dressed and placed in a coffin. The rite is inspired by Hirata Atsutane's thoughts on life and death, where the beginning of a person's life is compared to the rising of the sun and his or her death to its setting. During the ceremony the chief mourner conjures the evil spirits to depart and leave the soul of the deceased in peace. He purifies the house and all those present, sprinkling them with salt water. Then the spirit of the departed is bidden to enter the *tamashiro*, or small shrine, which holds the tablet on which his or her name has been inscribed. Purification, prayer and a sacred meal are essential elements in the Shinto ritual. The mourners share a meal and food is also offered to the deceased. The final prayers, before burial or cremation, imply that the soul will survive and express the hope that it will rest in peace.[5]

Bereavement in Japan

In Japan, the bereaved are not expected to sever their relationship with the dead by the grief work recommended by Western psychologists. Japanese culture encourages the living to maintain a relationship with the dead and the continuance of the relationship is facilitated by the presence of the family shrine. If the family shrine is not Shinto it is likely to be Buddhist, and both may be found in the same household. The family altar is used as though it is a 'hot line'. The living can light incense and symbolically make a telephone call to discuss current problems with a loved and cherished ancestor, the *kami*, of the shrine. When happy they can smile and share their good feelings with him; if sad they can shed tears in his presence. The ancestors can be cherished, fed, berated and idealized by all the family members. By this means the living maintain a continuous relationship with those they have loved and lost.[6]

Some Japanese homes have small private shrines in their gardens, but in most cases there is only a high shelf in a quiet, convenient place, to act as the family altar. If this is a Shinto shrine it will contain symbols of local *kami* and in the centre a *taima*. This is an inscribed board from the main Shinto shrine at Ise, which represents a universal *kami*. A lower shelf is provided for the ancestral spirits. On this is placed a small box containing the memorial tablets of dead relatives and a small mirror.

It is difficult for an outsider to distinguish between the worship the Japanese offer the universal *kami* and their veneration or worship of the ancestors. Nor can one easily distinguish the stage at which the grief of mourning moves into an acceptance of death and a new relationship with the ancestor. In considering these uncertainties, three factors need to be kept in mind. The rites associated with death, and the ancestors, are not merely rites of passage that enable the bereaved to detach themselves from the dead. They are seen as an essential service for the departed soul if it is to become a *kami* and not merely disintegrate in an impure land. Also, the Japanese see divinity in all things, and in honouring individual *kami*, including the ancestors, they may be doing so in a universal as well as a specific sense. Finally, a high proportion of Japanese widows feel that their dead husband is still close to them here on earth.[6] These perceptions enhance the meaningfulness of the rites for the dead that are performed at the family shrine.

Worship at the shrine is preceded by an act of purification, with a ritual washing of the face and a rinsing of the mouth. Food is offered at the shrine to the ancestors and the *kami*. The offering is normally of clean rice, water and salt, but on days of special significance to the ancestors the type of food they preferred when they were still alive will be offered instead. As a token of gratitude the worshipper may place a monthly pay cheque or a recently acquired diploma before the shrine, thus both acknowledging the help received from the *kami* and informing them of recent happenings within the family. The offerings are made with a slight bow and then two deep bows. A prayer is said either silently or aloud. This is followed by two deep bows, two handclaps at chest level, a deep bow, a light bow and the rite is over. Later the special food offerings are removed and served at mealtimes. These are accepted with a slight bow and handclap, the recognized way of saying 'thank you' to the *kami*.[7]

Bon Festival

Each summer there is an exodus of people from the cities to their home town for the Bon Festival, an occasion for fêting and consoling the spirits of the dead. The festival, which is observed mainly in small towns and villages, was introduced to Japan by the Buddhists. It is the Japanese equivalent of All Souls' Day but the occasions differ in two important ways. Firstly, unlike the Bon Festival, All Souls' Day is not an event of real importance in Western countries. Secondly, Christianity has never been easy with the idea that the dead may retain a close relationship with the living and has always tended to look upon such ideas as superstitious and sinful.

In Japan when the spirits return to their former homes for the Bon Festival, they are warmly welcomed. Family members provide a *mukaebi* or 'welcoming fire' and place offerings on the household altar. Two days later, the *okuribi* or 'sending-off fire' is lit to guide the spirits back to their ghostly abode. In some places, instead of lighting a fire people float candles down a nearby river. The Bon Festival has considerable social and domestic importance. Apart from the holiday atmosphere it engenders, it enables the living to consult with the dead about important ventures for which the co-operation of the ancestral *kami* is considered desirable.[8]

The ancestors' tablet

The ancestors' tablet is a uniquely oriental device, which has an honoured place in many Chinese and Japanese homes. Because of the socio-political changes that have taken place in the East, it is difficult to assess the importance that is given to tablets nowadays but they are of more than just historical interest. The purpose of the tablet is to provide a special place in the family home for the most important of a person's souls – it is commonly believed in some oriental countries that a person has more than one soul – so that they can watch closely over the activities of the family and receive offerings from its members.

A tablet is a length of wood, about 30 cm high, inscribed with details of the deceased. It carries the inscription 'the place of the spirit of . . . ' and one character in the inscription is at first deliberately omitted. The most important part of the tablet is the 'dot' or 'stroke', written in vermilion pencil to replace the character that has been left out. This 'dotting' of the character attracts the deceased's spirit to the tablet, and because of its importance the dot is normally inserted by a person of authority or high rank.[9] The tablet is then placed on the family altar with the other ancestral tablets.

Daily offerings are placed before the altar by the women of the household and an 'eternal' light illuminates the shrine. On more important days, especially the lunar New Year and the ancestors' birthdays, the man of the house presents more elaborate offerings. If the number of tablets in the shrine becomes excessive – five is considered to be the optimum number – the oldest tablets are removed and ritually burnt or buried. With increasing antiquity the ancestor is less able to help the family and accordingly the importance given to their welfare decreases. If, however, the ancestor has been an important member of the clan, the tablet cannot be discarded. It is then placed in the ancestral hall with the tablets of the senior members of the clan. Within this hall, which is managed by a small council, the ancestors continue to receive proper respect and gifts but with more formality and ceremony than at the family shrine.

The Chinese only care for and venerate the spirits of adult ancestors. No provision is made for the support of the souls of dead children and they are not honoured by a tablet in the family shrine. There are probably two reasons for this. Firstly, before China became a republic in 1912, its laws, customs and social structure were determined, as they had been for thousands of years, by Confucian principles, and these placed a very low valuation on young children. Secondly, the perceived relationship between the family and ancestors was the practical one of mutual support and no such reciprocal help would be expected from a child.

Chinese Attitudes to Death

The most significant event in China during the twentieth century was the accession of a communist government in 1949. This has had widespread repercussions. For instance, the sale of women, female infanticide, polygamy and concubinage – all previously common practices – have been made illegal. A later development was the unleashing by Chairman Mao of the Cultural Revolution in 1966. This, with its attacks on the four Os – old beliefs, old customs, old habits and old ideas – totally disrupted most aspects of Chinese society, being especially destructive in the spheres of education and religion. The one aspect of religious life that the communists did not strongly attack was the veneration of the ancestors. However, this forbearance applies only to practices in the family home and not to those associated with the larger kinship group or clan. The ancestral halls, which functioned as clan centres and temples, have been converted into schools and social centres, and the trust lands which financed these ancestral halls have been taken from the clans by the government.

The cult of the ancestors has always been one of the most distinctive features of Chinese life. Respectful veneration of the dead is as important to them as it is to the Japanese. Death is not considered to sever the bonds of kinship, it merely alters the way the relationship is maintained. Moreover, this relationship cannot be maintained by women even though they provide food offerings at the family shrine. The important sacrifices, which are essential for the wellbeing of the ancestors whether they are male or female, can only be offered by sons. This tradition extends back thousands of years and has always underpinned Chinese attitudes to the hereafter whatever philosophy or religion had been favoured by the government of the time. Whether the cult of the ancestors will survive the present changes is a matter for historians and sociologists to determine in the future. One thing is clear, however: the importance of maintaining a respectful relationship with the ancestors and providing them with the appropriate sacrifices, was most clearly defined in the teachings of Confucius, one of the great thinkers and reformers of the sixth century BC and a contemporary of Buddha, Pythagoras and Māhavira.

Confucianism

Confucianism has almost disappeared during the twentieth century. It was not a religion nor a speculative philosophy, though it possessed some aspects of both. It was the code of behaviour of an educated Chinese gentleman based on the Confucian concept of the 'Superior Man'. More importantly, it was the ethical and social code of the mandarins, the senior bureaucrats who administered China for almost 2,000 years.[10]

The Confucian ethic placed great importance on family relationships. Large sections of the legal code were concerned with the regulation of relationships in the family, between the wider kinship groups and with the provision of proper rites for the ancestors. It laid down detailed regulations for the type of mourning clothes that different members of the family should wear after a death, and failure to observe these rules was severely punished. The first duty of each person was to serve the family unit. This applied throughout life and continued after death. The child's duty to the parents did not end when the parents died; death merely altered the form the duty took. Filial care was reciprocated by the blessings the ancestors provided from the world of spirits.[11] Confucianism did not create these beliefs but it did prescribe the way the duties should be carried out.

Taoism

Taoism provided the Chinese people with the indigenous mystical philosophy and religion that Confucianism lacked. Its origins are obscure, but its roots probably developed within ancient Shamanistic practices and the cult of an earth or water goddess. It is closely linked with the Chinese concept of *Yang* and *Yin*, the interplay of masculine (*Yang*) and feminine (*Yin*) principles, which form the basis of much Chinese thinking. Early Taoist literature contains many references to

Yin, the dark feminine principle which is closely associated with the earth and water, but few references to *Yang*, which has close connections with the air and light. This early emphasis on *Yin* appears to have been replaced by a later preference for *Yang*, possibly because *Yin* became associated with death.

Taoism has a philosophical tradition and also a religious dimension with its own pantheon of gods. The latter stresses the importance of devotional worship as a means of attaining a favourable afterlife. Taoists have always been concerned with longevity and immortality. In its pursuit of longevity, Taoism is closely linked with traditional Chinese medicine, self-defence, charitable organizations and welfare. Longevity is striven for by various means, including the use of diet, medicines, gymnastics and breathing exercises. Immortality for the ancient Chinese meant physical immortality. Spiritual immortality was a concept they acquired only later from Buddhism. Physical immortality could be attained by the practices prescribed for longevity and by obtaining the mythical elixir of life. It was believed that by these means the existing body could be changed into a new body, but one of more durable and lighter materials than the normal physical body. At death the person would discard his or her worn out body as a snake sloughs off its skin and, within the new body, move into the abodes of bliss that were not outside but within the physical world.[12] This view of the afterlife has long been discarded and replaced by more spiritual concepts.

The Afterlife

The Chinese believe that an individual has more than one soul and, in accordance with the principles of *Yang* and *Yin*, at least one soul is masculine and another feminine. At death the souls separate and go different ways. The female soul sinks into the earth as *kwei* (a ghost) and disintegrates. The masculine soul rises and become *shen* (a spirit). The *shen* is the most important of the souls and it requires special veneration, though the *kwei* is not neglected and is visited during the *Quing Ming* festival when the graves are cleaned, joss sticks burnt, and the family picnic at the graveside. *Shen* souls reside in the spirit world after death, but they are also present in the tablets that are placed on the family shrine.

The Chinese believe that the dead are judged and then punished. One soul, which may be the *shen*, goes to Hell before moving to its allotted place in the spirit world. If this soul is generously provided with funds, it can use them to bribe the official custodians of Hell in order to receive more favourable treatment. Wherever they live, the spirits have the same needs as men and women. They require food, clothes, shelter, money and status symbols, and it is the duty of the living to provide them with these essentials. Food is offered to them at the family altar and their other needs are provided symbolically by the means of paper replicas. These are inscribed with the names of the ancestors, then burnt and dispatched to them in the smoke. The dead are commonly considered to be present when these gifts are offered. The support provided is mutual because the dead have vast though undefined powers. If displeased their anger can inflict disaster but, if treated with proper respect, they guarantee success in the activities of life. The special needs of the ancestors are determined through oracles or spiritual mediums. Through their agency a long shopping list may be presented by the dead, and the items may include money, clothes, a bed, or a motor car.

A family has to provide only for its own ancestors; it has no responsibility for the dead of other households. If there is no son to perform the necessary offices the ancestors become hungry and malevolent ghosts. To placate these demons, the Buddhists introduced public ceremonies of propitiation when offerings are made to the sonless dead. These offerings are not given for any charitable reason but to ensure that these ghosts do not become too malevolent and destructive. The ceremonies, which are held during the seventh lunar month, may be looked upon as an exercise in public mental health, or spiritual sanitation.

People without male descendants have an obvious problem within the Chinese perception of the afterlife. Young Chinese parents still attach great importance to having sons and it is known that female infants have a higher mortality rate in China than male infants. Also, when adjustments are made for differing life expectancies and fertility rates between countries, it is conservatively estimated that there is a deficit of 29 million women in China.[13] Some childless groups have managed to circumvent the problems caused by having no male offspring. Taoist monks and nuns elevate their deceased elders to the status of ancestors and provide them with appropriate veneration and sacrifices. While in some expatriate communities 'halls of all faiths' have been established which provide residential accommodation and funeral benefits for the childless elderly. They also enable the residents to establish a pseudo-kinship system that ensures ancestral respect for the dead and the proper care of the tablets of deceased members.[11]

Chinese Mourning Customs

Until the beginning of the twentieth century, mourning customs were strictly defined in Chinese law. Age, sex and marital status were the main determinants of the style of mourning followed by the bereaved. The mourning required of a husband and wife for a death in the wife's natal family was minimal. That required when a relative of the husband died was considerable. Deep mourning followed the death of an older member of the family, whereas the loss of a younger member, even the loss of a young son, required little or no mourning.

The mourning regulations were known as *wu-fu*. This term means the 'five kinds of clothing' and refers to the five kinds of mourning garments that were to be worn as prescribed by Confucian edicts. Each type of clothing was associated with a prescribed period of mourning. The longest period was 27 months and during this time the clothes authorized were made of undyed, unhemmed, coarse hemp, with grass sandals and a mourning staff. The shortest mourning period lasted three months and during this time mourners wore a dress of plain silky hemp.[14] Failure to follow the correct procedures of mourning was severely punished by fines, beatings, imprisonment or temporary exile. These laws were abolished when China became a republic in 1912, and a much shorter period of mourning became the norm. The wearing of a black armband is now the usual sign of mourning in Chinese communities.

Traditional Chinese Funerals

The traditional rites following a death involve the family only; they are not the concern of the wider community. These rites are elaborate and expensive. Apart from the family mourners, the funeral procession will include professional mourners, musicians and costumed figures. Papier mâché replicas of objects the deceased might need in the world of spirits will be a prominent feature. The obsequies may be Buddhist, Taoist or those of the popular religion. (In China there are recognized 'state religions' such as Buddhism, Christianity, Islam and Taoism, but the 'popular religion' has been banned and its practices declared illegal. It is a mixture of animism and spiritual mediumship, with elements of Taoism and Buddhism and its own local gods.) In the latter instance the local earth-god must be propitiated with offerings as he is the registrar of births, marriages and deaths for the Heavenly realms, and will conduct the soul on its passage through the dark regions.

Meanwhile the coffin stands in an elevated position surrounded by burning candles and the smoke of incense. Vast quantities of paper money are burnt for the soul to use in its new abode. A paper bicycle or other vehicle may be burnt for the soul to use as transport in the afterlife. Professional bearers carry the coffin to the chosen burial site, followed by the white-clad mourners lamenting loudly and sometimes crawling on their knees in grief. After the internment an inscribed tombstone with a photograph of the deceased marks the body's final resting place.

Immediate burial is not considered appropriate. This would be a sign of poverty and lower the prestige of the family in the eyes of the community. The corpse may be interred immediately but only as a temporary arrangement until a geomancer can determine the most auspicious date and place for burial. The deceased will then be disinterred, washed, cleansed with incense and buried in the new grave. Alternatively the corpse may be embalmed and kept in an earthenware urn, or a sealed coffin until an auspicious date and place for burial has been determined

Feng-shui

Most people agree that buildings, and places like cemeteries, should be appropriately sited. The Chinese believe that the position should be more than just a good physical location; it should also have a good *feng-shui*, a propitious balancing of the subtle forces of *yang* and *yin*. Underlying this idea is the belief that a correctly sited house enhances a family's health and prosperity. Similarly, the wellbeing of a family is considered to be affected by the *feng-shui* of the ancestors' graves.

The normal way of determining the *feng-shui* of a site is by geomancy, a form of divination. Once the site has been chosen, care is taken to enhance the *feng-shui* by altering nearby features where this is deemed desirable. If the site is subsequently damaged the opposite effect is achieved and the *feng-shui* is soon lost unless the damage is quickly repaired. As a consequence of these beliefs, *feng-shui* fighting became a common feature of Chinese life. Such conflicts are rare nowadays, but in the past hostile clans would not only attack a rival's crops and villages; they would also deliberately destroy the *feng-shui* of the graves by felling nearby trees and displacing masonry. They thought that by these means the *feng-shui* associated with graves would be diminished and a rival's power and prosperity weakened.[15]

Although the original site of a grave will have been carefully chosen, its *feng-shui* may be deemed unacceptable later, possibly because of a decline in the family's fortunes. When this happens a new site will be found, again with the help of geomancy, and the body will be disinterred and reburied.

Modern Funerals

China is a vast country with an enormous population and many different ethnic and cultural groups. There is some evidence that traditional rites and customs have been maintained, to various degrees, in some rural areas but not so in the cities. In Chinese cities, funerals are now simple and relatively cheap affairs. The pattern seems to conform closely to that in Western countries with undertakers organizing the funerals on behalf of the families. The body is taken to a funeral parlour, where wreaths and flowers may be sent and where friends and colleagues may also gather to pay their last respects to the deceased. Their tribute may take the form of a eulogy after which the mourners walk past the coffin and may later meet together for a meal.

In urban areas, cremation has replaced burial as the preferred method of disposal of the dead. Funeral processions to the crematoria are discouraged but are still seen sometimes in Chinese cities. After the ashes have cooled they are collected in a box and handed to a relative. The name of the deceased is inscribed on the box, which also carries his or her photograph. The box is then taken to a funeral hall where it is stored with the ashes of other people. If they wish, the relatives are allowed to place a small tray on the box of ashes, and some memento of the deceased, such as a watch or fountain pen, may be placed on the tray. Although these articles could be easily stolen, they are not disturbed by visitors to the hall. Finally, relatives may visit the ashes whenever they wish. Those who do so usually stand quietly in front of the box, remembering the dead in the silence of their own thoughts and feelings.

Sea Burial

During the 50 years of Communist rule the population in China has increased twofold and there are now 10 million deaths each year in the country. Cremation, though widely practised, is still unpopular but burial space is very limited and the only people who can be legally interred in cities like Shanghai are overseas Chinese who are willing to pay inflated prices for burial plots in the special cemeteries reserved for them. Everyone else has to be content with very limited space – only 1.5 square metres is allowed for the disposal of their ashes, and the cheapest site costs as much as a month's wages.

To ease the pressure on available land, the Government has been actively promoting the practice of sea burials since the year 2000 – these are carried out free of charge. The first mass sea burial was undertaken at the mouth of the Yangtze river in April 2000 when 230 Chinese families scattered the ashes of their loved ones on the sea.

The burial was carefully organized by the Shanghai funeral department. The boat, decorated with black ribbons and banners, sailed far out into the river mouth, and there the families emptied the ashes into shutes suspended over the water.[16] This innovatory form of disposal has environmental and costs benefits but is still unlikely to be popular with the Chinese.

Chapter 5
African and Afro-Caribbean Beliefs and Customs

We carry within us the wonders
we seek without us. There is all
Africa and her prodigies within us.

Sir Thomas Browne; Religio Medici

Afro-Caribbeans

In every country the population tends to be a mixture of races, each with its own cultural tradition. This is apparent in the West Indies where people of African, Asian and European origin have intermarried with each other and with the indigenous people, the Caribs. There, most people are now Afro-Caribbean in origin and Christian in religious adherence. But it would be strange if their spiritual beliefs did not display something of the people's African heritage. It does so, perhaps most clearly in the way many Afro-Caribbeans view the world of the spirits, which is for them not a vague concept or a far-away place but a living reality. Many believe that the ancestral dead can continue their existence alongside the living and so after the initial burial they hold a second funeral service, just as they do in Africa, to make sure that the 'hovering spirits' are at rest and do not disturb the living.[1]

The funerals of Afro-Caribbeans tend to be very warm-hearted occasions and they also last for quite a long time. When a West Indian dies, the death is treated as a community event in which everyone, including the children, is involved. Neighbours support the bereaved family emotionally and by the provision of food. They attend the preceding wake and fill the church at the funeral service. Expressions of grief with lamentations and tears are much in evidence, but less obvious are the sashes close relatives may have wound around their waists to ease 'the pain in their stomach' caused by the loss of their loved one.[1] In spite of the grief, there is a strong sense of rejoicing based on the expectation that the deceased is going to heaven. The mood can be so joyous that a West Indian youth, speaking in a discussion group, said that he had never been so happy as he had been at the funeral of his uncle. He felt particularly uplifted by the music and the singing of gospel songs.

Burial is the normal mode of disposal. Observances at the grave-side are likely to show traces of former African customs; for instance, it is common for mourners to throw money on to the coffin to help the dead on their way, and the grave is likely to be filled in before everyone leaves the cemetery to make sure that the spirits cannot escape. A second service is held nine days after the interment to help the spirits find rest.[1]

Some distinction needs to be made between Rastafarians and other Afro-Caribbeans. The former belong to a political and reli-gious group which was founded in Jamaica in the 1920s by Marcus Garvey. Its members can usually be distinguished by their dreadlocks (uncut hair, washed and braided) and woolly hats in the Ethiopian colours of red, green and gold. They follow the Nazarite Vow of Separation which forbids certain foods and activities, including contact with dead bodies. Consequently, unlike other West Indians, Rastafarians place little emphasis on attendance at funerals or the performance of the last rites.

African Religions

Whilst more sophisticated people may deny the existence of a spiritual dimension to life, Africans affirm it. They see the world as a spiritual arena in which great psychic forces interplay and the spirits of the dead take a close interest in family affairs. This attitude exists even among the large proportion of Africans who have discarded ancient tribal beliefs and embraced Western religions and ideologies. The advance of Western religions, education and commerce may have weakened the authority of traditional religions but it has not destroyed them.

The situation is complex as one of the most dynamic phenomena in Africa today is the growth of independent churches and new reli-gious movements. Estimates of the number of these sects vary, but they probably exceed 10,000 – spread over such regions as Nigeria, Ghana, central Kenya, Zaire and South Africa, and about 15 per cent of all Christians in Africa belong to such groups.[2] They form a bridge between Western and traditional African religions which enable the ancient customs and beliefs to retain a place within modern African society. Moreover, there is inevitably a diffusion of ideas when different cultures meet. This exchange of ideas is not unilateral, it occurs in both directions. Africans, for instance, are interested in developing their own Christian theology, which uses classical African images to portray the essential tenets of Christianity. At the same time the animistic belief in nature spirits that Christian missionaries had tried to eradicate in Africa appears to be gaining ground in Western countries as part of the New Age philosophy.

Africa is a continent with many different tribes and nations, and its religious traditions are equally varied. Although Islam has dominated North Africa for 1,200 years and Roman Catholicism is now pre-eminent in the rest of Africa, most tribes have their own indigenous beliefs and customs. These are often seen by people from other countries as primitive and debased, but this misjudges a rich and vital spiritual resource. The size of the continent precluded the establishment of a uniform belief system, but an underlying pattern can be detected. These beliefs are not recorded in sacred Scriptures nor discernible in great temples, but they are integrated into the daily lives of the people and have their own basic structure. The spirit world is seen as a pyramid, with a supreme Creator at the apex, nature gods and ancestors on the sides, and a base which is formed by superstition and magical practices.

The attitude of Africans to life is essentially religious and, despite the apparent polytheism, they have a monotheistic view of Creation. Tribal religions recognize the existence of a Supreme Creator but he is usually considered to be too remote to be concerned with the affairs of men and women. When they have problems, they turn to local spirits, gods and the ancestors for help. The latter have great importance in African cultures, being seen as a large invisible community extending beyond, yet close to, the human sphere.

Tribal Africans recognize no sharp distinction between the sacred and the secular. Material and spiritual forces are considered to intertwine, the former as a vehicle for the latter.[3] Death scarcely separates the living from the dead, who are sometimes referred to as the living dead. The ancestors inhabit their own spirit world but they still visit their families and retain an interest in them. Family property belongs to the ancestors and they must be consulted by dreams or oracles if there is any question of selling land. They are especially interested in the birth of children, as a newborn child may enable some aspect of their spirit to be reincarnated.[4]

Belief in reincarnation

Belief in reincarnation is reported in many African societies but their concept of it differs from that taught by the Indian religions.[5] They do not share the Hindu and Buddhist belief that the world is a place of suffering and illusion, from which one will eventually be liberated only after many incarnations. They see the world as a place of light and warmth, to which the dead are only too glad to return from the spirit world of cold and darkness. The African's attitude is world affirming not world renouncing; this is the best of all possible worlds, it is a punishment to be detained in Hades and a curse for a woman to be barren as it blocks the channels of rebirth.[3]

Africans reject the Indian view that after people have died their essential nature is reincarnated fully into a new physical body. For the African, death is a reality and the end of life as such. Consequently reincarnation is usually seen as an incomplete or fragmentary event. The living dead continue their lives in the spirit world – tending cattle, raising spirit children, eating and drinking – but some of their characteristics may also be reincarnated when a new child is born into the family. This has nothing to do with, and should not be confused with, the transmission of genes; these can be acquired from outside the family unit by a casual sexual encounter, but the essential characteristics of a dead relative can only be reincarnated in a child conceived within a marriage that has been blessed by the proper family rites.[6]

The African concept of reincarnation is difficult to understand, but it seems to be based on a perception of individuality that is similar to the beliefs of the ancient Egyptians and the teachings of Jungian psychology – that each person has many psychic constituents and that the mask each person presents to the world hides many personalities. The African believes that some of these personal characteristics retain their individuality after death and can be reborn in the children of kinsfolk. As a consequence, a person may be reincarnated simultaneously in several individuals regardless of sex. It is as though the living dead are able to imbue some people with aspects of their own psyche, whilst continuing their own separate existence in the spirit world.[5]

Ancestral spirits

It is difficult for the European or American to understand fully the importance of the ancestral spirits to the Africans. Mbiti expressed it thus: 'Whatever science may do to prove or disprove the existence or non-existence of the spirits, one thing is undeniable, namely for the African peoples the spirits are a reality which must be reckoned with, whether it is clear, blurred or confused reality. And it demands and deserves more than academic recognition.'[7] Africans believe that many other spirits are in close contact with the physical world. There are nature spirits inhabiting fields, trees, stretches of water, and mountains. There are also demi-gods and spirits whose special concern is with the tribe or nation.

The character of the relationship between the living and the spirits varies throughout the continent but it is a real, active and powerful relationship, especially with the spirits of those who have died recently. Various rites are performed to maintain this contact; these may involve the sacrifice of animals, offerings of food, or the pouring of libations of beer, water, milk or coffee. In some areas this is done daily but most Africans do it less often. Failure to observe these acts is a sign that the people have broken their links with the departed and have forgotten the spirits. This is regarded as extremely dangerous for the individual, the family and the tribe.[8]

The living dead are the closest links that people have with the spirit world. They sometimes reappear to their relatives, especially the older members of the family, but rarely to those outside the family unit. When they do reappear the response of the living is likely to be ambivalent. They are both wanted and not wanted, as people realize quite clearly that death has erected a distinct barrier between them and the living dead. They are welcomed, but not with the normal spoken courtesies of every day life, and though they are treated with respect and supplied with food and libations these, para-doxically, are also a way of informing them to move on.[8]

Attention is given to only five generations of the ancestral dead as these are considered to be still part human as well as part spirit.[7] After the sixth generation the living dead lose the remnants of their human nature and become pure spirit. This paradoxically involves a loss of status as it is believed that they can no longer influence the lives of people. With this loss of status the living dead lose their personal names and become an 'it' and no longer a 'he' or 'she' known by name. The traditional belief is that these 'pure spirits' no longer possess a personal immortality, because they have entered the state of collective immortality. There is no judgement in the spirit world, neither is there any evolution or even disintegration. It is a static changeless state that continues for eternity. God does exist, but is so far distant that in African beliefs there is no hope or possibility that the soul will attain anything of the divinity of God.[5]

Rites of passage

There are many different ceremonies associated with death, burial and the living dead in Africa. These ceremonies are often long, complex and expensive. Some customs and beliefs are common to all parts of tribal Africa. Death, for instance, is never considered to be due just to natural causes; it is always believed to have been brought about by some other agency, usually human, most commonly by magic or witchcraft.[9] Mbiti explains it in this way: 'a bereaved mother whose child has died from malaria will not be satisfied with the explanation that a mosquito, carrying malaria parasites, stung the child and caused it to die. She will wish to know why the mosquito stung her child and not somebody else's child. The only satisfactory answer is that "someone" sent the mosquito or worked other evil magic against her child. This is not a scientific answer but it is reality for the majority of African peoples.'[10] As a consequence, attempts will be made, probably with the help of a witchdoctor, to identify the guilty person so that the latter can be made to make reparation. If the accused, although innocent, cannot prove their innocence, they will accept their guilty status and provide redress, though there may be a period of bargaining in which the amount of compensation to be paid is agreed.

When death is imminent everyone known to the family is expected to visit the dying person. Those who fail to do so are likely to be suspected of having caused the death by witchcraft. Attendance is also promoted by the belief that non-attenders may be troubled by the dead person's spirit. Close relatives maintain a constant vigil with the sick person during the terminal phase of the illness. This enables them to show their solidarity and concern, and provides the patient with an opportunity to say farewell and apologize for any offences he or she may have committed. A sacrificial meal may be eaten at this time of crisis. An animal – ox, goat or sheep – is slaughtered, cooked and served to members of the family. This sacrifice serves two purposes. If sick people are lingering in pain, it may help to hasten their death. The sacrifice is also the last gift of the patient to the living-dead, who are considered to be present and partaking of the meal. It is the traditional African method of asking the living dead to receive the newcomer into the spirit world peacefully and provide them with a place in a friendly community.[11]

After the death the first task of the bereaved family is to dispose of the body. This must be done quickly for corpses rapidly putrefy in a hot climate and soon become a source of pollution for the entire village. Infusions of the leaves of scented shrubs may be used to wash the body. If the head is shaved – a custom in some tribes – great care will be taken to ensure that all the hair is buried with the body so that there is no possibility that an enemy might steal it and use it for witchcraft.[10] The corpse may be buried naked, or first dressed in its best clothes and finery and photographed surrounded by the family. The traditional practice of the Zulus was to bind the corpse in the foetal position in his or her blanket or hide mat, and sit it in its hut until burial. Meanwhile the women wail loudly, for immediately after the death the funeral wail commences.[11, 12]

There is a wide variety of funeral practices, but corpses are usually buried. Internment normally takes place soon after death, the grave being dug by close male relatives. Graves vary in shape and size throughout the continent. Elaborate coffins reflecting the rank and skills of the deceased are constructed in some areas, but burial procedures are becoming increasingly standardized in most places. The box coffin is now widely used even by those tribes that previously did not use coffins. They are easy to obtain and prevent the earth falling directly on the body, which some tribes would consider a defilement of the dead.

The men lead the funeral procession, the women, now silent, following. In many societies, money, food, clothes and tobacco are placed in the grave for the dead to use on their journey into the next world. This applies even though for the majority of African peoples the next world is geographically 'here', being separated from this world only by virtue of being invisible to human beings.[13] One former custom has been abandoned. This was the killing and burial of wives and close attendants of a powerful king so that they could accompany the deceased into the spirit world. A man's weapons may be broken before being placed in the grave with him. This is to ensure that he doesn't fight with the ancestors if he becomes troublesome in the world of spirits. The eldest son throws in the first handful of earth, then each male and female relative does the same. Finally the whole grave is filled in and firmed down, or covered with stones and bushes.

Mourning customs

There are many different tribes and kingdoms in Africa, each with its own mourning customs, so the subject cannot be dealt with comprehensively here, but certain common attitudes and practices can be mentioned. For instance, in tribal Africa death is not seen as an event, occurring on a particular day, but as a process that continues long after the physical body has been interred.[14] It includes the traditional 'mourning period' in which grief work may be publicly undertaken, and continues for many years, even decades, until no memory remains of the individual. This period is greatly curtailed if there is no son to mourn, remember and offer sacrifices to the deceased.[14]

When a death occurs, all the normal activities of the village are set aside and a number of strict taboos are observed. Death defiles the whole village and everybody is weakened and endangered by it. After the burial all the villagers take strengthening medicines and they also give them to their cattle. Purification ceremonies are essential for cleansing the village. The people wash themselves in rivers, or with special herbs, or may walk through smoke to be purified by the fire. The day after the funeral an animal may be killed to 'wash the hands' of those who took part in the ceremony. This is not a sacrifice, as no meat offering is set aside for the ancestors nor are they addressed in any way. It is simply a purification ceremony known amongst the Zulus as *imbuzi yokuges' izandla* (goat for the washing of hands).[12]

Having strengthened and purified themselves, the people of the village are relatively safe though they are still in a dangerous situation and have to observe many taboos. At this time all unnecessary activities cease and no one works, not even in the fields. There is no singing or rejoicing and all marriages are postponed. Close relatives may vacate their homes and sleep in the open air for weeks after the funeral. In some tribes, widows and widowers have to undergo a prolonged period of mourning during which they remain chaste, unwashed, dress only in old clothes and sleep in different places at night. The last directive is important for a widow as it protects her from her dead husband who may wish to continue his earthly married life and seek sexual intercourse with her. Some months later she will bathe, dress in her best clothes and remarry, often a member of her late husband's family.[15]

In central Africa, a widow may have to undergo a 'cleansing ceremony' to drive away the husband's ghost; this ceremony involves having sexual intercourse with a close relative of the husband and this could be one possible explanation for the particularly rapid spread of AIDS in Uganda. The custom of inheriting the wife of a deceased brother is fairly common in Africa. Children born after this inheritance generally belong to the deceased man. A few tribes have sororate marriages, in which a husband marries one of his deceased wife's sisters. In Africa, the terms brother and sister embrace a much wider kinship than in Western countries, and each person may have literally hundreds of siblings. This is of great social and psychological value as it provides a deep sense of security in the otherwise insecure world in which African peoples live.[16]

After the mourning period a widower may slaughter an animal as a further act of purification and as a sign that he can remarry if he so wishes. Months or years after the burial, a second ceremony is arranged 'to make the grave firm'. This is an important ceremony and close relatives living overseas will fly back for the occasion. It is a festive occasion involving the whole community. There is drinking, singing and dancing, and it was once customary in some areas to drive cattle over the grave to firm it down. Sacrifices and prayers are offered asking the living dead to be helpful and not troublesome. Although the deceased is now recognized as an ancestor who may be called upon for help, the aim of this rite is to separate them from their earthly family. The ceremony is also intended to ensure that the deceased remains content in the spirit world and does not become a dissatisfied ghost.[17]

Chapter 6
Jewish and Muslim Funeral and Mourning Customs

Lay her i' the earth:
And from her fair and unpolluted flesh
May violets spring.

Hamlet

Judaism

Generalizations are usually flawed but it is probably true to say that no other race has been so sustained by its mourning customs as have the Jewish people. With no country of their own for 2,000 years, and often persecuted within the lands in which they have settled, their ability to maintain a separate identity as a race is remarkable. Their survival is partly explained by Rabbi Rabbinowicz in his rhetorical question, 'Can people disappear and be annihilated so long as the child remembers the parents?'[1] The question demands the answer *no*, and the mourning and burial customs of Judaism have been uniquely important in helping to maintain the separate identity of this people.

The codes for mourning and for the disposal of the body are precise. Central to these customs are *Kaddish* (the mourner's prayer) and the set periods of mourning known as *Shiva* and *Yahrzeit*. It is said that nothing unites the Jewish people so much as *Kaddish*, affectionately called 'the watchman and guardian of the people'. It is the traditional prayer of mourners, but its words are of sanctification and praise. Few Jews will refuse a request to form a *minyan* (congregation of 10 adult male Jews) for *Kaddish* in the synagogue. It is proclaimed in the home by the eldest son when a death occurs, and monthly in the synagogue during the 11 months of mourning. It is always said standing and, when completed, the mourners take three steps backwards as though in the presence of a king. It begins with the affirmation:

> Let us magnify and let us sanctify the great name of God
> in the world which He created according to His will.

and ends with the verse:

> May He who makes peace in the high places make peace for us and for all
> Israel, and say ye Amen,

It is an expression of faith by the mourners that although they are
distressed, they still believe in God and that life is worthwhile.[2]

Jewish funeral rites

There are discernible differences in mourning and funeral rites
within every religion, and such variations are to be found in Judaism
also. Whilst the underlying pattern is true for all Jewish sects, the
account given here applies particularly to Orthodox Jews.

Respect for the dead is a basic principle of Judaism. When a death
occurs, the corpse is covered with a sheet and laid on the floor with
the feet pointing to the door, and a lighted candle is placed near the
head. The body is never left unattended, verses from the Psalms
being recited by those present. The rites of purification and
the clothing of the body are undertaken by at least two members of
the *Chevrah Kadisha*, an association of Jews that is concerned with the
burial of the dead. Following the established custom they pour copi-
ous quantities of warm water over the sheeted body, dry it with clean
sheets and wrap it in a shroud of fine linen. The body is dressed and
the deceased's prayer shawl (*tallit*) is torn to render it ritually unfit
before being spread out in a plain unvarnished coffin. The body is
lifted, face upwards, into the coffin to lie upon the shawl. Sometimes
earth from the Holy Land is placed inside the coffin with the corpse.
This is in accord with a traditional Jewish belief that when the
Messiah appears those who have died, but have lived a pious life, will
roll underground to the Holy Land and be resurrected from the
dead in that country. The earth is sprinkled in the coffin as a
symbolic preparation for this longed-for journey.[3]

Cremation and embalmment are forbidden to Orthodox Jews.
The body must be buried – and within 24 hours of death. At the
Jewish cemetery the coffin is taken to the *odell* (a hall) for the first part
of the burial service. Then during the passage to the grave, several
stops are made for lamentation and the recitation of Psalm 91.
Garments are ritually torn at the graveside, if the mourners have not
done so previously in the house. The coffin is interred with a short

prayer and each person present places three spadesful of earth in the grave to symbolize the threefold nature of man: soul, spirit and breath. When the grave is filled, all those present wash their hands and return to the hall where Psalm 91 is recited followed by *Kaddish*. The mourners pluck a few blades of grass as they leave the cemetery and say: 'And may they blossom out of the city like the grass of the earth' or 'He remembereth that we are dust', which are customary allusions to the resurrection of the dead. Flowers are not placed on the grave as this is regarded as *Chukat Hagoy* (a pagan custom).

Jewish mourning

Immediately after the funeral, the family return to the house of the deceased for *Shiva*. This is a unique institution, a seven-day period of family reunion in which no tasks are undertaken and only certain parts of the Scriptures can be read. The house is lit continuously by candles, mirrors are covered and the family sits only on low stools. Friends and neighbours will visit but, for the first three days, the mourners do not greet people or reply to them, nor do they say the daily prayers. The first meal is provided by the visitors. This is a traditional meal called *Sudat Havra'ah* (meal of consolation), which always consists of hard boiled eggs and rolls of bread brought in wicker baskets. The meal is symbolic, eggs being the symbol of life and birth, and bread the most staple of foods. Salt is excluded from the table. In Judaism the family table is seen as a sacrificial altar where salt is used in the meal offerings, and mourners are not permitted to offer sacrifices.

Shiva is the first and most intense part of a 30-day mourning period (*Sheloshim*), during which the change from the sadness of bereavement to normal life is allowed to take place. It is not necessarily a time of intense gloom, though it does provide an opportunity for deep grief to be explored and dealt with. If the deceased has led a rewarding life and died within the fullness of age, the atmosphere is likely to be, if not celebratory, at least sufficiently relaxed for happy memories, and perhaps even jokes, about the deceased to be exchanged. During *Sheloshim* the mourners' hair is kept uncut and they may not use scissors to cut their nails.

The anniversary of a parent's death (*Yahrzeit*) is observed punctiliously. It is a day of study for the mourner, amusements are avoided and donations made to worthy causes. The house is lit by a memorial lamp or candle for the 24 hours of the anniversary and *Yahrzeit* is often observed as a fast day. Like *Kaddish*, *Yahrzeit* reinforces the unity of the Jewish people by drawing the mourner back to the synagogue where customarily he conducts the service and the mourner's *Kaddish* is recited. A year after the death a simple tombstone is placed on the grave. It is thought to be psychologically undesirable for the family to visit the grave during the first year of mourning, but thereafter visits to the grave are traditionally made before the High Holidays and during *Seret Yemei Teshuva* (the Ten Days of Repentance).

In Reform and Liberal Judaism the observances are much less strict than for Orthodox Jews. Cremation is accepted and the mourning rituals viewed with flexibility. Members of these branches of Jewry are encouraged to give equal status to women in the observation of mourning customs. *Shiva* is often reduced to one night and its effectiveness as an emotional and psychological support is sometimes questioned. Garments are not likely to be torn, nor mirrors covered, but the throwing of earth on the grave is considered helpful; mourners often say that this simple act provides a very direct way of acknowledging and accepting the death.[4]

Islam

There are two main Muslim sects, the *Sunni* and the *Shia*. Breakaway sub-sects include the *Ismaili* with the Aga Khan as its spiritual leader, and the *Alawite* sect to which the ruling party in Syria belongs. Most Muslims belong to the *Sunni* sect and the descriptions given here apply particularly to that group.

The first words spoken to a Muslim at birth and the last they should utter, or hear, when they die are the *Shahada*, the Muslim declaration of faith, 'there is no God but God and Muhammad is his prophet' (*Lailaha illa Llah, Muhammedun rasula Llah*). Muslims will undertake their own spiritual preparation for death by prayer and reading the *Qur'ān*. At the moment of death they should be facing towards Mecca. The corpse is considered to belong to God and is treated with great respect. It should not be touched by a non-Muslim, but if this cannot be avoided the attendant should wear gloves.

Burial is mandatory and this should be done as soon after death as possible. Post-mortem examinations are forbidden unless specifically required for medico-legal reasons.[5] One outcome of this respect for the corpse is that Muslims have been reluctant to donate organs for transplant operations. In some countries this problem has been resolved by the issue of local *fatwahs* which allow surgeons to take organs from the brain dead for transplant purposes. Such a *fatwah* was issued in the UK in 1995.

Muslim funerals

There is a strict procedure for washing the body and covering it with a shroud. It must be washed at least three times with soap or detergent and water, starting with the parts of the body normally washed by a Muslim before prayer. These ablutions are undertaken by a male relative for a man, and by a female relative for a woman. The eyes are closed, the feet tied and the jaw bound to the rest of the head with religiously pure material. Perfume may be used, or camphor placed, in the orifices and armpits. During these offices prayers are said and passages read from the *Qur'ān*. The body is clothed in simple cotton garments and covered with a white shroud of poor material.

It is customary for the enshrouded body to be placed directly into the grave. In Western countries local by-laws are observed, and the body is placed in a simple box-coffin before burial. Loud lamentations and the tearing of clothes are discouraged, and usually only men accompany the funeral procession to the grave. In Muslim countries the body is placed on a bier and carried shoulder high to the mosque, or directly to the burial ground, for the *Salat-ul-Janazah*. This funeral prayer is an essential element of the service for all Muslims. It is said in congregation with the bier lying in front of the Imam, who stands facing Mecca whilst the people stand facing him.

There is no bowing or prostration with this funeral prayer. It consists of four *takbirs* or recitations of *Allah Akber* (God is Most Great). After the first *takbir*, praise is offered and the *Al-Fatiha*, the opening chapter of the *Qur'ān* read. After the second *takbir*, the *Ibrahimi* prayer is recited asking God to exalt Muhammad and the family of Muhammad. After the third *takbir*, there is a prayer for forgiveness for the deceased. The fourth *takbir* is followed by *Taslim*, the turning of the head first to the right and then to the left, a gesture meaning 'peace be on thee and the mercy of God'.[6] At the interment the body is buried with the head towards Mecca. The grave is filled with the earth raised slightly. In Saudi Arabia the graves are left unmarked; elsewhere, graves are often marked with a headstone, sometimes carrying a photograph of the deceased. Members of the family visit the grave each Friday for 40 days and visits are also customary on *Eid* (festival) days. Graves are a reminder of death and the hereafter. The Prophet visited graves himself and encouraged his followers to do likewise.

Mourning in Islam

Muslims show great solidarity with the bereaved in times of grief. Relatives and friends will visit the home of the deceased to comfort the family, recite from the *Qur'ān* and pray that the deceased may have God's forgiveness and mercy. Failure to attend a wedding may be forgiven, but every effort has to be made to attend a funeral, even though this usually takes place within 24 hours of death. If attendance at the funeral is impossible then one must at least visit the family at the earliest opportunity.[7]

Mourning usually lasts for about a month but may vary with the degree of kinship and in different communities. The family stays indoors for the three days following the funeral, and during this time friends visit to provide companionship, prepare food and give whatever help is required. Donations are made to good causes on behalf of the dead person. The mourning customs are more stringent for women than for men. This is because a woman may remarry and it is important for the family, and any future husband, to know if she is pregnant with her dead spouse's child. Consequently, she is expected to remain in her own home for the first 130 days of widowhood; during this time she must not wear bright clothes, jewellery or cosmetics. If she is pregnant the restrictions last only until the child is born. If she is the sole breadwinner, she is allowed to go out to work during the day but must return home before nightfall. Prolonged grief is discouraged because of the expectation that the deceased will meet God and find eternal peace. Islam recognizes, however, that grief needs to be expressed and, during the first few days of mourning, professional mourners (*Kriah*) may visit the family to help them in their grieving.

Chapter 7
The Funeral Rites of Christians

Nothing in his life
Became him like the leaving of it; he died
As one that had been studied in his death
To throw away the dearest thing he owned,
As 'twere a careless trifle.

Macbeth

Funeral Directors

The part played by professional mourners, musicians and, in China, of funeral parlours in the ceremonies for the dead has been mentioned in earlier chapters. In the West, the main functionary is usually the funeral director and their contribution to the disposal of the dead, and to helping and supporting the bereaved, though often overlooked, needs to be recognized.

Once the province of the jobbing carpenter or small family firm, funeral directing is now a large-scale business mainly organized by a few major companies. Employees of these companies receive appropriate training and are encouraged to take the examinations set by the Association of Funeral Directors. Their function is to act as the agent, technical adviser, contractor, master of ceremonies and custodian of the body for their client.[1]

As adviser, funeral directors explain to the bereaved relatives the procedures for the days ahead and the various documents that are required. They make contact with the clergy, cemetery or crematorium, place notices in selected newspapers, arrange for the printing of service leaflets and for transport. If the officiating clergy have had no previous contact with the family, as happens quite frequently, the funeral directors provide them with relevant details about the deceased and the principal mourners.

Funeral directors accept direct responsibility for the care of the corpse and for delaying putrefaction by refrigeration or embalmment. If the last rites have not been performed by a nurse or the family, they will arrange for the body to be washed and clothed before being placed into the coffin. They make sure that the deceased lies supine in the coffin with the head resting high on a pillow and the hands on the abdomen or chest. A small napkin is placed upon the face and clean linen spread over the rest of the body. When handling the body, funeral directors are expected to behave as if the next of kin were present, or as if the deceased was a member of their own family.[2]

The role of funeral directors is such that their services are required only when a family is confronted with the crisis of death. This provides them with a unique opportunity to support and comfort the bereaved, a function that is becoming increasingly important in communities where close ties between neighbours are no longer the rule. Funeral directors need to be tactful and support-ive, knowledgeable and in charge, and yet relatively inconspicuous. They seem to achieve these ends as, if asked who has been support-ive, relatives will often say how helpful the funeral director has been. Their professional skills are also recognized by the clergy and I know of one chaplain who advises young curates to observe how funeral directors approach and speak to relatives; he considers this to be the most effective way of teaching them how best to behave towards mourners and at funerals.

Despite their useful and specialist role, there is no legal require-ment in many countries for a bereaved family to employ a funeral director. In the UK for instance, if the family wishes it can arrange its own funeral at a much reduced cost. This entails obtaining the appropriate documents, making arrangements with the cemetery or crematorium, and placing the body into a coffin. Then the coffin has to be taken to the church for a funeral service, if this is desired, or just directly to the place of disposal.

Eastern Orthodox Church

The central doctrine of Christianity is based on the life, death and resurrection of Christ. This is celebrated most clearly in the burial service of the Eastern Orthodox Church. When members of this church are dying, they will wish to confess their sins to God in the presence of a priest. After death the body is washed and clothed in fresh garments so that the deceased may appear clean before God at the resurrection. An icon of Christ is placed in the hand as a token that they have believed in Christ and surrendered their soul to him. A chaplet is placed upon the brow. This strip of material carries depictions of Jesus Christ, Mary his Mother, and St John the Baptist, together with the words, 'O Holy God, Holy Mighty, Holy Immortal, have mercy upon us'. Thus the deceased is symbolically adorned with a wreath, like a warrior who has won a victory.[3]

In some Orthodox churches there may be a separation of sexes within the church, with the men standing on the right and the women on the left side of the church. It is customary for the women's heads to be covered with a scarf or shawl. During the burial service the coffin lies in the centre of the church facing the altar. It is usually left open so that the body is in full view of the congregation. Here the ultimate tragedy of death is revealed. Death destroys the individual not just the body. It shatters the unity of body and soul, making the body a corpse and the soul a ghost. It is symbolic of humanity's separation from God. This open evaluation of death leads to a true appreciation of Christ's resurrection. The great tragedy is overcome by Christ's victory. The funeral rite is permeated by the celebration of Christ's resurrection. Light-coloured vestments are worn by the priests. An abundance of lights, burning candles and incense dominates the external actions of the service. The inner pattern of the Liturgy is the Easter Hymn,

> Christ is risen from the dead
> Trampling down death by death
> And upon those in the tomb bestowing life.

The body of the deceased is repeatedly incensed as a sign that 'the redemption of our bodies has already begun'. Psalm 119, the praise of the law of God, forms a large part of the text of the service. The funeral dirge is the singing of 'Alleluia', which glorifies the presence of Christ even in death. The service reveals the destiny of each member of the Church. They are confronted by death in all its reality but, through their sacramental unity with Christ, already possess the token of their deliverance.[4] Before leaving the church, each member of the congregation will kiss the deceased, or the coffin if it is sealed, as a last farewell.

At the interment, the priest scatters a shovelful of earth crosswise upon the remains as a token that everything in the world belongs to God. Then he pours in oil from the shrine lamp and ashes from the thurible as symbols that the life that is extinguished on earth is still acceptable to God. After the grave is filled in and before the people depart, further prayers are said for the soul of the deceased.

Roman Catholic Church

In the Roman Catholic Church the ritual associated with death is both a preparation for death and a rite of passage for the deceased into the next phase of life. It begins when the terminal nature of the illness is accepted by the sick person. The priest then offers the invalid the *Viaticum* – food for a journey – and the Prayer of Commendation, 'May the Lord Jesus Christ protect you and lead you into eternal life'. Ideally these acts should take place within the context of a full Eucharist, and with the family, friends and representatives of the community present. This helps to emphasize the unity of the Church with the dying person. The relationship is reciprocated. Dying people can provide support and the essence of their life's experiences to those about them. In this special context the *Viaticum* is food for the journey towards death, and beyond that into the next life. Although the moment of death may still be some time away, every subsequent communion possesses this distinctive nature of the *Viaticum*.[5]

There have been important changes in Catholic funeral rites since the Second Vatican Council in 1962. Black is no longer the required colour, and priests can now celebrate the requiem mass in the white vestments of the resurrection. The emphasis is no longer on grief and loss but on God's faithfulness and the Christian hope. The central rite is the Eucharist, which, like the Eastern Orthodox Liturgy, is rooted in the Easter Mystery of Christ. The mass is no longer said in Latin but in the vernacular, and members of the family are encouraged to take an active role in the service, especially in reading the appointed portions of the scriptures.

The service offers praise and thanks to God for the gift of life, and it includes prayers for the bereaved as well as the dead. The rite recognizes the spiritual bond that still exists between the living and the dead, and proclaims the Catholic belief that all the faithful will be raised up and reunited in the new heavens and a new earth, where death will be no more.[6]

The funeral mass is full of symbolism. The service begins at the church door where the priest welcomes the funeral procession and sprinkles the coffin with holy water as a reminder of the deceased's baptism. The procession inside the church is symbolic of the deceased's journey through life, and into and beyond death. A white pall, symbolic of baptismal garments, may be placed upon the coffin. A lighted Easter candle stands in the sanctuary, or next to the coffin, as a sign of the deceased's baptismal dignity and a pledge of Christian faith.

These rites of welcome are followed by the liturgy of the word, when the priest speaks to the congregation of God's compassionate love and the risen mystery of the Lord as proclaimed in the Scripture readings. In the intercessions, which follow, the people pray for the deceased and all the dead, for the bereaved and all who mourn, and for all those present in the congregation. Then follows the Eucharist and the rites of commendation and farewell. At this stage a friend or member of the family may speak in remembrance of the deceased, but the main purpose of these last two rites is to commend the deceased to God one final time and bid a formal farewell.

The final rite is the act of committal, which normally takes place at the burial ground. As the coffin is lowered into the grave, those present again pray for the dead person and the bereaved. If the family and friends wish to make one last gesture of farewell, they may throw earth or flower petals into the grave, sprinkle the coffin with holy water or sing a farewell song.

Other Christian Churches

The Anglican Communion is a loosely knit association of Christian Churches – including the Episcopal Churches of America, Canada and Scotland, which hold the same essential doctrines as the Church of England. The latter's status as an Established Church means every citizen living in England has the right to a funeral in the parish church, however tenuous his or her association with the church may have been. This applies in English parishes only and not elsewhere in the British Isles.

An Anglican funeral may be a simple affair at a crematorium, or it can be more elaborate, with a church service preceding burial or cremation, or may even take the form of a requiem mass with a Eucharist. Whatever the pattern of service, it will recall the promise of the resurrection, entrust the dead person to the love and mercy of God, and ask for comfort and strength for the bereaved. The final committal takes place in a cemetery or crematorium. In the crematorium the deceased is committed to God's care as the coffin disappears from view. In the cemetery, the lowering of the coffin into the grave is accompanied by the ancient words, 'we therefore commit his (her) body to the ground; earth to earth, ashes to ashes, dust to dust; in the sure and certain hope of the Resurrection to eternal life.' Many Anglicans follow the Catholic and Orthodox traditions of praying for those who have died, but Evangelical Anglicans consider such prayers to be inappropriate and ineffective.

In other branches of Christianity, burial or cremation is usually preceded by a service in the chapel, with prayers, readings from the scriptures, hymns and a funeral oration. The service will not include a Eucharist nor are there prayers for the dead, but great importance is placed on supporting the dying person in his or her distress and the family in their loss.

Funeral customs are not fixed they can be changed and many adaptations have been made throughout the twentieth century, the most noticeable being the widespread replacement of burial by cremation. Churches have also introduced different liturgical rites to make them better suited to modern idiom and expectations. One instance of change among the Free Churches is the increasing practice of having a short committal service at the crematorium for family and close friends, followed by a full service in the chapel that anyone may attend. This is a popular innovation: people like the more relaxed atmosphere this allows, with the chapel service now concentrating on the life of the deceased rather than the death. Another advantage is that the chapel service is no longer constrained by the time factor, with the need to be at the crematorium at a fixed hour.

Some other points may be mentioned here. In many Christian countries, people are seeking alternatives to church funerals and, to reverse this trend, Peter Jupp[7] suggests that certain issues should be addressed urgently. First, there is a need to develop a theology of cremation. Second, the present theology of burial needs to be revised and new liturgies/services developed which are relevant for the twenty first century. Finally, and perhaps most importantly, there is a pressing need to establish an effective teaching on the nature of life after death. This is a topic many clergy avoid discussing and their inability to do so seriously diminishes their role in supporting the bereaved.

Chapter 8
New Religions and
New Sects

I never did repent for doing good,
Nor shall not now.

The Merchant of Venice

Running like a connecting thread through all religions is a steadfast belief in the existence of an afterlife. The sacred texts may describe the nature of this afterlife differently, and some choose not to speculate about the subject at all, but central to religious teaching is the idea that life follows death. As a consequence of this belief, followers are taught to see this present life as a preparation for the next one, and, to use a biblical phrase, 'to love their neighbours as themselves'. These are fundamental ideas that are found in all religions including those that have appeared in recent centuries. This chapter deals mainly, but not exclusively, with those Christian sects which emerged in the nineteenth century and are still flourishing today.

The Bahá'í Faith

Just as Christianity arose from within Judaism, so the Bahá'í Faith developed from within Shi 'a Islam. Some Muslims still regard it as a heretical sect and treat its members with the disdain, and at times the rigours, that apostasy from Islam is considered to merit. This has resulted in the periodic persecution of Bahá'ís, most noticeably in Iran the country of the Faith's origin. Although the Bahá'ís do not actively proselytize, numbers are increasing rapidly particularly in Africa and South East Asia. There are now more than six million believers in over 200 countries – a wider distribution than any religion apart from Christianity.

A brief history of the Bahá'í Faith would say that it was founded in 1844, when a young Persian (called the Báb) started to preach that the Day of God was at hand: and that he – like John the Baptist, was

71

the forerunner of someone greater than himself who would intitiate a new age of peace and justice. The Báb was publicly executed in 1850 and his followers imprisoned and exiled. Among these followers was Mirza Husayn-Ali Nuri, later known as Bahá'u'lláh (the Glory of God) who, in 1863, announced that he was a 'Manifestation', a messenger from God, the person whose coming the Báb had foretold. He taught that previous messengers included Krishna, Buddha, Moses, Jesus and Muhammad, and that each 'Manifestation' has a particular task for his time. Bahá'u'lláh's was to unite all people in friendship, and to establish peace and justice on earth. This emphasis on unity is indicated by the following observation:

> Judaism brought to people the knowledge of God's law.
> Christianity brought grace, salvation and a relationship with God.
> Islam brought submission to the will of Allah.
> The Bahá'í Faith brings unity to all God's people.

Bahá'u'lláh appears to have been a man of considerable spiritual stature who, in his writings, emphasized the essential unity of all religions. He taught that religious truth is not absolute but relative, and that divine revelation is a continuous process both in this world and in the afterlife. The social themes he stressed were the need to work for world peace, world unity and justice, Bahá'í morality is rooted in justice, mercy, compassion and loving kindness to every person. It is essentially a pacific belief system but it recognizes the fickleness of human nature and the need to control aggression, both individually and collectively. Whilst renouncing the personal use of force or violence, it advocates the establishment of a system of collective security by means of a world police force whose main purpose would be to deter acts of aggression by nation states. Bahá'u'lláh also proposed the establishment of an international court of justice, a federal system of world government, universal education, protection of the environment, a fairer distribution of wealth, and an agreed international language to be learned by everyone in addition to their own.[1]

The Bahá'í Faith looks forward to the ultimate unity of mankind and an eventual state of world peace. Its members work for the evolution of society on earth, and yet regard this present life as just a transitory stage in the development of the soul. They believe that life after death is as different from this earthly life as that of a foetus and a newborn infant. There is no heaven or hell in the traditional Christian or Islamic sense. Death merely enables each soul to find its rightful place within the universe and continue its journey towards union with God.

The Bahá'í community

The Bahá'í community is organized on democratic lines. It has no priests, gurus or imams. All members are equal and all have a say in decisions taken at the local level, and in selecting representatives for the national and international assemblies. There is no racial or sexual bias. A high priority is give to education: ideally this should be equally available to all children but where a choice has to be made the girls should have preference.

Every Bahá'í is expected to pray daily, to fast 19 days each year, to abstain from alcohol and to meet regularly with other Bahá'ís. They usually meet every 19 days to read the scriptures, pray together, discuss community activities and to enjoy one another's company. These group meetings are simple and relaxed occasions and normally take place in the home of a member of the community. There is no set ritual to Bahá'í worship but the meetings do have a basic, tripartite format with devotional, administrative and social elements; within this format the content of the meeting is largely determined by the host or hostess. They also arrange 'firesides' when they invite friends who are not Bahá'ís to similar gatherings.

Bahá'ís have no designated meeting place, such as a church, chapel, mosque or temple. However, there are six regional Houses of Worship; these are situated in Wilmette in Illinois, Frankfurt am Main, Kampala, Delhi, Sydney and Panama City. These centres are open to people of all traditions, and contain, in their decorative motifs, the symbols of the various world faiths. Services there comprise readings from the scriptures of all religions. Bahá'ís are also encouraged to worship with followers of other faiths and to promote inter-faith activities.

The soul

Bahá'ís believe in the immortality of the soul. They teach that life begins at a conception and does not end with death as the soul just continues on its spiritual journey hopefully drawing closer to God. Sometimes the transition of the soul at the moment of death is likened to a bird in a cage released when the cage door is opened. Another analogy compares the change to that of a foetus in its mother's womb, which enters an entirely different dimension of being at the moment of birth.

At birth each soul is pure and then during life it acquires positive or negative attributes. Its nature after death can never be properly described but human souls continue to recognize and associate with each other at appropriate levels. The distinctions existing between them are determined by soul quality and conscience. Prayer facilitates a co-mingling of souls at different levels of evolution, so we should pray for the departed souls as they pray for us. Finally we are told: 'Know thou of a truth that the worlds of God are countless in their number, and infinite in their range. None can reckon or comprehend them except God, the All-Knowing, the All-Wise.'[2]

Bahá'í funerals

If someone asks a Bahá'í, 'How should one look forward to death?' the answer would be: 'How does one look forward to the end of any journey? With hope and expectation.' The simplicity of the Bahá'í faith is reflected in its burial service. Since they have no clergy or recognized liturgy, the final rites are devised and conducted by the family and friends of the deceased person. The structure of the service is likely to vary between communities, reflecting the cultural differences that exist among Bahá'ís living in various parts of the world. Certain constant factors are discernible, however. These are the placing of a ring on the finger of the deceased: the use of a special communal prayer and the preference for burial. Bahá'ís do not favour cremation or embalming but will always comply with any national regulation requiring these procedures.

Before interment, the normal procedure – though this is not currently practised in Western countries – is for the body to be washed by a member of the family and wrapped in a shroud of white silk or cotton. Five sheets of silk or cotton are normally used, but if the means are limited a single sheet of either fabric is considered acceptable. A distinctive ring – worn only after death, is placed upon the finger before the body is lifted into its coffin. The ring bears the inscription: 'I came forth from God, and return unto Him, detached from all save Him holding fast to His Name, the Merciful, the Compassionate.' A specific prayer for the dead is also said before the interment of an adult. When children below the age of 10 years die, this prayer is omitted and a ring is not placed on their finger.

The communal prayer for the deceased is the only one that should always be included in the service and it is said with everyone standing. It begins with a short prayer commending the deceased to

God. This is followed by the greeting Alláh-u-Abhá which is repeated six times. Then the following verses are said.

> We all, verily worship God.
> We all, verily bow down before God.
> We all, verily are devoted to God.
> We all, verily give praise to God.
> We all, verily yield thanks unto God.
> We all, verily are patient in God.

Each verse is repeated 19 times,[3] as 19 is a significant number for the Bahá'ís. One other requirement is that the corpse must be buried within one hour's journey of the place of death. The burial itself should be conducted with 'radiance and serenity'.

The coffin is important for Bahá'ís and it should preferably be made of as durable a material as possible. Modern materials, such as concrete, may be used but in earlier times coffins were expected to be of crystal, resistant stone, or fine and durable wood, depending on the means of the family. The significance of this provision is to show respect for the human body which 'Was once exalted by the immortal soul'. Bahá'ís believe that the soul continues to evolve after death and that this process can and should be assisted by prayers seeking forgiveness, mercy, advancement and blessings for the dead. Children are also taught to express their love for their deceased parents by doing good works in their names.[4]

The Church of Jesus Christ of Latter-day Saints

More commonly known as the Mormons, the Church of Jesus Christ of Latter-day Saints was the first important religious movement to originate in the USA. Founded by Joseph Smith (1805–44) in New York State, it is best known for the polygamy which was widely practised in the nineteenth century, the great 1,000 mile trek to Utah under the leadership of Brigham Young in 1846–7, for its vigorous proselytizing and missionary activities and for its interest and expertise in genealogical research. The Church has a world membership approaching 11 million and now occupies a respected niche in Western society, particularly in the USA. Among its most interesting but less well-known beliefs and practices are those concerning the welfare of the dead.

For a proselytising church, Mormons are suprisingly tolerant of other religions. Whilst many Christian denominations reject the idea, Mormons insist that they are true followers of Jesus Christ. They regard mainstream Christian churches as misguided, lacking in spiritual gifts, and in need of the new insights and revelations that Joseph Smith was granted. In 1820 Smith had a vision in which he saw God the Father and Jesus Christ (two separate beings), this was followed by an encounter with the angel Moroni in 1823, and one with John the Baptist in 1829. Central to Mormon teaching is the *Book of Mormon*, which the angel Moroni disclosed to Joseph Smith and which was published in 1830. Believers consider this book to be as much the word of God as the Bible. It tells of two early migrations to the American continent, the first after the fall of the Tower of Babel, the second about 600 BCE. It also records in detail the appearance of Jesus in America after his resurrection.

The Mormon religion is millennialist, expecting the 'Second Coming' of Christ on earth. This is clearly stated in Article 10 of its creed, which says: 'We believe in the literal gathering of Israel and in the restoration of the Ten Tribes: that Zion will be built on the American continent, that Christ will reign personally upon the earth and that the earth will be renewed and receive its paradisical glory.' The main activity in this millennium will be 'temple work' especially baptism on behalf of the dead.

Faithful members of the Mormon Church will eventually become as gods, but other people will also obtain their appropriate share of glory and will be assigned to eternal kingdoms. That said, salvation in its fullest sense can only come through membership of the Mormon Church. The essential prerequisites for salvation are a belief in Christ, repentance of sins, baptism in water, receiving the Holy Spirit – and with it the gifts of prophecy, revelation and speaking in tongues, and persistence – enduring to the end.

The Mormon community

The Mormon Church is episcopally constituted, each bishop being responsible for a congregation of between 200–600 members. Only men can become bishops as women are excluded from the priesthood. There are two orders of priests – the Aaronic and the Melchizedek. Boys are ordained into the Aaronic order as deacons at the age of 12, become teachers at 14, priests when 16, and are eligible to enter the Melchizedek order at 18. A similar hierarchical system exists within the Melchizedek priesthood. Most active, adult, male Mormons are elders, the lowest rank of the Melchizedek order. When a young man receives the Melchizedek priesthood, he may at the age of 19 elect to serve a two-year mission for the Church. This mission is self-funded, and may be at home or overseas, wherever he is assigned. Women and older couples also have opportunities to serve as full-time missionaries.

The Mormon Church is a tightly knit organization and expects a high moral standard from its members. Tobacco, alcohol and drugs are banned, as are coffee and tea. Meat is eaten sparingly, and sex before marriage and infidelity within it are condemned. Mormons tend to work hard and play hard. Despite the apparent asceticism, they enjoy a wide range of recreational activities and are socially and politically involved.

The soul

Mormons believe that life on earth is part of a never-ending journey that begins long before birth. They believe that all of us lived as spirits in a pre-existent life with heavenly parents. At an appointed time, each spirit has the opportunity to come to earth and to take up a physical body provided by its earthly parents. This is an opportunity to live by faith and to grow and develop in face of mortal experiences.[5] In this way the spirit becomes more than just a spiritual entity, it is now a 'living soul' with the capacity to become a god. Humanity's potential for divinity is also recognized in Catholic teaching. The Benedictine priest, Father John Main put it this way: 'Our redemption by Jesus Christ has opened up for us levels of consciousness that can be described by St Paul only in terms of a totally new creation. God became man so that man might become God, as the early Fathers of the Church expressed it. It is our destiny to be divinized by becoming one with the Spirit of God. Divinization is utterly beyond our imagination and our powers of understanding to comprehend. But it is not beyond our capacity to experience it in love.'[6] Mormons believe that in this spiritual development within the individual and the family, both in this life and the next, the temple has a unique role.

The temple

Every Mormon community has its local chapel for Sunday worship and weekday activities, but in addition there are 52 temples worldwide. For Mormons, these are the most sacred places on earth where every believer can experience a special closeness to God. Here also, certain important ordinances can be performed. Each temple is made of the finest materials and with expert craftsmanship. When they enter the building, members change into white garments to symbolize purity, cleanliness and the setting aside of earthly things.

Everything done in the temple – ordinances, instruction, promises and prayer – is done in the name of Jesus Christ because he is the Saviour and his atoning sacrifice made possible every hope and blessing in the temple.[7]

Non-members are not allowed into the temple. The one exception to this rule occurs a few weeks after the building has been completed and before the new temple is dedicated. There was such an occasion in 1998 when the temple at Chorley in Lancashire UK was opened to the public. Temples are beautifully furnished with many pictures on the walls displaying incidents in the life of Jesus. There is no large assembly room other than the dining area, but many relatively small rooms are available for discussions, instruction and the sealing of ordinances. The most impressive area of all is the baptistry with its large font: this stands on 12 bovine figures, symbols of the 12 tribes of Israel.

Temple rites

The temple is the only place where certain sacred rites can be performed for those who have died. These rites include sealing, eternal marriages and the baptism of the dead. Sealing unites children to their parents and parents to their children for eternity. Similarly, a married couple can take a vow of eternal fidelity to one another and live as husband and wife throughout eternity. However, these ordinances are not restricted to the living. Mormons believe that the dead can also benefit from them. This means that the bereaved who failed to have their marriages sealed while their spouse was still alive can do so with the appropriate temple rite. Similarly with other family relationships: at the temple members can be sealed with their dead parents, brothers, sisters or grandparents for eternity. The Church recognizes that it is up to the dead whether they accept the ordinances or not.

Mormons consider surrogate baptism to be an important redemptive work for the dead. They support this contention with the words St Paul wrote in his first letter to the Corinthians 15:29: 'Now what about those people who are baptised for the dead? What do they hope to accomplish? If it is true, as some claim, that the dead are not raised to life, why are those people being baptised for the dead?' and a few verses later: 'But if the dead are not raised to life, then, as the saying goes, Let us eat and drink, for tomorrow we will die.' Members believe that being baptized in the place of a dead relative enables that relative to receive the full blessings of Christ's atonement if they choose to do so. For those who hold this belief, surrogate baptism is a vital work that should include distant ancestors. This is why the Church of Jesus Christ of Latter-day Saints is so interested in genealogical research. Its genealogical database is the best of any organization worldwide and it willingly provides the information it has to other researchers. By using this information, Mormons are able to seek and identify their ancestors and arrange for the temple ordinances to be performed on their behalf.

Funerals

The temple is not used for funerals. These services take place in the neighbourhood chapel. Mormons prefer interment to cremation as they believe in the physical resurrection of the dead when the physical body and the spirit will be made whole in a perfect and inseparable unity. If the deceased has visited the temple, and about one quarter of members will have done so, the corpse is dressed in sacred clothing, in particular a set of ritualistically significant underclothes. This service to the deceased is performed by a member of the Church. If the deceased has not entered the temple there is no such requirement. Support for the bereaved is provided by friends and the sacred ordinances of the Church.

Jehovah's Witnesses

This Church can trace its origins to the 1870s when an American businessman – Charles T. Russell, became interested in biblical studies and later established the International Bible Students Association and a successful publishing firm – the Watch Tower Bible and Tract Society. This publishing house remains an important part of the Church and produces books, tracts, recordings and periodicals chief of which are *Watchtower* and *Awake* which have a circulation of 10 million copies in over 80 languages.

Jehovah's Witnesses have been described as people 'who live by the Scriptures' and 'who stress family togetherness'. They have their own modern-language version of the Bible, the *New World Translation of the Holy Scriptures*, which is available in the vernacular of 50 per cent of the world's population. Their 32-page brochure, *Enjoy Life on Earth Forever*, is available in 237 languages. Their aim is the establishment of God's Kingdom, the Theocracy, which will emerge following the great battle of Armageddon. This is not expected to happen in the near future though the exact date is not known.

Like other sects that originated in the USA, the Jehovah's Witnesses is a millennialist Church expecting the 'Second Coming' of Christ, and anticipated dates for this event have included 1914, 1920, 1925, 1940, 1975 and 1984. Many of these apocalyptic expectations are based on interpretations of the book *Revelation*, and it is here that the number of the 'elect' – the righteous congregation, is given as 144,000. This is now regarded as a symbolic number which includes men and women from all races, cultures and backgrounds.

Witnesses regard Jesus Christ as inferior to Jehovah: He is the first of Jehovah's creation and a 'son of God' but he is not God the Son. They also deny the existence of the Holy Spirit as a separate entity and regard the term merely as a synonym for 'God in action'. [8] They believe that Christ was born in October – not December, and make a point of not celebrating Christmas or Easter, which they regard as pagan festivals. The name Jehovah's Witnesses was only adopted by the Church in 1931, and it did this to clarify where their allegiance lay. Their God was the Jehovah of the Old Testament.

There are about six million Witnesses worldwide, distributed in over 200 countries. They are best known for their doorstep mission work and their steadfast refusal to accept blood transfusions. The spread of AIDS by the use of blood products, among haemophiliacs for instance, will have strengthened their conviction in this matter.

Witnesses are not interested in party politics or in attaining positions of power in governments, which they regard as the sphere of Satan and his devils, They tend not to vote in public elections and do not undertake military service even when required to do so. Not surprisingly, they are often persecuted by dictatorial regimes. The firm stance they took in Nazi Germany resulted in many deaths in the concentration camps, and was the subject of a special conference at the United States Holocaust Museum in September 1994. They were persecuted in the Third Reich not, like the communists, gypsies and Jews, because they were deliberately targeted but because they held to their beliefs and refused to comprise them. These principles included a refusal to swear allegiance to the state or to utter the words 'heil Hitler'. As a consequence, many were sent to the concentration camps and killed. Their intransigence resembled that of early Christians who could have escaped martyrdom by sprinkling incense on a brazier, in recognition of the divinity of the Roman emperor, and refused to do so.

Death, heaven and hell

Jehovah's Witnesses regard the apocalyptic books of the Bible, especially Daniel and the Revelation of St John the Divine, as God's timetable for world affairs and as the only authentic insight into human destiny. Soon, they believe, there will be the great battle of Armageddon, which will be followed by the 'Second Coming' of Christ and an idyllic period of 1,000 years when the earth will revert to its original paradisical state and there will be universal peace. During this time there will be a general, physical resurrection of the dead. After this millennial period, Satan and his followers will be completely destroyed, and Christ will return the Kingdom to his Father so that God may be all things to all people. Most human beings will live on earth in human perfection but the 'elect' will live in heaven – close to Jehovah.

In their belief system, there is no Hell and no place of eternal torment. Heaven is where Jehovah is, and this includes the spirit realm where Jesus ascended after his death on the stake – not, Witnesses say, on a cross; but when ordinary people die they remain in the grave until the 'Second Coming' and the resurrection of the dead. Not everyone lives for ever. For some death really is the end of life, and they remain dead for ever.

When a Jehovah's Witness dies the funeral rites are simple. The main service is conducted at the local Kingdom Hall and will include a eulogy by a member of the committee. Burial and cremation are equally acceptable.

The Society of Friends

The Society of Friends was founded in England, in the mid-seventeenth century, by George Fox, a devout shoemaker and mystic, who became an itinerant preacher. Probably nicknamed the 'Quakers' because shaking was often a feature of early meetings, the Society of Friends has become a byword for respectability and philanthropy. Never a large organization, it is not a proselytizing Church and its worldwide membership is less than one quarter of a million people, its influence has consistently exceeded the size of its membership.

Originally a Christian sect that rejected both formalized worship and an ordained ministry, Quakers are diverse in their religious beliefs and their unity is not expressed in credal statements but in the shared experience of 'Meeting for Worship'. Few are cradle Quakers: most UK Friends will have joined the Society from other churches attracted in part by the freedom of worship, the social concern, the pacifism and the involvement with the Campaign for Nuclear Disarmament that characterized the Quaker movement during the twentieth century. One well-known saying that illustrates the traditional Quaker attitude to other people is 'There is that of Christ in every man.' The modern Friend is careful to substitute the word 'everyone' for 'every man'; indeed gender discrimination has never been a feature of the Society of Friends and women have always had an equal say in Quaker meetings for worship and business.

In Britain, and this is true of 'unprogrammed' meetings in North America too, Quakers meet for worship in silence. On entering the meeting house, they walk to their place and sit down quietly. No one speaks unless he/she feels moved to do so by the Holy Spirit, but usually some people present have something they wish to say, and will stand up to minister (speak) and then sit down. They are heard in an attentive silence. After a set period, usually an hour, two Elders (Friends appointed for a three-year period to exercise responsibility for the conduct of worship) shake hands, others do likewise and the meeting breaks up for conversation and refreshment.

Friends are exhorted in their *Advices and Queries, A Booklet of Guidance*, to be sensitive to one another and supportive. They are also comfortable with silence and used to encountering others in its depths. For those who are Christ-centred, every meeting, in the home or the street, can be one in which they feel the presence of Christ. Perhaps reflective of many Friends' attitude to death is this verse from the poem The Departed:[9]

> As to their living in some other sphere,
> I cannot say –
> I only know they left the country here
> Of every day

It is sometimes said that a Quaker funeral is just like a normal Quaker meeting. That is only partly true, for whilst a special meeting will be held in honour of the deceased the Friends who attend will be more likely to speak than on other occasions. This is because they will use this opportunity to offer consolation to the bereaved, to draw inspiration from the life of the deceased and to pay tribute to the loving care provided by the bereaved relatives.

A seventeenth century, Quaker funeral

There have been considerable changes in funeral customs since the seventeenth century and we are lucky to have an eyewitness account of George Fox's death and burial; it was written by Thomas Ellwood, who was a close friend and the editor of' Fox's journals. As a young man, he was also reader to the blind poet, John Milton, and suggested the writing of *Paradise Regained* to Milton.

Ellwood tells us that Fox's final illness occured quite unexpectedly with a sudden feeling of coldness in the heart followed by great weakness. He died three days later, I think most probably from a coronary thrombosis. Friends who visited him during his last days found him content and at peace. To some he said: 'All is well: the Seed of God reigns over all, and over death itself. And though I am weak in body, yet the power of God is over all.'

A very large number of people came to the meeting house for the funeral service. We are told that this lasted about two hours, 'with great and heavenly solemnity, and was manifestly attended with the Lord's blessed presence and glorious power.' Many testimonies were given during this meeting. After it, the body was carried by Friends to the burial ground where Ellwood said: 'his body was committed to the earth: but his memorial shall remain and be everlastingly blessed among the righteous.' [10]

Friends are more likely to be cremated than buried nowadays, although some regard burial in a biodegradable coffin as more environmentally friendly, and less wasteful of energy resources. Many old Quaker burial grounds are located in the UK and these are often visited by Friends from overseas. A feature of former Quaker burials was that they only rarely used headstones to mark the individual graves.

Seventh-day Adventists

This is another Church that has its roots in America and looks for the 'Second Coming' of Christ. It adopted the name Seventh-day Adventist at a conference in 1860 but it traces its origins to a slightly earlier date and celebrated its 150th anniversary in 1994. Its most significant leadership was provided by a visionary, Ellen G. White (1821–61), which makes the present-day refusal of the Church to admit women to the ordained ministry extremely puzzling.

Church membership now numbers about 10 million in over 200 countries. Brazil has the largest number of Adventists, but growth is rapid in Central and South America, Africa and Asia. Its theology is mainstream protestant Christian, and it has a very active humanitarian arm – the Adventist Development and Relief Agency (ADRA) which has been closely involved with relief work in Third World countries devastated by civil wars and famines.

Besides observing the Saturday Sabbath – from sunset on Friday to sunset on Saturday, they have two unusual teachings about the fate of believers which are similar to those of the Jehovah's Witnesses. Firstly, they believe that the soul is mortal and that life does end with death. When people die their soul dies with them, hence the need for the resurrection at the 'Second Coming' of Christ when the saved are made whole again. Secondly, they do not believe in Hell or eternal damnation. When the wicked die, they have no torment or resurrection just the eternal sleep of death.

Ministers are advised to say little but to do much when visiting the bereaved. They are reminded that a funeral is a fruitful time for evangelizing. The funeral service is similar to that of other protestant Churches with a reading from scripture, prayers, hymns, an overview of the person's life and perhaps a sermon. Burial in the ground or cremation are equally acceptable as God created all things and will have no problem with the raw materials he has to use at the resurrection.[11]

Spiritualist Churches

Whilst the modern spiritualist movement can trace its origins to March 1848 and to a farmhouse in New York state where Kate Fox is said to have established contact with a discarnate spirit, any discussion of Western spiritualism would be incomplete without some mention of the persecution of witches and mediums in medieval Europe and America. In fact, antipathy to such practitioners in Judaeo-Christian societies can be traced back to biblical times when Saul, King of Israel (c.1030 BCE) expelled all fortune tellers and mediums from his kingdom.

Before the Reformation, two types of witchcraft were recognized in medieval Europe: white witchcraft, which involved the practice of healing, and *maleficium*, black magic which included sorcery. After the fifteenth century a third form of witch became identified, one who had made a pact with, and sold her soul to, the devil. The use of the female gender is particularly relevant here as most of the people accused of practising witchcraft, and subsequently burnt at the stake, were women. During the sixteenth and seventeenth centuries witch hunts became a common occurrence, first in Europe and later in North America. The causative factors seem to have been the rise of nation states, the rapid development of printing and literacy, the emphasis on personal salvation, and a shift from 'restorative justice' (when a case against a witch would be brought by the injured party) to 'retributive justice' (when the case was brought by the state). The result was an upsurge in witch trials amounting to almost epidemic proportions. The most severe persecutions were in Germany and France. Notable witch hunts occurred later in Scotland, Ireland, Scandinavia and America. The hounding of witches was less rigorous in England, whilst Spain – except for the Basque country – and southern Italy almost avoided it altogether.

The first repressive Act against witchcraft in England was passed in 1542. As a direct consequence of this law English witches were persecuted in large numbers but, because the legal system had developed in a different way, they were not subjected to the full logic and relentlessness of Continental law. English witches were rarely tortured to extract confessions; English lawyers maintained throughout the distinction between white and black magic and this was reflected in the severity of the punishment meted out; and the demonic pact was rarely mentioned.[12]

In England and its colonies the revised Witchcraft Act of 1563 imposed the death penalty even on those found guilty of merely consulting a witch or a medium and a new Act in 1642 was more severe. The British Parliament repealed these and all other Acts against sorcery in 1735, but the Witchcraft Act of 1735 still made it illegal to act as a spiritualist medium, practise telepathy, clairvoyance or any similar power. This Act was repealed only in 1951 when it was replaced by the Fraudulent Medium Act, which permitted the above practices but only if they were not undertaken for any reward, or were practised solely for the purpose of entertainment. It is within this repressive environment that the spiritualist Churches were founded and mediumship developed.

Most spiritualist Churches subscribe to seven principles. These are:

- the Fatherhood of God;
- the Brotherhood of Man;
- the Communion of Spirit and the Ministry of Angels;
- compensation and retribution hereafter for all the good and evil deeds done on earth;
- eternal progress open to every soul.

One organization, the Greater World Christian Spiritualist League also acknowledges the leadership of Jesus Christ.[13]

Apart from social events, three types of activity take place in a spiritualist church. There are healing services – often held in midweek; circles for psychic development; and a church service led by a medium. Healing has always had a high profile within the spiritualist movement and this aspect of its work has flourished, and from it has developed the World Federation of Spiritual Healers.

Members of the Church who wish to develop their psychic abilities join a 'development' circle. This is a group of like-minded people who meet regularly and sit together with the intention of contacting spirit guides and developing their sensitivity to the spirit world. These circles are like Quaker meetings, as everyone sits quietly until someone is moved to speak and the other members of the group listen attentively to what is said. Circles are held in well-lit rooms, in an open and relaxed manner.

Sunday services in spiritualist Churches are low-key affairs. The proceedings are usually led by the Church president and include words of welcome, hymns and prayers. The president then introduces the visiting medium who may preach or just chat to the congregation for 10–15 minutes before contacting a spirit guide. This he/she does in full consciousness, standing in clear view of the congregation. There is no dimming of lights and the medium does not go into a trance but just stands in front of the congregation and talks with them, making comments, asking questions and receiving replies. The conversation will go something like this.

Medium   The gentleman over there in the blue pullover. I've got an
           elderly man here: he looks like a farmer; the name Bert is
           coming through, Bert Greenway.
Man   Yes I can accept that.
Medium   Does the name May mean anything to you?
Man   Yes she was Bert's wife.
Medium   Well he says May is with him now, and all is well.
Man   Thankyou.
Medium   The lady in the centre with the brooch. I've got a young woman
           here, she says you were at school together.

The service usually ends with the old Sankey and Moody hymn 'Till We Meet Again'. The medium has two main objectives. The first is to provide evidence to the bereaved that their loved ones have survived death. The second is to examine with them the implications of this evidence. All parties recognize that it is impossible to prove that life continues after death. The aim is merely to consider the available evidence and the teachings given by the spirit guides on the afterlife and how one's actions on earth are likely to affect the pattern of life in the hereafter.

Death

For the spiritualist, death is not a frightening event. It is the culmination of life's journey, a change of situation, a gateway into another sphere of life. Spiritualists expect the moment of death to be painless and pinpoint that moment to the severing of 'the silver cord', the umbilical-like attachment that clairvoyants say unites the body and the spirit in life. The transit into the spirit world is seen as a birthing process, with spirit guides receiving the newcomer in a way reminiscent of midwives attending a childbirth. Then the individual is taken to a place of rest to sleep.

Life in the spirit world

When the spirit regains consciousness, it realizes that the absence of a physical body is no inconvenience. It has retained its own individuality, and experiences a greater freedom of movement and a higher level of awareness than was possible when incarnate. Every thought and emotion acquires its own specific appearance and embrace the individual as tangible realities. Consequently, one has to learn to control one's thoughts and feelings to protect oneself from these thought forms.[14]

Memory of one's earth life gradually returns. Eventually, the entire sequence of life events unfolds in a kaleidoscopic series of pictures. There is no judgement apart from self-judgement.[15] Everyone is their own accuser, judge and jury, and each person gravitates to that state/place that is most appropriate for them. The situation is not fixed however; the soul can progress to other levels and is helped to do so by more enlightened spirits.

Chapter 9
The Reburial Issue

Of comfort no man speak;
Let's talk of graves, of worms and epitaphs;
Make dust our paper and with rainy eyes
Write sorrow on the bosom of the earth,
Let's choose executors and talk of wills.

King Richard II

Funeral rites usually have a great psychological impact. This is realized by individuals and by society as a whole. People often say that they needed the finality of casting earth into the grave, or seeing the coffin entering the furnace to accept the reality of their loved one's death. Sometimes the grieving process is unnaturally prolonged, perhaps by the need for a coroner's inquest or, as often happens in wartime, because the body has never been found. In the latter instance, the mothers of these young men are likely to cling to the hope that their sons are still alive, perhaps in some distant prison camp. Governments are sensitive to these yearnings and more than 40 years after the Korean War, the combatants – including the Americans, British and Koreans – are still negotiating for the return of their war dead. So we should not be surprised that other nations are also deeply concerned about the treatment of their dead, a concern that, in some instances, is particularly focussed on the proper disposal of anthropological remains held by museums and scientific institutions. This is known as the 'reburial issue'.

Reburial and Museums

An almost unnoticed change is taking place in the museums of First World countries. It is the consequence of the 'reburial issue', a demand by ethnic people that the human skeletons and mummified bodies of their ancestors should be returned to their homelands to receive the respect and proper funeral rites that befits their human status. Linked to this is the demand that ancestral burial sites should be protected and no longer excavated for archaeological purposes. North American Indians and Australian Aborigines have been particularly insistent that these requests should be met, whilst archaeologists and museums have responded with varying degrees of enthusiasm.

The nineteenth century was the century of the great collectors and a time when public museums were established in many countries. The skeletons and remains of people who were considered to be of particular interest were brought to these collections, often from distant countries. Consequently, with increasing international travel, it is now possible for people to visit a museum in another country and find the skeleton or mummified body of one of their tribal ancestors on public display. Many find the experience degrading for the ancestor and for their own tribal traditions. They feel that the soul of the ancestor cannot dwell in peace in a foreign land, and that the soul's wellbeing depends on the bodily remains being returned to the homeland and disposed of in accordance with tribal customs.

One of the largest anatomical collections in the world is the Murray Black collection, which contains over 1,800 human exhibits, mainly of Australian Aborigines. The most famous remains were those of Truganini, who died in 1876. She was the last survivor of one of the most disreputable episodes in Australian history, the annihilation of the Tasmanian Aborigines. Truganini realized that after her death her body was likely to be exploited by people who might seek to sell or study it. She expressed a wish to be cremated but her body was buried soon after she died. Two years later the body was disinterred and sent to Melbourne, and then to England. In 1904 it was returned to Melbourne, where her body was on public display in a museum until 1947, when it was placed in the vaults available only to scientists. Eventually, after pressure from the Aboriginal community and the Australian Institute for Aboriginal Studies, the Tasmanian government agreed that Truganini should be cremated. This was done on 30 April 1976 and her ashes were scattered on the sea.[1]

Public response to the demands of similar pressure groups has been increasingly sympathetic. The Smithsonian Institute in Washington and the Pitt Rivers Museum in Oxford are two centres that have removed all North American Indian remains from public display and they have also returned Aboriginal remains to Australia for burial or cremation.

Excavating the Dead

The excavation of burial sites by archaeologists is causing concern to people as far apart as the Philippines and Sweden. Frequently there is local opposition to these digs and this often succeeds in halting them. In Zimbabwe, for instance, the Museum Service stopped the excavation of a site when the local people complained that the diggings were disturbing the local Shona spirits, and excavations have also been stopped in Israel for religious reasons.[1] A similar concern is discernible in the UK where the Protection of Military Aircraft Act 1986 makes it illegal to excavate the remains of aircraft that crashed in the war as these planes are regarded as war graves.

There is an enormous difference between people unearthing their own dead to honour their ancestors and having their burial grounds desecrated by outsiders. Eighteenth-century documents show the great affection North American Indians had for their dead, and record some of the strange mourning customs they practised. On the Feast of the Dead, it was customary for the Western Iroquois to disinter the dead, wash and reclothe the bodies, and re-mourn the ancestors before reburying the remains. Similar rituals are still practised in Mexico and Madagascar, where people even dance with the corpse. These are occasions of high festivity and of great expense for the family concerned.

In Madagascar the date of the festival is determined by an astrologer. Hundreds of guests attend and are fêted. The bodies of the ancestors are taken from the tombs and carried joyously through the dancing crowds to the sound of drums, whistles and the music of bands. The joy is mingled with grief. Everyone connected with the family will wish to touch the ancestors. For those present there is nothing macabre about the occasion. The predominant mood is one of joy. The family have had an opportunity to draw close to the ancestors, and to show their respect by washing and reclothing them before returning the corpses to the tomb. Many of the people attending the ceremonies are Christians, and their presence indicates an interesting synthesis of Christian belief with traditional customs.

Socio-political Issues

Concern for the dead person is the main reason for local communities halting excavations or demanding the return of their ancestors' remains. In some instances there is also a political motive but this is usually secondary. Archaeologists who are also members of tribal communities can find themselves in a particularly difficult position.

They appreciate the need to continue the scientific studies but they are also bound by the traditions and indignation of their own people. To resolve the problem, attempts have been made to formulate a policy that is acceptable to both the scientists and the tribal communities. Most of these compromises are based on a recognition by both parties of the legitimate claims of science and education, and the desirability of not disturbing sacred burial grounds and of returning ancestral remains to their native lands.

Another aspect of the reburial issue is what may be called a 'green issue'. Some communities and ethnic groups see a close relationship between the proper care of ancestral remains and the welfare of the people and the Earth. They believe that when burial sites are desecrated and the ancestors have not been properly buried, the result is sickness among the people, an alienation from the environment and disaster in the land. The validity of these ideas cannot be proven but the beliefs are often deeply rooted and are very difficult, if not quite impossible, to disprove.

The reburial issue has gained considerable support in influential circles. In 1991, the United States Congress passed a law that set out time limits for museums to catalogue all the human and cultural remains of America's native peoples. The law also required museums to consult, and be directed by, the surviving communities, on the ultimate disposal of these remains. A resolution of the United Nations requires its signatories to return to indigenous peoples any ancestral remains that are held by museums or similar institutions. These requirements do not mean that valid scientific/archaeological research will cease – there is current research, for instance, on population affinities, diet, disease and environmental adaptation. Fears that this might happen have been expressed but present trends show that, once the native peoples are given a real voice in the decision making, they do not automatically demand the cessation of scientific research but carefully assess its ultimate value before giving or withholding their consent.[2]

Chapter 10
Freud, Mourning
and Death

We are such stuff
As dreams are made on, and our little life
Is rounded with a sleep.

The Tempest

Introduction

Sigmund Freud died over 50 years ago and most of his innovative ideas were published long before that. Despite this lapse of time, a book dealing with the psychology of death and bereavement would be incomplete without examining his contribution to these subjects. He had a tremendous influence on public opinion, particularly in the first half of the twentieth century, and made an outstanding contribution to our understanding of the psyche and to the development of modern psychology.

Freud is best known as the founder of psychoanalysis, and as a physician who believed that neurotic illnesses were mainly caused by the repression of infantile sexual fantasies. But, more importantly, it was he who provided the basis for many of the ideas and insights on which bereavement counselling is now based. He was largely responsible for the development of 'talk therapy', though in his own practice he explored people's experiences at a much deeper level than present-day counsellors. He introduced terms like 'grief work', the 'death instinct', and 'pathological mourning' which are still widely used today. In addition to all this, he was responsible for coining commonly used psychological terms such as *ego, superego* and *id,* and for making the idea of an unconscious mind generally acceptable.

Oddly enough, his ideas have not been well translated from the original German into English. Bruno Bettelheim discusses this problem in his book, *Freud and Man's Soul.*[1] He points out that whilst Freud often used the noun *die Seele* (the soul), this meaning is rarely present in the English translations. Instead the word is usually translated as 'mind'. Similarly, where Freud spoke about the 'structure of the soul' (*die Struktur des seelischen Apparats*) this almost always becomes 'the mental apparatus'. The result is twofold. Not only is the style and elegance of the German prose lost but, more importantly, the true meaning of the passage is not conveyed. For German speakers *die Seele* implies the essence of a person's humanity, including their spiritual and emotional nature, in fact everything that is not physical.

The same problem arises with other words. *Todestrieb* is the German word for 'death drive'. It is usually translated as 'death instinct' but this obscures Freud's real meaning. In German there is a word *Instinkt*, which is used for the inborn instincts of animals, but Freud is not referring to a basic animal instinct when he uses the word *Trieb*; but to an inner urge or drive that, as *Todestrieb*, provokes people into aggressive, destructive and self-destructive actions. Making this point may seem pedantic but instincts are basically unalterable whilst an inner drive can be changed, sublimated or suppressed.

Ambivalence to the Dead

One of Freud's achievements was to reveal the turbulent nature of the psyche, and the power that ambivalence wields within the human mind. He considered that ambivalence – the coexistence of love and hatred – is such a common attitude that he wrote of: 'the law of ambivalence of feeling which governs our emotional relations with those we love most'.[2] In his view any intense emotional attachment to a person is associated with a hidden hostility. A person's love is not simple, it is tarnished by hatred, and outward shows of affection by repressed desires to harm. This ambivalence of feeling is associated with an inner conflict, which becomes more intense when a loved person dies.

Bereavement increases the outward appearance of affection for the deceased but inwardly there is a corresponding increase in hostility. This often lies dormant, being repressed into the unconscious where it creates inner turmoil and a general mood of depression. When it is released, as sometimes happens, then angry outbursts occur in which the repressed anger is directed at other people, including, relatives, friends, professional carers and even the deity. It may also be projected onto the dead person, and Freud suggested that it was this projection of anger on to the dead that gave rise, in very early societies, to the collective belief that the dead could become malevolent spirits.

He then suggested that this innate tendency to regard the dead as potentially hostile had gradually diminished with the evolution of society. Likewise, people's ambivalence to the dead had slowly decreased over many centuries. As the ambivalence diminished, mourning taboos, which had been quite severe in primeval communities, became less relevant and began slowly to disappear. Despite these changes, some unconscious hostility to the dead remains deep within the psyche and Freud taught that these angry feelings must be recognized, accepted and dealt with if the mourning process is to have a good outcome.

Mourning and Grief Work

Freud taught that mourning has a specific psychical task to perform. Its function is to detach the survivors' memories and hopes from the dead.[3] When this has been achieved, the inner distress grows less and any associated feelings of remorse and self-reproach diminish. To the task of mourning, Freud ascribed the term 'grief work'. Grief work forces the ego to give up the loved one by accepting that the person is dead, and offering the individual the inducement to live contentedly, albeit in a restructured lifestyle. It is a long process as all attachments have to be withdrawn from the dead person. This is done reluctantly with much inner pain and emotional effort, and the opposition may be intense. If the reluctance to accept separation is too great, the bereaved may avoid the reality of death by means of a hallucinatory wishful psychosis.

Psychosis is not a common feature of bereavement but depression is frequently associated with grief. Bereaved people often appear to be depressed and, if the grief is severe, psychiatrists are likely to make a diagnosis of 'reactive depression'. It is not surprising then that Freud should write specifically on this subject and entitled one of his works *Mourning and Melancholia*.[4] Sleep disturbances, a feeling of painful dejection, a diminished capacity to love, and a reduced involvement in external activities, are frequently reported both by the bereaved and by those who are depressed for other reasons. Both experience a sense of loss but, whilst mourners have suffered a real and tangible loss, the loss of those with other depressive states is not so easily described. Freud also taught that *melancholia* (clinical depression) is associated with a loss of self-respect. This is not usually a feature of mourning, even when people feel very sad, but if present he called the reaction 'pathological mourning'.

The Soul and the Afterlife

One of Freud's more interesting ideas is the 'theory of unconscious immortality'. This states that 'in the unconscious everyone of us is convinced of his own immortality'.[5] In other words, in the depths of their unconscious no one can accept the possibility that he or she will die. This theory is particularly interesting as it points to the ambivalence that even Freud was subject to. Philosophically he was a materialist. He was dismissive of religious beliefs and rejected the possibility that there is a life after death. Yet at the same time he was propounding as a theory the idea that something exists in the depths of each person that makes them quite sure that they are immortal.

Freud used the theories of 'unconscious immortality' and 'ambivalence of feeling' to explain how the myth of a soul could have arisen in the early history of mankind. He believed that a relationship existed between the emerging concept of a soul and the primeval attitude to death. He suggested that our remote ancestors were ambivalent towards death. They recognized the reality of death for other people because they killed them but they were so in tune with their own unconscious, and its deep denial of death, that they could not accept the possibility that they themselves might die. These opposing attitudes came into conflict in the distant past when our forebears first encountered death in someone they loved. This was a seminal moment in human evolution because the lust to kill had existed for a long time but love was a new experience. At such a moment people were aware of a new conflict of feelings. They were grieving the loss of a loved person and simultaneously feeling pleased that their unconscious death wishes for that person were being fulfilled.

This conflict of feeling forced prehistoric people to accept the possibility that they might die, but they did so reluctantly and with the help of a compromise. They accepted the reality of their personal mortality but denied death the significance of annihilation. Whilst they were mourning someone they loved, they invented the soul and spirits, and because their inner mood was a mixture of sorrow, anger, satisfaction and guilt, these spirits were not perceived as kindly but as fearsome demons. The emerging idea of a soul was reinforced by the physical changes of death, for instance the cessation of respiration would suggest that the individual had separated into a body and an animating spirit. Persisting memories of the dead provided a further reason for assuming the existence of spirits, and helped to formulate the belief that life continues after death.

Initially, souls or spirits were thought to be no more than shadowy spectres dwelling in the underworld. Later, religious teachers managed to portray some of them as highly evolved spiritual beings. Then the teachers succeeded in making the afterlife seem more desirable than life on earth, and so reduced this present life to a mere preparatory stage. After that it was merely logical to extend life backwards into the past, to create a belief in previous existences and in reincarnation, all with the purpose of depriving death of its significance as the terminator of life.

As a belief in immortality emerged, and with it the doctrine of the soul, ethical commandments began to be formulated. The first commandment was 'You Shall Not Kill'. This arose as a reaction to people's profound sense of guilt at their hostility towards people they loved who were now dead. In Freud's opinion, unconscious death wishes for loved ones, and ambivalent moods when they die, are still part of the human experience; but they no longer produce ethical and metaphysical doctrines. In this modern era they are more likely to give rise to neuroses.[5]

Religion: A Universal Neurosis

The teachings of religious leaders, and the various practices associated with religion, have had a great influence on people's attitudes to death. Freud did not consider this influence to have been particularly benign but he was interested in religion as a phenomenon of civilization and wrote extensively about it.[3,6,7] He was disdainful of religious beliefs, referring to them as collective examples of childhood regressions and wish-fulfilling illusions, which differ from those of children only because they are held by society as a whole.

He perceived a similarity between the psychological growth of children towards adulthood and the emergence of civilizations. Just as, in his opinion, a child cannot complete its development successfully without passing through a phase of neurosis, so humanity had to pass through various neurotic episodes during the evolution of mankind. It was in one such neurotic phase that religions made their first appearance. They did so as a collective *Oedipus complex*, and were the external manifestation of humanity's repressed desire to kill a supreme father figure, possibly some outstanding tribal leader such as the Jewish patriarch Moses.

People started to believe in God (or gods) because society needed a supreme parental figure; someone who would protect them, both individually and as a community, from the dangers inherent within nature. Deities arose as a result of people's inner needs and performed three important tasks: they exorcized the terrors of nature, helped to compensate individuals for the sufferings and privations that life has imposed upon them, and helped to reconcile men and women to the cruelty of fate and in particular to death.

Whilst Freud respected the historical worth of certain religious doctrines, he regarded religion as a social disease and specifically as a universal, obsessional neurosis. He believed that the time had arrived for religious beliefs to be regarded as neurotic relics and replaced by the rational operation of the intellect. In his opinion there was no evidence that life persisted after death and he rejected any such possibility.

Eros and the Death Drive

Freud believed that there is a deep urge (a death drive) in all forms of life to revert to an earlier state of being, to become inorganic or dead again. The goal of life is therefore death, and this innate pursuit of death is the ultimate expression of what is called the 'Nirvana principle', the constant striving for a state which is free from external and internal stimuli, a state of eternal peace.

The death drive (*Todestrieb*) is one of the two basic drives inherent in all living organisms, whether it is a simple cell or a complex civilization. The other is Eros, the creative force. A constant struggle exists between Eros and the death drive, between the forces of creation and destruction. They can be in direct opposition or operate in harmony. The sexual act is a prime example of the two working in tandem as it is an act of aggression with the purpose of the most intimate union. The interplay between the two basic urges gives rise to the whole variety of the phenomenon of life.[8]

The death drive may appear in various forms. One aspect is aggression, most notably the aggression and destruction of war. Freud realized that people can obtain enormous pleasure from being aggressive and destructive. He did not see men and women as gentle creatures who only defend themselves if attacked, but as individuals with powerful and innate tendencies to be aggressive. Moreover, wilful destruction can produce an extraordinarily high degree of narcissistic enjoyment, providing the *ego* with an opportunity to indulge its wish for omnipotence. Because of this, other people are perceived not only as potential helpers or sexual partners, but as opponents who arouse an instinctual urge to be aggressive. As a result people are exploited, humiliated, sexually used, tortured and killed for pleasure. This innate aggression, which is part of the death drive is perpetually threatening society with wars and disintegration.[7]

However, the aggressive tendency can be sublimated and directed into harmless channels. Competitive sports provide one obvious outlet for these inner drives. Less socially acceptable ones are certain criminal activities. Young offenders, for instance, have often mentioned to me that they get a 'buzz' or 'kick' out of burglaries and stealing cars, particularly if the latter involves a police chase in which they manage to elude the 'cops'.

Freud taught that the externalization of the death drive is essential for the preservation of an individual's life. This does not mean that people should behave aggressively towards one another; instead they must learn to sublimate the aggressive aspect of *Todestrieb* and this is best done by physical activity. Whilst the death drive is usually directed outwards, some portion of it continues its secret work within and eventually succeeds in killing the individual.[8] This means that people eventually die because of their own inner conflicts.

There is no point in looking beyond death as nothing exists of the individual as a living entity afterwards. However, death has its compensations. There is nothing to fear after death as it is a state of everlasting peace, free from all anxieties, stimuli and discomforts.

Chapter 11
Jung and
Self-realization

If I must die,
I will encounter darkness as a bride,
And hug it in mine arms.

Measure for Measure

Introduction

When depth psychology was emerging as a new discipline, Carl Jung and Sigmund Freud were close colleagues, probably even friends, but their attitude to life was so different that, inevitably, there was a clash on fundamental issues and the relationship came to an end. Freud, the elder man, was a Viennese and had specialized in neurology. Jung was Swiss and had trained as a psychiatrist. Their understanding of death was also quite different. To Freud, death simply signified the end of life. Jung's views were more complex and, whilst being vague about the possible nature of an afterlife, he considered that death involved more than just biological extinction. He also believed that the psyche has two separate goals during the life of the individual, one for the early years and another for the latter part of life. Until middle age the psyche is mainly concerned with establishing the individual's role in society. Thereafter its primary concern becomes increasingly focused on preparing for death.

Many of the psychological terms now in common use, for instance *introvert* and *extrovert*, owe their origin to Jung. He was an introvert, and he always considered his inner experiences to be more important than the external events of his life. He had many psychic experiences, in some of which he perceived apparitions of the dead, and at the age of 49 he had a heart attack that induced such wonderful visions that he described them as the most tremendous experiences of his life.[1] One of his books, *Septem Sermones ad Mortuos*, was written to instruct the spirits of the dead. He felt impelled to write it by a feeling that the dead were asking questions that could only be answered by the living, and that the answers would help the dead in their further spiritual development. The book, which was written in an archaic style, was published privately and is not included in the English edition of his *Collected Works*.

The Function of Religions

Jung had a deep interest in the psychological insights inherent in religions, both Eastern and Western, and was largely responsible for popularizing in the West such esoteric texts as the *I'Ching* and *The Tibetan Book of the Dead*. He had a particular admiration for the psychological techniques and spiritual insights possessed by the Eastern religions. They showed, he thought, a much greater understanding of human nature than the Western religions, but in making this assessment he was careful to point out that his opinion was of limited value, as he could speak only from the viewpoint of a psychologist. He realized that whilst he could make useful comments about the emotions which religions touched and the symbols they used, he was not competent to pass judgement on their essential nature.[2] Within Christianity, he considered that the Roman Catholic Church provided more psychological support for its adherents than the Protestant Churches but, in view of his interest in Eastern religions, he had surprisingly little to say about the Eastern Orthodox Church.

He used to encourage those patients who could do so to return to their root religion, as he considered all religions to be guardians of collective and therapeutic truths.[3] He saw them as the repositories of humanity's understanding of the significance of life and death, and as centres of learning for the second half of life. All contain elements of psychic truth which enable them to act as agents of public health. Christianity was, in his opinion, 'a beautiful system of psychotherapy as it is capable of healing the suffering soul'; and Christ's statement 'the kingdom of heaven is within you', 'a great psychological truth'.[4] These opinions differ greatly from those held by Sigmund Freud, so it is not surprising that the two men found it difficult to get on with each other.

Archetypes and the Psyche

Jung's views on death were closely linked with his understanding of the nature of the human psyche. This he considered to be a much more complex structure than the one described by Freud. He enlarged Freud's concept of the unconscious to include, in addition to a personal unconscious, a much larger and deeper level which he called the collective unconscious. The collective unconscious is an attribute common to people of all races and is not restricted by time and space. Jung described it as the psychic equivalent of the vast galaxies of planets and stars, which one sees in the night sky. Another image he used when describing the collective unconscious was that of a house with deep cellars, built on ancient foundations. The cellars conceal the foundations that support the house and these foundations have their own form and structure. They are rarely perceived by the people inhabiting the upper rooms of the house, but they have existed in the basement and supported the house over many centuries. In the same way that the foundations have always supported the house, the collective unconscious provides the unchanging substrata of the psyche. This deeper layer of the psyche is composed of instincts and archetypes, but essentially of archetypes.[5]

Archetypes are primordial forces, hidden within the collective unconscious, which normally lie dormant and unnoticed but which can suddenly irrupt into the conscious mind and produce the most unexpected results. They represent the psychic origins of mankind, the matrix from which the patterns of thoughts and feelings arise. Their number is relatively limited but they represent the sum of the latent potentialities within the human psyche. Among their various attributes, they act as powerful balancing mechanisms within the psyche when conscious activity becomes too dominant. They are activated when people, either individually or collectively, are confronted with problems that cannot be dealt with in a standard way. Then they appear in dreams, fantasies and delusions, but usually first as part of a dream.

The language of the collective unconscious is the language of images. Consequently, archetypes make themselves known to the conscious mind as the events and personalities which are commonly recorded in myths, religions and fairy tales. The best known archetypes are the shadow, the anima and animus, the child, and the wise old woman who is often portrayed in fairy tales as the good fairy. The most important archetype is the Self. It is from this archetype that the ego arises in early childhood

Life's Two Phases

According to Jungian psychology, the psyche has two separate goals during the life of each individual, one for the early years and another for the latter part of life. Initially the psyche is mainly concerned with the growth of the ego, the development of the personality and the establishment of the individual's role in society. When this has been accomplished the psyche becomes increasingly focussed on preparing the individual for death. These two phases are not necessarily of equal duration. Jung used to liken them to a parabola in which the upward arc represents the first stage of life and the downward one, which may be longer or shorter than the upward curve, represents the second stage of life.

Whilst the first phase of life tends to be expansive and concerned with relationships with other people, the second phase is governed by restrictions and by the need to concentrate on inner realities. In this later stage, individuals seem to be alone and increasingly absorbed in re-evaluating the past. They learn to see things from a new perspective, and become aware of the errors that are present in former certainties, and to realize how much antagonism and even hatred existed in what was once regarded as love. This process of re-evaluation, and with it an acceptance of the contrary aspects of one's nature, is an important preparation for death.

Jung was amazed that the psyche does not appear to be concerned about death as an event. Yet, he said, the unconscious mind is deeply interested in how one dies, in whether the conscious attitude is adjusted to dying or not. Although death is the goal and fulfilment of life, it does not signify the end of life. Life has a purpose and meaning that extends beyond the physical sphere because, among other reasons, the psyche is not restricted in space or time, either in life or death.[6]

Self-realization

The Self is the most important archetype. From the Self the ego arises in childhood, and the ego's ultimate aim is to apprehend clearly and vividly this archetype. This quest is usually known as 'Self-realization' or the 'Individuation Process', but is sometimes referred to as a 're-rooting in the Self', as it is a return of the ego to its source with all the characteristics that it has acquired in life.[7] During the quest the conscious ego will encounter other archetypes, first the shadow, then the anima or animus, and then progressively perhaps the other archetypes until possibly an encounter with the Self is attained.

The inner struggle towards Self-realization occurs naturally throughout life but its importance increases as death becomes imminent. Moreover, Jung believed the process continues beyond death as the psyche is not restricted by the intellectual concepts of space and time. It involves an exploration of both the outer and inner worlds, and eventually the integration of the outer world of consciousness with the inner world of the unconscious.[8]

Implicit in Jungian psychology is the concept that the beginning and end of life are inseparable, like two sides of the same coin. This close connection between birth and death is underlined by one of the many descriptions Jung gave to the Self, calling it the 'total timeless man'.[9] The Self is simultaneously the centre of the psyche and its periphery, embracing all conscious and unconscious contents. It possesses enormous intensity and power of irradiation but, because of its transcendence, remains beyond human comprehension. Jung was not prepared to postulate the existence of a creator God, but he considered that the Self approximates closely to people's concept of God, and for this reason he also called it the God-image.[10] He drew a close parallel between the Self and Christ, considering that for occidentals the Self is Christ, as Christ is the Westerner's archetypal hero, representing their highest aspirations.

As awareness of the Self develops, symbolic images of it may appear in dreams and active imagination. Its most universal symbol is the mandala or magic circle. The structure of the mandala may be extremely complex or as simple as a flower with four petals. It often has a healing quality and effect. Whether or not this healing quality is present, the symbol of the Self has an intrinsic significance that only the person concerned can really evaluate.

Archetypes of Transformation

As death approaches, the psyche may prepare the conscious mind for its impending end through the archetypes of transformation. These usually appear in dreams as symbolic motifs, plants, animals, or places and situations that typify change. Often they are symbols of creation, fertility and new birth.[11] In my experience they are not frequent occurrences, but then I rarely enquire about a patient's dreams. Two reported incidents may give some indication of how these archetypes are likely to present. Both occurred within 48 hours of death.

In the first a middle-aged married woman dreamed, the night before she died, that she was going to heaven as a bride. The second archetype featured the green man. This did not appear in a dream but as a conscious percept to an intelligent man in unimpaired consciousness. He had not been taking any hallucinatory drugs and his mental state was good despite his terminal illness. He realized that the experience was unusual and asked me not to tell other members of the hospice staff about it. The person he saw was a green pixie man with pointed ears, who stood about 5 feet high. The green man is a fertility symbol representing birth, death and renewal.

Bereavement

Jung called the grief work associated with bereavement, the 'transcendent function'.[12] Its dynamics are similar to those of the grief work of Freudian psychology. He wrote less specifically about bereavement than Freud did but, when he did so, he illustrated his accounts with many more personal experiences.

Occasionally, he had dreams that presaged the death of a close friend or relative. This happened the night his mother died, a sudden and unexpected event. He dreamt he was in a dense, gloomy forest and suddenly a gigantic wolfhound tore past him and he knew that it belonged to the Wild Huntsman and had orders to carry away a human soul. He awoke in terror. The next morning he received the news of his mother's death and immediately returned home with very mixed emotions. He found himself experiencing great grief and yet he did not feel mournful. Throughout the journey he heard dance music, laughter and other sounds of jollity, as though a wedding was being celebrated, and this made it impossible for his sorrow to overwhelm him. He had simultaneously a feeling of warmth and joy, and of terror and grief. He resolved this paradox by supposing that death was being represented at one moment from the point of view of the ego, and at the next by that of the psyche. In the first case it appeared as a brutal catastrophe that had destroyed a human being and an important relationship. From the other point of view death appeared to be a joyful event, almost like a wedding in which the soul achieves complete wholeness.[13]

Jung's views on bereavement differed from those of Freud in one important aspect. He considered that the spirits of the dead, which the bereaved perceive, are psychic facts. He realized that these perceptions can be interpreted as real presences, or as illusions, or superstitious fantasies, but whilst not being dogmatic he gave his support to the traditional, and universal, belief that they are living entities. He considered this to be the psychologically correct interpretation as it enables people to retain their connection with the depths of the psyche. In his opinion, people who deny the authenticity of these experiences are in danger of standing opposed to something very basic in their nature.

The Afterlife

When Jung was terminally ill, a friend asked him 'whether it was important to know if there was something beyond death'. He replied that the question was badly put and would have been better phrased 'Is there any reason to believe that there is life after death?' He expressed his own views on this subject mainly through accounts of personal experiences. 'When I speak of things after death', he said, 'I am speaking out of inner promptings, and can go no further than to tell you of dreams and myths that relate to the subject.' He had many such dreams including one in which his deceased wife was continuing to work on her spiritual development in the afterlife. That, he said, 'Struck me as meaningful and held a measure of reassurance for me.'[14]

He was careful to point out that we lack concrete proof that anything of us is preserved for eternity, and that we are dependent for our belief in a life after death upon the spontaneous revelations of the unconscious. However, he was equally careful to point out that, since the unconscious psyche is not restricted by space or time, it possesses better sources of information than the conscious mind which has only sense perceptions available to it. On balance, he thought it probable that some aspect of the psyche would continue to exist beyond physical death. He also thought it likely that, in such an event, this remnant of the psyche would act as a conscious personality. He was not inclined to view the afterlife as a state of unmitigated bliss. There the rule of opposites would apply. It would be, he said, both grand and terrible, like God and like nature.[15]

Chapter 12
Shakespeare, Death and Grief

Now boast thee, death, in thy possession lies
A lass unparallel'd.

Antony and Cleopatra

It is sometimes said that the scientific mind and the artistic one are psychologically quite distinct. This is a difficult idea to sustain when one considers the artistic and scientific genius possessed by Leonardo da Vinci, or the close ties that exist between the practice of medicine and creative writing. Chekhov, Conan-Doyle, A. J. Cronin, Somerset Maugham and Axel Munthe are all well-known twentieth century authors who were also students or practitioners of medicine. John Keats and the seventeenth-century physician and author, Sir Thomas Browne, are earlier names that could be added to the list. The Thirteen Articles of Faith of Orthodox Judaism were codified by the great twelfth-century physician and philosopher Maimonides, but the best known name of all is that of St Luke – physician and writer – and patron saint to both artists and doctors.

Depth psychologists have always shown a great interest in the visual arts and literature, partly because of the insights into human nature they provide but also because the doctors who were first associated with Sigmund Freud were people with wide cultural interests. Freud's own 'intellectual passions' included a deep interest in and knowledge of the works of William Shakespeare.[1] Carl Jung was a polymath, and his writings include an assessment of the works of Picasso and of the novel *Ulysses* by James Joyce, who also happened to be one of his patients. Jung considered that a wide understanding of literature, myths and religious symbols was essential for the practice of analytical psychology. Despite these close associations between healing and the creative arts, there is some truth in Aldous Huxley's remark that 'one of the most extraordinary and gratuitous pieces of twentieth century vanity, is that nobody knew anything about psychology before the days of Freud'.[2] The same view has been expressed, though less abrasively, by Dr D.R. Davis, a professor of psychiatry. Of Ibsen's plays *Romersholm* and *Ghosts*, he wrote: 'These two plays, written before Freud began his psychoanalytical work, epitomize for me the dilemma psychiatrists find themselves in. We discover in literature, and particularly drama, descriptions of disorders of behaviour more revealing, and in some cases more carefully analysed than anything contained in textbooks and monographs of psychiatry. There is much more of interest in Hamlet, than in a standard textbook of psychiatry.'[3]

The sources of inspiration that sustain a writer were explored in detail by Jung. In *The Spirit in Man, Art and Literature*, he says that there are two distinct types of creative writing. One type he calls psychological and the other visionary. In 'psychological' creative writing, the contents are derived from the author's conscious experience. Everything in the work belongs to the realm of clearly understandable psychology; this is the main form of literary output, whether it deals with social problems, romance, crime, poetry, comedy or drama. In contrast, when the writing is visionary in nature the author is in contact with a much deeper level of the human psyche, and then the oeuvre appears less familiar and has something strange about it. Such work arises from the deep recesses of the psyche where the author's individual experience is less important than the common experience of humanity. This universal experience underlies every great work of art and, as a consequence, the writing tends to be objective, impersonal and yet profoundly moving.[4]

Shakespeare was not a psychological writer in the way that Jung defines this term. He was a visionary, and it is therefore difficult to find in his plays any clear indication of his personal experiences or lifestyle. In contrast the plays are full of battles, shipwrecks, and foreign and faery lands that Shakespeare never encountered. The plays proceed with strange conjunctions of the comic, bizarre, beautiful, unworldly, murderous and profoundly wise. These reflect the human condition in the full range of its violence and tenderness, love and hatred, ambition and fear. Here we find insights into man's attitude to death, which enable us to place our own concepts within a wider, literary and historical perspective.

Shakespeare and Death

In the same way that death touches everybody, so the works of Shakespeare have significance for all who read or see his plays. His contemporary Ben Johnson aptly wrote of him, 'he was not of an age, but for all times'.[5] He remains a contemporary writer and his understanding of human nature is as valid now as it was in the sixteenth century. Shakespeare's plays, like modern television dramas, are full of death. His first play (*King Henry VI*) begins with the funeral in Westminster Abbey of King Henry V, and the opening stage directions read: 'Funeral March. Corpse of King Henry Fifth, in state, is brought in.' To add to the gloom, a messenger rushes in with reports of battles and disasters in France, where 6,000 Englishmen had been killed or taken prisoner. With such a start, it is not suprising that the deaths of countless other people feature in later plays. Some die from grief but relatively few die from natural causes or old age. Most die unnatural deaths, in the field of battle, by execution, murder or suicide. Even today, such events are considered a good source of news whilst death from natural causes receives little press coverage unless the person concerned is well known.

In the plays Julius Caesar is murdered, Hamlet is poisoned, King Lear dies of grief, Macbeth and Richard III die in battle, Romeo and Juliet, Cleopatra, Ophelia, Othello and possibly Lady Macbeth all commit suicide. Among the principal characters, only King Henry V and Falstaff die from natural causes. The death of King Henry V is not even mentioned in the play of that name and is acknowledged only briefly in *King Henry VI* by the funeral service and the words 'the king is dead'. So violent death is over represented in the works and this makes understanding of death more difficult, but not impossible or unrewarding. There are enough instances of natural death among Shakespeare's secondary characters, such as John of Gaunt, Cardinal Wolsey and Katherine of Aragon, to provide a balanced picture and to enable a useful comparison to be made.

One of the best known soliloquies written by Shakespeare is spoken by Jaques in *As You Like It*. In this speech Jaques reviews the life of a man, describing in all seven stages. He explains how a man begins his life as a crying, vomiting infant, then becomes in turn a reluctant schoolboy, a lover, soldier, successful lawyer and an elderly man with thin legs, slippers and spectacles. Finally he reaches senility, a dotard without teeth, sight, taste or any really human attribute. This is a description of a long varied life ranging from infancy to old age. But in Shakespeare's time, even more so than in our own, not every child reached adulthood and death usually came at an early age for those who were weak or disadvantaged. Then as now the runt of the litter was particularly at risk. In *The Merchant of Venice*, Antonio compares his own hazardous state to that of the weakest of lambs.

> I am a tainted wether of the flock
> Meetest for death; the weakest kind of fruit
> Drops earliest to the ground; and so let me.

Shakespeare's characters display the same attitudes towards death as people do in real life. In *Measure for Measure*, the youthful and life-loving Claudio tells us that 'death is a fearful thing', while the elderly John of Gaunt (in *King Richard II*), realizing that his end is near, wishes to help those close to him, particularly the young king.

> Will the king come, that I may breathe my last
> In wholesome counsel to his unstaid youth

Natural death

The longest description of a natural death is given by the hostess of the Boar's Head Tavern in *King Henry V*. She tended Sir John Falstaff during his last hours and was present when he died. As befits her humble status, she speaks in a simple prose and not in the blank verse that is more characteristic of the plays. Her immediate reaction to the death is a strong conviction that despite his drunken and dissolute lifestyle, Falstaff has not been consigned to Hell but lies 'in Arthur's bosom'. She describes his death as that of a christened child that ended at the turning of the tide, a reference to the old sea-faring belief that people died with the ebb tide. She observed how he fumbled with his sheets, played with flowers, smiled at his finger tips, and talked incoherently about green fields. He complained of feeling cold and asked her to put more clothes on his feet. He called out to God repeatedly and the hostess, wishing to comfort him, advised him not to think of such things. Then he died, his terminal illness being 'quontidian tertian' a medieval term for malaria, which was endemic in sixteenth-century England. The woman confirmed Falstaff's death by testing the temperature of his body to see if it was cold. She placed her hand on this feet, then his knees and 'so upward and upward, and all was cold as any stone.' So Falstaff's death was confirmed by the temperature of his body, but King Lear recognized that respiration too was a vital sign of life. When he enters with the murdered Cordelia in his arms, he knows that she is dead but hopes that she may live, and uses a mirror and later a feather in a vain attempt to show that she is still breathing. Kneeling besides his dead daughter, Lear calls out,

> Howl, howl, howl, howl! – O, you are men o' stone:
> Had I tongues and eyes, I'd use them so

> That heaven's vault should crack.– She's gone for ever!–
> I know when one is dead and when one lives,
> She's dead as earth. – lend me a looking glass;
> If that her breath will mist or stain the stone,
> Why, then she lives.

One needs to remember that the pattern of mortality in sixteenth century England was very different from that of today. Then infant mortality was high and not all children reached adult life. Epidemics were rife, simple infections were likely to become fatal, and death often followed soon after the onset of an illness. There is no mention of cancer in Shakespeare's plays though it accounts for over 20 per cent of present deaths. In contrast, Shakespeare certainly mentions grief as a cause of death, with Romeo's mother and Constance (*King John*) among the lesser characters who died because of it. Despite the difference in mortality patterns, there are hints in Shakespeare's plays of insights similar to those of modern psychiatrists like Elizabeth Kübler-Ross.

Anger, bargaining and acceptance

In her portrayal of death as an event occurring in five stages, Kübler-Ross suggests that the dying normally experience episodes of denial, anger, bargaining, depression and acceptance. Emotions tend to run high in Shakespeare's plays, and anger is often expressed at the time of death. When, in *King John*, Prince Henry learns that his dying father has expressed a wish to be in the open air, he replies

> Let him be brought into the orchard here. –
> Doth he still rage?

The word 'rage' is rather ambiguous, it could mean being angry or feverish, but there is no doubting the anger expressed by the elderly John of Gaunt (*King Richard II*) on his deathbed.

> And thy unkindness be like crooked age
> To crop at once a too-long wither'd flower.
> Live in thy shame, but die not shame with thee! —
> These words hereafter thy tormentors be! —

To which King Richard replies:

> And let them die that age and sullens have;
> For both hast thou, and both become thy grave.

When, later in the play, King Richard has been mortally wounded, he still manages to strike down some of his assailants and curse them soundly.

> Villain, thine own hand yields thy death's instrument.
> Go thou, and fill another room in hell.
> That hand shall burn in never-quenching fire
> That staggers thus my person.–

That anger can give way to acceptance is apparent in the *King Henry IV, Part 2*. In Act IV, the king speaks bitterly to his son Henry.

> Thy life dost manifest thou lov'dst me not,
> And thou wilt have me die assur'd of it.
> Thou hads't a thousand daggers,
> Which thou hast whetted on thy stony heart,
> To stab at half an hour of my life.
> What! can'st thou not forbear me half an hour?
> Then get thee gone and dig my grave thyself.

But the King's bitterness is eased by the Prince's kind and modest reply, so that he can respond,

> Come hither, Harry, sit thou by my bed;
> And hear, I think, the very latest counsel!
> That ever I shall breathe.

Confusional states are common in terminal illnesses and the ravings of Cardinal Beaufort (*King Henry VI, Part 2*) are indicative of such a state. Vaux informs Queen Margaret:

> That Cardinal Beaufort is at the point of death;
> For suddenly a grievous sickness took him,
> That makes him gasp, and stare, and call the air,
> Blaspheming God, and cursing men on earth.
> Sometimes he talks as if Duke Humphrey's ghost
> Were by his side; sometimes he calls the king,
> And whispers to his pillow as to him,
> The secrets of his overcharged soul.

When, later the King visits the Cardinal, Beaufort tries to bargain for his life.

> If thou be'st death I'll give thee England's treasure,
> Enough to purchase such another island,
> So thou wilt let me live and feel no pain.

Bargaining, in the form of a secret contract with God, is not found in the plays, but characters threatened with death do strive for deliverance in other ways. In *Measure for Measure*, Claudio tries to persuade his sister to bed his judge to save his life, and in *Othello*, Desdemona pleads with her murderous husband, 'kill me tomorrow let me live tonight' and later asks for 'but half an hour' and 'but while I say one prayer'. Similarly, in *King Henry VI, Part 3* the youthful Rutland pleads with his murderer: 'O let me pray before I take my death' and later, 'Ah let me live in prison all my days' but to no avail.

Denial is not a feature of the plays, but this is understandable in an age when death was often swift and seen as a normal part of family life. On the other hand, there are many instances of people accepting death quietly and with apparent unconcern. King Edward IV, in *King Richard III*, tells his companions

> I every day expect an embassage
> From my Redeemer, to redeem me hence:
> And now in peace my soul shall part to heaven,
> Since I have made my friends at peace on earth.

And in *King Henry VI, Part 1*, Bedford can say,

> Now, quiet soul, depart when heaven please,

and later, in the same play, Talbot, himself mortally wounded, takes and holds the body of his son, with the words:

> Soldiers, adieu! I have what I would have,
> Now my old arms are young John Talbot's grave.

Depression and suicide

Depression does not make for good theatre. It is rarely depicted in the plays, though Lady Macbeth's decline from an ambitious and energetic queen, who demanded the murder weapon from Macbeth, to a guilt-ridden insomniac obsessed with her own uncleanliness, makes for high drama. Shakespeare obviously understood the intractability of a deeply rooted depression. When Macbeth asks a physician

> Can'st thou not minister to a mind diseased;
> Pluck from the memory a rooted sorrow;
> Raze out the written troubles of the brain
> And with some sweet oblivious antidote
> Cleanse the stuff'd bosom of that perilous stuff
> Which ways upon the breast?

the physician replies

> therein the patient must minister to himself.

That Shakespeare was also aware of the contribution that a priest might make to the healing of a troubled mind, is apparent from the physician's remark to the queen's gentlewoman.

> More needs she the divine than the physician: –
> God, God forgive us all! – Look after her;

The exact cause of Lady Macbeth's death is not clear. It may have been due to grief or dementia, or she may, as so many other Shakespearean characters did, have chosen suicide as the most acceptable way out of her predicament, In contrast, Cardinal Wolsey in *King Henry VIII* died from natural causes. He fell ill whilst travelling from York to London and died three days later in a monastery. He knew he was dying, accepted the fact and foretold the exact hour of his end. Such a faculty is not portrayed by any other character in the plays. This idea was not necessarily a product of Shakespeare's imagination. Trelease has observed that Alaskan Indians are often able to foresee the time of their death.[6]

Everyone hopes for a peaceful and easy death. This desire underpins the arguments both for legalizing euthanasia and improving the care of the terminally ill. Although euthanasia is not mentioned in Shakespeare's plays they do contain examples of assisted suicide. In *Julius Caesar*, Brutus persuades his servant, Strato, to hold a sword so that he can impale himself upon it; and the clown, in *Antony and Cleopatra* brings the queen a basket containing venomous snakes, though he does so with some reluctance. He warns her that the snakes are dangerous and distances himself from her intended suicide with the words, 'I should not be the party that should desire you to touch him, for his biting is immortal'. While the clown carries out his task with uncharacteristic seriousness, Cleopatra speaks more lightly, 'Hast thou the pretty worm of Nilus there, That kills and pains not?'

In her acceptance of death, Cleopatra remains regal yet lighthearted. She retains her dignity and control of the situation, and displays no fear or sense of guilt. She does not see her intended action as an escape from life – 'I have immortal longings in me', but as a way of being reunited with Anthony in eternity. As she clasps the snake to her breast , she quietens her distraught attendant Charmian with the words,

> Peace, peace!
> Dost thou not see my baby at my breast,
> That sucks the nurse asleep?

Deathbed visions

In a Shakespearean world full of fairies, ghosts and spirits, one might
expect to find scenes depicting deathbed visions and archetypal
dreams of transformation. Such a scene occurs in *King Henry VIII*,
where the ailing and sleeping Katherine of Aragon has a dream
which Shakespeare calls a vision. In the vision Katherine sees six
people, clad in white robes, wearing garlands of bay leaves and
carrying leafy branches in their hands. When discussing the vision
later with her attendants, Katherine tells them how this 'blessed
troop' had brought her flowers, invited her to a banquet and
promised her eternal happiness, whilst their 'bright faces cast thou-
sand beams upon me, like the sun'. She then goes on to discuss her
impending death, how she wishes her body to be treated with
honour, and embalmed and covered with flowers before she is
interred. The reference to embalmment is both interesting and
unexpected as this is not a procedure that is normally associated with
Tudor England.

Funerals

Shakespeare provides many descriptions of funerals and burials.
After the battle of Agincourt, King Henry V orders the burial of the
dead with all holy rites and the singing of *Non Nobis* and the *Te Deum*.
In *Hamlet*, Ophelia describes her father's burial in the song

> They bore him barefaced on a bier;
> Hey nonny, nonny, hey nonny;
> And in his grave rained many a tear,
> Fare you well, my dove!

And she also sings,

> He is dead and gone lady,
> He is dead and gone;
> At his head a grass green turf
> At his heels a stone.

In a later scene, at Ophelia's funeral, we are reminded of the
punitive attitude towards suicides that has been a feature of Western
societies until recent times. There is obviously a strong suspicion that
Ophelia committed suicide. She had been distraught and died by
drowning but, because there is no suicide note and her relatives held

positions at court, she is allowed a Christian burial. But this is a trun-
cated affair, carried out against the better judgement of the clergy. As
the priest pointed out to her brother, Laertes:

> Her obsequies have been so far enlarg'd
> As we have warranties: her death was doubtful;
> And, that but great command o'ersways the order,
> She should in ground unsanctified have lodg'd
> Till the last trumpet . . .

The final words are consistent with the doctrine, then generally held
by Christians and still held by Orthodox Jews and Muslims, that
there will be a final Day of Judgement and with it a bodily resurrection of the dead from their graves.

Reviving the dead

Bringing the dead back to life is mentioned twice in the plays. One is
the successful resuscitation of an apparently dead person: the other a
wise decision not to revive a demented old man, who had longed for
death. In *Pericles, Prince of Tyre*, Queen Thaisa dies in childbirth
during a stormy sea voyage. At the urgent behest of the sailors, her
body is sealed into a coffin and thrown overboard. Soon afterwards,
the coffin is washed ashore by the tide and is found by Cerimon, an
Athenian nobleman. He opens the coffin, sees the Queen and
decides, because of the freshness of her complexion, that she must
have died that night and therefore could possibly be revived.

> Nay, certainly to-night;
> For look how fresh she looks!– They were too rough
> That threw her in the sea.– Make a fire within:
> Fetch hither all my boxes in my closet.–
> Death may usurp on nature many hours,
> And yet the fire of life kindle again
> The o'erpress'd spirits. I heard of an Egyptian
> That had nine hours lien dead,
> Who was by good appliance recovered . . .

With the aid of his companions, Cerimon revives the Queen with
music and warmth, which suggests that Thaisa may have been
suffering from hypothermia. She recovers, enters a convent and
eventually is reunited with her husband and daughter. The second
mention is in King Lear. Soon after the murder of his fool and his
daughter Cordelia, the grief stricken king dies, surrounded by his

friends. One of them, Edgar, makes a move to revive the old man but is restrained by Kent's wise words,

> Vex not, his ghost: O, let him pass, he hates him,
> That would upon the wrack of this tough world
> Stretch him out longer.

In these few words, Shakespeare says something of importance to doctors, nurses and paramedics of the twenty-first century, people who have the equipment and skill to resuscitate elderly, demented patients who have just died. Professional carers and ambulance workers need to be reminded that for many older people death is not a fearful thing but often a blessed relief. There are times when someone, like Kent in the play, must be allowed to take the decision not to intervene.

Shakespeare and Grief

Shakespeare's plays are based on relatively few themes. The plots are usually about struggles for power, family feuds and frustrated love. The comedies deal mainly with love, initially thwarted but eventually joyfully realized in the final Act. There is much rivalry both between and within families. This is most obvious in the plays dealing with the warring Plantagenets, but similar tension is found in *Romeo and Juliet* and *King Lear*. Even in two of the comedies such rivalries form a subplot. In the *Tempest*, Prospero is ousted from the Dukedom of Milan by his brother, and, in *As You Like It*, Duke Senior is banished to the Forest of Arden by his brother, Frederick. Within the context of these themes there is much loss, death and grief. Shakespeare knew that bereavement is the most potent cause of grief but shows that it is not the only one. In the plays, the characters also experience grief following shipwreck, imprisonment, banishment and general mishap. Whatever its cause, the grieving process remains the same and Shakespeare provides many insights into it.

In *The Merchant of Venice*, Shylock, a Jewish widower, suffers many losses. First, his daughter Jessica elopes with the Christian, Lorenzo, taking Shylock's money and jewellery. The most hurtful aspect of this robbery was that Jessica took his turquoise ring and swapped it for a monkey. The ring was the most precious memento Shylock had of his wife Leah and when he learns that it has been given away, his response is bitter. 'Out upon her! Thou torturest me, Tubal: it was my turquoise: I had it of Leah when I was a batchelor: I would not have given it for a wilderness of monkeys.' But this is just the beginning of Shylock's problems. Later, he loses a lawsuit and is forced by the court to allow his daughter to marry Lorenzo, and he is also required to forfeit half his goods to the state. He is bereft and humiliated, and must have felt dreadful. His request to the court, 'I pray you give me leave to go from hence; I am not well', is totally understandable, and reminds us that people frequently fall ill after a bereavement or any other deeply felt loss.

Some of the most moving passages written by Shakespeare are to be found in his sonnets. These were probably addressed to two separate people though there is considerable dispute as to who they might be. The theme is of love first accepted and then spurned. As a rejected lover, Shakespeare knew the agony of such a role. We can find in the following extract from *Sonnet XXX* some characteristic features of grief – the pangs that memory brings, a tendency to sigh and weep, and the possibility that grief may be assuaged by an openness to a new loving relationship

> When to the sessions of sweet silent thought
> I summon up remembrance of things past,
> I sigh the lack of many things I sought,
> And with old woes new wail my dear times' waste:
> Then can I drown my eye, unus'd to flow,
> For precious friends hid in deaths dateless night,
> And weep afresh love's long since cancell'd woe,
> And moan the expense of many a vanish'd sight.
>   ....
> But if awhile I think on thee dear friend,
> All losses are restored and sorrows end.

Stages of grief

Some bereavement counsellors say that the grieving process has four recognizable stages that, though distinctive, tend to overlap. These feelings are first numbness, then pining and searching, followed by disorganization and despair, and finally some degree of recovery. There is little reference in Shakespeare's plays to the first stage of numbness. This is not surprising. Numbness is an early feature of grief, it is of short duration and is not easily expressed in words. It is a state of relative silence in which the inner resources are being mobilized to deal

with the new situation. It can be more aptly expressed on the stage by
gesture and stance than by words. But Shakespeare still managed to
capture the mood exactly when, in *Twelfth Night*, Viola says,

> she pin'd in thought;
> And with a green and yellow melancholy,
> She sat like Patience on a monument,
> Smiling at grief.

Smiling at grief is an unusual phrase, which describes two conflicting
emotional states in three simple words. Perhaps a better known, but
more clumsy term, is 'putting a brave face on things'. Whichever
expression is preferred, bereaved people are indeed sometimes
surprised to find that outwardly they appear placid or even cheerful,
whilst their inner state is one of turmoil. The same short quotation
contains the phrase, 'she pin'd in thought'. Pining is synonymous
with yearning, and both conditions are said to be linked with an
impulse to search for the loved person. At the death of Falstaff, his
companion, Bardolph, expresses a wish to be with him 'where-
some'er he is', either in Heaven or Hell whilst Pistol feels the need to
share his grief for 'we must yearn together'. Yearning is often associated with a tendency to sigh. Edmund draws attention to this sign of
grief in *King Lear*, with 'my cue is villainous melancholy with a sigh'.

Searching

The state of numbness does not facilitate a reunion with the lost
person; for this the search is needed. The features of searching are
anger, crying and restlessness. All are described in Shakespeare's
plays, though the searching is more often for a lost lover than a dead
relative. Anger may be directed towards individuals, as when King
Lear rages against the murderers and traitors who killed Cordelia, or
against the deity as in Juliet's more gently expressed,

> Is there no pity in the clouds
> That sees into the bottom of my grief.

Sometimes mourners cannot find an external target for their
anger and so it remains within or directed against themselves. This is
likely to result in depression or suicide. When Othello discovers that
the wife he has just murdered was an innocent victim of his jealous
accusations, he curses himself, and demands to be flogged, and
roasted in sulphur and blown to the winds. This is didactic theatre: it
highlights the intense guilt and anger that is often associated with

grief; an anger that is closely linked with tears. 'Speak of me,' Othella says before he finally commits suicide, as

> Of one that lov'd not wisely, but too well,
> Of one not easily jealous, but being wrought,
> Perplexed in the extreme; of one whose hand,
> Like the base Indian, threw his pearl away
> Richer than all his tribe; of one whose subdued eyes,
> Albeit unused to the melting mood,
> Drop tears as fast as the Arabian trees
> Their medicinal gum.

Tearfulness in Shakespeare's time was considered to be the prerogative of women; men were expected to be less demonstrative in their grief. However, Shakespeare knew that deeply felt grief could overcome a man's normal reactions to loss even on the battlefield. In *King Henry V*, Exeter tells the king how the death of Suffolk,

> forc'd
> These waters from me which I would have stopp'd
> But I had so much man in me,
> And all my mother came into mine eyes,
> And gave me up to tears.

Exeter was a combatant at the Battle of Agincourt and an eyewitness of Suffolk's death in the fray. In the *King Henry IV, Part 2*, when Percy is killed in battle, the news of his death is brought to his father, the Earl of Northumberland, by Morton. On seeing Morton, the Earl realizes immediately that his son is dead, but hopes that his intuition is mistaken. He encourages Morton to speak;

> Tell thou thy Earl his divination lies,
> And I will take it as a sweet disgrace,
> And make thee rich for doing me such wrong.

As Morton hesitates, the Earl sees in his eyes a further confession of the truth and, realizing Morton's difficulties, expresses the messenger's predicament for him

> Yet the first bringer of unwelcome news
> Hath but a losing office; and his tongue,
> Sounds ever after as a sullen bell,
> Remember'd knolling a departing friend.

Then strangely, the Earl of Northumberland, though mournful and angry at his son's death, finds himself enlivened by the news

> and these news,
> Having been well, that would have made me sick,
> Being sick, have in some measure made me well;
> And as the wretch, whose fever-weaken'd joints,
> Like strengthless hinges, buckle under life,
> Impatient of his fit, breaks like a fire
> Out of his keeper's arms; even so my limbs,
> Weaken'd with grief, being now enrag'd with grief,
> Are thrice themselves

Thus Shakespeare describes poetically what modern psychiatrists might call an atypical grief reaction.

Death of a child

The sudden death of a child is a devastating experience for parents. Death and serious injury are accepted as the risks of battle, and Morton's demeanour also helped to prepare Northumberland for the news he hoped not to hear. In contrast, a mother who goes to her child's bedroom in the morning and finds that the child, who was alive and well the previous night, is now dead, is totally unprepared for such a catastrophe. Such is the experience of parents when their child is a victim of a cot death. The nearest approach to such a death in Shakespeare's plays occurs in *Romeo and Juliet*, when Lady Capulet is summoned by the cries of Juliet's nurse and on entering the bedroom finds her teenage daughter apparently dead. Her grief is immediate and intense:

> O me, O me! - My child, my only life,
> Revive, Look up, or I will die with thee! –
> Help, help! – call help.

The death is apparent not real. Juliet has drunk a potion that induces a death-like sleep, so that she can be placed in the family tomb and from there escape to join her banished husband, Romeo. But Romeo, on entering the tomb, believes that Juliet is dead and kills himself, while she, on awakening from her sleep and finding Romeo dead, stabs herself with a rusty dagger. The parents are overwhelmed with grief after the lovers' deaths. Romeo's mother dies as a direct consequence whilst Juliet's mother predicts that she herself will not live long. The feuding fathers become reconciled in their joint sorrow, and place in the city golden statues of Romeo and Juliet as a memorial to the lovers.

The purpose of shrines and memorial tablets is not to erase memories of the dead but to reinforce them. Even in the absence of a shrine painful memories persist and, paradoxically, may remain a welcomed aspect of grief. Moreover, only those people who have had a similar loss can understand the anguish experienced by the parents. All this is stated succinctly in *King John*, by Constance, whose son is imprisoned by the King and later dies attempting to escape. Constance tells Cardinal Pandulph and King Philip of France how

> Grief fills the room up of my absent child,
> Lies in his bed, walks up and down with me,
> Puts on his pretty looks, repeats his words,
> Remembers me of all his gracious parts,
> Stuffs out his vacant garments with his form;
> Then have I reason to be fond of grief.
> Fare you well: had you such a loss as I,
> I could give better comfort than you do . . .

She becomes neglectful of her appearance and longs to be dead, or even insane, so that she may lose the burden of her grief in madness. Bereft mothers may, like Constance, long to be dead but they do not usually share her desire for madness; they are more likely to be afraid of going insane with grief.

Madness and blackness

Bereavement is often followed by a period of depression but insanity is a very unusual outcome. When it does occur it indicates the presence of an extreme form of atypical grief. This happens to Ophelia after the accidental killing of her father by her beloved, Hamlet. Trapped in a situation with such conflicting loyalties, it is not surprising that Ophelia escapes into a psychotic, depressive illness. Like other bereaved people, she also wants to talk about her loss and 'speaks much of her father', but people do not want to listen to her. At first the queen refuses to speak to her, which is a nice Shakespearean pointer to the social isolation experienced by the bereaved, but she is persuaded to do so. A similar intolerance of grief is found in Lady Capulet's remark to Juliet after Tybalt's death and the banishment of Romeo:

Therefore have done: some grief shows much of love;
But much of grief shows still some want of wit.

There are no stage directions in *Hamlet* to indicate that Ophelia is
wearing mourning clothes after the death of her father, but in a
conventional presentation of the play she will normally be dressed in
black. However, the mourning garb that Hamlet wears is clearly
described. It is the black cloak that in the sixteenth century was
customarily put on over a person's normal clothes. But black clothes
are only the visible sign of mourning, they do not reveal the true feelings, which may be of intense or, as is sometimes the case, of little
grief. Hamlet recognizes the difference between the inner reality and
outward show when he tells his mother

'Tis not alone my inky cloak, good mother,
Nor customary suits of solemn black.
Nor windy suspiration of forc'd breath.
No, nor the fruitful river in the eye,
Nor the dejected haviour of the visage,
Together with all forms, moods, shows of grief,
That can denote me truly: these, indeed, seem,
For they are actions that a man might play;
But I have that within which passeth show;
These but the trappings and the suits of woe.

Spirits of the Dead

A central character in the first act of *Hamlet* is the ghost of Hamlet's
murdered father. The ghost appears first to three soldiers, who
report the incident to Hamlet's friend, Horatio. He displays a
natural scepticism for as one of the soldiers says:

Horatio says 'tis but our fantasy,
And will not let belief take hold of him
Touching this dreaded sight, twice seen of us.

Horatio's attitude changes when he sees the ghost himself:

Before my God, I might not this believe
Without the sensible and true avouch
Of mine own eyes.

He goes to tell Hamlet and finds him absorbed by thoughts of his
father

Hamlet	Horatio! – My father, – methinks 1 see my father.
Horatio	O where my lord?
Hamlet	In my mind's eye, Horatio.

The relatively calm way in which Hamlet mentions these images of his father differs markedly from his explosive 'angels and ministers of grace defend us!' when he is confronted by the ghost. The ghost is bitter and vindictive and has come to persuade Hamlet to exact revenge on his murderers, Hamlet's mother and Claudius, her newly married husband. Although Hamlet's father is the most famous of all theatrical ghosts, apparitions of the dead also appear in *King Henry VI, Part 1*, *King Richard III*, *Julius Caesar*, and *Macbeth*. All tend to be the angry and vindictive ghosts of murdered men and women. This is in keeping with Freud's idea that apparitions of the dead are projections of deep seated and powerful emotions, of which anger and hatred are the most prominent. It does not support recent findings that many bereaved people find perceptions of their dead loved ones helpful. However, whilst Shakespeare was willing to use ghosts for their dramatic effect, he realized that most people do not wish to appear to be overcredulous about such matters and that they would rather adopt the approach of Antigonus in *The Winter's Tale*, when he informs his child

> I have heard, – but not believ'd, – the spirits o' the dead
> May walk again: if such things be, thy mother
> Appear'd to me last night; for ne'er was dream
> So like a waking.

Shakespeare's Audience

Within the walls of the old Globe theatre – destroyed by fire 350 years ago and recently rebuilt, Shakespeare and his fellow actors created the illusion that thousands of people had been killed in battle or died from other causes. In Shakespeare's time there were no actresses, all parts – male and female – were played by men or boys, so we can only speculate on the ease with which they assumed the female roles. This required more than a readiness to put on women's clothing. The characters had to be presented in a demanding situation, for the Globe theatre was a boisterous arena, open to the elements, with members of the audience strolling and chatting in front of the stage, and hawkers shouting and selling their wares as the actors played their parts.

The playgoers were probably responsive and often noisy, ready to express approval or distaste, just as children do at Christmas pantomimes. We know that the plays were popular but we have no means of determining how the audience responded to particular lines, such as these spoken by Claudio in the comedy *Measure for Measure*, where he declares:

> If I must die,
> I will encounter darkness as a bride,
> And hug it in mine arms.

These are serious lines even though the play is a comedy, so did the audience smile and laugh, or were they more thoughtful, perhaps thinking 'that's a good way to meet one's end'? How did they react when the Duke, also in *Measure for Measure*, came on to the stage disguised as a friar and advised the imprisoned Claudio to

> Be absolute for death, either death or life
> Shall thereby be the sweeter.

Did they listen in silence as we do, silently assenting, or did they react differently. Probably not, for even in his comedies Shakespeare set out ideas that audiences throughout the ages surely recognized as being irrefutable.

The Tragedies

Then as now, Shakespeare's tragedies would have stirred the emotions in a different way from his other plays. The burial of the dead demented Ophelia, and her brother Laertes's anger with the priest dealt with the sad consequences of bereavement, and these are skilfully portrayed in Laertes's speech

> Lay her i' th' earth; –
> And from her fair and unpolluted flesh
> May violets spring!– I tell thee, churlish priest,
> A minist'ring angel shall my sister be,
> When thou liest howling.

These few lines touch on a whole range of human responses to the tragedy of death. Anger and the ability to accept the reality of the loss are expressed with equal vigour, Here too is remembrance, and hope – the recollection of Ophelia's physical beauty and good nature, and the expectation that she will find a place in heaven whilst the priest, who so reluctantly provided the Christian funeral rites, would obtain his own deserts, howling somewhere in Hell.

Not everyone enjoys going to the theatre and that was true in Shakespeare's lifetime. The puritans of his era considered entertainments to be so morally subversive that they tried to close the theatres, and succeeded in doing so 50 years later. They would certainly not have approved of the rompings of Antony and Cleopatra nor of the Queen's suicide. Yet how tenderly does Shakespeare express the suicide's desire as Cleopatra gazes on the body of her dead servant Iras, and speaks the words

> Dost fall?
> If thou and nature can so gently part,
> The stroke of death is as a lover's pinch
> Which hurts, and is desired . . .

People who are frightened of dying, and long for a swift and easy death, may feel an empathy with those last words of Cleopatra. Alternatively, advocates of euthanasia may find their own thoughts more fully expressed in the Duke's advice to Claudio, in *Measure for Measure*:

> Be absolute for death, either life or death
> Shall thereby be the sweeter. Reason thus with life: –
> If I do lose thee, I do lose a thing
> That none but fools would keep: a breath thou art,
> Servile to all the skyey influences.

Yet somehow these lines are too rhetorical and lack the simple delicacy of Cleopatra's 'lover's pinch'. They are not out of place within the context of a Shakespearean comedy, but it is in the tragedies that Shakespeare expresses his clearest insights into the sad aspects of human life. These insights may have been the result of personal experiences, or based on ideas widely held in England at that time, but whatever the explanation it needed the genius of Shakespeare to write such lines as

> Give sorrow words: the grief that does not speak
> Whispers the o'er-fraught heart, and bids it break . . .

His Epitaph

Shakespeare wrote many verses that would have graced the epitaph of any man, but no such felicitous phrases are found in the lines he is said to have written for his own gravestone. They might easily be dismissed as doggerel. They contain no hint of his poetic genius, his generosity, or cheerful personality, and there is no indication of the high esteem in which his contemporaries held him. Inscribed over the tomb, visited each year by hundreds of thousands of people from many countries, are the simple words:

> Good friend for Jesus' sake forbear
> To dig the dust enclosed here:
> Blest be the man who spares these stones
> And curst be he that moves my bones.

Chapter 13
Dying
The Last Months

This fell sergeant death,
Is strict in his arrest.

Hamlet

Introduction

Almost 2,000 years ago, the Roman historian, Pliny the Elder, wrote: 'so uncertain is men's judgement that they cannot determine even death itself'. Pliny was possibly overstating the point he wished to make, but his words are interesting as they underline the fact that, even in Roman times, people believed that some agreed standard for determining the death of an individual was essential. Nowadays, it is necessary for three reasons. First, it is important for those who are terminally ill that their death, when it occurs, should be clearly established before they are buried or cremated. Second, the relatives need to be sure that the person is really dead before they can accept the loss. Third, this knowledge is of importance to other interested parties. These include the registrar of births and deaths, lawyers, the police and any person who might benefit from the deceased's possessions, including someone waiting for a heart or kidney transplant.

Strict criteria now exist for diagnosing death, but the moment at which an illness becomes terminal cannot be so clearly or objectively defined, particularly now that the moribund often recover and patients with cardiac arrest are readily resuscitated. Yet a consideration of the psychology of death requires some agreed understanding of what a terminal illness is. The definition I use is as follows: 'A person is terminally ill when, following correct diagnosis and appropriate treatment, the disease remains progressive, death is inevitable in the short term, and the practical need is for care not cure.' The phrase 'death is inevitable in the short term' envisages a period of weeks and months, not just of days, hours and minutes. Despite its shortcomings, this definition provides a useful framework within which practical judgements can be made. It stresses the importance of 'care' and this requires the adoption of a holistic approach to the problems confronting patients and their families. These problems are usually multifarious. They may be physical, mental, emotional, spiritual and social in nature or, as is usually the case, a combination of these different components.

Physical Distress

A study of the psychology of death would be incomplete without some reference to the physical distresses associated with dying. A relationship obviously exists between the thoughts, emotions and bodies of individuals, and this relationship becomes more apparent during the physical decline that precedes death. Moreover we are social creatures, and people who are dying have family and friends who care about them and become upset when they see their loved ones suffering. To illustrate the distress patients and their families are likely to experience, I have included in this chapter extracts from letters I wrote to family doctors after I had visited their patients at home. All the patients had terminal cancer though many had other diseases as well.

> *(F age 48)* Following your telephone call, I visited B. today. I found her restless, and in great distress from pain and pruritus. The family were distraught.
> *(F age 57)* The situation seemed tense in the house today, with the daughter tearful, complaining that mother was not eating, was vomiting, needed more nursing care, and that there were inadequate discussions within the family.
> *(M age 67)* Pain is the major problem. This is most severe in the perineum but radiates into the penis and right leg . . . Vomiting is a more recent problem occurring once or twice a day . . . He is very concerned about his wife and how she will manage when he dies. He says she is depressed and awakens during the night crying. He describes his own mood as equable.

Some people see a close conceptual relationship between birth and death. When a pregnant woman goes into labour, she does so with mixed feelings of relief and apprehension. Similarly, dying patients accept the approach of death with varied thoughts and emotions. Even if the individual is not afraid of death itself, or perhaps longs for the release it promises, he or she is likely to have doubts about his or her ability to cope with severe pain and the other trauma that people associate with dying. These include incontinence, dementia, being a burden to other people, behaving badly, choking to death and dying alone.

Various surveys have shown that a high proportion of terminally ill patients have episodes of unrelieved pain. The hospice movement has done much to improve terminal care in hospitals and the community, and the basics of palliative medicine are now taught in all medical schools, but the dying still experience unnecessary pain particularly with movement. Doctors still need to be reminded that their assessment and management of pain is incomplete until they have seen the patient move or be lifted.

> *(F age 70)* Mrs M is confined to the first floor of her house and her only excursions are by ambulance to the hospital. At first glance she appears to be a lively, cheerful, well preserved lady. Her considerable disability and discomfort are apparent only when she walks. This she manages with the aid of a stick and holding on to the wall. Pain is fairly generalized below the waist, being greatest over the left hip and leg.

A well-known axiom in palliative medicine states that the dosage of analgesic drugs given to a patient needs to be titrated against the patient's pain. It is also accepted that, once pain has been controlled, the appropriate dose is the minimum amount that will prevent the onset of pain, and that drug requirements vary with age. Perhaps less well known is the finding that the effective dosage of opioids for terminal cancer pain decreases in a regular manner from a high requirement in young adults to a low level in the very old. Among the likely explanations for this progressive fall is that the perception of pain decreases with age.[1]

Other factors play a part in determining people's assessment of the intensity of pain they feel. The duration of the pain is one such factor; another is the patient's psychological attitude. The latter is determined not only by a person's innate character but by environmental conditions – whether these are strange and stressful, or familiar and comforting – and the attitude of people close by. All these factors can affect a person's response to pain and to the other distresses associated with dying. Terminally ill patients feel most comfortable and peaceful in caring environments where they are supported by familiar and competent people. Often, the best environment for them is their own home provided the patient and family receive adequate nursing and social support.

> *(F age 79)* Thank you for referring this elderly spinster with cancer of the bronchus. She lives very happily with her unmarried sister in the house

where they were born. She is a weak, uncomplaining lady who is breathless on effort and obviously terminally ill . . . They are pleased with the care and attention you are giving. The Home Care Team will continue to visit.

(M age 48) He talks easily about his disease, his increasing weakness and poor prognosis. He is content at home and well supported by his wife.

(M age 21) Although extremely weak he seems perfectly content at home with his mother.

If the atmosphere is cheerless and the attendants unsympathetic or incompetent, the patient is less likely to feel comfortable in body or spirit.

(M age 73) The home conditions are bad and the sister distraught. She is threatening suicide unless adequate help is provided, viz. admission to a suitable unit. He is a very weak, incontinent man who is just capable of walking unaided. His breathing is noisy and he is breathless on slight effort. He doesn't like hospitals. I have suggested to him that he should come into St Mary's Hospice but at present he prefers to stay at home.

Although unbearable pain is the most feared aspect of dying, terminally ill patients are more likely to complain of weakness and exhaustion. These symptoms are often associated with *cachexia*, the wasting away of body tissues, which may lead to the development of pressure sores. Terminal weakness is not a condition which responds to drugs, psychotherapy or the practices of alternative medicine. It requires good, basic nursing care, the presence of individuals who are competent to lift, carry, wash and feed the patient.

Finally, patients are often frightened of dying alone and have a right to expect someone to be present at the moment of death. It is a personal journey but, even if they are comatose, they seem to be aware if someone is sitting close by to watch over them. If the imminence of death causes an upsurge of panic, as happens occasionally, the presence of a close relative is more likely to bring peace to a dying person than any other measure.

The Psychological Stages of Dying

The insight professional carers have into patients' inner experiences is likely to be enhanced if they have been in similar situations, but relatively few working doctors and nurses have been close to death themselves. An exception is Dr Elizabeth Kübler-Ross, who published a book in 1969 entitled *On Death and Dying*.[2] Her book is now regarded as a classic as it provides important insights into the experiences of dying people. Dr Kübler-Ross's empathy with the dying can be attributed to a close encounter with death in childhood, her psychiatric training, and an early involvement with suffering when she worked in Poland with the victims of a German concentration camp. She was greatly influenced by the attitude of a Jewish girl she met there. Although this girl had been a prisoner in the camp, she had chosen to remain after its liberation to help the other victims. Like other Jewish survivors she had lost her entire family, but she had remained surprisingly free from anger, bitterness or self-pity. More importantly, she demonstrated a capacity for personal growth in these appalling conditions that Kübler-Ross found impressive. Later Kübler-Ross found a similar potential for growth in many disadvantaged people, including the terminally ill. She noted that this capacity for growth, even in the face of death, was most discernible when people had the courage to look at themselves objectively, to set aside trivialities, and to examine basic issues in painful but revealing ways.[3]

These characteristics were exhibited by Sue, a 30-year-old woman who asked to be referred for hospice care when she realized that she was terminally ill. Sue was unmarried, had no children but many friends, and lived alone. At our first meeting, she told me in a straightforward manner that she had been treated for cancer of the cervix, that the disease had spread to the vagina, that she was awaiting chemotherapy and that she knew this further treatment would not affect the progress of the disease. She realized that the chemotherapy would have unpleasant side effects but thought it proper to accept the advice of her radiotherapist. At the same time she wished to make arrangements with the hospice for her subsequent care. When I left the house, she offered me a chocolate bar, which I accepted. This gesture was typical of her. Whenever one visited Sue, and whatever the situation or state she was in, she would offer some small gift to her visitors. She never complained about her lot and enjoyed life as fully as her circumstances permitted. A few weeks before she died, she persuaded two hospice nurses to take her to a swimming pool for a final swim, even though her appearance was almost skeletal. When I knew her better, I asked her whether she ever felt angry or bitter at dying so young, and she replied no. When I asked her why this was so, she replied that she had lived half her normal life span very fully and was ready to go. Perhaps the most important contribution she made during her final illness was that those who knew Sue saw her as a role model in the art of dying.

Kübler-Ross's main contribution to the management of terminal illness was to point out that patients nearing death are likely to experience five distinct psychological states, which she called the stages of

dying. They are generally known as the stages of 1) denial and isolation, 2) anger, 3) bargaining, 4) depression and 5) acceptance.
Although these five stages are set out in sequence, they do not necessarily occur in the order listed and features of more than one stage
may be present at any given time. Patients' moods quite often fluctu-
ate so that someone who has reached the stage of depression may
suddenly produce an outburst of anger, and a patient facing a new
crisis may regress from a later to an earlier stage. However, the list
does provide a useful description of the psychological states that
commonly occur in terminally ill patients, and their likely sequence.
Some health workers make the mistake of pressing patients to reach
the stage of acceptance. This can be psychologically destructive. The
aim should be to elicit the patients' needs at any given time, to find
out how they are coping with the situation at that moment and to
help them at that stage. All patients handle their problems to the best
of their ability, and if they happen to feel most secure in denial or
anger, no one should destroy the barriers they have erected to
protect themselves.

Denial and isolation

The first stage is one of denial and isolation.

> *(M age 71)* According to his wife, they have both been told that he has
> cancer of the pancreas with a life expectancy of about 6 weeks. However,
> he seems to be denying this.
> *(F age 65)* There is massive enlargement of the liver from secondary cancer
> but her only complaint is of recent weakness. She seems remarkably uncon-
> cerned about the nature of her illness and although willing to give her as
> much information as she desires, we found that she really wanted to know
> very little at this visit. She has not been specifically told that she has cancer,
> but when the time is right no doubt she will ask the appropriate person and
> the information can be given then.

Denial is a natural response to bad news. Most terminally ill people
realize they are dying but when they first become aware of that
possibility they need time to accept its implications. In addition to
denying the seriousness of their illness, people are likely to mobilize
their psychological defences in various other ways.

> *(M age 83)* This retired psychiatric nurse is becoming bed bound. He needs
> help to stand and walk. He knows the nature of his illness but intends to
> fight it and remains buoyant in spirit.
> *(F age 62)* She looks an old woman but is still capable of walking unaided.
> Her problems include deafness, vomiting – especially when changing the
> colostomy bag – loss of appetite, lassitude and interrupted nights. She has a

mucoid discharge from the rectum and, gets out of bed 3–4 times per night to make sure she does not dampen the bed. She is determined to fight the cancer and get better but sometimes wonders whether it is worth doing so.

Some patients supplement orthodox medical treatment with faith healing, the practices of alternative medicine, special diets and by attending support groups. All these initiatives are likely to improve morale and reduce the sense of helplessness, isolation and defilement.

(M age 64) Although severely disabled by metastatic renal cancer, C. was dressed and sitting in the garden when I visited yesterday. Whilst I was with him, an art therapist arrived from the AP Clinic [an alternative therapy centre] so I had an opportunity to observe his technique. Present treatment seems to consist of (1) massive doses of vitamins; (2) carrot juice; (3) a near vegetarian diet; (4) mistletoe injections given by E. [a homoeopathic doctor]. *(F age 47)* Her condition seems to have deteriorated fairly quickly during the past eight weeks. Her main complaints are of pain, nausea, vomiting, weakness and sweating. Headaches are also sometimes troublesome. She walks with a stoop, supporting her back with both hands. Recent treatment has included acupuncture once a week, attendance at the B — Clinic [an alternative therapy centre] and a weekly visit by a faith healer. The last she considered particularly helpful in assisting her to gain some inner control. *(M age 41)* Thank you for referring this 41-year-old man with inoperable cancer of the rectum. Two years ago he survived a coronary thrombosis and lives in hope that he will recover from his present condition. He is already receiving support from Al [a cancer support group], intends visiting the B — Clinic [an alternative therapy centre] and hopes to find a faith healer.

Denial is the most common psychological defence employed. It enables people to avoid accepting the reality of their situation. They find it more helpful to believe that the diagnosis must be wrong, or that a new cure will be found soon, or that they have not been told that the growth is malignant and has spread throughout the body. Denial provides patients with a breathing space in which they can collect their thoughts and mobilize their inner resources. It is a temporary defence that is usually soon replaced by partial acceptance. Sometimes it is used selectively, with expectations of recovery being expressed to some acquaintances and not to others. A minority of patients do not wish to move out of this stage; denial is too important a defence for them to relinquish and their wishes must be respected.

The stage of denial and isolation is the only one in which Kübler-Ross says that two factors are present. Isolation can be considered either as a psychological or as a social phenomenon. Patients use the isolation of inner withdrawal instinctively as it helps them to come to terms with their grief. They withdraw introspectively to consider their plight and deal with their inner turmoil. But the word can also be understood in a wider, social context. Unless patients have a close network of friends and relatives who visit and maintain contact, their illness can make them not only housebound but socially isolated. This is a particular problem for the widowed and elderly, and for patients whose illness is disfiguring or socially unacceptable.

> (F age 61) Thank you for referring this lady with lung secondaries, the primary being a hypernephroma. She is weak and breathless on effort but describes her main problem as 'sheer boredom'. Despite good support from her daughter, she is in the house most of the day by herself and then becomes depressed.
>
> (M age 75) This 75-year-old widower was referred to us by the QE Hospital with cancer of the bladder. He says his main problem is 'being alone by himself'. He is a social person who lacks company. He has few visitors and is no longer able to visit his local club.
>
> (M age 66) He was with the Grenadier Guards during World War II and has retained his soldierly bearing but is now breathless on slight effort and emaciated. He lives alone in a high rise flat and is totally isolated apart from visits by the district nurse. Because of the DHSS strike he is receiving no pension, has no money and his food is being paid for by the nurse. He has agreed to come into the hospice when a bed is available.

The realization that one is alone and isolated may be associated with a fear of unwanted intruders, particularly if one is weak and helpless. This fear is not mentioned by Kübler-Ross but a number of incidents come to mind where intruders have broken into the homes of dying patients. The first involved an octogenarian lady who, though terminally ill, was still just capable of living alone. Fortunately the young man she found exploring her bungalow did her no harm and left immediately. The second incident was a break-in at the house of a doctor, whose wife was in the final stages of a terminal illness. The damage caused by the intruder and the knowledge that their privacy had been violated added to the distress of the family. Another intruder broke into the house and walked into the bedroom of a dying academic but left without causing the patient any physical harm. The fourth incident, which involved the theft of a television set, had a slightly ironic aspect as a son of the household was currently serving a prison sentence for theft. Sometimes a break-in can be viewed with surprising equanimity by the family as the following letter shows:

> (M age 62) We were able to discuss the nature of his illness quite easily and he informed me that he had 'some form of cancer of the lung'. Following

this we discussed how radiotherapy can kill the cancer cells in the leg. I saw him at perhaps an unpropitious moment as he was sitting on the bed half naked, having just had an enema from the district nurse. We also learnt that the house had been burgled two days previously and property worth approximately £2,500 stolen. This latter incident did not seem to disturb the harmony of the household.

Anger

The second stage of dying is associated with anger. It is characterized by a general feeling of envy, bitterness and resentment against the whole situation in which the patient is enmeshed. The dominant questions in the patient's mind are, 'Why should this happen to me?' and 'What have I done to deserve this?'. Anger is not always openly expressed, but an upsurge of resentment may arise as the illness passes through each new crisis point and the patient is forced to accept an increasing disability. Younger patients are more likely to express their anger openly and they usually direct it at the people closest to them, causing them much distress.

When anger is present but suppressed it has a destructive effect on the patient and, if it cannot be sublimated, its release should be facilitated and, if necessary, its fury accepted. This may be done by encouraging patients to talk about their feelings or to express them on paper, in words or pictures. Pummelling a pillow or any other inanimate object may help to release pent up feelings. Some patients find that the use of active imagination, in which they picture themselves mobilizing the defence mechanism of the body against the disease, also provides some level of catharsis and gives them the feeling that they can control the situation. Although a patient's anger may be hurtful, the outburst should be seen as something impersonal. It is easier for people to be angry with their carers than with the less tangible cause of their distress, the disease itself. Terminally ill patients have various reasons to be angry; these include the fact that they are seriously ill and dependent on other people and, in the case of younger people, that they are going to die before their lives have been fulfilled. Sometimes the only way they can deal with this distress is by projecting their anger on to those looking after them.

(M age 64) The principle problem is that he has outbursts of aggression. These are directed against his wife but no one else. She says he is aware of these outbursts and regrets them afterwards.
(F age 67) Last February she was found to have myxoedema and in May, cancer of the lung with secondary spread. She is fully aware of the nature of her illness. Her mood is one of bitterness and anger. She feels very

depressed but is unable to cry. She has death wishes but no suicidal thoughts. She is worried lest the cancer has spread to the brain . . . She is frightened of dying and afraid of having her face cut. She wants to be told that 'the whole damn thing is not true'.

(M age 18) Thank you for asking me to see Jim who I visited at home today. He has improved with steroids and although ataxic is able to walk without help. He asked searching questions and expressed considerable bitterness though not in a vehement manner. The family is managing but the situation is difficult with the epileptic sister having recently become a single-parent mother.

Much of the anger is directed towards hospitals and doctors:

(M age 35) His main problems are widespread pain and fear. His mood is 'as low as I could be'. He is clearly very angry and feels let down by the doctors, having been told there was probably not very much the matter, then within a month, that he had incurable cancer.

(F age 63) She is the main carer of her husband who has been a cripple for the past 9 years. She realizes there is something seriously wrong with her lungs but does not want to know the details. She expresses some anger towards the hospital but in general appears to be a pleasant and placid person.

(F age 57) There is a lot of anger in the household. Mr F feels that the hospital should have diagnosed the condition earlier. He also has the added problem of recently seeing his business close down. Mrs F is normally an energetic person who goes out to work, and now feels lonely and isolated in the house . . . These problems apart, the relationship between Mr and Mrs F appears good.

(F age 38) She is aware that the disease has metastasized to the lung. She is adamant that her husband should be given crucial information first and that he should act as her informant. She is angry that the reverse has happened from time to time and that she was the person who told her husband that she had secondaries in the lung.

Bargaining

The third stage of dying is characterized by bargaining. This is a device that people use to postpone death. It is an unspoken contract, with oneself or God, which enables the person to achieve a short-term aim. This may be the chance to attend a daughter's wedding in a few weeks time, see the autumn colours, or be present at an annual function which they have attended for years. The bargain, which carries the implication 'If I can only go to . . . I shall die happy', is limited to a specific event but once the goal has been achieved it may be followed by another bargain. Patients with insight sometimes use this approach to add purpose to life, setting themselves small goals that they intend to achieve. This ability to postpone death was observed by Frankl among the inmates of German concentration camps. He noticed a significant fall in the death rate before Christmas and Easter, which was counterbalanced by an increase in deaths once the festival had passed.[4] A similar variation in mortality rates has been reported amongst Jews before and after Passover,[5] and in Chinese women before and after their Harvest Moon Festival.[6]

Depression

The fourth stage of dying is one of depression. This is a mood that can occur any time during life, but its incidence becomes more frequent with ageing. Its presence in the dying is therefore not surprising. Some terminal patients need antidepressant drugs but most respond to simple psychotherapy, an opportunity to discuss their feelings and the chance to deal with outstanding financial and family problems. Kübler-Ross describes two forms of depression in the terminally ill, a reactive depression and a preparatory one. The first type is a reaction to the losses that have already occurred. These include loss of employment, financial loss, disfigurement, the inability to do things for oneself and the losses associated with social isolation.

(F age 31) I have, at last, had an opportunity to visit L. whose sarcoma has been treated by radiotherapy. Secondary deposits are present in the brain, lungs and skin. She has been almost totally blind for 4–5 weeks though previously her vision was good. Nights are disturbed by nocturia and her husband helps her to the toilet every 2 hours at night. She says her main problem is depression because she can no longer see.

(M age 31) Since Christmas, when he learnt that he would be unable to work, he has become very dispirited. He cries a lot. He knows he easily becomes frustrated and angry, and this upsets him as it affects his wife and children. He says his problem is not being able to sleep. He lies awake through the night with a very active mind . . . There are considerable anxieties about money in the household . . . I shall arrange for our social worker to visit next week to discuss the family's financial problems.

(M age 38) His wife says his main problem is very severe depression and I am sure this is correct. He admits to being depressed, is restless, has disturbed nights, loss of libido, and although he is not suicidal there are times when he wishes he was dead. He resents not being able to undertake his previous wide-ranging physical activities, but at least he does go out each night to the pub and has resumed drinking Guinness.

(M age 54) Following our telephone conversation, I visited C. today. He has obviously deteriorated a great deal since the initial diagnosis was made 12 months ago. He knows he has cancer and seems to have become very despondent. He admits to being depressed, feels he will never get better, and at times asks God to take him.

(F age 68) She admits to being depressed and at times wishes she was dead though she would like to get better for the sake of the family.

(F age 71) Her condition and morale have deteriorated rapidly recently, and she is so despondent she reiterates that she does not want to be kept alive.

The second type of depression that occurs at this stage is preparatory in nature. It looks forward to future losses and tends to be silent. It is a form of anticipatory grief. It looks forward to the eventual loss of home, friends, family and of life itself. The successful negotiation of this phase is essential if the patient is to die in a state of acceptance and peace.

A depressed person is likely to have suicidal thoughts. Some terminally ill patients do kill themselves and one study in England showed that 4 per cent of suicides had an incurable illness which would probably have ended their lives within six months. I cared for a few dying patients who had attempted suicide before being admitted for hospice care, but once they felt safe and had had their symptoms relieved, their mood improved.

(M age 66) Mr J. was referred by BD Hospital following a recent attempt to commit suicide. As you know he had an oesophagectomy for cancer in 1987 followed by an emergency resection of the ileum, necessitated by post-operative gangrene of the gut. He says his wife died of cancer 15 years ago but a report from the L — Clinic says she was a manic-depressive who committed suicide in 1976. J. seemed a relaxed, cheerful man who likes company and talks easily in a long winded way . . . He describes himself as being content in his present situation and that he has all the help he needs.

One patient did kill himself. He was an elderly man with no family, whose main interests were his sailing and shooting clubs. He was not depressed nor in pain, and his main problem was increasing weakness. He was keen to attend the annual dinner of his sailing club and arrangements were made for him to do so. Instead of returning to the hospice the next day as expected, he went home and shot himself. He was a person of strong character who had decided to end his own life.

Sometimes the suicidal person is not the patient but a close relative:

(F age 29) Thank you for referring this young woman with extensive cancer whose husband committed suicide 6 weeks ago. She is recovering from her second course of chemotherapy and yet, despite so much physical and emotional trauma, does not seem greatly distressed though she does admit to occasional panic attacks. Her daughter attended school today for the first time since the husband's death. There is good support within the family from two siblings, the younger being a nurse.

Acceptance

The last stage of dying is one of acceptance. This does not mean that the state is one of happiness. This stage is almost devoid of feelings. It is the time of final rest before the long journey. Patients' circles of interests diminishes. They wish to be left alone and not disturbed by news or problems. They are no longer talkative and now appreciate the silent visitor. Most people die in the state of acceptance without fear or despair. Some elderly people describe it quite succinctly: 'It is like this,' they say, 'I have had a good life and I am ready to go.'

Kübler-Ross does not think of a terminal illness simply in terms of its destructive power. She sees it as one of the many windstorms of life that can enhance a person's inner growth if they allow it to do so. In this sense her psychology seems to be based on Jungian rather than Freudian principles. Dying is seen not just as an end point but as a growth point. It can have a transforming power that enables patients to treat even the most adverse events with relative composure.

(F age 50) The history is of an adenocarcinoma, of uncertain origin, with widespread involvement of the skin and liver. She seems to accept her illness very philosophically and says, 'You've got to accept it, you can't alter it.' She spends much of her time alone as her husband is a long-distance lorry driver and is sometimes away at night. Despite his enforced absences, the family are supportive and have organized a rota of helpers to care for their mother.

(F age 76) Her condition is deteriorating and although still ambulant, she is very weak. She is fully aware of the diagnosis and seems unperturbed by the closeness of death. Fortunately pain is not a problem, her most troublesome symptom being vomiting.

(F age 76) She is a naturally cheerful person whose main complaints are of breathlessness, weakness, constipation and slight pain. She accepts the disease philosophically, knowing the fatal prognosis.

(M age 37) He has improved considerably since attending hospital for radiotherapy and remains pain free. Recently he has noticed a tendency to deviate to the left when walking. He lives on the 3rd floor of the Salvation Army hostel and is able to walk upstairs. He knows he has bronchial cancer and only a few months to live. He accepts the situation with remarkable urbanity and cheerfulness. He is pleased with our involvement and we will maintain contact through the Home Care Team.

(M age 60) He questioned me about the diagnosis and now knows he has cancer of the lung. He accepted this information with equanimity and says he has 'had a good innings'.

(M age 80) He is a pleasant, contented man with few complaints who feels well prepared for death. He is cared for by his daughters, his wife being disabled by rheumatoid arthritis and angina.

Hope

Even though a person may accept the closeness of death with equanimity, throughout the illness some form of hope persists. The nature of this hope does tend to vary with the stage of the illness. In the initial stage of the disease, hope is almost exclusively associated with the possibility of a cure or at least the prolongation of life. This is true for the patient, the family and those involved in the therapy.

> *(M age 47)* He knows the nature of his illness and at first 'was shattered' when he realized he had cancer. He now takes a positive attitude and hopes that medical science will make a breakthrough and he will get better.
>
> *(M age 67)* His wife says he is more irritable; he admits to being depressed and at times thinks life is not worth living. However, he tries to be positive and is hoping for some miracle cure. He walks with two sticks and still goes upstairs, albeit on hands and feet, being very breathless by the time he reaches the top.

When cure becomes an unlikely outcome, patients' hopes change and become focussed on other objectives. These may include being able to share in family achievements, or visiting a favourite place. For many the final hope is centred on the possibility of life after death and a reunion with those whom they have loved, who have predeceased them.

> *(M age 70)* He now receives the equivalent of 360 mg of morphine every 24 hours. Apart from pain, he feels fairly well though he is becoming increasingly weak and now walks with two sticks. He hopes to be able to drive his car again and perhaps go on a short holiday with his wife.
>
> *(F age 80)* She has become breathless and her voice is feeble. She knows that she has a 'tumour on the breast' and is looking forward to 'waking up in heaven'.

A few terminally ill people are remarkably cheerful, even euphoric. The following cases involved patients who were not taking drugs that might have produced the euphoria:

> *(M age 77)* Although fully aware of the disease he is surprisingly cheerful, almost euphoric, but his wife says this has always been his nature and there has been no personality change.
>
> *(F age 72)* I visited Mrs E at home today. The contrast between husband and wife is marked. She, though desperately ill, is cheerful and constantly singing. He is worn out by sleepless nights, anxiety and despondency. Nevertheless he is determined to keep his wife at home. Apart from her seeming euphoria, she is dehydrated with incontinence of urine and faeces. She seems to have polydipsia and polyuria so the bed is constantly wet. The district nursing sisters are visiting frequently and providing incontinence pads, but the situation would be better controlled by a self-retaining catheter and I am asking our home care nursing sister to insert one.

Anxiety

In *On Death and Dying* Kübler-Ross has surprisingly little to say about anxiety. Yet when confronted with the unknown, most people are likely to be anxious or even fearful. This is natural and such feelings are aroused by the contemplation of any stressful event, including approaching death. Some are frightened of dying, a few are frightened of death itself:

(F age 63) She dreads the night, is frightened of the future and is frightened of death. She has a recurrent nightmare of going down a dark passage alone and screaming silently. She says she has encountered much horror and terror in her life. Her husband died from misadventure (suspected cyanide poisoning caused by his work as a jeweller); her childhood was difficult.

(F age 66) She feels weak and, though ambulant, finds standing and walking difficult. She was able to tell me she had cancer though she had not been officially told the diagnosis. Apart from immediate problems she talked at length of her unhappy childhood, saying that nowadays she would have been described as a 'battered baby' . . . She is frightened of death and is frightened of sleeping at night, partly because she has bad dreams but also because she fears she will not wake up. As a young woman she was so ill-informed that in her first pregnancy she expected to give birth through her umbilicus.

(F age 73) Although Mrs D does not know her diagnosis, her opening remark to me was 'I think I am dying'. Pain is a persistent problem and keeps her awake at night. For the past two nights she has not gone to bed and has spent the night in a chair downstairs. She is a frail, despondent lady who feels very frightened. She assesses her sense of fear as in fact worse than the pain.

(F age 74) She is a very frail lady who is deteriorating rapidly . . . She recognizes the severity of her illness as she has informed her husband that she is dying and has cancer. She is an anxious lady who is frightened of being left alone and makes considerable demands on Mr G.

(F age 44) She is a nurse with two young children . . . Apart from weakness, her main complaints are of breathlessness and discomfort in the liver. Her fear for the future is that she will not be able to cope, that her appearance will become unsightly and that she will have unrelieved pain. She is also, of course, naturally worried about her husband and children.

(F age 60) She displays separation anxiety about leaving her husband and family but otherwise her main complaints are of . . .

(F age 68) Her complaints include a feeling of hopelessness. She is frightened the disease will affect the brain and this fear has been exacerbated by a recent deterioration in the vision of the left eye . . . She obtained some consolation from my finding an early cataract in the left eye which provided a rational explanation for her failing vision.

(F age 67) Thank you for referring this quiet 67-year-old widow with cancer of the ovary. She has been vomiting daily for the past week. Her other main problems are breathlessness and increasing weakness. She is frightened that she might suddenly collapse in the house without anyone being present to help.

In many instances, dying patients worry more about their relatives than about themselves.

> *(M age 68)* He is very concerned about his wife and how she will manage when he dies.
>
> *(F age 72)* She says she worries more about her husband than herself.
>
> *(M age 77)* He is an alert, uncomplaining man who is trying to be positive in his attitude towards what he knows is a terminal illness. He is unsteady when walking, has poor vision, weight loss and pain in the left shoulder. An even greater problem for him is his wife who is suicidal and worried about her personal future.

Significance of Death

The significance a person gives to dying is based on the personal philosophy he or she has acquired during life. The attitude may be spiritual or materialistic, life affirming or nihilistic, or unformulated and uncertain. People whose philosophical attitude is based neither on clear religious convictions nor on nihilistic tenets may have learnt to accept life as it comes and to handle each new situation as best they can. This is a pragmatic attitude, which is close to the life-affirming approach, but lacks its strongly positive attitude to new situations. Sometimes uncertainty denotes inner turmoil, and when this is the case the individual has no firm basis on which to confront death. Some very religious people fall into this category, they may fear Hell as much as they long for Heaven, or they may not even be sure that there is life after death.

A firm nihilistic approach that denies any significance to death is rare, particularly in older people, but it has its compensations for those who truly hold this view. It enables a person to see death as a state of eternal peace, undisturbed by the problems of life. To them it is a state akin to sleep but bereft of troublesome dreams. This is the 'nirvana' state of Freudian psychology and its philosophical roots can be traced back as far as the ancient Greek Sophists.

Within the terms of Jungian psychology, people who meet death in a life-affirming way have developed a positive attitude to life and seek to find meaning in every situation. Although they may not be able to say clearly what they think the outcome will be, they expect from death a new and creative aspect of life. Such patients have three basic characteristics in common. The first is a willingness to discuss their experiences. Second, they are ready to share with others their philosophy of life and understanding of reality. Finally, they accept the good and the bad in life uncritically and with a continued sense of the wonder of life itself. These attitudes are said to be attributes of maturity and to represent in sequence the Jungian concepts of 'an expanding Self', 'the realization of the Self', and 'union with the Self'.[7] People with these attributes are likely to share Kübler-Ross's belief that death is the final stage of growth, that only the body dies, and that the Self or the spirit, or whatever one calls it, is eternal.

Cognitive Impairment

Kübler-Ross's stages of dying have important practical applications but they present only one view of the changes likely to be observed in a dying person's condition. Various other stages of dying can be formulated. One of these might depict a late stage as loss of consciousness, a state that is implied rather than described by Kübler-Ross. As death approaches, stupor and coma become the norm, with few people passing from life to death in a state of clear consciousness. A year-long study of all the people who died in a rural community showed that only 12 per cent were fully alert 24 hours before death occurred and that 40 per cent were comatose.[8] Another study in a London hospital found that 34 per cent of cancer patients were unconscious for at least 24 hours before death and only 6 per cent were conscious shortly before death.[9] As death approaches, the number of patients who slip into a comatose state increases. So the penultimate stage of dying may be seen as loss of consciousness, and the final stage as cessation of cardio-respiratory activity.

Impairment of intellect can be an important landmark in a terminal illness though it is less easily diagnosed than impairment of consciousness. Its onset is often insidious and in its early stages it is often overlooked. In its gross form it appears as dementia or confusion. It is common in the later stages of a terminal illness, especially if the patient becomes dehydrated, has brain damage, or a biochemical disturbance:

(M age 40) Thank you for referring this 40-year-old headmaster with metastatic cancer of the rectum. His condition is worsening rapidly. His main problems are weakness, cachexia and intermittent pain beneath the right ribs. He realizes that his intellect is less sharp than usual and that his memory is failing.

(M age 69) He has deteriorated rapidly in the past 4 months and the family report marked personality changes with intellectual impairment. His wife is particularly concerned that he might set the bedclothes alight whilst smoking.

(F age 78) I saw this lady today in the Day Centre as the staff report a personality change. Apparently the family have been expressing increased

concern about her mental state. She is a pleasant, tidy lady with a diagnosis of oat cell cancer based on biopsy of the supraclavicular glands. She says she feels bewildered, does not know what she is talking about and does not know who she is. The replies she gives to questions are invariably correct, but she often does not know the answer and then she says 'I don't know'. She is obviously becoming increasingly demented, perhaps quite quickly, and we shall try to monitor the situation through her visits to the Day Centre.

The incidence of intellectual impairment among terminally ill patients is rarely assessed but it is said to be high in AIDS. This does not imply the presence of violent or antisocial behaviour but of poor concentration, memory loss and a slowing of motor function. The more severe the HIV infection the worse the cognitive dysfunction. Over 50 per cent of patients with AIDS have some impairment of intellect[10] and 75 per cent have evidence of central nervous disease at autopsy.[11] In determining the extent of an individual's decline, these neurological factors need to be assessed together with the psychological stages described by Kübler-Ross and the physical state of the patient.

How Long Have I Got?

One of the difficulties doctors encounter is assessing accurately possible outcomes. They are so often wrong. People will recount years later how mistaken their doctors were and how they outlived the pessimistic prognoses given to them in the past. A large-scale survey in Chicago looked at this aspect of care and found that doctors are not good at assessing the life-expectancy of terminally ill patients. Usually they are too optimistic and this is particularly noticeable among less experienced doctors.[12]

The report was based on forecasts given by doctors to research workers, not to patients or their relatives, so the need to explore the subject sensitively with the patient did not arise, but the findings do have important implications. One probable result of undue optimism is that patients are referred for hospice care later than is desirable: this may deprive them of effective pain relief, and encourage the continued use of aggressive treatments aimed at prolonging life when it would be kinder to stop such therapy. In Chicago, people with a life expectancy of six months or less are eligible for hospice care, but the actual length of stay is usually one month, and 7 per cent die within hours of admission. Most patients enter the hospice during a period of rapid physical deterioration and often in crisis, when the overriding need is to control symptoms and support the family. Securing a physically comfortable death is a worthy goal but more could be done for the patient both emotionally and spiritually if a longer period of time were available.[13]

We are told that 'obtaining prognostic information is often the highest priority for seriously ill patients, eclipsing their interests in treatments options or diagnostic details'.[12] I am not sure if this is true but there is an obvious need to improve the accuracy of the information given to patients and their families. New instruments are being developed, and Morita's palliative prognostic index and Maltoni's palliative prognostic score have both been shown to predict short-term survival reasonably well.[14] However, as Smith points out, people's decisions at the end of life are not guided solely by doctors.[13] A complex interaction exists between what the doctor says to patients, and their families, what they actually hear, the unspoken landmarks – like increasing weakness and becoming bedridden – and the input provided by other people like nurses, clergy, alternative therapists, paramedics and lawyers. All of this information is processed by patients as they come to terms with their approaching death and take steps to put their affairs in order at the end of their life.

Chapter 14
Caring for the Dying

. . . and we'll talk with them too,
Who loses and who wins; who's in, who's out;

King Lear

Establishing a Relationship

In order to gain some insight into the deeper needs of dying patients, we must be able to communicate with them at more than a superficial level. Good communication is a two-way process, it implies giving and receiving. It is not simply imparting information or instruction; nor is it merely exploring the other person's psyche, looking for areas that they may wish to keep secret. It involves establishing a relationship of mutual respect, in which both participants may be vulnerable yet still able to learn from each other. It is a relationship in which patients feel free to disclose their most pressing fears and needs, and health care workers are able to impart, with care and sympathy, information the patients and their families need to deal with the situation, and to plan for the future.

It has been said that next to pain, poor communication is the most common cause of distress to dying patients.[1] This assessment is probably correct. Poor communication is often the result of haste, of being concerned with the next task or activity instead of concentrating on the present one. Good communication starts with sitting down and slowing down, and thereby creating a time–space interval in which the patient's areas of concern can be expressed and dealt with. In these situations the ability to listen and be silent is an essential aspect of good communication. The silent gesture conveys its own meaning. If the patient offers no questions or comments, open-ended observations may result in unspoken worries being expressed and discussed. The aim is to enable patients to talk about their problems, express their anxieties and wishes, and have access to the information they need for their own decision making.

146

The amount of information given should be that desired by the patient at the time. The patient's need for further information or discussion can be assessed by asking if there is something else they wish to talk about, or whether there is anything else they wish to know. Most people want to be fully informed, but any limits to the information given should be set by the patient. The problem for the doctor, nurse or relative is not what to say, but how best to share with the patient the information they possess. The professional should be wary of giving a specific answer to the question, 'How long have I got to live?' because predictions of death are notoriously inaccurate and the prognosis is likely to be wrong. It would be wiser to respond with a question: 'Would you prefer it to be a longer or shorter time?' If the person is really terminally ill, often the reply is 'shorter'; that this is likely to be so can then be gently affirmed. The same general principles apply in any discussions with the family.

Sometimes information has to be gently extracted from people. When calling at the house of a terminally ill patient, the doctor or nurse, especially on a first visit, may be asked by a relative not to tell the patient the nature of the illness. If this happens, the relative, who should be present during the consultation, should be asked not to interrupt any discussion that takes place between the doctor, or nurse, and the patient. This is to ensure that the relative knows exactly what is said but does not block the conversation by speaking for the patient. During the consultation, it is also necessary to respect, and bear in mind, the relative's expressed wishes.

Sometimes it is apparent that the patient is so confused that meaningful conversation is impossible and nothing much need be said. If patients are mentally alert, it is important to find out what they know or suspect about the illness. The conversation may go something like this:

'How are you today?'
Answer: 'So so.'
'What do you make of this illness?'
Answer: 'I don't know and I don't want to know.'

Such a reply expresses the patient's wishes clearly, and no more need be said. On other occasions the patient may open a gap with the reply 'I don't know, I haven't been told anything'. The question may then be put, 'How much do you want to know?' The most frequent reply to this is 'I want to know everything.'

It is sometimes helpful to ask patients what other doctors and nurses have told them about the illness, and what the information meant to them; or one may point to a lump and ask specifically

'What did they tell you about that?'
'They said it was a growth'.
'What sort of growth did they say it was?'
(Pause.)
'They said it was a cancerous growth.'

This approach often enables the relative to know that the patient knows as much as the family about the illness, even though they have not discussed it together.

Although the relative was asked initially to allow the health worker to have an uninterrupted conversation with the patient, it is important that all parties should be involved in the discussion during some stage of the consultation. Similarly, when patients are in hospital, communication between them and their families can be facilitated if staff members learn to communicate with families as a group and not just with individuals.

Home, Hospital or Hospice?

In Third World countries, terminally ill patients for whom no more can be done are likely to be discharged from hospital so that they can die at home. This is considered appropriate for a number of reasons but mainly because it allows people to die within the bosom of the family. In Western countries, the reverse applies: the dying are likely to be admitted to hospital if no more can be done for them at home. This was not always the custom in affluent countries.

Fifty years ago it was much more common for people in First World countries to die at home than in hospital, but probably less than 20 per cent do so nowadays. These changes have produced their own benefits and problems. Most people say that they would prefer to die at home, but when it comes to organizing care for relatives, eventually the decision is taken that probably the best place for 'gran' is in hospital. Also, as the illness progresses and their health deteriorates, many patients change their minds and no longer want to die at home,[2] or reluctantly agree to go into hospital.

Home is usually best if adequate care and resources are available. On the other hand, it is extremely difficult to provide satisfactory terminal care for an elderly pensioner living alone in a small high-rise flat, when that person becomes bed-bound and has no support from friends and relatives. Never mind how keen the patient is to stay at home, eventually a decision will have to be made to provide in-patient care. When admitted, such patients often feel as though a heavy burden has been taken from them; now they will be cared for, kept warm, dry and comfortable. Concerned relatives, unable to help because they live at a distance or have jobs to hold down, are also likely to feel that a burden has been taken from their shoulders.

My own preference has always been to care for people at home, when this is feasible. Improved nursing aids, such as syringe drivers, have made symptom control much easier, but the main problem is that families can no longer provide enough able-bodied adults, on a regular basis, to lift and change bed-bound patients. In my experience, one of the main differences between home care and in-patient care is that patients experience a change of status when they move from the care of the family into hospital. At home, the patient is usually the central and often dominant person. In hospital, their role as an individual becomes more peripheral even though the staff may be very dedicated people. I have found too, that my own ability to communicate with patients diminishes after they had been admitted, even if it is to one of my own hospital or hospice beds. Probably because of the more public setting, our relationship seems to become more distant, and conversation tends to become more constrained and stereotyped. It is likely that relatives experience similar difficulties.

The allocation of resources to patient care is an economic decision that has important ethical, social and psychological implications. Health care will absorb all the resources that are made available to it, so economic boundaries have to be defined, even when people are terminally ill. In the USA the highest medical costs are incurred during the last week of a person's life in an acute care hospital. Even a sudden death, which is defined as a death occurring within one hour of the onset of symptoms, incurs a medical cost of over $9,000.[3] Other better, and more economic, ways of caring for the dying need to be developed. One answer to the problem has been provided by Dr Cicely Saunders and the hospice movement.

Hospices

The end of the twentieth century has seen a remarkable upsurge of interest in the care of dying patients and their families. This is most evident in the work of the 'hospice movement', a term that embraces a wide range of people and organizations who are interested in the specialist care of the terminally ill. Since 1967, hospices have been established in over 100 countries – including states in South America and Africa, India, Japan, Poland, New Zealand and Russia. The number of hospices, the standard of care they provide, and the means by which they are funded vary greatly between countries depending upon the socio-economic resources available. Some hospices have a clearly defined admittance policy and provide facilities only for particular groups such as cancer patients, sick children or people with AIDS, but most are flexible and willing to admit a wide range of patients.

The first person to use the term 'hospice' in connection with the care of dying patients was Mme Jeanne Garnier who founded the 'Dames du Calvaire' in Lyon, France, in 1842. The modern hospice, however, is a late twentieth-century phenomenon, which has its origins in nineteenth century Dublin, where the Irish Sisters of Charity opened a hospice for dying patients in 1879. The sisters called their unit, 'Our Lady's Hospice' and the term 'hospice' has been widely used since then. In the UK the term 'hospice' tends to be used mainly for purpose built units with in-patient facilities, but in other countries the name is often given to community care programmes for the terminally ill or to special wards in hospitals. Whatever form the system takes, the common theme is a philosophy of holistic care that focuses on symptom control, on integrating the psychological and spiritual aspects of care, and offering support to families both during patients' terminal illness and their bereavement.

The care given to the family may be seen as an extended act of good neighbourliness. It should also be regarded as an effective form of preventive medicine. Bereavement is a protean state with many aspects and these include features that are usually associated with the presence of physical disease. It has a substantial morbidity from both physical and mental disease, and an appreciable mortality in men though probably not in women. Fortunately, it appears that good social support can mitigate some of the physical and mental ailments that often accompany bereavement. Volunteers who work in, and for, hospices may also derive some benefit from their experiences. One volunteer indicated the symbiotic nature of her involvement with a hospice when reacting to some unwelcome management decisions: 'but I shall not leave' she said, 'I know that I need the hospice more than it needs me.'

Death is not seen as a disaster in a hospice. Neither is it an enemy to be constantly fought against. It is accepted as a natural occurrence and the fulfilment of human life on earth. It is an event that occurs only once for each person and its uniqueness means that great consideration should be given to the circumstances surrounding it. The technological improvements that transformed medical practice during the twentieth century did nothing at first to ease and enhance the process of dying. In fact the reverse was true: they appeared merely to prolong the distress of terminally ill patients and their relatives. This has been a cause for real concern and many people were angered and dismayed by it. They realized that conventional medical and nursing services were failing dying patients and were determined to do something about it. When Dr Cicely Saunders showed that a high standard of care could be provided in special units, they recognized immediately that this was the way forward and the modern hospice movement was born.

It began, to be more exact, when Dr Saunders undertook clinical work in St Joseph's Hospice and then, in 1967, opened her own hospice in South London. The establishment of this unit, St Christopher's Hospice, inaugurated a new era in the care of dying patients and their families, initially in the UK but soon afterwards in many other countries. The work at St Christopher's was not confined to in-patient care. It soon established a research programme, a community service for the care of patients in their homes, and an educational programme, which may be seen as the prototype for the academic departments in palliative medicine and thanatology that have been established in various countries in recent years.

Modern hospices have shown that doctors and nurses need to develop special practical and interpersonal skills for the care of terminally ill patients and that these skills are best learnt and taught in specialist units. A multidisciplinary approach to care has been developed, which gives important roles to artists, clergy, occupational therapists, psychologists, physiotherapists and social workers. Any therapy, including alternative medicine, which is likely to help the patient is encouraged. Art classes and music therapy are commonly employed, and some hospices have resident creative writers to help their patients express their feelings. Even the type of picture placed on the wall can affect a patient's wellbeing. Pictures of trees and of stretches of water such as the works of the Impressionists can reduce anxiety and pain, but paintings like those of the Cubist Picasso are often associated with greater anxiety and more physical pain than if the patients look at bare walls.

Most hospices have a day centre for patients who live at home. Transportation is arranged to and from the centre where they are provided with regular nursing care, baths, lunch, hairdressing salons, entertainments and excursions. Some patients prefer to sit quietly alone, while others find that attendance at the centre enables them to develop supportive relationships with other patients. The main purpose of a day centre, however, is to provide the housebound patient with a day out, and the caring relative with a day off.

Although in terminal care the dying patient's needs are of paramount importance, the burden carried by the family is also great and needs to be recognized. Close relatives have to cope with the ordinary stresses of life as well as caring for, visiting and being concerned about, the dying person. Like the patient, they may experience states of denial, anger, depression and acceptance. The key carer is usually a woman and if she is coping alone she may find it difficult to lift and move her patient. She is likely to have sleepless nights and become physically exhausted. Weariness of body and spirit is likely to continue into bereavement and here the hospice may be of further help. Part of its ethos is that care does not cease when the patient dies. Support for the family continues after death through its bereavement service. Not everyone needs this help, most people cope with support from friends and family, but hospices do provide ongoing support for those in need and this can be particularly useful during the early stages of bereavement.

Domiciliary Care

The crises that carers find most difficult to bear occur when their relatives have severe pain, intractable vomiting, extreme breathlessness or become incontinent, especially of faeces. These crises can usually be anticipated and prevented. If the community health care team fails to do this, the caring relatives are likely to reach a breaking point where they can no longer cope physically or emotionally. This often occurs quite suddenly and is usually resolved by the admission of patients to hospital/hospice when they would have preferred to stay at home.

The standard of domiciliary care provided by doctors and nurses for the terminally ill is highly variable. It ranges from the excellent to the almost negligible. A consistently high standard can be expected when the primary care team is supported by a hospice-based domiciliary care team. The latter will consist of a number of specially trained nurses, who are often Macmillan nurses, supported by a doctor and social worker. Macmillan nurses care mainly for cancer patients but their special role enables these nurses to visit the patients regularly and spend plenty of time with them.

A visit by a Macmillan nurse is not likely to be a breezy 'in and out' affair. They spend enough time with the family to assess all the relevant problems and organize effective help. This includes dealing with financial worries and ensuring that the family receives all the benefits to which they are entitled. They liaise closely with the relevant health care teams, arrange for the provision of appropriate nursing equipment and for a 'night sitter' to stay with the patient at night, if this is necessary. They do not undertake 'hands on' nursing duties, which remain the province of the family carer and community nurse. Instead, they monitor the effectiveness of the drugs being prescribed for the patient and help to ensure that the symptoms are adequately controlled. Most importantly, they are trained to be particularly aware of the emotional and mental distresses that patients and relatives experience, and have the skills and time to help them to surmount these problems.

Incontinence and pain have been mentioned as two of the main afflictions that distress the dying patient. Incontinence of urine can be readily controlled by means of a self-retaining catheter attached to a drainage bag. This procedure is normal practice in hospitals and hospices but seems to be rarely used by general practitioners or community nurses. The ability of doctors to control the patient's pain at home has been transformed by the availability of the light weight syringe driver. This simple device, which mobile patients can carry in their pockets, enables analgesic and other drugs to be given continuously, by subcutaneous injection, throughout the day and night. As death draws nearer and the breathing becomes more stertorous, hyoscine may be placed in the syringe driver to ease the breathing.[4]

A Good Death

When people die they wish to be at peace with themselves, their family, friends and the God they worship. This is less easily achieved in hospitals than in their own home but in many countries death has been so institutionalized that the main players in the drama are not members of the family but nurses and doctors with little time to spare for the deeper needs of the dying patient. This failure has been rectified to some extent by the establishment of hospices, of special services for the terminally ill and a greater understanding of their needs.

But what steps can people take themselves to ensure a good death and what more can society do to help? These questions were considered by Age Concern,[5] which convened a special 'study group' to examine the problems and provide the answers. The study group identified 12 principles which they say should be incorporated into the codes of health professionals, the aims of health services and into the personal plans of individuals. They believe that the terminally ill should be able:

- to know when death is coming, and to understand what can be expected;
- to be able to retain control of what happens;
- to be afforded dignity and privacy;
- to have control over pain relief and other symptoms;
- to have choice and control over where death occurs (home or elsewhere);
- to have access to information and expertise of whatever kind is necessary;
- to have access to any spiritual or emotional support required;
- to have access to hospice care in any location, not only in hospital;
- to have control over who is present and who shares the end;
- to be able to issue advance directives that ensure wishes are respected;
- to have time to say goodbye, and control over other aspects of timing
- to be able to leave when it is time to go, and not to have life prolonged pointlessly.

The emphasis here is on personal control though the ability to relinquish control and accept what is, after all, the inevitable are necessary attributes as death approaches. Control of their own medication is especially difficult for the dying but this can be facilitated, as Grogono[6] points out, if the patient has an '*amicus fortis*, a friend at death' – usually a relative – who has the time and love and prescribing power to undertake the 'privilege of care'. This personal control is most easily achieved in areas with good palliative care services and the need to integrate these or, a national level is beginning to be recognized, notably in Spain[7] and Wales.[8]

Time for Grief!

When the end does finally come, the family finds itself in a new situation. Suddenly they are no longer carers but mourners. They may have been grieving for some time beforehand but death creates a new pattern in their lives and with it a change in status and duties. In the midst of their sorrow they are confronted by new practical challenges. The death has to be registered, arrangements made for the disposal of the body, and the condolences of friends and acquaintances received and responded to. At the same time mourners are expected to behave as though their lives have not been seriously disrupted. Wage earners are still expected to work and are only rarely allowed any time off in which to come to terms with their loss.

The provision of a statutory period of mourning/readjustment for the recently bereaved seems overdue. Many societies with longstanding traditions have always considered it to be a necessary provision and it could be of great psychological benefit to many recently bereaved relatives in our modern societies. Such a period may also prove to be cost effective by reducing the time eventually taken off work because of unresolved grief reactions and any associated physical and mental illness.

Chapter 15

Bereavement

The Basics

Canst thou not minister to a mind diseased,
Pluck from the memory a rooted sorrow,
Raze out the written troubles of the brain
And with some sweet oblivious antidote
Cleanse the stuff'd bosom of that perilous stuff
Which weighs upon the heart?

Macbeth

Introduction

When we look at the origin of the word bereavement, we find that it is derived from the Anglo-Saxon word *beriafien*, meaning to be robbed. Even today there is a close relationship between being robbed and being bereaved. In both situations something precious has been taken from us, and the sense of deprivation produces a deep emotional response often with feelings of anger. The intensity of the reaction depends on the importance that is attached to the lost object, for few people place an equal value on all their possessions or personal relationships. Among the most difficult losses to bear are loss of health, loss of freedom, loss of home or employment, and most commonly the loss due to the death of a loved person. Although the causes for the ensuing distress are diverse, people's response to these different losses is sometimes remarkably similar.

Bereavement has been considered a special state in most societies since prehistory. The Western attitude to bereavement is based, in part, on Jewish ethics, and one of the first known statements on bereavement is recorded in Exodus (c.1250 BCE) where the injunction 'ye shall not afflict any widow or fatherless child' is given to the Jews.[1] Some 600 years later an even more positive commandment is given in, Deuteronomy: 'and the stranger, and the fatherless, and the widow, which are within thy gates, shall come, and shall eat, and be satisfied'.[2] This helpful attitude contrasts sharply with the strictures imposed on widowers in nineteenth-century New Guinea.

156

In the Makeo District of New Guinea, a widower lost all civil rights and became a social outcast. He became an object of fear and horror. He could not cultivate a garden, appear in public, cross the village or walk along the paths. If he wished to hunt he had to do so alone and at night.[3] It seems that whilst bereavement is generally seen to be a special state, people's response to it can vary. People may be helpful, antagonistic or unconcerned in their attitude towards the bereaved. Modern societies do accept some collective responsibility for the care of widows and orphans, mainly through the financial benefits provided by state or company pensions, and the gifts of charitable societies. This financial help is the minimum support the destitute widowed and orphaned need. They also need help to adjust to the new situation, to develop new personal relationships, and to remain socially integrated in spite of having lost a central figure in their lives.

Freud's Seminal Ideas

Sigmund Freud's concept of 'grief work' established the basis for the modern psychological approach to bereavement. This sees mourning as a prolonged and inner struggle to adapt to and accept the irreversible loss of a loved person. Although painful, it is a normal process with a discernible pattern that leads to inner healing. Freud believed that the distress of bereavement is due to the survivor's struggle to both retain and relinquish their attachment to the deceased. This distress is exacerbated by the ambivalent feelings that exist between people who are closely related. The prevailing emotions are a mixture of overt love and suppressed hatred, and these are reinforced in bereavement by the anger that is generated by the sense of deprivation. Healing comes by recognizing, accepting and integrating these conflicting feelings, and by learning to free oneself from all emotional attachments to the loved person. Failure to make the appropriate adjustments may result in a prolonged or atypical grief reaction. When this is associated with a deep depression Freud called the condition 'pathological mourning'.

Whilst Freud's ideas provide a base for our present understanding of bereavement, other workers have made important contributions to this field. One of the first to provide new insights into the subject was the American psychiatrist, Lindemann.

Lindemann and Atypical Grief

In 1944, Lindemann published a paper on the symptomatology and management of acute grief.[4] This paper was based on the experiences of a diverse group of 101 bereaved people: they included war widows, psychiatric patients, and the relatives of victims of the Coconut Grove Fire in which almost 500 people were killed or injured. Although Lindemann's paper included many bereavements with unusual features, he made no attempt to distinguish between the reactions of people who were bereaved as a result of a violent death from those where the death was due to natural causes. Nevertheless, his paper proved to be a landmark in studies on bereavement as it helped to clarify the differences between 'normal' and 'atypical' (or abnormal) grief.

Lindemann listed five characteristics that are usually present in normal grief. These are 1) physical distress, 2) preoccupation with the image of the deceased, 3) guilt, 4) hostility and 5) loss of established patterns of conduct. Three of these characteristics – guilt, hostile reactions, and preoccupation with the image of the deceased – are in line with psychoanalytical theory. This is not surprising as Lindemann's therapeutic technique was based on the Freudian idea of uncovering the ambivalent feelings the survivors had towards the deceased and helping them to resolve this inner conflict.

His paper gave new emphasis to the physical distress and the loss of established patterns of conduct that follow bereavement. He showed that the bereaved were surprised to find how large a part of their normal activities was dependent upon a meaningful relationship with the deceased, and that these activities lost their significance after bereavement. He also referred to the amount of physical distress that is sometimes associated with bereavement, mentioning in particular the exhaustion, weakness, loss of appetite and the marked tendency to sigh that people display. Other common symptoms of normal grief that he recorded were a sense of unreality, restlessness, a rush of speech when talking about the deceased, and a painful incapacity to initiate and maintain normal patterns of behaviour.

Atypical grief reactions occur when the normal grief process has been suppressed. The suppression may be deliberate or unconscious. It may be the result of people wishing to maintain a social convention of appearing stoical, or simply because they do not wish to upset others by an overt display of grief, or because they are naturally undemonstrative individuals. Young prisoners often make a conscious effort to suppress overt grief. These young men have a remarkably high incidence of sudden loss to cope with but the macho environment of a prison does not facilitate grieving. When counselled they will often say that they cannot grieve properly in prison and intend to mourn properly when they are released. Whatever the cause may be, the result is the same. The grief work is delayed and the bereaved are unable to express their distress fully and come to terms with their loss.

This postponement of effective grieving may span a few weeks or many years. Eventually, the reality of the loss may be accepted only when another, perhaps less significant bereavement, occurs or at a date that is particularly associated with the deceased. Delayed grief reactions can therefore be expected when there has been no marked distress after an important loss. Lindemann pointed out that, despite the apparent lack of response, certain subtle changes occur that point to the presence of an unresolved grief reaction. He called these less obvious changes 'distorted grief reactions' and said that they often respond to simple psychotherapy if they are recognized and treated early.

He classified distorted grief reactions into nine types which he listed as 1) overactivity without a sense of loss but with an increased sense of wellbeing and zest for life; 2) the development of symptoms similar to those experienced by the deceased; 3) the development of a recognized medical illness; 4) alterations in relationships with friends and relatives, with progressive social isolation; 5) furious hostility towards specific people; 6) a deliberate restriction of hostile feelings, so that the person appears to be cold, wooden and formal; 7) a loss of initiative and of the ability to make decisions; 8) the development of undesirable traits such as spending money recklessly, and antagonizing friends and relatives; and 9) the development of an agitated depression with restlessness, insomnia, feelings of guilt and worthlessness, and suicidal tendencies.

Lindemann also demonstrated that the severity of a grief reaction can be predicted, and mentioned two important pointers to the likely outcome. The first is the intensity of the relationship a person had with the deceased before death. The other indicator is the importance of the deceased's role within the family. Because the relationship that exists between a mother and her baby is very close, severe grief reactions can be expected in mothers who lose young children. Likewise, the loss of a key person, such as the sole wage earner, may have such a profound effect on the living standards of the survivors that adjusting to the new economic situation adds a further burden to the grief process itself. Both of these factors are more important indicators of the likely outcome of bereavement than any previous tendency to deal with the stresses of life in a neurotic way.

Lindemann was the first person to describe anticipatory grief. This occurs in people who, when faced by a probable bereavement, pre-empt the situation and undertake their grief work before the death occurs. In anticipatory grief people may go through all the phases of mourning whilst the person for whom they grieve is still alive. It enables people to come to terms with their loss at a very early stage. This has obvious advantages when the expected death can be foreseen some weeks or months ahead. However it has one important disadvantage. Some terminally ill people make unexpected recoveries after long illnesses, and in these instances the close bonds that have been severed by the grief work will need to be reformed.

Grief as a Process

The term 'grief process' refers to the inner turmoil that follows bereavement and the individual's subsequent adaptation to the new situation. People's response to bereavement can vary considerably, but many therapists believe that there is a discernible pattern and that this pattern consists of overlapping but distinct stages. Various attempts have been made to classify the grief process but the model suggested by Bowlby[5] is one that is widely accepted. A principle component of his theory is that bereaved people have a strong urge to look for and find the lost person.

Bowlby's original classification consisted of just three phases – yearning and searching, disorganization and despair, and reorganization of behaviour, but he later added a brief first phase, the stage of numbness.[6] In his model, mourning is seen as a process, often extending over many months, in which a succession of clinical patterns blend into and replace one another. The distinction between the phases is not clear cut and elements of one tend to intermingle with those of other phases. The pattern is complex and is based on the successive stages of:

1. numbness – in which the reality of the death is not fully appreciated;
2. yearning and searching – in which the urge to recover the lost object predominates and searching takes place. This phase may last months and sometimes years;
3. disorganization and despair – in which the loss is accepted and attempts to recover the lost object are relinquished;
4. reorganization of behaviour.

This model is, of course, applicable only when an important and meaningful relationship has been broken.

Mourning usually begins with a sense of numbness. This normally lasts from a few hours to a week though it may persist for over a month. Parkes found that over 45 per cent of the London widows he interviewed mentioned this as their first reaction.[7] The feeling of numbness is frequently associated with a sense of disbelief but whilst numbness is a relatively transient phenomenon some form of denial often persists for many months or even longer.

Numbness is characterized by an inner emptiness. Everything seems to be unreal and the bereaved may feel too confused and bewildered to cope with their immediate problems. Tearfulness is common. Panic attacks may also occur, or restless periods of 'busyness' and, rarely, a mood almost of elation. There may be outbreaks of extreme distress and anger; such emotional outbursts may be therapeutic as they provide a natural and effective way of expressing grief. If the psychological trauma is sudden and severe, people may be so numbed that they are incapable of any immediate response other than sitting quietly and nursing their grief and bewilderment.

As the feelings of numbness fade, the pain of grieving increases. Grief is now experienced as pangs of severe anxiety and psychological pain. The predominant mood is one of yearning (or pining) for the dead person. This feeling occurs episodically; it begins within a few hours or days of bereavement and usually reaches a peak within 5 to 14 days. It then becomes less frequent and spontaneous, though it can still be triggered by anything that recalls the deceased to mind.

Yearning is not just a passive longing for the departed, it is the emotional component of the urge to search. Whilst Bowlby emphasized the importance of crying and angry protestation in this second stage of mourning, Parkes considered that the impulse to search is the more important. He realized that a bereaved adult is likely to know that there is no point in searching for the dead person but he maintained that this does not prevent them from experiencing a strong urge to do so. He also points out that whilst crying and protesting are important features of bereavement, they are relatively non-specific phenomena because bereaved people may have other reasons for crying and being angry. It is only when the anger and tears are clearly related to the deceased person that they can be regarded as a specific part of the grief process.[8]

Searching, by its very nature, implies the loss or absence of the loved person and consequently must be an essential component of grief. In their search, bereaved people display more than just a rest-less tendency to move about and scan the environment. They think intensely about the deceased, call for them by name, and develop a perceptual 'set' for them by concentrating their attention on aspects of their surroundings that may suggest the presence of the deceased. Some psychiatrists have a problem with this emphasis on 'the search' as it is at odds with Freud's assertion that the function of mourning is 'to detach the survivor's memories and hopes from the deceased', and no one can simultaneously look for and disengage themselves from another person. Parkes explains this paradox by pointing out that the intensity of pining and searching diminishes with time, and that the bereaved have to undergo these painful experiences before they can 'unlearn' their attachment to the deceased.[9]

Bowlby shared Freud's opinion that anger is an important aspect of grief. He also believed that it features in mourning more often than is generally realized. Anger is a fluctuating emotion, which is not easily sustained. Its presence is not always apparent and if left unexpressed it may be internalized, with the bereaved person experiencing feelings of guilt and self-reproach. These may lead to an apathetic attitude to life and a state of clinical depression needing psychiatric help.

The third stage is one of disorganization and despair. The permanent nature of the loss is now being accepted and attempts to recover the deceased relinquished. It is a period of uncertainty, aimlessness and apathy, in which the bereaved find that they have to reassess their position in society and adjust to a new pattern of life. People often feel depressed during this phase but are not necessarily suffering from a depressive illness. When healthy people are subjected to severe stress they may experience moods of depression, but Bowlby believed that these are indicative not of an illness but of a subjective state of disorganization, which is best seen as having an adaptive function. Patterns of behaviour, which developed as a result of interactions with the deceased, now cease to be appropriate and, if continued, become maladaptive. Consequently, some inner disorganization is an indispensable preliminary to the achievement of a new lifestyle. The process is painful but the bereaved must accept the destruction of part of their former personalities before they can reorganize themselves along new lines.[10] Not everyone is prepared, or able, to tolerate this disorganization and Bowlby considered this should be seen as a 'failure' of the grieving process.

This failure to grieve properly was considered to be particularly, evident if the bereaved remained orientated towards the deceased and continued to live as if the dead person was still present and retrievable. However, when it was later shown that a continuing sense of the dead person's presence is a common and normal feature of healthy mourning, Bowlby accepted this finding. He also accepted the later findings of Glick and his colleagues that persistent feelings of attachment to the deceased helped widows to maintain their sense of personal identity and to reorganize their lives in a meaningful way.[11]

The fourth stage in the grief process is a 'greater or lesser degree of reorganization'. With the passage of time, alterations in behaviour patterns occur as people learn to discriminate between attitudes that are no longer appropriate and those that can be reasonably retained. Ideally, recovery occurs when there is complete acceptance of the loss and a reintegration of the personality, but this should not be expected in all cases. Incomplete acceptance of the loss should not automatically be seen as a sign that the grief work has not been properly done. Some losses, particularly those experienced by parents when a young or teenage child dies suddenly, are too great for a full recovery to be achieved. In such cases, pangs of grief may still be experienced years after the death, even though the bereaved parents may have adapted themselves successfully to a new mode of life.

That Freud recognized this truism became apparent only in 1961 when his correspondence was published. In a letter to Ludwig Binswanger, a friend who had lost a son, he wrote in 1926: 'Although we know that after such a loss the acute stage of mourning will subside, we also know that we shall remain inconsolable and never find a substitute. No matter what may fill the gap, even if it be filled completely, it nevertheless remains something else.'[12]

Freud was 70 years old when he wrote that letter and by then had suffered many bereavements himself, including the death of his daughter Sophie, aged 27, but the most grievous loss was the death of his 4-year-old grandson Heinele, in 1923, and in another letter to a friend Eitingon, he wrote: 'I am obsessed by impotent longings for the child' and 'a stranger to life and a candidate for death'. At this time, Sigmund Freud was a very depressed man.[13]

Worden: The Tasks of Mourning

The ideas advanced by William Worden, a professor of psychology at Harvard Medical School, form the basis of much of the counselling work done with bereaved people. He distinguishes between grief and mourning, defining grief as the personal experience of loss and mourning as the process that occurs after the loss. He says that because mourning is a process, it can be depicted as occurring in stages: though he points out that this type of presentation can be taken too literally by the novice, as happened with workers in terminal care when Kübler-Ross's book *On Death and Dying* was first published.

Worden does not dispute the four phases of mourning described by Bowlby and Parkes but considers it more helpful to think of mourning as involving four basic tasks which overlap, a model which is based on Freud's idea of grief work. Although the recently bereaved may already be overwhelmed by grief, he believes that confronting their despair in this way can, with the help of a therapist, offer hope that something can be done to alleviate their misery and assure them of an end to their pain.[14]

Worden's four tasks of mourning are to:

- accept the reality of the loss;
- work through to the pain of grief;
- adjust to the environment in which the deceased is missing;
- emotionally relocate the deceased and move on with life.

This last task, he says, is the one people find most difficult to accomplish. It has its origin, as does much bereavement counselling, in Freud's famous dictum that: 'Mourning has a precise psychical task to perform: its function is to detach the survivor's hopes and memories from the dead.'[15] The truth of this assertion is, however, debatable and Worden has adjusted his views on this subject. In the second edition of his book *Grief Counselling and Grief Therapy*, he is able to say of Freud's dictum 'I believe this to be true': but he is also able to write 'one never loses memories of a significant relationship' and later: 'the counsellor's task becomes not to help the bereaved give up their relationship with the deceased, but to help them find an appropriate place for the dead in their emotional lives – a place that will enable them to go on living effectively in the world.'[16]

Worden writes clearly and concisely. But he does more than provide an interesting and useful approach to grief and mourning. He discusses the principles and techniques used in counselling; helps counsellors to cope with their own grief and includes twelve 'grief sketches', for trainee counsellors to use in role-play, thus creating a training manual for counsellors.

A Simple Classification

Sometimes it is helpful to have complex ideas expressed simply. My own classification of bereavement is simple and is put forward to complement the ideas that have been considered already. In this classification, bereavement has the following possible outcomes:

1. no appreciable change;
2. improvement in mood and health;
3. increased morbidity
    A. psychological . . . immediate
                          anniversary
                          delayed
                          chronic
    B. physical illness;
4. increased mortality;
5. perceptions of the dead – these common experiences of the bereaved are dealt with in Chapter 22;
6. socio-economic changes.

Before considering these different aspects of bereavement, we shall first examine the relationship between outcome and kinship.

Outcome and Kinship

We have noted already Lindemann's view that the two most important predictors for the likely response to a bereavement are the intensity of interaction with the deceased before death, and the significance of the deceased's role within the family. We also commented on his failure to distinguish between the reactions of those people bereaved by a violent death and those by a natural one. This was a surprising omission as people who are suddenly bereaved by murder, or a drunken motorist, are likely to be more distressed than those whose relatives die naturally in old age.

Lindemann did point out, however, that kinship can be an important predictor of outcome. This view was confirmed by a survey undertaken at St Mary's Hospice, Birmingham, of the relatives of patients with terminal cancer. Most frequently the next-of-kin (NoK) was a son or daughter (40 per cent): the next most common relationships were a spouse (35 per cent), a sibling (11 per cent), or some other relationship (14 per cent). In an attempt to find out how well people were coping with bereavement and whether they needed further help, the hospice contacted the NoK of 148 patients four weeks following the deaths. The results showed that 78 per cent of siblings and 65 per cent of offspring were coping well and needed no further help but only 37 per cent of widowed people thought that they were managing adequately. [17]

No Appreciable Change

When relationships are not close, people tend to be less deeply affected by bereavement. In these instances there is no great grief, no subsequent illness, no financial hardship or overwhelming sense of loss, and once the funeral is over life proceeds very much as before. This relative non-reaction is quite common, normal and understandable. Close relationships are often weakened by the relocations inherent in a modern, mobile population, and the subsequent need for people to establish new roots and support systems. Affection remains but when an aged relative has languished for years in a nursing home or chronic geriatric unit, death can assume the mantle of kindness. Often the grief work is commenced, or even completed, months or years before the death occurs. In this situation an excessive display of grief would be false.

Improvement in Mood and Health

An improvement in mood and health is not common but it occurs occasionally and needs to be recognized as a possible outcome. It has to be carefully distinguished from the overactivity and increased zest for life that is sometimes indicative of a 'distorted grief reaction'. An example of the latter is recorded by the artist Augustus John in his autobiography, *Finishing Touches*.[18] He describes how he returned to his flat in a state of euphoria after the death, in a French hospital, of his young wife. The euphoria did not last. For months afterwards he drank heavily and refused to see his friends. Another distorted grief reaction was apparent in the behaviour of the mother of one of my young cancer patients. She was excessively happy both before and after the death of her daughter. When questioned about this unusual response, she replied that she had already done her grief work and had come to terms with her daughter's impending death. A few months later she wrote to say that she was feeling despondent. More remarkable was the improvement in health of a schizophrenic woman, who was showing signs of relapsing before her husband's death. He died suddenly at night from coronary thrombosis. Everyone felt concerned for the widow and her two young children but her improvement was dramatic. She became a vivacious person who was helpful to her neighbours; she also took a new interest in her appearance. So too did the relatively young wife of an elderly man who had been a chronic invalid for years. Shortly after his death both the wife and her house appeared to be transformed from a state of dinginess to one of brightness. In both the latter cases the initial improvements persisted.

Immediate Grief Reactions

Typically, the immediate response to the sudden loss of a loved person is a sense of numbness followed by intense pining. The reality of the death may not be totally accepted until the corpse has been seen or interred. The classical symptoms of numbness followed by crying, restlessness and anger were demonstrated vividly by an elderly woman immediately after her husband had committed suicide. When the body was discovered I was asked to visit the family in their isolated home and found them sitting together in total silence. Speech seemed inappropriate and it appeared more fitting just to sit and share their grief with them. Eventually I was asked to prescribe a sedative for the widow but this she chose not to accept. During the night she kept the family awake by rushing outside and crying out, 'Oh John, why have you left me?' This persisted through-out the night and by the morning the whole family was exhausted. But this demonstration of her distress appeared to have been helpful and cathartic. During that one night the widow poured out all her anguish and discharged her grief. Subsequently, she managed her business affairs ably, maintained a good relationship with her friends and relatives and showed no evidence that the mourning process had been cut short or was inadequate.

The isolation of the house was also helpful as it ensured that there were no close neighbours to be disturbed. It is doubtful whether a widow could have behaved in such a way in a town or city without being restrained by social convention, force or tranquillizers. In many other countries different social conventions apply and an open display of acute grief is both accepted and encouraged. Its therapeutic value seems to have been appreciated in rural Wales. I am told that old Welsh parsons, who knew their flock and understood the dynamics of grief, would try to ensure, possibly by the power of their preaching, that the family cried during the funeral service if they had not done so previously.

Anniversary Reactions

Anniversary reactions occur on those occasions when the bereaved are particularly likely to remember the deceased. They frequently occur on the anniversary of the deceased's birth or death, or on festive occasions such as Christmas when the survivor is most likely to feel lonely and despondent. They are likely to appear as a transient depression, lassitude or as a physical symptom requiring medical advice. In the latter instance, doctors are more likely to assess the problem correctly if they know the family history. One such example occurred on a September afternoon when a robust farmer walked into my surgery. I could find no clinical cause for his symptoms and eventually asked about the date of his brother's death. It was an event neither of us would forget as we had stood together on the hillside and seen the brother lying with his chest crushed by an over-turned tractor. My patient was consulting me on the first anniversary of his brother's death but had not mentioned that fact and probably would not have done so if I had not asked him about it.

Delayed Grief

Sometimes overt grief is deliberately avoided. Three months after the sudden death of her father, a 16-year-old girl came to the surgery complaining of headaches, being low spirited, unable to sleep or concentrate on her school work. She also had an early seborrhoeic dermatitis of the face. It would have been easy merely to prescribe an analgesic, sedative or, on the evidence of an interrupted sleep pattern and flattening of affect, an antidepressant drug. Instead, we talked about her father and her feelings about the loss. With a little encour-agement she started to cry and then to weep freely. This was the first time since his death that she had been able to cry, as she had felt previously that her father would have disapproved and also she had not wanted to upset her mother. In addition to being allowed a permissive consultation the dermatitis was treated and she was given a mild sedative. When seen a month later, the skin was clear, the mood much improved and the sleep pattern normal.

Delayed grief might also have have played a part in the following incident. Some months after his father's sudden death, a young man was seen exposing himself indecently in front of young children. The police looked upon this as a serious offence and intended to prose-cute but eventually agreed not to do so provided the young man sought psychiatric help. Whether this unfortunate episode was a direct result of his father's death and indicative of a distorted grief reaction is debatable. However, it is in keeping with the known fact that bereaved people have a high incidence of emotional problems and an increased referral rate to psychiatrists.[19]

Chronic Grief

Every family doctor has a number of 'thick files'. These are the medical records of patients with multiple and intractable problems.

In some of these cases the underlying cause is 'chronic grief', a persistent pining for a person who has died many years previously and a failure to adjust adequately to the new situation. Many of these patients are referred to psychiatrists and Parkes says they invariably show intense separation anxiety and strong, but only partial, attempts to stop grieving.[20] Typical of such patients was a woman who came to me about 30 years after the death of her only child. She had a history of attempted suicide, arthritis and muscle pains. She was invariably depressed and never felt well. Her medical folder bulged with reports from various specialists including psychiatrists. Her son had fallen off his bicycle whilst riding on a towpath and drowned in the adjoining canal. The woman blamed her husband for the death, retaining a constant bitterness towards him and never forgiving either him or herself. They remained married but never talked about their child. Even when the son would have been old enough to leave home and marry, the mother still remained engrossed in the feelings that had become dominant years previously. The pattern had become so permanently fixed that any chance of recovery was remote whilst, unfortunately, further suicide attempts could not be discounted.

Emotional Responses

Some of the emotional consequences of bereavement feature also in Kübler-Ross's stages of dying, viz. denial, anger, bargaining, depression and acceptance. Denial and bargaining are less apparent in mourning, though bargaining can be a feature of anticipatory grief, often in the form of a plea to a saint or God such as 'if you let him/her get better then I will do . . .'. Bouts of anger and depression, and some degree of acceptance are common to both situations. This similarity is not surprising as the process of mourning and the inner preparation for death are closely related. Both are expressions of grief. In bereavement there is grief for the death of a loved person, whereas terminally ill patients grieve for aspects of their lives which have been lost already and for the further losses that death signifies.

In both situations there is likely to be some anxiety. Parkes considers anxiety to be a salient feature of mourning, but most psychiatrists prefer to classify the grief of bereavement not in terms of an anxiety state but as a 'reactive depression', and depression is certainly a prominent feature of mourning. Those who are depressed frequently experience guilt, insomnia and feelings of unworthiness. Sighing was mentioned by Lindemann as a feature of acute grief and, occasionally, people with this tendency consult their doctors complaining of pain in the chest. Physical disease has to be excluded but the diagnosis is easily made by observing the person sigh.

Physical Changes

The distinction between the emotional and physical responses to bereavement is not always clear and is sometimes arbitrary. Crying, for instance, has both a physical and an emotional component, yet it is usually considered to be an emotional reaction. Some of the physical responses – a quickened heart rate, increased muscle tension and dryness of the mouth – occur when the sympathetic nervous system is activated by pangs of separation anxiety. When a depressive mood predominates, the appearance will tend to be more lethargic and dull. Impairment of appetite and weight loss are also common, and the bereaved may feel, or even become, physically ill.

There is obviously a close connection between the emotional stresses that accompany bereavement and the various physical changes that may follow. The endocrine and sympathetic nervous systems are just two of several internal regulatory mechanisms that are involved, and there is a growing body of evidence that the immune system may also be affected. Psychoneuroimmunology (PNI) is the term given to the study of the interactions that occur between the nervous, endocrine and immune systems of individuals who have been subjected to stress. Many PNI studies have been undertaken in animals, and also in people with AIDS, cancer, depressive illnesses and post-traumatic stress disorders[21] but only a few such studies have been undertaken in the recently bereaved. This type of investigation may eventually provide important pointers for our future understanding of the effects of bereavement.

In one study, 15 men were investigated before and after the death of their wives. Although there had been much stress prior to the death, a significant suppression of the immune function occurred only after bereavement.[22] Another study compared women who had been recently widowed with a group of controls. The results showed that depressive symptoms were significantly elevated and the immune function significantly lowered in the widows.[23]

Emotional distress and emotional involvement are usually important predictors of increased activity of the suprarenal cortex. A study of 67 middle-aged and older people, who had either been bereaved or threatened with such a loss, showed evidence of increased cortisol levels in those with increasing separation distress. Bereaved people and those anticipating a loss also had increased levels of urinary cate-cholamines.[24] Fifty-two of the original 67 subjects were followed up for two years, to see if any of the psychological or endocrine changes observed increased the likelihood of subsequent illness. A few positive findings emerged and these mainly linked adrenal cortical activity with an increased sense of hopelessness.[25] Despite these positive findings there is still no evidence of a direct relationship between altered endocrine activity, or impaired immunity, and subsequent physical illness in bereaved people. However, this is a new field of study and the possibility has only just started to be explored.

Chapter 16

Bereavement

Medical and Social

Issues

If you have tears, prepare to shed them now.

Julius Caesar

Bereavement is the most devastating of social losses but it also has adverse health implications and sometimes we need to be reminded of this. Engel did so in 1961, when he pointed out that bereavement fulfils all the requirements of a disease and that the psychological trauma experienced when a loved companion dies is analagous to the physiological trauma of a severe injury.[1] From this perspective, bereavement can be classified as a psychosomatic disease and possibly the most important of the psychosomatic diseases. The therapeutic approach therefore needs to be different from that usually provided by allopathic medicine where physical remedies are the normal means of treatment: instead there is a need to concentrate on the inner hurt that is the hallmark of grief. Health-care workers are not the people most closely involved in this form of care. The healing word and helpful hand are provided mainly by family and friends, but clergy and funeral directors, colleagues and bereavement counsellors, and many others also have a role in comforting the bereaved.

Bereavement can be classified as a disease because it makes people ill and can even lead to their death: there is a clearly demonstrated morbidity and mortality associated with it. Sometimes the pain is repressed and not immediately apparent and then it resembles the subclinical infections that can occur in certain illnesses such as glandular fever, an infectious disease that affects mainly children and young adults. Glandular fever is caused by the Epstein–Barr virus, and it has a wide range of clinical presentations. In some cases it is extremely debilitating and may leave the individual weak and depressed for many months afterwards. In contrast, some people are so mildly affected that they may not be aware that they have had the infection until the diagnosis is made, often inadvertently, by a blood test years later.

People who have had glandular fever, even at the subclinical level, will be immune from the disease for the rest of their lives but the same principle does not apply to the bereaved. A person who has been bereaved and passed through the grieving process does not become immune from the grief of further loss. In fact the distress may become more severe as happened to Sigmund Freud when, at the age of 67, he grieved longer and more deeply for his young grandson than he had for a well-loved daughter who had died three years earlier.[2]

Morbidity of Bereavement

The most serious physical illness associated with bereavement is coronary thrombosis – the broken heart syndrome. Repeated studies have shown that married men have fewer heart attacks than widowers, and that the increased risk of coronary thrombosis following bereavement seems peculiar to men.[3] The explanation for this finding remains a subject for continuing debate, but the emotional and caring support provided by most wives is probably an important factor in maintaining their husbands' good health.

People who have been bereaved often feel unwell and are more likely to consult their doctors than previously: this has been demonstrated by studies in Australia, the USA and the UK. A comparative study of widows in Australia and the USA found that 21 per cent of widows in Boston and 32 per cent in Sydney reported a deterioration of health during the 13 months following bereavement, whilst the comparable figure among control groups was 7 per cent.[4] In England, a deterioration in health was reported by 43 per cent of widows living in London,[5] and the number of medical consultations increased by 63 per cent during the first six months of bereavement: much of this illnes was psychological but it included a high incidence of musculo-skeletal complaints.[6]

Clinical depression is often a feature of bereavement and sometimes it is difficult to distinguish this from a normal grief reaction. The Beck Depressive Inventory (a questionnaire) is a useful tool for monitoring depression and the physical changes – anorexia, sleep disturbance, weight loss and loss of libido – that may accompany it. Margaret and Wolfgang Stroebe used the inventory in the Tübingen longitudinal bereavement study, an in-depth survey over a two-year period of younger widows and widowers living in Germany. They found that four to seven months after bereavement, 42 per cent of the widowed were depressed compared to only 10 per cent of a control group of married people; and two years after the loss, 27 per cent of the widowed were still depressed. During the same period, 21 per cent of the bereaved reported an increase in the use of psychotropic drugs whereas none of the controls did.[7] Other surveys show that the bereaved tend to show a variable increase in the use of drugs and alcohol, depending on their social situation and cultural tradition.

Most studies find an increase in ill health following bereavement but not all do so. In Tübingen, 32 per cent of the widowed reported new illnesses during the six-month period following the loss; the comparable figure for the control group was 7 per cent.[7] Similarly, in the University of Southern California spousal bereavement study, where sociodemographic and other factors known to influence health were carefully controlled, poorer physical health was recorded in the bereaved than in the non-bereaved.[8] However, different results were obtained elsewhere in California: a study of 70 widowed people in San Diego County found no increase in acute illnesses within the month of interview, nor any increased anxiety about personal health.[9]

Mortality of Bereavement

Many people are not comfortable with the idea that bereavement should be regarded as an illness, and in most instances it is not appropriate to do so. But the ultimate test is whether bereavement can be shown to contribute directly to the death of surviving relatives. Popular folklore tends to support the legend of the lover who dies from a broken heart, an idea that is embodied in a couplet written in the seventeenth century by Sir Henry Wooton:

> He first deceased, she for a little tried,
> To live without him, liked it not and died.

Modern science, however, requires more than legend or folklore to validate such an idea. A significant difference between the mortality of the bereaved and a control group is an essential prerequisite for the general acceptance of such a theory. Some investigations have been done but the results from different surveys are variable, ranging from a high mortality[10] to no increase in deaths[11] during the first 12 months of bereavement. However, most show that there is an increased death rate during widowhood, especially among widowers, but it is not yet clear whether the increase in mortality occurs mainly soon after widowhood or over a prolonged period of years.

The balance of opinion seems to be in favour of the former view.[12] One long-term study of 4030 white residents in Washington County not only confirmed an increased mortality for widowers but showed that the trend was not due to potentially confounding variables, such as cigarette smoking and socio-economic level.[13]

Various suggestions have been put forward to explain the increased mortality in the bereaved. First, the results are dismissed as spurious and due to statistical bias in the sample. Second, the risk is attributed to a shared lifestyle with married partners eating the same diet, taking the same physical exercises and breathing the same clean or dirty air and therefore being equally at risk of dying. Third, stress – and the need to adapt to changed circumstances are blamed as important contributory factors. Stress is known to depress the immune system and increase the level of certain chemicals in the blood; this may be sufficient to bring about the death of a vulnerable individual but the evidence is not conclusive. Fourth, there is the broken heart theory, which focuses on the loss of the loved person, *per se*, not on other changes associated with the loss. Perhaps a typical example of this syndrome occurred in an elderly man who had looked after his wife for many years. She had multiple physical disabilities and a history of depression and attempted suicide, but he was always cheerful, active and physically fit. She died suddenly at home, there was an inquest and this showed that death was from natural causes. There was one child to the marriage, a caring daughter. She lived some distance away but she helped with the funeral arrangements and a few days later 'phoned me to say that her father was not well and to ask me to visit him. I went immediately and was surprised by his appearance, which had changed dramatically since I last saw him. He looked ill and was breathless at rest, yet he smiled and said he felt alright. He had auricular fibrillation and was in cardiac failure so I admitted him to hospital. If I remember rightly, there was no previous history of heart problems but he died that weekend whilst I was on holiday. I have always regarded this as a typical case of broken heart syndrome, characterized by the rapid decline and death of a previously fit man soon after the death of his wife.

Almost all the studies on the adverse effects of bereavement have been carried out in First World countries, so little is known about the level of risk in the Third World. It seems likely, however, that the level of risk may show regional differences, worldwide. There is too much variation in geographical, cultural and economic systems, and in the availability of medical services, for similar observations to be made in all regions. Statistics on bereavement mortality are also likely to be affected by the speed and efficiency with which the victims of near-fatal heart attacks can now be resuscitated. This improvement in care will probably result in lower mortality figures being recorded for bereaved people, some of whom might have died from coronary thrombosis before these techniques became widely available.

Oddly enough the trend towards cremation, rather than burial, may also affect the statistics. Newly qualified doctors are less likely to be summoned, as I was, to sudden deaths at funerals. When I worked as a family physician in rural Wales I was called out on three occasions within 10 years to such a death. Each of them occurred at bleak, hillside cemeteries, two in bad weather. This traditional way of disposing of the dead is becoming less common as cremation becomes more acceptable. It seems reasonable to assume that people who pay their last respects while sitting in the warm chapel of a crematorium are less likely to have a fatal heart attack than those who do so standing on a wet and windy hillside.

Social and Economic Changes

Social and economic changes are the hallmarks of widowhood. Usually the economic change is for the worse, though a well-insured death can result in a financial gain for the surviving partner. In many countries the full force of the economic loss for widows is made less severe by the availability of state benefits and company pension schemes, but despite these provisions some loss of income is common. A widow usually suffers a greater fall in income than a widower. In San Diego County, California, widowers are likely to retain 90 per cent of their income immediately after the death of a spouse, whereas the income of widows falls to 60 per cent.[9] This discrepancy bears out the well-known fact that men tend to earn more than women. It also indicates that many Californian women either continue working or find a job after widowhood, as the level of their income is higher than would be expected if it was solely derived from state or company pension schemes or their husbands' insurance policies.

Whilst financial loss is important it is not the only deprivation associated with widowhood. There is the loss of an important relationship and the subsequent loneliness. Also there is often a loss of status and the added burden of the stigma that is still associated with the widowed state, for both men and women, in some cultures. The sense of stigma may be enhanced if the death is attributed to a socially unacceptable cause, such as suicide, AIDS or homicide. This

additional distress may not be a universal feature of such bereavements. In those countries where the AIDS epidemic is rife, to be
bereaved as a result of that disease may be commonplace and
accepted as such. Similarly in those countries with a high incidence
of homicide – the rate in Columbia is nine times that of the USA, 50
times that of Singapore and 125 times that of England and Wales,
there may be no stigma associated with being bereaved as a result of
such criminal activity.[14]

It is probably true to say that more help is given to widows than
widowers but Wortman and her colleagues suggest that, apart from
the increase in mortality, men are more vulnerable than women after
bereavement. They also say that 'widowhood is not the same event
for the two sexes', a conclusion they reached following a longitudinal
study of 616 widowed people over a three-year period. They found
that the effects of bereavement last much longer than expected and
that it takes about 10 years for the widowed to score the same as
controls on a 'life satisfaction scale.' Widowers tend to be more
depressed and their depressed mood lasts longer than that of
widows. They are much more limited in their social relationships
and have more difficulty in coping with tasks that were previously
undertaken by their wives. Within the family, they manage interpersonal relationships less well than widows and this tension is particularly noticeable between them and their children.[15]

Helpers

What help is available for the bereaved and how effective is it? In
traditional societies, the bereaved are mainly supported by family
and friends, and the social organization of this support, for instance
in Islam and Judaism, has been described in earlier chapters. But
with the influx of people into large towns and cities new patterns are
developing. A study in Chicago of the help available to widows
produced several surprises. Relatively little emotional support is
provided by friends and few widows help one another with the care
of children. Only 10 per cent regard a sibling as someone to whom
they can turn in times of crisis. It is mainly the children who supply
the support, and Chicago widows feel closest to their children and
happiest with them. Some are heavily dependent on their children,
usually a daughter, and live in a very restricted social space with few
outside interests. The links these people have with social and
emotional support systems within their communities is poor and
should be strengthened. The best way of doing this will vary with

locality but the first requirement is for representatives of existing services to identify people going through crises such as the death of a significant person and then to establish contact.[16]

Although support is often haphazard some organizations are particularly well situated to help. Most hospices provide a bereavement service, and funeral directors in New Zealand provide counselling and support for 12 months after the funeral as part of their contract with the bereaved. There are also groups such as Cruse Bereavement Care and The Compassionate Friends that were set up specifically for this purpose but they are heavily dependent on referrals from other agencies. General practitioners are ideally situated to identify and contact the recently bereaved and either provide personal support or refer them to such a support group. To do this most effectively, they need to develop a strategy for this purpose and one way of doing this is to use a bereavement protocol as suggested by Charlton and Dolman.[17] They devised the protocol for their primary care team but it might be adapted for use by other groups such as schools and churches.

The protocol requires that:

- all practice staff should know and understand it;
- patients are to have easy access to relevant leaflets. These will provide explicit information about the action to be taken at the time of death. They are to be updated regularly and will include contact numbers/addresses of supporting agencies such as The Compassionate Friends and Cruse Bereavement Care;
- a key worker is to be allocated to the family when a bereavement occurs. This will help to ensure continuity of care;
- the first bereavement consultation is to be as soon after the death as is practicable but not on the day of the funeral;
- most of this time is spent listening;
- the first consultation should be a home visit;
- if personal consultation cannot be established, then contact is to be made by telephone or personalized letter;
- the practice staff will maintain a register of all patient deaths. Case notes of patients will contain the birth, death and pertinent anniversaries of dead kinsfolk/partners. This is to facilitate their care on the anniversary of a death or other significant event.

We used a less precisely formulated system for contacting the bereaved at St Mary's Hospice in the 1980s. All the next-of-kin, who had not been phoned or visited, were sent a letter of condolence and a short questionnaire four weeks after their bereavement. There was a high (77.5 per cent) response rate. Commenting on this aspect of our work in *The Practitioner*, I drew attention to the general practitioner's role in initiating contact with the bereaved. I wrote: 'the problems of bereavement are an intricate blend of the social and medical and the general practitioner needs to maintain a positive and effective role. This he can achieve by initiating contact with the bereaved, perhaps in the pattern indicated in this paper. Doctors who do so will receive a warm response to their initiative. This is apparent from the letters of appreciation we receive from 33% of the relatives who return the questionnaire. Perhaps typical of such letters is one beginning, "Thankyou for your letter. It is a great comfort to know someone cares".'[18]

Bereavement in Combat

Surprisingly little attention has been given to the consequences of bereavement in war, even though this can have long-term effects upon the national morale as well as on those individuals most closely involved. Military codes of conduct have consistently refused to acknowledge the importance to a combatant of the death in battle of a friend. Casualties, though regrettable, are seen as an inevitable consequence of war and as such must be accepted philosophically. All ranks, and to a lesser extent the civilian relatives at home, are expected to abide by the military code that there is no place for mourning in a soldier's life. After the Vietnam War, the American people took several years to realize the extent of the mental distress that had been suffered by members of its armed forces. Of the 3,000,000 United States troops who served in Vietnam, an estimated 500,000 to 1,500,000 were later found to be suffering from various forms of psychiatric disorder, brought about by the grief and pain of that campaign. Most of these psychiatric casualties had close friends and relatives who also suffered as a result of their emotional ties with these servicemen, thereby multiplying the overall mental trauma caused by the war.[19] Perhaps even more poignant is the finding that the number of United States veterans who committed suicide after the Vietnam War (60,000) was greater than the number of their comrades who died during the campaign.[20]

Apart from any personal injury they may receive, the death of a friend is the most important loss suffered by a soldier in battle. This sense of loss is enhanced by the close bonding and esprit de corps that the military encourages within its personnel. The close ties and mutual dependency thus formed makes the sudden, irretrievable loss of important relationships difficult to bear. But military stoicism, the suddenness of the death, the absence of a recognized mourning period and appropriate funeral service, all hinder the normal grief process. Denial and repression of grief are also fostered by traditional attitudes. Men, and soldiers in particular, are expected not to display their feelings. This code of conduct is maintained even when the soldiers move out of the battle zone, for even in safe areas they find it difficult to speak of their experiences. When they do tell their stories, it is often in a tense and withholding fashion that does not facilitate the grief process. Anyone who seeks to help them should expect outbursts of anger, resentment and derisive comments such as, 'what do you know about it? You weren't there.' The last memory a soldier may have of a dead comrade is of a distorted body in a blazing vehicle or of a corpse in a body bag. Some soldiers, whilst still on the battlefield, may even have experienced a sense of relief, sometimes verging on euphoria, at having survived whilst someone else had died. This feeling cannot be easily confided to another person and it may be associated with a strong sense of guilt, with the soldiers believing that they had harboured dangerously murderous thoughts towards their dead comrades.

The death of close friends is just one of the losses that combatants have to bear. There may also be a loss of self-esteem at having killed another person, or they may have lost a limb or been severely burnt and disfigured; all these traumas need to be mourned yet there is no opportunity to do so adequately in the war zone. When hostilities finally cease the prevailing mood changes dramatically. The victors celebrate whilst the vanquished experience a sense of desolation and despondency. But for both victors and vanquished the dead cannot be forgotten. They are remembered in thoughts, feelings, nightmares and eventually by memorials, services of remembrance and the laying of wreaths. Everyone has been affected and the most deeply rooted griefs may only become apparent in later years. Veteran soldiers may find that many years after the war they still need to attend remembrance services, or to visit old battlefields and the cemeteries in foreign countries for the war dead. They do so often not realizing that these are not just acts of remembrance but also the means of completing their own mourning for their dead comrades.

Ethnic Cleansing

War does not only result in the killing and maiming of young combatants, it is also the spur for other atrocities. Each year we receive fresh reports of ethnic cleansing, of the massacre of civilians of all ages, of torture and rape, and of the destruction of homes and the devastation of the countryside. Refugees are forced into exile, leaving behind the unburied corpses of their loved ones. No one has yet assessed the grief of these people; probably it can never be determined but attempts are being made to do so.

The Department of Social Medicine and Pediatrics of Harvard Medical School has looked at the effects of ethnic cleansing on Bosnian children during the civil war of 1992–6, when more than 800,000 Bosnians became refugees in neighbouring countries and up to 250,000 were killed: of these 90 per cent were civilians. They interviewed 364 children aged six to 12 and obtained additional data from the parents or guardians: the families were mainly Muslim. Most children had faced bereavement, separation from other members of their family, close contact with conflict and extreme deprivation. Approximately 40 per cent reported witnessing the violent injury or death of parents or siblings, and 6.2 per cent had witnessed a massacre. All the children showed symptoms of significant distress including anxiety (95.5 per cent), post-traumatic stress disorder (93.8 per cent), sadness (90.6 per cent), feelings of guilt that they were responsible for the troubles in their family (66.6 per cent), anorexia (59.7 per cent) and extreme pessimism (56.8 per cent). The experience with the most dramatic and consistent after effects was witnessing violence to members of their nuclear family. The authors concluded their report, perhaps surprisingly, by pointing out that whilst the children were involved in a dreadful tragedy, they also showed considerable resilience and that 'two thirds of the children felt that life was worth living despite having experienced some of the harshest events that can befall a child.'[21]

Of the many incidents reported at the time, one comes to mind. Among a group of refugees who came to England from the former Yugoslavia there was a mother and her two sons. They had survived by hiding in a hole in the ground when their village was attacked and its inhabitants slain. In the morning, a ceasefire allowed the survivors two hours to leave the village and seek safety. The elder son found the body of his father and kissed him goodbye before walking past the other dead to the peace line. His one possession was a diary of recent events. This was taken from him by a journalist. Like many millions of others, this boy had experienced his own personal Holocaust and will have been permanently changed by the events he witnessed. What can this boy, who has to adapt to life in a foreign country, learn a new language, and face the regular developmental hurdles that are part of growing up, expect in the future? On the basis of evidence provided by Holocaust survivors, he will probably cope with daily problems in an effective manner, especially those that do not pose a problem to his health or life. Despite the past traumas, and continued bouts of anxiety, he will become an effective citizen in his new country. He may even achieve considerable wealth and social status, for in adjusting to his new situation he may try to compensate for his losses and inner emptiness by material achievement, and by 'climbing the ladder of success'.[22]

Bereavement as a Public Health Issue

The USA is a large country with a vast population. About 8,000,000 people who live there lose a close relative each year, whilst countless others, such as members of the gay community, suffer other significant bereavements. The stress associated with these losses is often exacerbated by the violence of the death. In 8 per cent of cases, death is not due to natural causes but to suicide, homicide or an accident, and the violent and sudden nature of these deaths is likely to affect the grief process adversely. Also, in some areas, sudden, violent death is so frequent an event that young people look upon it as a normal aspect of life to which they have to adapt.

The National Institute of Mental Health decided that the high incidence of bereavement, and the known mortality and morbidity associated with it, could constitute a major public health problem. It therefore requested the Institute of Medicine of the National Academy of Sciences to study the factors that affect the bereavement process, and the impact of bereavement on general health and mental health.

The Institute issued a lengthy report,[23] which can be summarized as follows. People's reactions to bereavement are highly variable. There are a number of interrelated responses – psychological, social and physiological – though their sequence cannot be predicted nor the time at which they will occur. Most people experience appreciable distress and some are at increased risk of illness and death. This risk is exacerbated by the health-compromising behaviour that can follow bereavement, such as an increase in alcohol consumption, smoking and drug usage. The ill effects of bereavement can persist over a long period. A year or more after their loss, 10 to 20 per cent of widowed people display clinical evidence of depression. Young and middle-aged widowers are particularly likely to die prematurely, and this increase in mortality is mainly due to an increased incidence of death from accidents, cardiovascular disease, suicide and some infectious diseases.

An impressive amount of advice is available to the public and to health care workers, and there are increasing numbers of lay and professional programmes available to help the bereaved. Many of these programmes and much of the advice they provide, appear to be based on sound conceptual principles. At present there are four main approaches to bereavement support and counselling: these are 1) mutual support or self-help groups: 2) hospice-based lay counsellors: 3) individual psychotherapy: and 4) the use of drug therapy. Few studies have been undertaken to test the effectiveness of these interventions and no serious attempt has been made to see which is the most helpful. Consequently much basic research needs to be undertaken. This should be done before further consideration is given to ways in which these programmes and other possible means of helping bereaved people are established and financed. Most studies in bereavement are limited to conjugal loss in white, middle-class people and this leaves many serious gaps in our knowledge of bereavement, especially in the case of children, impoverished ethnic minorities, recent refugees and migrants. There is reason to believe that members of these groups may be at particularly high risk if bereaved.

Much less is known about the physiology of bereavement than is known of the physiology of exercise and pregnancy. The changes that may occur in the cardiovascular, endocrine, immune and nervous systems after bereavement are not well understood and need to be looked at more closely. Basic work needs to be undertaken in this area and in the social factors that can influence the outcome of bereavement.

In general, this assessment remains true today. However, research workers are becoming increasingly interested in the problems of bereavement, and a comprehensive review of more recent research, both in practical and theoretical terms, is provided in the *Handbook of Bereavement. Theory, Research and Intervention*.[22] This is a multi-author work that covers all aspects of the subject and clearly illustrates the many perspectives from which bereavement can be viewed. It shows that work is being done on the particular problems experienced by ethnic groups, the older person and children. However, while the psychological and social consequences are becoming better understood, little progress has been made in our knowledge of the endocrine and immunological responses to bereavement. The Institute's finding that little is known about the physiological changes that accompany bereavement therefore remains valid.

New Ideas

One interesting development is the increasing awareness of the need to test long-held assumptions that have not been proven. For instance, while it is generally accepted that counselling is beneficial, few studies have been undertaken to validate this belief. Walfgang and Margaret Stroebe have even suggested that 'grief work' is not essential even after the death of a spouse.[7] They pointed out that the 'grief work' hypothesis, which claims that bereaved people have to work through their grief in order to come to terms with their loss, had never been tested. Consequently, they did so in the Tübingen survey of younger widows and widowers. They report that the findings for widowers were equivocal but those for widows did not support the claim that grief work is needed in bereavement: widows who avoided confronting their loss were not more likely to complain of depression or physical symptoms than those who did.

This conclusion is corroborated by the work of Kaminer and Lavie.[22] They studied Holocaust survivors and noted that the well-adjusted survivors had strong egos and a clear repressive tendency towards the past. Most had never talked about their experiences in the concentration camps, or when in hiding, and in some cases their close relatives did not even know that they had lived through the Holocaust. These findings contradict the widely held belief that painful memories should not be repressed and that unhappy experiences should be confronted and dealt with consciously. As Kaminer and Lavie point out, the well-adjusted survivor's ability to repress, and exclude from conscious thought, recollections of traumatic incidents is beneficial: and that repression can be a coping mechanism that helps people to live with the horrors and losses of the past.

A new approach to easing the distress of bereavement is being developed in the USA, using advances made in the treatment of post-traumatic stress disorder (PTSD). American psychotherapists say that many aspects of PTSD can be resolved rapidly if their patients move their eyes in a rhythmic way while focusing on emotionally charged elements of the disorder.[24] This technique, when used with the bereaved, requires the patient to focus on the dead person. I have no personal experience of this technique and cannot substantiate the claims made for it but one half-hour session is said to be usually long enough for complete acceptance of the loss and to relieve the negative feelings of guilt and anger. One surprising side effect of the treatment is that patients report a meaningful spiritual encounter with the person they are grieving, usually seeing or speaking to them.[25]

Chapter 17
The Death of a Child

Grief fills the room up of my absent child,
Lies in his bed, walks up and down with me,
Puts on his pretty looks, repeats his words,
Remembers me of all his gracious parts,
Stuffs out his vacant garments with his form;
Then have I reason to be fond of grief,
Fare you well: had you such a loss as I,
I could give better comfort than you do . . .

King John

Introduction

The most grievous form of bereavement for a parent is usually the death of a child. The word child has its origins in the Teutonic word, *kilthei*, meaning a womb, the place where all human life is nurtured. It is also the tomb for the many who die before parturition. These prenatal deaths can be more distressing and psychologically damaging to the parents than is generally recognized, and the distress is often increased by their realization that the foetus has never attained the status of a real child.

The precise moment at which human life begins is the subject of much legal and ethical controversy. The question is not a new one, there has been a long history of uncertainty on this point, but advances in medical technology and concern about the population explosion have polarized positions and made the debate more urgent. In this chapter the life of an individual is considered to begin at conception. This enables consideration to be given to the reactions of parents who suffer the loss of a child by miscarriage, termination of pregnancy or stillbirth.

185

Miscarriages

The exact incidence of miscarriages is not known but it may be as high as 20 per cent of all pregnancies. Many early miscarriages occur in women who are unaware of their pregnant state, and these miscarriages are not likely to be associated with any show of emotion unless the mother is actively seeking a child. The situation is different if the mother knows that she is pregnant and is looking forward to motherhood. Apart from the physical and emotional distress of the miscarriage and the disappointment of losing her baby, the mother is likely to feel guilty and inadequate. In dealing with these emotions, mothers are not helped by the dismissive attitudes some people display to an early miscarriage. Although the individuals may intend to be helpful, their brusque comments merely make the mother feel more isolated in her grief.

A miscarriage is often considered to be the loss of tissue rather than a child, and the dead foetus is never given the status of a proper child. Its existence is not officially recognized by a certificate of still-birth and, typically, there are no funeral or mourning rites. The mother is given little encouragement to express her feelings, to cry, to talk about the loss, or even to assume the role of a bereaved parent.[1] She will not have seen her baby and she can only fantasize about its appearance, sex and personality. The father's distress is usually less intense, but both parents are likely to suffer from the loss of a wanted pregnancy, and their grief can persist for years. There is some evidence that an act of ritual mourning can provide almost immediate relief for this grief,[2] but such a potentially helpful measure is rarely brought to the notice of, or made available to, the parents.

Termination of Pregnancy

Each year over 150,000 pregnancies are terminated legally in England and Wales. Most involve women aged 16–29, with teenagers forming a quarter of the total group. None find the experience pleasant, but the amount of distress does vary and is dependent on a number of factors. These include firstly, whether the mother was aware of her pregnant state; this is relevant, as a small number of abortions are performed on mentally incompetent mothers on the authority of the courts. Other factors are the mother's attitude towards the pregnancy, her involvement in any decision to terminate it, the reasons for the termination, her religious beliefs, and the level of social support and counselling she receives.

Before the pregnancy is terminated, the mother will have discussed the situation with her medical advisers and reached her own decision. The level of counselling and support she receives will depend upon the commitment of the staff at the clinic she attends, but there will be some preliminary discussion and an opportunity for her to undertake some preparatory grief work.

Most terminations take place during the first three months, which psychoanalysts call the 'narcissistic stage of pregnancy'. During this phase, the mother is said to experience the developing pregnancy not so much as a separate entity but as an integral part of herself. The narcissistic stage is characterized by an ambivalence towards the pregnancy, with an early tendency to depression that later turns to joy. If the pregnancy miscarries or is terminated before this normal psychological development takes place, the woman may feel devalued and contemptuous of herself. Should this happen, she needs to be adequately supported if she is not to suffer long-term psychological damage. Having said this, it must be stated that most pregnancies are terminated because the mother does not want the baby, and so her distress at undergoing an abortion is balanced by her relief at relinquishing the responsibilities of motherhood.

The readiness with which women accept a termination of pregnancy is highly variable and often dependent on the religious tradition to which they belong. In Islamic, Orthodox Jewish and Roman Catholic societies, a termination is considered permissible only if the life of the mother is put at risk by continuing the pregnancy. In many other communities the attitude is more permissive and, in some countries, terminations are made freely available as a means of limiting the growth in population. The differing response of women to the prevailing policies is interesting. Chinese women who have one baby, particularly if it is a girl, often regret being coerced into having subsequent pregnancies terminated because of governmental policy restricting families to one child. In Poland, on the other hand, there was a widespread use of the state abortion services, despite the opposition of the Catholic church, when these services were provided by the communist government.

Although most terminations are carried out on the initiative of the mother for purely social reasons, some are the result of unfavourable prenatal diagnoses. Prenatal screening enables the condition of children who are at risk of inheriting congenital abnormalities to be assessed before birth. The incidence of birth defects is high and 2–5 per cent of all live born infants have genetic disorders or congenital malformations. Implicit in prenatal diagnosis is the

understanding that, if a serious defect is found in the foetus, the pregnancy will be terminated if the parents agree to this decision. Unless
there are religious objections, early abortion is an acceptable form of
management for most mothers. When, for example, a Down
syndrome foetus is detected most mothers ask for the pregnancy to
be terminated,[3] and over 70 per cent of parents who have a Down
syndrome child consider this to be the right decision.[4]

Some mothers find that the success of prenatal screening is
producing a new form of stress, as there is an increasing pressure on
pregnant women to have foetal testing. Women, who have been
asked to do so and refused to comply, say that they have been made
to feel morally irresponsible for refusing a test that might lead to
their being advised to have an abortion.

Death in a Multiple Pregnancy

It is not generally known that there is a high incidence of intra-
uterine death in multiple pregnancies. Ultrasound scanning has
shown that 50 per cent of the twin pregnancies detected in the first
12 weeks of pregnancy end up as single deliveries. In many instances
one foetus disappears completely, in the remainder the dead foetus is
delivered as a single foetal papyraceous when the live twin is born.
Scanning techniques sometimes show the presence of a severely
deformed foetus alongside a normal one. This has created ethical
problems as it is now possible to kill the deformed foetus in utero
whilst leaving the normal foetus unharmed, and this option is
becoming increasingly available to obstetricians and parents. Apart
from the ethical and technical problems involved, such an act is
likely to leave the parents and some members of the obstetric team
with a sense of guilt, and this feeling will remain with the parents
even after childbirth.

Although it may be thought that their joy in having a live baby
would help the parents to forget the dead one, this is not so. The
presence of the live child increases the difficulty the parents experience in forgetting the death and forgiving themselves for it. The live
child is a constant reminder to them of their dead child. Consequently the parents' distress is often greater than that of parents who
lose a child by the termination of a single pregnancy. They have
special problems even during the pregnancy. The mother, in particular, is likely to have disturbing thoughts of the dead foetus lying
alongside the live baby. The maternity staff, on the other hand, are
inclined to forget the dead twin if they can, and this failure by the

professional attendants to acknowledge and respect the dead baby adds to the distress of the parents.[5]

Stillbirths

A stillborn child is one that is born dead after the 24th week of gestation. In contrast to earlier intra-uterine deaths, there is a legal requirement for such deaths to be registered and for the baby to be cremated or buried. Stillbirths are not uncommon and about 3,800 are registered in England and Wales each year. In technologically advanced countries, the expectations of the safe delivery of a healthy baby are so high that the effects on the parents of a stillbirth are correspondingly great. Many of these mothers may have already realized that something has gone wrong and that something has happened to the baby. They may be alerted by the absence of foetal movements or by a change in the attitude of the doctors and midwives who are attending them. Their anxiety may be apparent, even though it is not expressed, and if a mother shows any sign that she believes her baby is at risk, it is better for her to know exactly what is happening than for her fears to be left unexplained and unresolved.[6]

A stillbirth is a shattering event in which the only certain outcome is misery, grief and shame. The grief is heightened by the absence of a real person to mourn, as a stillborn child is someone who never actually existed, just a non-person with no identity or name. Both parents feel bereaved but the mother suffers a double loss, the loss of the baby from her womb and the loss of the compensating live baby. The question 'why did my baby die?' is constantly in her thoughts, and this question needs to be answered on more than one occasion so that she has the chance to absorb fully the information that is given to her.

About 50 per cent of mothers blame themselves for the death. As in other forms of bereavement, grief for a stillborn child begins with numbness and a sense of disbelief, and parents need time to come to terms with this initial phase. Feelings of guilt and shame are common and they are exacerbated if other people fail to react adequately to the loss. Accepting the reality of the death is not easy at first, but it helps if the parents are able to hold or touch the dead baby. This contact gives them someone tangible to remember, and for a similar reason they should be encouraged to name the baby, take an active part in the registration of the stillbirth, and make the funeral memorable.[7] It also helps if they can be given a memento of the child, such as prints of the baby's hands and feet.

The parents of stillborn children are often young and too immature emotionally to deal with their loss without considerable support. They need people to spend time with them, to answer their questions and explain what went wrong. One mother's fears were ignored for two weeks after she had reported the absence of foetal movements. She told her friends when she returned home after the stillbirth: 'We do not want to sue the hospital, we know that there is always a risk. We just want someone to sit down and tell us what happened.'

Obstetric units are becoming more flexible in the arrangements they make available to parents following perinatal deaths and are placing greater emphasis on the support they give to these parents.[8] Whenever possible, they offer bereaved mothers the choice of where to be cared for in the maternity unit whilst they remain in hospital. Most mothers prefer to go into a single room, but it is important that they should not feel isolated from the rest of the unit. Bereft mothers are usually glad to be allowed near to other people's babies and especially to hold them, as their confidence as mothers has been seriously damaged. It also helps if they can meet nursing mothers, so that they can learn to deal with their aggressive feelings of envy and jealousy, and allay any possible fears they may have that they might harm or steal another woman's baby.

It is only in recent years that stillborn infants have been given what might be called a proper burial, with a family funeral and prayers. It is not all that long since they were likely to be placed in a shoe box, or wrapped in paper, and given to the father to bury. If the child was buried by an undertaker, he or she would have been placed in a common grave without any ceremony or memorial. Since 1991, the Roman Catholic Church has authorized a 'Rite of Final Commendation for an Infant' to be used for a stillbirth, or for a newborn infant who dies shortly after birth, and which may be adapted for use following a miscarriage. Other Churches are also developing support services for the parents of stillborn children.

Women who had a stillbirth many years ago can still grieve for the child. If the baby was born in a hospital, the records may still be available and mothers who wish to consult them are likely to be treated with great sympathy. Details are often available of the baby's birth weight, postmortem findings and place of burial. It is possible, if the mother so wishes, to have a headstone placed on the grave.[9]

Neonatal Deaths

The grief for a baby that dies soon after birth is very similar to that following a stillbirth, though parents grieving a neonate have a better understanding of why their baby died than parents of stillborn children. The incidence of neonatal deaths and stillbirths is similar, with about 3,800 of each occurring annually in England and Wales. Parents who experience a neonatal death tend to emphasize that their babies did live, if only for a few hours, and seem to take comfort from this fact.

It makes a difference to the parents if they are able to see and hold their baby whilst it is still alive. Sometimes it is not possible and when the birth is very premature, parents may find it difficult to relate meaningfully to the tiny creature they see connected to tubes in an incubator, and who appears to belong more to the nurses than to themselves. Nevertheless, they do not feel the same sense of defilement that distresses those whose babies died in utero.[6]

The loss of a newborn baby is a tragedy and everything possible needs to be done to support the parents. They need something tangible to remind them of the child and this should be provided by the hospital staff. This memento may be a lock of hair, a name band, or a photograph of the baby taken when it is dressed and in its most attractive pose.

The parents leave hospital and return home empty handed. The mother will not only be grieving, she will also be physically tired and may be lactating. The expected joy has turned to sorrow, friends and relatives are upset and uncertain as to how they can best help the young couple. Toys and baby clothes waiting in the house are sad reminders of what might have been.

The parents will probably experience emotional tension and sexual frustration. They are likely to reproach themselves and quarrel easily. The unbearable pressures may cause a fragile marriage to break up, though the shared grief brings some couples closer together. The first step towards any subsequent recovery is for the parents to talk together, but because of their emotional turmoil they may not find this easy. They will also need to decide what to tell any other children in the family, a decision they may find difficult to reach. Mystery and secretiveness should be avoided. If a photograph is available, this should be shown to the other children and they should be allowed to attend the funeral.

Having other children is both a consolation and a strain for parents grieving for the death of a baby. Young children are very sensitive to their parents' moods and any change makes them feel insecure and therefore more demanding. Their increased demands are at odds with the parents' sadness and need for a quiet space in which to come to terms with their loss. In contrast, the children need to work out their unease in play activities. Friends, keen to be of assistance, can usefully provide a place where young members of the family can be noisy and boisterous without disturbing their parents.

Friends have to adjust themselves to the new situation if they really want to support the bereaved. They must be prepared to help and to listen – often to a reiteration of what they have heard before – whenever this seems necessary. In their desire to ease the pain, they need to avoid certain common pitfalls. They have to be careful not to suggest that the parents should be grateful for any other children they may have. This advice will not be appreciated as the parents will still miss the child that died. Neither should the parents be told, if the lost child was severely disabled, that he or she is probably better off dead as they would never have grown into a healthy adult. They may get round to this view at some later stage but not at the beginning, when they are still wondering why their child was born disabled in the first place.

One subject the parents will need to discuss is whether to have another child. If they seek advice, they should be discouraged from rushing into a new pregnancy. They first need to mourn adequately the loss they have sustained and so allow their inner wounds time to heal. This will help to reduce the likelihood of further psychological problems occurring in the next pregnancy. Some parents decide to have no more children and opt for sterilization. Other parents deliberately seek a replacement baby, and herein lies a subtle danger and an added burden for any subsequent child. No child should be expected to play a replacement role for any other person, for every child needs to be accepted, as and for, him or herself. If possible the birthdays should not be obviously close together, and the new child should not be given the name of the dead child but its own individual name, so that its separate identity is established from birth.

Cot Deaths

Before 1988, the sudden-infant death syndrome (SIDS) was the third most common cause of infant death in many countries. Commonly known as 'cot death', each year it killed one in 500 of all live babies in First World countries. However, thanks to the pioneering work done by Dr Ed Mitchell in New Zealand, developed countries now report a dramatic fall in the incidence of cot deaths – a drop of 80 per cent in England and Wales. This success is the direct result of national 'Back to Sleep' campaigns which were based on three recommendations. The first and most important recommendation was that babies should be put to sleep on their backs or sides, not on their front. More recent work suggests that it is best for babies to lie on their backs, when placed on their sides it is too easy for them to roll on to their fronts.

The other two recommendations were that babies should not be exposed to tobacco smoke and they should not be overheated. Governments continue to advise against parental smoking. The increased risk from smoking begins during pregnancy as infants of mothers who smoke in pregnancy are almost five times more likely to die from SIDS than those of non-smokers. Although overheating was implicated, recent work suggests that thermal factors are not important when babies sleep on their backs.[10]

The incidence of cot deaths has always been low in certain Asian communities, such as Hong Kong, Japan and the Bangladeshi community of the UK. This is probably because Asian parents have always preferred to place their babies on their backs. It has also been suggested that, because the houses are so overcrowded, there is greater environmental stimulation and that this is a protection for the child. Health workers in Third World countries do not consider SIDS a major problem as infections are still responsible for most infant deaths in those regions.

Apart from the hazards mentioned above, other factors increase the likelihood of infants dying in this way. The risk is increased 50-fold when parents sleep with their baby on a sofa,[11] possibly because of an increased likelihood of the mother rolling onto and smothering the child. There is also a clear seasonal variation with most deaths occurring in the winter months and fewest during the summer: they are also more likely to occur at weekends. Cot deaths are more common in male infants, prematurely born babies, the babies of teenage mothers and of the economically disadvantaged. They occur less frequently in Asian than in white or black families. Eighty per cent of SIDS victims are babies aged between one and six months with a peak incidence around three to four months.

The grief of parents following a cot death is similar to that which follows the death of a neonate, but the suddenness and unexpectedness of the death and the inability of doctors to say why it happened, make the shock and bewilderment much more severe. There is also the fear, often unspoken, that other people may suspect them of having in some way brought about their child's death. The parents, though blameless, are tormented by guilt and constantly ask themselves if there was anything they did, or did not do, that caused the death. Similar feelings of culpability and grief are likely to affect people associated with the family such as relatives, health visitors and social workers. Friends will be upset and not know how to react. They may try to help by telling the parents not to feel guilty but a more useful approach is to say something along the lines of, 'I am sorry this happened to your baby. You did everything possible by caring for him/her so well. This was a tragedy that could not have been foreseen or prevented.'

The baby is usually found by the mother, who may be alone in the house at the time. Her immediate reaction is one of numbness, fear and disbelief. If she has experience in resuscitation techniques, she may attempt to revive her child but without success. She then has to call for help and tell people that her baby is dead. The police will visit the house to document the evidence and arrange for the baby to be removed for autopsy. If the parents are able to see their child again, the body will be disfigured by the pathologist's scalpel. The law requires them to register the death in person, and this will probably be in the same office where a few months earlier they had joyfully registered the birth. They may find that their personal tragedy has become headline news in the local paper, as the police liaise closely with the local press and keep it informed of all sudden deaths in the neighbourhood. The whole event can seem like a bizarre nightmare.[10]

The emotional and physical reactions of mothers caught up in such a tragedy are intense. They may still be lactating and their daily routine, which was centred around the baby, is destroyed. The parents are likely to get upset with each other at a time when they most need one another's support. Dark moods of depression may erupt into outbursts of anger. This is perfectly normal in their situation but it makes living together more stressful. They should be encouraged to retain some mementoes of their child and they may wish to turn the child's room into a shrine, but such a course is best avoided. They will feel a desperate need to talk to someone who has suffered in the same way and knows how they really feel. It will take them years to come to terms with the tragedy and they will never get over it completely even though they may appear to do so. The emotional turmoil that follows the death of a child leaves its mark: the grief will diminish but the tortured feelings remain deep within the psyche and are painfully re-experienced intermittently throughout life.

Only one of my patients, a nurse, had a child who died in this way. I can still remember the occasion, 30 years ago, when she telephoned to say that her baby was dead. I received the call during surgery hours and the news brought mixed feelings of despair and anxiety. She lived in an isolated farmhouse and was alone with the dead infant and his twin brother. She had tried to resuscitate the child without success, and when I arrived at the house she was obviously upset but not, if I remember clearly, distraught. Being a trained nurse she knew what to do in moments of crisis but in fact neither of us knew how to behave in such circumstances. The infant was dead and had been so for some hours. We both felt distressed and guilty, and there was no practical help or even consolation that I could give. My immediate task was to return to the patients I had left in the surgery, inform the police so that a post mortem and inquest could be arranged, and let her closest friends know of the disaster. These things I did. A few years later, she died quite suddenly from a coronary thrombosis. I was called out to the farmhouse when she collapsed. Her husband was full of anger.

Infanticide and Filicide

It has to be acknowledged that though few parents deliberately harm their children a small proportion of child deaths are due to this cause. A quarter of all victims of legally proved murder in England and Wales are under the age of 16, and 81 per cent of these are killed by their parents. Children in the first year of life are at greater risk of being the victims of proved homicide than any other age group.[13] In 1994, 37 child deaths in the UK were confirmed as caused by the child's carers; in a further 14 cases, the evidence was highly indicative of a death associated with child abuse. Emery has estimated that between 1:50 and 1:10 cot deaths are probably caused in some way by those responsible for the child. Babies are extremely vulnerable and it is vital for all agencies to try to reduce the risk to which they are exposed. These attempts are not always successful. In a 1994 review of suspicious child deaths Reder and Duncan report an instance in which the death of a first child was certified as SIDS, and this was followed by the deaths of two further children aged 19 months and 5 months despite close monitoring and professional intervention aimed at preventing a recurrence of the syndrome. The mother was convicted of their murders.[14]

Although the word infanticide is used loosely to refer to the killing of a baby, it also carries a specific legal meaning in the UK. In 1933, infanticide was defined by law as the death of a child under one year of age at the hand of its mother. The purpose of the Act was to ensure that the mother was not charged with murder and this protected her from the then automatic sanction of the court for homicide: death by hanging. A more general, though not widely used term, for the killing of a child by either parent is filicide.[13]

According to Emery and Waites[15] filicide is most likely to occur when an exhausted parent (usually the mother) suffocates the baby while trying to quieten his or her crying. These parents usually barely know what they are doing and do not want, or intend, to kill their child. Emery points out that after the child's death a considerable amount of effort is put into bereavement counselling, but very little work is done on the mental state of parents before their child's death. He asks, and it is a pertinent question, 'Is it pure chance that the period at which cot deaths are most common largely coincides with the periods when mothers are most likely to be depressed?'[13]

Emery, who died tragically whilst rescuing his dog from a burning house, believed profoundly in providing support for bereaved families and advice on the care of their next child. Much of the literature issued by the Foundation for the Study of Infant Deaths (FSID) was based on his work and he was closely involved with the 'care of the next infant' (CONI) programme which is funded by FSID. The purpose of CONI is to help parents who have suffered the sudden death of a child. It does this through a network of local coordinators who arrange for Health Visitors to call on families at risk. A report on its work with 4,182 families shows a highly significant improvement in the survival rate of children, the value of supporting families after a cot death, and the need for confidential, in-depth, non-judgemental enquiries into all unexpected child deaths.[16]

Disease and Famine

Worldwide, most childhood deaths are from infectious diseases. Each year a million children die from malaria alone. Many more die from bacterial and viral infections, such as diphtheria and poliomyelitis, which have been largely eliminated from First World countries. Infectious diarrhoea still kills countless infants who rapidly acquire, from dehydration, the appearance of malnourished and starving children – a picture we have become sadly familiar with on the television screen. The despair of the mothers is clearly etched in their faces, and theirs and the children's desperate needs apparent in their emaciated bodies.

In First World countries, few children who live beyond the age of 12 months die as a result of illness. This makes their deaths more poignant and the grief of the parents possibly harder to bear. A disproportionate number of those who die come from the least privileged groups in the community, a fact that is likely to increase both parental and class bitterness.

Childhood deaths in prosperous communities are either fairly sudden and unexpected, or the final outcome of a chronic disease, such as cystic fibrosis or leukaemia, with which the child has had to contend for many years. There will have been many admissions to hospital, with life-threatening crises interspersed with phases of relative wellbeing. Both the child and the family will have learnt to cope, with varying degrees of effectiveness, with the uncertainties associated with the illness and the physical and emotional strains it causes. The pattern of relapse and recovery may have become so accepted that when death finally supervenes it has ceased to be anticipated.

Although the parents will have cared for, and fought for, the child over many years, they are still likely to have quite irrational feelings of guilt when he or she dies, that in some way they should have done more for the child. They will not be helped by people suggesting that the child's death is for the best, as their suffering is now over. This may be an acceptable comment when an elderly person dies, but not for someone whose life appears unfulfilled. Nor does it help to be told that the death is part of God's plan for the child, when to the parent's eyes he could just as easily have arranged a cure.

Some parents lose children who have reached adult status. These deaths may be from cancer, AIDS, a heart attack or some sporadic infection such as meningitis or legionnaires' disease. All will be a grievous blow. There is something in a parent's psyche that says their children will survive them. No amount of 'coming to terms' with their child's death can ease the pain when that conviction turns out to be illusory.

Accidents, Murder and Suicide

Death in older children and young adults is usually due to 'unnatural causes', that is accidents, suicide or murder. The most common of these is the road traffic accident. The parents of such victims tend to be older than those who lose young children and, perhaps contrary to expectations, are likely to be less resilient and less able to adapt to the loss than younger parents. The sudden death of an adolescent or adult child is a devastating experience for parents and it remains a dominant preoccupation of their later life.[17] On the few occasions when I have visited parents immediately after the sudden death of an adolescent, their grief has been the most intense that I have ever witnessed.

Whatever the cause of death, the impact on the family is overwhelming. Their happiness is shattered by a knock on the door, or by the front door bell, or by noises indicative of a nearby road traffic accident. The sight of a uniformed police constable standing on the doorstep produces immediate feelings of apprehension, which are confirmed by the dreaded news and the resultant physical weakness, disbelief and inner numbness. The family does not know what to think, believe or do, and will at first tend to react automatically.

A member of the family will probably be asked to identify the body. This is a difficult assignment, though the parents may later choose to see their dead child and say farewell. In some instances, especially when the death occurred in a foreign country or when the deceased had been murdered, there may be a long delay before the body is returned to the parents for burial. Meanwhile they will be subjected to many other stresses. Friends will not know how to approach or support them. The media will have learnt of the death and may become intrusive. Certain legal procedures will have to be followed. The coroner will have to be informed and an autopsy and inquest arranged. Surgeons may request permission to remove organs from the brain-dead child so that they can be used for transplant operations. Some families find this idea abhorrent. Others obtain consolation in the fact that their dead child is able to provide the gift of life to other sufferers.

If murder was the cause of death, there is a criminal to be caught and punished. This will be followed by the prolonged stress and uncertainty of a murder trial, a process that may be extended by an appeal against the conviction or sentence. The entire procedure may last many months or years. The sense of relief that follows a successful conviction can be great. Then everything may fall to pieces. Irene Baldock gives a vivid description of her reactions after the sentencing of her son's murderer: 'Almost immediately I went to pieces. I literally could not swallow. The doctor could not find anything wrong. He said it was the effects of the trauma causing the symptoms and suggested counselling. I approached my vicar who immediately agreed to weekly sessions. I found them very beneficial and very gradually the "swallow" became easier.'[18]

There are always unanswered questions and strong feelings associated with these 'unnatural' deaths. 'I was so angry at the time' says the mother of a young man who killed himself. 'I kept saying to him: "Come back and tell me what went wrong".' These situations are also associated frequently with the 'if only' syndrome: 'If only he had not gone to the pub that night'; . . . 'if only we had not let him have a motorbike'; . . . 'if only I had seen her crawling towards the pool' . . . and all the other 'if onlys' with which distraught relatives torment themselves.

Support Services

Obstetric and paediatric units are usually well geared up to support the parents of children who were stillborn or who die from congenital disabilities or illnesses later in life. The same cannot be said about hospitals when the death is due to an accident or assault.

Some victims die immediately at the site of injury, others survive for a short time but die later in hospital or in the ambulance while in transit to the hospital. If the death occurs soon after the assault or accident, the family will have had no opportunity to prepare itself and the unexpectedness of the loss is likely to exacerbate their distress. The level of support and understanding that the relatives will receive at the hospital cannot be predicted, but one thing is certain: staff working in accident and emergency units usually feel inadequately trained to deal with death, grief and bereavement,[19] and find that they have neither the time nor the facilities to do so. One-third of hospital deaths occur within a few hours of the patient's admission, and many of these deaths occur in the accident and emergency department. Bereaved relatives are usually taken to a special room by a nurse whose sole task is to care for them, but in many hospitals the nurse is untrained and the room is also used for other purposes. When the relatives return home, they are rarely contacted again by the hospital.

Hospital managers are becoming increasingly aware of the need to provide better facilities and support for the relatives of accident victims, and some innovatory steps are being taken. For example, the Accident and Emergency Unit at the Hope Hospital in Salford[20] has been equipped with a specially furnished room for relatives, and a nurse has been appointed as counsellor to support relatives who are visiting severely ill or dying patients. Support is given in the critical period preceding death and it is continued by means of domiciliary visits during bereavement. The counsellor liaises closely with community services such as Cruse, The Compassionate Friends, the Samaritans and FSID. When not engaged in the primary task of supporting relatives, the nurse undertakes normal duties in the unit and provides training in bereavement support for doctors, nurses and administrative staff. Support for the nurse-counsellor is provided by a professional counsellor at regular monthly meetings.

The law courts are also developing provisions for the support of the families of victims. This is being done through the Victim Support Scheme, a national and mainly voluntary organization. After March 1996, each of the 72 Crown Courts in the UK will have a properly staffed Witness Support Service available to support witnesses and relatives through the stresses of a trial. The Crown Court in Maidstone, Kent, which pioneered this service now has its own offices, 30 volunteer workers and an organizer who is paid by and reports to the Home Office. It is expected that similar schemes will be developed for the magistrates' and coroners' courts.

The Other Children

The other children of the family will be hurting too. It is not their fault that their brother or sister has died, yet they are likely to feel guilty about it. They are suffering a double loss, the death of a sibling and the change that they perceive in the parents. These parents, in their yearning for the dead child, tend to overlook the presence and needs of the children they still have. Eventually, the surviving children may even feel that they are no longer loved because all the emotion is centred on the lost child.

The surviving children need their parents at more than the basic level, that is, more than just as providers of food and shelter. They need to feel physically close to them. They want their parents to talk to them, to be open and honest and to discuss their feelings with them, and to examine the questions that cannot be answered . . . like why did this happen to our Jane or John or Dick. They are also likely to be overwhelmed by the constant references to the dead child, as if he or she was the only person that really mattered.

Some parents may be aware at the time that they are rejecting or neglecting their remaining children, but just lack the physical and emotional strength to support them. Sometimes this realization comes later in life, and it can then cause parents intense feelings of guilt and anxiety as they come to the conclusion that they have let down their other children.

Contacting the Family

When a family loses a child they may be inundated by letters, telephone calls and personal approaches. This can be trying but it is far better than being ignored and avoided. The most helpful letters are those that recall the child in some personal way, and that help to enlarge the picture that the family already has of their loved one.

Speaking to members of a family that has lost a child is not easy. It requires an effort and a step into the unknown as one doesn't know what to say or how the other person will react. It is an emotional experience for all concerned and the emotions are likely to be inhibiting. But some recognition of the loss is required, even if it is only a quiet shake of the hand or a few words such as, 'I am so sorry, I just don't know what to say.' Shared tears and hugs are most helpful when given by those who feel free to do so.

Coping

Everyone copes with their loss as best they can and there is no right or wrong way of doing it. There is a place for tears and despondency, and at times a place for forgetting and laughter. No one gets over the death of a child, and pangs of yearning are still experienced 20 and 30 years later. Some people establish their own strategy for coping. One friend has found these two simple rules helpful:

1) I don't place myself in situations with which I cannot cope;
2) I have stopped asking questions that no one can answer.

Another useful aid is to undertake some charitable act in memory of the deceased. This is a long-established Jewish tradition and may take the form of raising money for a charity by organizing a concert, or establishing a new service like a local, or national, self-help group. Some people try to forget in a whirl of social activities, and this too can have its place.

Counselling has become an accepted part of the bereavement scene and people can benefit from it. Counsellors help mainly by providing a listening service and enabling people to tell their own story. Whilst some bereaved parents may be reluctant to unburden themselves to strangers, others have a need, which Freud designated 'compulsive repetition', to retell their stories at length to anyone who will listen.

Bereaved parents say that the only people who can really understand and empathize with them are those who have had similar experiences. They are likely to meet kindred souls through groups such as The Compassionate Friends and FSID. The Compassionate Friends is an international organization that was established in 1968 by a young hospital chaplain, Simon Stephens, and bereaved parents, Joe and Iris Lawley and Bill and Joan Henderson. By talking, comforting and crying with each other, the Lawleys and Hendersons discovered that bereaved parents can help one another as no one else can, and that parents need a friend who is always available, day and night. Simon Stephens transformed this insight into an international mutual support group, The Compassionate Friends, who are not counsellors, but simply bereaved parents who just befriend other bereaved parents. They listen to them, allow them to tell their story, let them cry, and say one very important thing: 'We are here as long as you need us, for as long as you want us.'

Some people find they are helped by church services, or by other meetings of a spiritual nature. Some find that they can no longer go to church, or to the church they previously attended. In the latter instance they may just change their place of worship.

People of different cultures have their own way of coping with bereavement. Iroquois Indians, when bereaved, go into a forest and select a tree, which they cut deeply several times with an axe. This tree then becomes their special place. They identify the cuts with their own grief, and will visit the tree whenever they feel the need to be quiet, or sad or when they particularly want to remember the loved one who has died. As time goes by, they see that the wounds in the tree heal and that the tree continues to grow and flower. They know that they have been changed and that, like the tree, though their lives will continue they will always carry the scars of their grief deep within.

Chapter 18
A Child's Response to Death

Give sorrow words; the grief that does not speak
Whispers the o'erfraught heart and bids it break.

Macbeth

Introduction

Children's understanding of death is determined by their age, intelligence, and life experiences. Children learn to accept the reality of death at an early age but they may still lack the conceptual understanding to appreciate its significance. Their understanding of the significance of death is acquired gradually. Thus most five-year-old children know that they will die, but only a third realize that death is irreversible and not a state, like sleep, from which they will reawaken.[1] At this age they accept most experiences at face value.

Except in highly intelligent or experienced children, the onset of deductive reasoning is fairly late.[2] This usually begins between the ages of six and 10. Children then often show an increased interest in death and its associated phenomena such as ghosts. They accept the irreversible nature of death and become aware of its social implications and its effect on survivors. They also have a good understanding of the outward appearance of a dead person.[1]

Explaining Death to a Child

Parents, doctors and nurses are not taught to talk to children about death and have to rely on their own experiences and common sense when doing so. This applies most particularly in crisis situations such as when a death is imminent within the family or has just occurred. Children's questions should be answered honestly and carefully but Goodall suggests that with the under-10s it is probably better, whilst telling the truth at all times, not to tell it all at once.[3]

When young children seek an explanation about death, a story based on a natural transformation may be helpful and appeal to their imagination. Well-known examples on which such a story can be based are the metamorphosis of caterpillars into butterflies, or of waterbugs into dragonflies.[4] A patient of mine explained her approaching death to her young children in terms of moving house. She felt that the children would understand this as they had lived in various houses and realized that the essential person remained the same even though their surroundings might change. Such explanations are preferable to just saying that grandma died in hospital or in her sleep. Whilst these are seemingly harmless explanations, they sometimes result in children becoming frightened of hospitals, or of going to bed, as they associate them with places where people die.

Older children need more detailed, age-appropriate explanations, which enable them to accept the reality and irreversibility of the death. Sometimes words are just not adequate, and the most eloquent statements may be made by the ritual of the funeral service. Even adults can find it difficult to accept the death of a loved person until they have witnessed the disposal of the body, and being present at the funeral and saying goodbye can be just as helpful for the child. It also helps to enhance their self-esteem and confirm their status as full members of the family.

Immediate Grief Reactions

When someone they love dies, children experience grief just as intensely as adults. They too will be numbed by the loss, feel anger and yearning, become internally disorganized, and eventually learn to readjust to the death with varying levels of effectiveness. At the same time they may be attempting to support the surviving parent and their siblings. They will probably be unable to express their grief in words, and though they may not appear to be much affected they will be grieving, often very deeply.

One immediate effect of bereavement in young children is that they may regress to an earlier stage of childhood with, for instance, a display of temper tantrums or a loss of toilet training. They may start to have nightmares or become fearful if separated from significant carers. They will express their grief in the ways they best can. This may be with an apparent lack of concern (denial of the death), by episodes of naughtiness (anger), wheedling (bargaining) or withdrawal (depression). Some children will feel guilty because they are still alive, or because they consider themselves to be responsible for the death. Others will have panic attacks, fearing further losses, or that they themselves might die. Those who vent their anger on the people and objects around them are likely to be labelled 'difficult children'.

Older children tend to be less overt in their grief. Most shed tears but not many express anger, and a few – the badly treated and sexually abused children – may experience a sense of relief at a parent's death. Some need to be alone whereas others seek support from family or friends. About a third have sleep problems and there is an increased incidence of physical complaints – mainly of weariness, headaches and stomach aches – and even of serious illnesses. Distinguishing the latter from more trivial problems is not always easy. One 13 year old, who was brought to me with tummy problems soon after the death of a much-loved grandfather, appeared to be suffering from a psychosomatic reaction to her grandfather's death. This diagnosis was supported by a normal physical examination, chest x-ray, urinalysis and blood tests. A few weeks later she was admitted to hospital with an epileptic fit and was found to have a rapidly extending intra-abdominal cancer, with brain secondaries. She died in hospital shortly afterwards, under my care. I still feel guilty about the death even though an earlier diagnosis would not have altered the course of the disease.

Children spend a considerable amount of energy in maintaining some form of relationship with the deceased. They think a lot about them, keep things that belonged to them and visit their graves. When children aged between six and 17 were asked in the Harvard child bereavement study what they believed happens after death, most said that their parent had gone to a specific place, and they mentioned Heaven. Fifty-seven per cent spoke to the deceased parent and 81 per cent felt that their parent was watching them. The deceased was definitely a real presence in most of the children's lives and seemed to retain the role they had adopted while they were still alive, such as a protector or disciplinarian. Some children found this association comforting but others felt uneasy in case the parent did not approve of what they were doing.[5]

Later Grief Reactions

Many children cope with bereavement satisfactorily, but the available evidence suggests that early bereavement greatly increases a child's susceptibility to depression, difficulties at school and delinquency.[6] In saying this one realizes that the results of the various surveys can be conflicting. For instance, in the Harvard study of children bereaved when aged 6 to 17 years old, Silverman and Worden found that most of the children were not functioning poorly either at four months or one year after the death.[7] In contrast, Pettle and Lansdowne[8], using a well-researched behaviour scale, found that two to three years after the death of a sibling a high percentage of children show sufficient difficulties to be labelled 'in need of psychiatric help'. Similarly, Elizur and Kaffman found that 40 per cent of Israeli kibbutz children who had lost a father in the Yom Kippur War of 1973 continued to show severe maladapative behaviour more than three years after the death.[9] They also found that other factors such as preceding marital discord were important in determining the likely outcome.

Among the kibbutz children, behaviour problems – including soiling, social isolation and learning difficulties – peaked in the second year after the father's death. Sixty-five per cent of all symptoms persisted at a moderate to severe level $3\frac{1}{2}$ years after the loss. Less than one-third of the children had adapted satisfactorily to the new situation throughout the $3\frac{1}{2}$ years of the study. The researchers also noted that the onset and duration of severe and persistent symptoms was variable and could not be predicted.

In their comparison of bereaved kibbutz and urban children, Kaffman and Elizur also noted that children living in a kibbutz did not fare better than those from an urban environment. This suggests that the social support available in a kibbutz and the perceived less central role of the parents that is a feature of such a community did not help the children when bereaved.[10]

Rutter[11] and Van Eerdewwegh[12] are among those who have found a high incidence of depression among adolescent boys whose fathers had died, and Cain et al.[13] reported that, in a group of disturbed $2\frac{1}{2}$–14 year olds who had lost a sibling, half had guilt reactions, accompanied by trembling and crying, for five or more years after the death.

There is general agreement among clinicians that the loss of a parent has an adverse effect on a child at school, both in terms of academic performance and social behaviour. Delinquency has also been found to correlate with parental bereavement, particularly in adolescents. Also, a number of studies have shown a link between childhood bereavement and attempted suicide in adult life.[14]

One needs to balance these adverse findings with more positive attitudes to bereavement. Death is part of the normal life cycle and bereavement is an aspect of life to which people are capable of adjusting. Many children respond with a resilience that is often overlooked in studies that are more concerned with the problems of bereavement than with the child's ability to cope and adjust to the new lifestyle that bereavement brings. An example of a child who appears to have coped well with bereavement is provided by Pope John Paul II. His mother died when he was eight and his elder brother a few years later. His country was invaded by Germany and Russia when he was aged 20 and his education was then interrupted. Despite these handicaps, something in his upbringing or character enabled him to deal successfully with all these stressful life events.

Supporting the Child

Children who have lost a parent or sibling are likely to find themselves isolated in an inner world that they cannot readily share with other people. They find it difficult to talk about these events but they need to do so. They do not know how to broach the subject and worry about upsetting other family members if they do so. But talking about the deceased is a critical part of a child's grief work and one that adults do not sufficiently appreciate.[7] Both the surviving adults and children need to realize that this talking about and remembering the deceased is an important means of resolving grief. It is a time when tears are appropriate and physical contact helpful, and these aids to inner healing need to be encouraged and not repressed. Within this context, talking includes repetition and it is better that questions should be repeated, even if no answers can be given, and that the same things should be said over and over again rather than that they should remain unspoken. There will of course be times for silence and these moments must be discerned and respected.

Not many people are experienced in the care and support of bereaved children, and we are not yet sure which methods work best for those in most need. Using experienced counsellors from Cruse, Black found a significant difference in outcome between bereaved children whose families had received counselling and a control group which had received no such support. Among the treated children, 20 per cent had behaviour problems sufficient to cause concern, whereas in the control group the figure was 41 per cent.[15] Two other factors affected the outcome: the mental state of the surviving parent one year after bereavement, and the extent to which the child cried following the death. When parents were depressed and functioning badly one year after being widowed, the children were more likely to be disturbed in their behaviour at home and school. Also, those children who cried the most were found at follow-up to have adjusted best to their new life pattern.

Some families obtain help from child guidance clinics. A more recent development is the establishment of children's bereavement groups.[16,17] These have a high ratio of staff to children and are producing innovative ideas. They welcome children from the ages of four to 16 but try to arrange the groups so that they contain children of similar ages. Games, music and play materials are used to help communication, and a sealed question box is available for children to ask questions that they cannot verbalize. Materials are provided that can be destroyed such as brown paper to tear, and cardboard boxes that can be battered, or balloons that can be popped. Other useful play materials include building blocks that can be built up and knocked down. They can also be used creatively as was shown by a four-year-old whose sister had died. He built coffins with the bricks and would then lie down inside them like a corpse. Toy nurse or doctor kits, or just paper, pencils and crayons are also useful. The latter enable young children to express their feelings in pictures, and these may provide a sympathetic adult with some understanding of the child's thoughts and his or her view of the situation.

The purpose of the bereavement group is to enable children to meet in a safe environment where they can explore and express their feelings and be reassured that the way they feel at this difficult time is perfectly right and normal. Members find that they can talk more openly about their experiences in the group than they could do at home or at school. They say that they cannot communicate at such a deep level with family members for fear of upsetting them, and greatly value the support and understanding of others in the group.[17] The effectiveness of this approach remains to be properly evaluated, but it does provide an opportunity for children to share experiences with others in a similar situation. The support children receive from one another also reduces their feelings of isolation.[16]

The Childhood Bereavement Project

A new development in the UK, launched in April 2000 with backing from the Princess Diana Fund, is the Childhood Bereavement Project. This has the specific aims of coordinating services for bereaved children, setting ethical and practice standards and providing a central access point for services throughout the UK. The intention is to ensure that all children who have experienced the death of a close relative will have prompt access to expert counselling and support services.[18]

At present, although facilities are available the distribution of these services is patchy and uncoordinated. Research on the effects of bereavement is scant and because of the haphazard manner in which services have been developed, they are often unpublicized and underfunded. One area that needs to be investigated is the different ways boys and girls deal with bereavement, and why so many boys who have suffered a bereavement are expelled from school, turn to crime and end up in prison. The lack of appropriate support for children is perhaps underlined by the large number who contact Childline – the telephone help line. Each year, it receives about 1,400 calls from children trying to cope with bereavement[19] – it would be interesting to know how many of the 1,400 are from girls.

Sex Differences

It is often assumed that boys and girls will react in a similar fashion to bereavement. This is not so and greater attention needs to be paid to the different ways in which children respond to grief. Understanding this is basic if we are to offer the optimum support to children at this crisis in their lives. For instance, girls are more likely to respond to 'talk therapy' and boys to 'activity therapy'. Dyregov says that the difference between the sexes becomes more pronounced as the children progress through school age and is particularly noticeable during adolescence. After a bereavement girls tend to cry more, have more difficulty concentrating and are jumpy and anxious. Boys are more likely to suppress unwanted thoughts and lack the ability, possessed by girls, to express their feelings in speech and writing. The boys tend to be more taciturn.

Boys also lack the environmental support available to girls. Almost all girls have a best friend in whom they can confide and who supports them. Less than 40 per cent of boys have established friendships of this calibre. Girls are also able to talk more easily about the death at home than the boys. Dyregov speculates on the reasons for these differences pointing out that girls play in pairs, that their play is centred on close human relationships and they build up a language for feelings. Boys' play focuses on group activities, sticking to the rules and the suppression of feelings.[20]

Whatever the explanation for the differences, one needs to be aware that they do exist and that at present the type of support given to bereaved children is tailored mainly for the needs of girls, being largely based on words and conversation. The inability to express themselves in non-aggressive modes may help to explain the large number of bereaved male adolescents who commit crimes and end up in prison.

Back to School

No national statistics exist on the numbers of children affected by bereavement, but it is estimated that 2 per cent are bereaved before the age of 18. In a secondary school of 800 pupils it is thought that about 24 children will have experienced a close death in the family. Most children return to school very soon after the funeral, some without having taken even a day off from school. It might be more helpful to encourage them to take more time to grieve. Their loss should be regarded as a psychological injury, which, if not properly dealt with, could produce long-term disabilities. School communities could help by recognizing the significance of the loss to the child, perhaps in assembly, class or in a particular way that meets the special needs of the child.

Whilst a child's grief may be overlooked at home because of the communal grief, it is likely to have an overt affect on their behaviour at school and will at least be noticed. Most bereaved children will have some difficulty in concentrating on their school work but only a minority will realize that it is affecting their performance. Teachers find that bereaved children look tired and worried and appear restless, but they rarely know how best to help or cope with the child. Common signs of stress include scratching, fiddling and frequent visits to the toilet. Some children may 'put on a brave face' or become the 'class clown' but more commonly they stop mixing with their peers, tend to do things alone and appear to be avoided by the other children. The death of a sibling tends to lower the self-esteem of surviving children and this effect appears to be related to the length of the illness. The more sudden the death the greater the loss of self-esteem.

Schools are not designed to be counselling centres but teachers are sympathetic to the needs of their pupils and wish to be helpful. If asked, most bereaved children say that they would like someone to sit with them in school and talk about their loss. It is a subject they find difficult to mention themselves and they want other people to introduce it into the conversation. Teachers and classmates often seem unable to do this, and as a consequence may give the appearance of not caring or not knowing how to care, when they are just being careful not to intrude into another person's grief. A few schools are dealing with this problem by including the topic of death into their social awareness courses. It is a subject pupils seem to find both interesting and important, and its presence in the curriculum may increase the awareness of all staff members of the need to support bereaved children, never mind how badly the latter may behave. Schools wishing to explore this possibility will find that they can borrow books dealing with bereaved children from the various national libraries maintained by The Compassionate Friends.

Working with Schools

Some charities, including Cruse Bereavement Care and Childline, have well-established programmes to help schools with the subjects of death and bereavement. The children's charity Winston's Wish works with 300 schools: its psychologist, Julie Stokes, says that about 70 per cent of the bereavements suffered by children are the result of sudden deaths involving heart attacks, accidents or suicides. These issues have to be handled sensitively by the teachers particularly as death means different things to different children depending on their religion and culture.[19]

Teachers receive more guidance now than formerly on how best to tackle death and bereavement but many still feel ill-equipped to do so in the school environment. But their ability to handle it is crucial. All schools have to deal with deaths and some have great tragedies to handle as at Dunblane in Scotland, Aberfan in Wales and Columbine High School in the USA. Mostly schools have to cope with bereavement at a more personal level and it is helpful for all concerned if clear guidelines have been formulated for these occasions. How the death is handled will depend on the circumstances. The death of a teacher or another student will have a greater impact on the school than that of a pupil's parent but the effectiveness of the care given will depend on how well prepared the staff are to deal with that situation.

I am told by a headmistress that church schools have a special advantage in dealing with deaths within the school community as the parish priest will provide support and lead special assemblies and that the Diocesan Director of Education has many times dropped everything else he was doing to support schools in these situations, and not only church schools. She also points out that much good practice is to be found in all types of schools although some young people have had bad experiences.[21]

The Death of a Parent

The death of a child's parent is always untimely. The parent may still be young or in early middle life and the death may be completely unexpected. Even if it is expected, it is still likely to come as a shock and may affect the way future crises are experienced and dealt with by the child. The structure of their life has been changed and a new one established that may be the mould for the pattern of the rest of their life. The main factor in determining their subsequent development is the way other people whom they love and respect react to the bereavement.

Most important for the child is the response of the surviving parent to their common grief, and the parent's ability to cope with the new situation. The child's primary need is to be cared for and respected. If this need is met, then his or her ability to cope with the immediate consequences of the present loss, and with any of life's future problems, will be much enhanced. Where roles are reversed and children are expected to provide support and care for the surviving parent, or younger siblings, then the outcome is likely to be less satisfactory even though the early acceptance of responsibility can be a maturing process.

It is not always easy for the surviving parent to make the right decisions. Andrew was four years old when his father died suddenly. They had had a particularly close relationship, possibly because Andrew was the youngest son in a largish family. His siblings seem to have coped with their loss quite well but Andrew became a tearaway, was drawn into drug taking during his teens and became a heroin addict with a history of attempted suicide. Since then, and with the aid of transactional analysis, he has managed to give up the drug habit and look to the future with confidence. Of his father's death he says, 'The 'phone went and something told us something was wrong. My Mum put on her coat and went out. When my Mum came back, she was very open. She sat us all around the kitchen table and said, "Your Dad won't come back, he has died." That completely finished me, but not the others. I ran away from the table, ran upstairs and barricaded myself in the bedroom. Ever since then I've been against everything. If I was told *no* it meant *yes*.' Later his mother remarried and he acquired a stepfather but their relationship was not a good one. 'The last thing I needed', he said, 'was to lose my Mum then. I needed my Mum.'

The Death of a Friend

One aspect of childhood bereavement that is often overlooked is the impact of the death of a close friend. Its importance became apparent to me only recently when I was encouraged to visit a local prison and talk to the young offenders. In an unpublished survey of 65 consecutive admissions to that institution, 38 were found to have suffered important bereavements. Twenty-three of these youths had lost a mate, by which they meant a close, male friend.

Most mates had died sudden and violent deaths, car accidents – often in stolen cars – being the single most common cause of death. Some had died through the injudicious use of drugs or inhalants, and seven had been murdered. One was electrocuted whilst crossing a railway line and another died whilst petrol-bombing a shop. They describe a subculture of violence in the UK that was not present 30 years ago and say that young children, who have not yet reached their teens, now commonly carry offensive weapons. They liken the situation in many English cities to that of Jamaica and New York, where some of them have lived.

The following accounts record some of their experiences. Alan lived in an apparently happy family of two parents and three younger siblings until his mother went off with another man, taking the younger children, but not Alan, with her. It was then that he started getting into trouble with some mates, just for the fun of it. One night they planned to steal some motor bikes and go joy-riding. Two of his mates, both aged 15, got killed when they crashed. 'That', Alan said, 'put me in a turmoil. I didn't care any more. I got into anything, and was doing house burglaries and stealing cars. I didn't care whether I lived or died. I got to the stage where every two days I did a house burglary and got £500, and I got to the stage where I couldn't live without being rich. I was always the one with the money.'

Martin's parents split up when he was two. He lived with his mother until he was 13 and then went into a foster home. At the age of 12, he was going to school by train with his best mate. When the train stopped at their station, his friend couldn't be bothered to walk over the bridge, so he jumped on the track to cross the line, tripped, fell against the live wire and was killed instantly. Martin witnessed this and the subsequent attempts to rescue and resuscitate his friend. He was then required to give evidence to the police. The immediate reaction of his friend's mother was to blame Martin for her son's death, though they were later able to re-establish a good relationship. He missed no school but was taunted by the other boys with remarks like, 'Where is your pal: he's fried isn't he'. He reacted by fighting with his taunters and was expelled from the school soon afterwards.

Two of Michael's friends were killed in a car accident. One, aged 16, died instantly, the other a few weeks later. He visited the 16 year old's family and found them devastated; the friend's mother and twin sister were too shocked to cry. The funeral took place two weeks later but before the interment the family had an Afro-Caribbean get together in a youth club. This reunion lasted nine days and nights; it was a quiet affair with a few drinks and soft music, so that the friends could share their feelings, express their sorrow and comfort the family. About 100 people were present on the last night of the reunion. Another of Michael's mates died at the age of 18. He was stabbed and died within 20 minutes. Michael says that 'these things are very common these days.'

Certain common factors emerged from the discussions I had with these teenagers. The first was their loyalty to the memory of their dead friend. Next, the punctilious way in which they showed their respect for the bereaved by visiting the family to offer support and express their own sadness. Equally striking was the regularity with which they visited their friends' graves taking flowers, and, in one instance, cannabis seeds to sow there.

It would be too simplistic to say that good bereavement counselling could have saved these young offenders from a life of crime, but it was not available and might have helped. What is certain is that they have expressed their anger against society in ways that are destructive to themselves and the community at large. Also, it is apparent that many of them continue to carry a heavy burden of unresolved grief.

The Dying Child

Death in the abstract, and coming to terms with the death of another person, even a loved one, are quite different from facing up to one's own death. Elderly people have many years in which to accept this reality but children can be confronted with it before they have started to develop their own potentials and explore the possibilities that life offers.

It is not surprising then that talking to children about their impending death is not easy. Moreover, few people have an opportunity to become skilful in such a difficult art. Some paediatricians say that it is more difficult to talk to a teenager about such a topic than to a young child, as the full implications are less well appreciated and not so feared by young children. In general, children's psychological adjustment to approaching death varies with age and with their experience whilst being ill. Even young ones may know that they are dying as increasing relapses tell their own story, and this awareness enables them to develop an insight and understanding ahead of their years. Their grief and fear of impending death will be similar to that of an adult. They would like to get better, they do not want to feel deserted, and they wish to avoid pain and distress.

Teenagers with chronic life-threatening illnesses will have learnt to live with varying degrees of discomfort and changes in their life-style. Most of them develop effective ways of coping with their disability, and some may even have had previous close encounters with death. Denial is common in this age group and many of them do not admit to any problems, even within weeks of their death.[22] This is partly due to their having learnt that a positive attitude helps them to survive. It is also their way of reducing the strain on their parents and siblings. Mood swings can be expected, with relapses being associated with episodes of anger and depression. Teenagers often find it difficult to communicate with adults and some will refuse to discuss their illness at home with their family. If this is so, the services of an outside counsellor may be helpful for both patients and their parents.

In recent years there has been an increasing interest in caring for the dying child at home and, given the choice, most teenagers choose to be at home for the last phase of their life. Martinson and Enos[23] say that the following conditions must be met before successful care at home is possible. First, cure-oriented treatment must have been discontinued, and the emphasis firmly placed on care and adding quality to life. Second, the child must want to be at home and the parents must want to have the child at home. Third, the family must be confident of their ability to care for the ill child. Fourth, a nurse must always be available and willing to be on call for 24 hours a day for professional consultation and support. Finally, the physician must agree with the plan and be willing to be on call as a consultant to the nurse and to the family.

The healthcare team must ensure that good symptom control is provided, and that the family knows that it can rely on them for regular visits and a prompt response to any emergency call. The strain on the family can be considerable as normal routines will be disrupted, wage earners may have to stay at home, and the family will be engaged in its preparatory grief work. Nevertheless, parents are usually glad to carry out their child's expressed wish to die at home. This powerful incentive is often reinforced by the parents' desire to retain a major role and not to become peripheral carers, as often happens in hospitals. There is one caveat however: Pettle and Lansdowne found that having the child die at home, and seeing the dead body, is of questionable benefit for the surviving children.[8]

Families differ greatly in their reaction to the death of a child, but three factors point to the likelihood of the family coping well. The first is the support of a 'significant other person' on whom they can rely. This may be a friend, a good neighbour or a professional carer. The second factor is an adherence to a philosophy of life that enables the illness and the death to be accepted by the family. Finally, they need to be sure that the child has received all the care and information he or she needed, and at a level consistent with the child's questions, age and stage of development.[8]

Chapter 19
Suicide

If thou and nature can so gently part,
The stroke of death is as a lover's pinch
Which hurts, and is desired.

Antony and Cleopatra

Introduction

Few people pass through life without at some time wishing they were dead. Most people are able to handle this intrusive thought, but others make a deliberate attempt to kill themselves, to commit suicide. In this, man is probably unique among all living creatures. There are reports of animals pining with grief after they have lost an important figure in their lives, such as a mate or their human owner, but in none of these instances do the animals deliberately destroy themselves. Why, then, do men and women do so? Various explanations have been put forward.

In medieval Europe, suicide was considered to be the result of demonic possession, and those who attempted it were seen as people who had made a pact with the Devil. Consequently, they were considered to merit severe punishment by both the Church and State. The origins of this belief can be traced to the Council of Arles in 452 AD and the Council of Nimes in 1184 AD. The first of these two Councils decided that suicides should be denied a Christian burial, and the Council of Nimes made suicide a culpable act in canon law. It is not clear when suicide was first declared a crime in England, but it had certainly become equated with murder as a criminal offence by the sixteenth century and remained a crime until Parliament passed the Suicide Act of 1961.

The first European country to legalize suicide was Prussia in 1751, followed by France in 1790; India, which inherited many

English laws, did so only in 1994. Before it was decriminalized, over 500 people were convicted each year of attempted suicide by English courts. Most were fined or acquitted but, each year, about 30 were sentenced to imprisonment. Amongst the latter group were people who had attempted suicide whilst already serving a prison sentence. Aiding, abetting or counselling suicide remains an offence in English law, and similar legislation exists in other countries including the USA. The existence, and possible rescinding, of this legislation has become of increasing importance in the debate surrounding euthanasia.

Underlying Causes

Whatever the apparent motive may be, an act of suicide is now considered to be due to a number of underlying causes. Psychoanalysts see it primarily as an act of aggression directed at oneself when hostile feelings towards other people cannot be dealt with adequately in any other way. Psychiatrists are likely to look for an underlying depressive illness, whereas sociologists are more likely to interpret an act of suicide as a person's response to social deprivation and the 'hopelessness' of their situation. A genetic predisposition to suicide has also been suggested, a possibility that is supported by the observation that double suicides are more common among monozygotic than dizygotic twins.[1] The pioneer in research on suicide was the French sociologist Durkheim, who published a book in 1897, *Le Suicide,* which pointed out the importance of social factors in suicide.[2] Durkheim classified suicides into three groups which he called *altruistic, anomic* and *egoistic.* Individuals rarely fit exactly into one of these three groups, but the classification remains useful even though it is now accepted that people who commit suicide do so for a multiplicity of reasons.

Altruistic suicide

People who commit suicide for altruistic reasons do so for the good of society. They often inspire respect and admiration and may later be honoured as martyrs. An altruistic suicidal act is sometimes carried out in public in order to draw attention to a particular social evil. Such a memorable instance occurred in 1963 when a Buddhist monk poured gasoline over his body and immolated himself in front of television cameras as a protest against the Vietnam war. This was the first suicide to be witnessed by millions of people worldwide. It helped to focus public attention more closely on the heartless destruction that was such a feature of that conflict, and possibly hastened the end of the war. Mahatma Gandhi made a similar gesture in 1947 during the partition of India, when many Hindus and Muslims were massacred by the opposing faction. Gandhi was so distressed by the violence and bloodshed that he commenced a fast to the death, a fast that he maintained until he was convinced that peace had been restored to the Indian subcontinent.

Some people might place suicide bombers in this category. These are usually political or religious extremists, whose deaths are regarded by their supporters as altruistic and by their opponents as acts of terrorism. Sometimes they target leading statesmen. Rajiv Gandhi, the former Indian Prime Minister, was assassinated in this way in 1991. More often, the attack is less discriminate. During the campaign to disrupt the peace talks between Israel and the Palestinians in 1996, Hamas and Islamic Jihad instigated a series of suicide bombings which claimed 40 lives and injured many other people. Later, in Pakistan on 19 November 1996, 15 people died in a suicide car bomb attack on the Egyptian Embassy in Islamabad. Militant Islamic factions opposed to the Egyptian government claimed responsibility.

The motivation for such attacks is probably a mixture of hatred anger, death wish and a firm belief in the rightness of the cause. Most suicide bombers are probably young men but women also volunteer to die in this way. A young woman was probably the first suicide bomber to die in the year 2000. It happened in Colombo, near the office of the Sri Lankan Prime Minister where the woman was being questioned by security guards. When she detonated the explosives strapped to her body 12 people were killed and 24 wounded. Tamil Tiger separatists are believed to have been responsible for this outrage.[3]

Anomic suicide

Durkheim named the second type of suicide, anomic. This term is derived from the Greek word *anomie*, meaning lawless, which implies the absence of normal social or ethical standards in an individual or a group of people. Durkheim widened the definition so that it included breakdowns in the social order, as he considered that both factors could lead to an increased incidence of suicide. That changes in social structures can increase suicide rates has been demonstrated in many parts of the world. In the island nations of the South Pacific,

for example, the transition from a traditional to a technological society is causing many socio-economic problems – in the cash economy,
the nuclear family, and the limited opportunities for upward mobility
– and this is reflected in a particularly high increase in suicides, especially among the young.[4]

Prison is another social disaster area, both in the antisocial stance
taken by the inmates and the underlying prevalence of drugs and
violence. That there is a high incidence of suicide in prisons is perhaps
not surprising, but it is odd that there are so many successful attempts
when prisoners have limited access to the means of self-destruction –
most do so by hanging themselves. The situation is not improving and
the suicide rate amongst prisoners in the UK is now higher than in
1880.[5] It is the most common cause of death in prisons, and one-third
of these deaths occur in the first few weeks of custody with those on
remand being at most risk. Long-term prisoners, who presumably
have adapted to the prison environment, rarely kill themselves.

Suicidal attempts by young prisoners are usually preceded by irri-
tations that in other situations may appear trivial. Visitors failing to
arrive, refusal of parole, court decisions, transfers, or any undesirable
change can be the trigger for a vulnerable inmate. Many are socially
disadvantaged young people who had mental health and drug problems before they were imprisoned. The sense of helplessness and
despair that imprisonment can produce, and the restrictions it places
on any show of hostility to those in charge, serve to increase the likelihood that susceptible individuals will direct their aggressive feelings
inwardly and try to commit suicide.

Egoistic suicide

An egoist is someone who is self-centred and selfish. Egoistic suicides
may be seen, therefore, as the acts of people who are concerned only
with their own problems. However, Durkheim included in this category those suicides that occur in people who are alienated from society
and who are not integrated into a collective unit such as a family,
neighbourhood or religious group. It is the suicide of the socially
isolated person and this isolation is often due to circumstances
outside the control of the individual. Among these uncontrollable
factors are bereavement, mental and physical illnesses, ageing with
its loss of supportive networks, and, in the case of refugees, forced
emigration. The opposite effect can be seen when people assume
responsibility for another person. Motherhood, for example, seems
to reduce the likelihood of suicide in women.

Some people can feel isolated and lacking in personal support even when they are working in what appears to be a caring environment. This may have been the experience of a professor of psychiatry who telephoned me one evening as he wanted to discuss a patient who was consulting both of us. This was our first and only contact, but whilst talking to him I received the impression that he was probably quite depressed. The situation did not permit me to comment on his mood, or enquire as to how he felt, but I wished later that I had done so. Early the next morning, our mutual patient informed me that the professor had committed suicide that night. His depressed mood was apparent to me on the telephone, so some of his colleagues must have been aware of it also and yet probably felt unable to offer any help.

Other Reasons for Suicide

Durkheim's classification of suicide is both useful and outdated. Fairbairn[6] offers a more detailed classification, which is also based on the reasons people have for killing themselves. He suggests that the most common reason is the 'no hope' suicide, which occurs when people decide that they would be better off dead than living the lives they do. Most of the suicides in prisons, and among the South Pacific islanders, would probably come into this category.

There is the 'dutiful suicide', of which the best known example is *suttee* – the self-immolation of Hindu widows, and the 'political or ideological' suicide that we have already met as Durkheim's 'altruistic' suicide. Fairbairn also speaks of 'revenge' suicide, in which the intention is to hurt other people. Then there is the 'other-driven' suicide, as exemplified by Field Marshal Rommel when he shot himself on Hitler's orders in order to protect his family from being interned in a concentration camp. Suicide pacts and mass suicides are other distinct types of suicide that will be considered in detail later.

Incidence

Suicide is not a medical diagnosis. It is a verdict reached by a court of law after that court has made enquiries into a death that doctors could not certify as being due to natural causes. The rules governing these enquiries vary between countries, Scotland – which has its own legal system – and England have different approaches, both methods being widely used in other countries. In Scotland, the procurator fiscal conducts a private enquiry and delivers a verdict of suicide when he or she considers this to be the most reasonable explanation. This system produces more verdicts of suicide for comparable situations than the one across the border in England. There the enquiry is conducted in public by a coroner, and they can only give a verdict of 'death by suicide' if it is beyond reasonable doubt that the individual has taken his or her life. If any doubt exists an 'open' verdict has to be given, a retrospective survey of 242 deaths on the London underground found that all were self-inflicted, but for only 143 were verdicts of suicide brought in by coroners' inquests.[7]

The reliability of official figures, as an index of the true comparative suicide rates between countries, is often questioned as they are dependent upon such variable factors as the legal rules employed at the enquiry, the certainty of diagnosis, effective record keeping and cultural attitudes. However, differences in national suicide rates remain fairly constant, persisting even when people emigrate to another country, so valid comparisons can probably be made. The age standardized suicide rate per 100,000 population of most countries is published by the World Health Organization.[8] These are the official statistics transmitted to the WHO by the competent authorities in the countries concerned, but comparative data are not provided by all countries. Those failing to do so include China, India and most African states.

Countries with the highest suicide rates are Lithuania (45.6), The Russian Federation (41.5) and Estonia (40.0). The lowest rates are provided by Iran (0.01) and Mexico (3.2). Corresponding figures for some other countries are Columbia (3.2), Israel (7.7), USA (12.1), Australia (12.8), Canada (13.3) and Singapore (13.4). In general the incidence of suicide appears to be relatively low in Roman Catholic and Muslim countries. Some figures for European countries are Greece (3.5), Ireland (9.1), Sweden (15.0), France (20.1), Austria (22.2) and Hungary (33.0). Variations may also occur within countries. In the UK, the highest incidence is in Scotland (12.1), then Northern Ireland (7.4) with the lowest being in England and Wales (6.9), where suicide accounts for just under 1.0 per cent of all deaths. According to Samson and his colleagues, the highest rate of suicide anywhere in the world is among the Innu (North American Indians) in Canada, and in particular the Innu living in Davis Inlet on the coast of Labrador. They estimate the suicide rate in this group at 178 per 100,000 people.[9] However, the validity of this estimate is questionable as it is based on very small numbers: the population of Labrador is only about 30,375 people, the Innu is a minority group there, and the population of Davis Inlet about 500 people.

Although the true incidence of suicide may be difficult to ascertain, certain patterns are readily discernible. Suicides are four times more common in men than women, and the incidence is higher in older than in younger people. They occur most frequently on Mondays and Tuesdays, and in the Spring and early Summer. In the British Isles, the incidence begins to increase in February, reaches its peak in May or June and gradually declines in July. No acceptable explanation has been given for this seasonal variation; and no clear explanation can be given for the decline in suicide rates that occur in war time and during periods of civil unrest. Various theories have been put forward by psychiatrists and sociologists. The former suggest that during war time people can legitimately direct their aggressive tendencies outwards at a discernible enemy rather than inwards at themselves. Sociologists suggest that the increased social cohesion occurring in war time reduces people's sense of social isolation and thereby the risk that they will kill themselves.

The methods used for committing suicide depend to a certain extent on the sex of the person involved, the country in which they live and the means available. Men tend to use the more violent methods such as hanging, firearms and car exhaust fumes. Women are more likely to take an overdose of drugs if these are available. In the USA firearms account for 61 per cent of all suicides, and in rural Australia three-quarters of all male suicides are carried out by this method. Access to guns is strictly limited in Japan, so few people shoot themselves. There, hanging is the method most frequently used and ill health is the most common motive. The methods used can change quite dramatically over a short period of time. In England and Wales between 1990 and 1997, there was an increase in male suicide by hanging and strangulation but poisoning by gases and vapours, including car exhaust fumes, fell by 60 per cent in both sexes. The fitting of catalytic converters to petrol powered cars probably accounted for some of this decline.[10] Also between 1990 and 1997 the previously rising rate of suicide in men reversed, and the suicide rate decreased in both sexes for all age groups. Possible explanations for the fall include a decline in psychosocial stress following an upturn in the national economy and improved employment prospects.[11]

Sex and Age

Women are less likely to kill themselves than men. This pattern is constant worldwide though variations in the male:female suicide rate do occur between countries.[8] In general, men are four times more likely to kill themselves than women, with the highest ratio of male:female suicides occurring in Mexico (5.5:1) and the lowest in Hong Kong (1.5:1). The relatively high incidence of female suicides in Hong Kong is reflected in the figures for Singapore (1.6:1), which suggests the likelihood that an increased risk of suicide exists among women of Chinese lineage. Unfortunately, comparative figures are not available for China itself. The need to care for their young children appears to be an important deterrent for women and this is reflected in the higher suicide rate that is found among married women who are childless compared with those who have children. The absence of a role in society and of someone to care for may be an important factor in the high incidence of suicide among elderly people.

There is an increasing tendency in many countries for young people to kill themselves, especially young men. The risk among among men struggling with their sexual orientation is particularly high.[12] During the past 30 years the suicide rate for people under the age of 25 has more than doubled in several Western countries. Suicide is the leading cause of death among young adults in France, and it is responsible for more deaths in Australia than road traffic accidents. Different trends have been recorded in a number of countries for men and women. For instance, between 1980 and 1990 suicide rates in England and Wales rose by almost one third for men aged 15–44 but fell by nearly a half among women of the same age group.

It is impossible to establish with any certainty the reasons for this divergence, as all the adverse social factors that might explain the increase in male suicides apply also to women. They have been exposed to the same level of family breakdown in childhood, the same likelihood of drug and alcohol misuse and the same increase in divorce rate that has been characteristic of their age group. The association between unemployment and suicide is well known and young men are certainly having more difficulty finding jobs than women. One possible explanation is that provided by the theory that links suicide with poor social integration. In recent decades, women appear to have become more successfully integrated within society and better supported by those around them, whilst the reverse seems to be true for young men.

Suicide is uncommon among children but it does occur. Exact figures are not available but bullying at school and examination pressure have been identified as the main reasons why Japanese children commit suicide. These may also be important trigger events for Western children who die in this way.

Social and Health Factors

A national survey was undertaken in Sweden to determine the personality and behaviour predictors of suicide in young men.[13] The survey was based on profiles obtained from 50,465 male conscripts, of whom 247 later killed themselves. The most frequently recorded predictors were poor emotional control, and evidence of early deviant behaviour such as running away from home and being involved with the police or child welfare organizations. Drug and alcohol abuse, a lack of friends and belonging to a single parent family were also often noted in the history of those who later committed suicide.

Social isolation and the death of a wife increase the risk of suicide. In some countries – Australia, Brazil and France for instance – the suicide rate is consistently higher in rural areas than in the towns. Veterinary surgeons and farmers are among the people who are most likely to take their own lives. Doctors, dentists and pharmacists also have high suicide rates. The association between suicide rate and social status is variable. In some countries there is no difference in the rate between classes, but elsewhere, as in the UK, suicide is most common in the highest and lowest socio-economic groups.

A strong association between unemployment and suicide has been described in various studies using different methods of assessment.[14] There is always concern, however, that the relationship could be confounded by other variables such as psychiatric disorder, and alcohol or drug abuse. In their study of 'suicide, deprivation and unemployment', Lewis and Sloggett allowed for these variables – as well as age, social class, access to a car, house tenure, educational level and permanent illness, and the preciseness of their methodology makes their survey of particular interest.[15] Their main finding is that the association between suicide and unemployment is more important than with any other socioeconomic factor. Unemployment doubles the suicide rate, and when this is taken into account there is little or no association between suicide and measures of socio-economic status such as social class and house ownership.

There is a close association between suicide and mental illness. The level of correlation probably varies between countries, but at least 90 per cent of the people who commit suicide in the UK are considered to have a psychiatric illness at the time of their deaths.[16] Suicide is the major cause of death among psychiatric patients. In most cases the patient has a depressive illness, but there is an increased risk for people with epilepsy and the suicide rate in alcoholics is 20 times greater than in the general population. Suicide is rare in the mentally subnormal and in people suffering from organic brain disease, such as brain tumours.

People with schizophrenia are particularly likely to kill themselves. Simon, a young man who had suffered from this condition for 12 years, eventually died in this way. Although there had been remissions, his condition tended to deteriorate and sometimes his behaviour was so troublesome and bizarre that the psychiatrists would have liked to have seen him admitted to prison. He received statutory social aid payments and the local authority had provided him with a flat in a tower block where he was sometimes happy and at other times suicidal. There were occasions when his mother felt almost overwhelmed by his demands and behaviour. He believed that he could fly and eventually jumped out of the window of his flat and was dead by the time passers-by reached his body. The coroner recorded a verdict of suicide. His mother, who cherishes his memory, sees the act as evidence of the strength of his conviction that he could fly.

Another possible reason for such aggressive self-destruction is suggested by Swedish researchers, who investigated whether there was a link between such suicides and traumatic birth experiences.[17] Using the birth records of 242 adults who had committed suicide by violent means, and comparing these with siblings who had been born in the same hospitals, they concluded that minimizing pain and discomfort to the infant during birth may reduce the risk of a subsequent suicide. Their findings complemented those of a study in the USA which found that adolescents who have committed suicide are more likely than controls to have suffered perinatal complications[18].

However their interpretation of the findings is controversial. They not only suggest that the pain experienced by babies during a complicated delivery is linked causally to violent suicide later in life but that the act of suicide unconsciously recreates the traumatic sensation of their birth. They believe the causal mechanism to be imprinting on the subconscious mind and point to the high violent suicide rate in males as supportive evidence, because testosterone is known to enhance imprinting in animal studies. However, other researchers are likely to suggest that any link between obstetric care and violent suicide is more likely to occur through mental illness, because considerable evidence exists that obstetric complications are associated with the incidence of schizophrenia.[19]

Suicide Pacts

Most suicides are solitary and private affairs but occasionally two people decide they want to die together. Such incidents are rare but they often attract extensive media attention, notably when the novelist/journalist, Arthur Koestler and his wife died in 1983. Koestler, who was a frail old man with leukaemia and Parkinson's disease had long advocated euthanasia – these factors made his suicide understandable. But his wife was a vigorous, much younger woman, and it was her death that make their joint suicide so intriguing.

Brown and Barraclough have published a useful report on suicide pacts.[20] They found that the average age of people who commit suicide together is higher than that of people who commit suicide alone. The ratio of men to women involved in such pacts is 1:1, a much higher proportion of women than in solitary suicide. Almost half are in social class 1 or 2, and 80 per cent in social classes 1, 2 and 3. In contrast to the solitary suicide where only half are married and a quarter live alone, suicide pacts are made by cohabiting couples, usually spouses, though they may involve pairs of siblings, lovers or friends.

In England and Wales, a seasonal excess similar to that for solitary suicide occurs in the spring. Clustering, which might suggest imitation of pacts reported in the media, tends to be absent. Most of the participants in such pacts are childless but some do leave dependent children. At the time, these are usually living with a surviving parent who had been divorced or separated from the parent who has committed suicide.

Suicide notes, a measure of premeditation, are left by over 80 per cent of couples, and are often signed by both partners. Painless, identical methods of self-destruction are usually chosen; again suggesting that the deaths are premeditated and agreed by both partners. A higher than expected proportion of such deaths are among people working in professions related to medicine, and many of these deaths are drug induced. The relationship between the couple tends to be exceptionally close and devoted, as is shown by the relatively high proportion (24 per cent) who are remembered by witnesses as talking of 'dying together' and 'not bearing to be parted'.

People who die in a suicide pact are more likely to be older, married, female and of a higher social class than those who commit suicide alone. With the increasing interest in euthanasia, one might expect the number of such deaths to be on the increase, but the opposite seems to be the case, at least in the UK, where the rate has declined by 27 per cent over the past 35 years.[20]

Mass Suicide

Suicide pacts involving many people are often referred to as multiple or mass suicides. The so-called Jonestown massacre is a well-known example of this type of pact. This occurred in Guyana in 1978, when hundreds of the followers (913 died) of the Reverend Jim Jones killed themselves and their children, mainly by the ingestion of cyanide. Perhaps a feature of this type of suicide is that many people, who do not wish to die, perish in the slaughter.

At the end of the twentieth-century there was evidence of a close association between multiple suicides and the activities of 'doomsday cults'. These cults, founded by charismatic leaders, had an apocalyptic expectation of life, foreseeing the imminent destruction of the world and seeking to ensure their own spiritual salvation by communal self-immolation. Three separate groups perished in this way between 1993 and 1997. David Koresh and 73 other members of the Branch Davidian sect, including children, died in a fire ball at Waco, Texas in 1993. In the following year, many members of the Order of the Solar Temple died at two separate sites in Quebec and Switzerland where it is believed that some committed suicide and others were murdered. In 1997, members of the Heaven's Gate movement committed mass suicide with the intention of riding on the comet Hale-Bopp to Heaven's Gate where they expected to live in peace whilst the rest of humanity perished. Are these incidents, one wonders, just a fin de siécle phenomenon or do they represent a more enduring trend?

Preventing Suicides

The early diagnosis and treatment of depressive illnesses is often considered to be the best way of preventing suicides. This aspect of care is important, but other means must be used to prevent these unnecessary deaths. If society wishes to reduce the incidence of suicide it has to address the problems of social isolation, deprivation and crises of despair. A particularly high proportion of suicides occur in those who have become isolated within society, the group referred to by Durkheim as egoistic. They include people who can be quite affluent and successful but if they have no friends and little social support they may still be at risk.

Welfare services provide a safety net for the most needy, but the only organization that specifically seeks to help the suicidal in the UK is the Samaritans. This is a voluntary organization that was founded by an English clergyman, Chad Varah, in 1953. He did so by establishing a telephone help-line service for those contemplating suicide, an idea that has been copied in many other countries. France now has SOS Amities, and Recherche et Recontres, which was established in 1958. Befrienders International undertakes similar work in the USA and there are over 600 suicide 'crisis centers' in North America. Japan introduced its telephone 'help-line' in 1971, and many Chinese cities now have suicide prevention centres. All these organizations are responding to an urgent social problem but, despite their commitment, it is difficult to assess the impact they make on suicide rates. An evaluation of the effectiveness of such organizations, based on reports published between 1964–1987, indicates that at best they may reduce it by about 1 per cent.[21] Other studies are more encouraging,[10] and Brown and Barraclough reported a drop in the suicide rate in England and Wales by 35 per cent since the 1950s – from 148 to 96 per million people each year.[20] Some of the credit must go to the Samaritans.

The relatively low suicide rate in women may indicate ways of reducing its frequency in men. Women, during pregnancy and the first year after childbirth, have a high psychiatric morbidity and some are so depressed that they wish they were dead. In spite of this, the suicide rate is small as the mothers feel that they have to stay alive for the sake of their children.[16] This overwhelming concern of a mother for her children points to one way in which society could help potential suicides particularly among the older population. Everyone needs a role in society but there are few worthwhile ones for older people once the family has left home and they have retired from work. These people need to be encouraged to be more active within their communities and more effort should be made to utilize their experience and understanding of life. Traditional societies have always given an important place to the 'elders', but developed countries place more emphasis on nurturing youth and advancing young adults to leadership roles. Establishing a proper balance between the needs of these two groups is not easy, but it may be that the scales have tilted too far against the aged.

Suicide is more common amongst recently bereaved people. This was first noted by Durkheim but has been confirmed by recent statistics. The risk is highest among widowers – especially among young widowers, but parents, sons and widows are also at increased risk.[22] Voluntary organizations concerned with helping the bereaved, such as Cruse and The Compassionate Friends, have much to offer these people if they can establish contact with them. Hospitals and hospices are particularly well situated to support the families of dying patients both with their anticipatory grief and later during bereavement. Many have established bereavement services for this specific purpose. Those bereaved as the result of an accident, or an act of violence, may expect some support from the Victim Support Services which have been established in the higher courts of law. The extension of this scheme to the coroners' courts might also reduce deaths from suicide in the recently bereaved.

Other approaches are being tried. It has been estimated, for instance, that 6,700 lives have been saved in the UK following the detoxification of domestic gas in the 1960s. Similarly, there was a remarkable reduction in suicide from barbiturate poisoning following changes in the prescribing patterns of family doctors. A marked reduction in deaths from car exhaust fumes is a welcome outcome of the introduction of catalytic converters to petrol driven vehicles. The usefulness of these findings has been questioned on the assumption that potential suicides would merely use an alternative method of killing themselves; but restricting access to an easy means of self-destruction does exploit the ambivalence felt by many of those who feel they want to die.

It is probable that some people who commit suicide would not do so if highly lethal methods were less easily available. This is one reason why pressure groups try to restrict the possession of firearms in countries where they are too readily available. Attention could also be usefully directed at introducing safety measures on underground railway systems and other suicide 'hotspots' such as the Golden Gate bridge in San Francisco, where over 1,000 people had jumped to their deaths before anti-suicide patrols were established in 1996. Drug-mediated suicides might be reduced by adding methionine to paracetamol, thereby limiting its toxicity in overdose, and it should be possible to redesign plastic bags, so that they do not so easily meet the purpose of the potentially suicidal.[21]

Most people who attempt suicide, whatever its outcome, give a prior warning of their intentions but only 16 per cent leave a suicide note. Such warnings, even if they are made in an offhand way, should be taken seriously as they are cries for help that need an instant response. Suicide is not usually attempted in isolated places but in settings where intervention by other people is possible, probable or even inevitable. It is as if the intended suicide were playing Russian roulette, willing to forfeit their life but also allowing chance the opportunity to intervene. For this reason a suicidal act is sometimes described as being 'Janus faced'. It is not only directed towards death and destruction but also towards human contact and life.[23] Apart from *seppuku*, carefully planned suicides are as rare as carefully planned murders; both tend to be impulsive acts.

Suicide in Eastern Countries

There are wide cultural differences in the incidence of suicide, the importance people attach to it, and the methods predominantly used to bring it about. A once notable feature of high caste Hindu funerals was the practice of *suttee,* when a widow mounted her husband's funeral pyre, cradled his head in her lap whilst the pyre was lit, and so joined him in death. The practice was outlawed in 1829 by Lord William Bentinck, Governor-General of India, and the Indian penal code has continued to forbid it. Despite this prohibition, *suttee* continues to be practised sporadically and about 20 cases have been reported since India became a Federal Republic in 1950. The spiritual inducements to commit *suttee* are strong, and were once considerably reinforced by the social pressures that were exerted on widows to follow this ancient custom. Hindus believe that when a widow dies in this way, she wipes out both her own and her husband's evil *karma,* thus releasing them from further physical incarnations and leaving them free to enjoy prolonged bliss in heavenly realms. Although *suttee* is now generally condemned and has almost disappeared from Indian life, a few Hindu extremists still support the practice.

There has always been a high incidence of suicide in China, and late nineteenth-century sources estimated that between 500,000 and 800,000 Chinese committed suicide each year. A favourite method of doing so, especially among Chinese women, was *tau-jeng* which literally means committing suicide by jumping into a well.[24] This method may have been chosen for the sake of simplicity – wells were readily available – but there may also have been important psychological reasons. In common with most suicidal attempts, *tau-jeng* was not carried out in an isolated place but in one where it was possible that the deed might be detected and the person rescued. It also polluted the well, a socially deplorable action that would have annoyed the community and increased the sense of guilt and grief of the surviving relatives.

Tau-jeng is not practised much nowadays – those determined to kill themselves are more likely to jump in front of trains or from high-rise flats – but the incidence of suicide in China remains high and is increasing. Many cities have opened suicide prevention centres to deal with this serious problem, which ranks second only to natural causes as the cause of death in China. In contrast to Western countries, the suicide rate among young Chinese women is reported to be particularly high. One can only conjecture why this should be so, but a possible explanation is that Chinese women may feel particularly stressed by the 'one child family' policy and all that this entails – for example, the necessity of subsequent abortions and sometimes the relative neglect of female infants.

Japan is the country most closely associated with the practice of suicide in Western eyes. The suicidal bravery of Japanese combatants is well known and the term *hara-kiri* is widely equated with the act of ritual suicide. But the Japanese word for ritual suicide is not *hara-kiri* but *seppuku*. The former term became familiar in Western countries in 1868 when 13 French sailors were injured in a brawl with Japanese *samurai*. The French government demanded that 13 *samurai* should be punished for the offence, whereupon 13 volunteers met a French delegation and one by one calmly began to cut open their abdomens (*hara-kiri*). By the time the third man began doing so, the French delegation was so distressed that they left the scene and the ceremony was stopped.

Seppuku has a special place in the culture and ethos of Japan. It has its own distinctive terminology and ritual, and is seen as a heroic and altruistic act in which the individual sacrifices his life for the good and honour of the community. It is a mark of courage and an honour reserved for the *samurai*, the aristocratic warriors of Japan. Lesser citizens could be executed for offences against the state or their hereditary lord but, if guilty of similar acts, *samurai* were allowed the privilege of performing *seppuku*. In these circumstances ritual suicide was known as *tsumbera*; it was removed from the list of death penalties in 1874. *Seppuku* is a particularly unpleasant way to die. It involves cutting the abdomen – transversely, horizontally or in both directions – sufficiently deeply to sever the intestines. Death is not instantaneous but prolonged over some hours. It was sometimes permissible to undertake *seppuku* with the aid of a second. He would be a person of equal rank, chosen for his skilled swordsmanship, who would behead his colleague once the act of disembowelment had been commenced.

The act of *seppuku* involves a stylized ritual that cannot be performed on a sudden impulse or in an alcoholic torpor. Although it is now rarely practised, it is a socially accepted and positively nurtured Japanese tradition with a firm basis in the Japanese hierarchical system and its attitude to death. Its place in Japanese culture owes much to the influence of Zen Buddhism, which teaches the importance of transcending both life and death. The *samurai* incorporated this ideal into a rigid code of social behaviour, a code of honour on which *seppuku* is based and which Durkheim considered to be a feature of altruistic suicide.

During the civil wars that took place in medieval Japan, thousands of *samurai* committed *seppuku* to avoid being captured by the enemy, and in the peaceful Tokugawa period (1603–1867 AD) many did the same out of loyalty to a feudal lord who had recently died. This latter custom was so honoured that every province took enormous pride in the number of *junshi* who chose to die in this way.[25] These suicides reflected the importance in Japanese society of honour, loyalty and social status. They were not seen as attempts to escape from life but as valorous affirmations of life. *Seppuku* enabled a *samurai* to live and die on his own terms and to become the active agent of his own death in a socially acceptable way. The ritual nature of the act made it also aesthetically acceptable within the Japanese culture. It required careful planning, mental preparation and a firm will. It was, and still is, part of the Japanese cultural heritage and is closely linked with Japanese ideas of self-esteem, honour and the significance of life.

Friends and Family

The Japanese see *seppuku* as part of their cultural tradition, and suicide is indeed a statement to society. It can never be regarded as a completely private event as it has an effect on the surviving relatives and the local community. In Western countries, suicide is rarely seen as a virtuous act that brings honour to the community. It is more likely to be seen as a sad event that some people may even perceive as a sinful escape from the problems of life. People's response to a suicidal act depends in part on whether it is successful or not. An unsuccessful attempt may result in increased sympathy and support for the person concerned, so that his/her situation is temporarily or even permanently transformed for the better. However, support is not always forthcoming, nor can the demands of the potential suicide always be met. Many years ago, I was asked to visit a young doctor who had taken an overdose of sleeping tablets. When I saw him he was deeply unconscious but he recovered later in hospital. He wanted to marry a nurse who chose to remain single and he responded by taking the tablets. He threatened to repeat the attempt if she did not relent but she would not agree to do this so a few months later he killed himself. Some years later the nurse became very depressed and isolated, and committed suicide.

Suicide is an act that cannot be isolated, it involves much more than the death of one person: other people are blighted by it. When a suicidal attempt is successful, the family is faced with a sudden and unexpected crisis. Whilst coming to terms with their grief, they also have to deal with a chain of events that are not associated with a natural death. There will be a police enquiry, an inquest, postponement of the funeral, publicity in the local newspapers and quite unpredictable reactions from friends and neighbours. Once the initial shock has passed, core members of the family will react to the death with varying degrees of distress. Some will be devastated for years, others may feel relieved that a difficult person is no longer there to trouble them. Most will feel in need of some form of help, which may be for emotional support, information and explanations, financial advice or help, or more intensive input by a trained counsellor, psychiatrist or priest.

Suicide carries a social stigma. Acquaintances do not know how to react and even close friends tend to avoid the family if they can. The psychological distress of adults bereaved by suicide has the same pattern as for other bereaved people during the first two months of bereavement. Thereafter, they improve more slowly and experience greater levels of depression, anxiety and anger.[26] The shock and disbelief so often associated with bereavement is likely to last longer in cases of suicide. Close relatives are likely to become depressed, feel guilty and want to know 'why' it happened, a question that cannot be answered.

The surviving relatives will find many reasons for feeling guilty. They may torment themselves with the thought that they had contributed in some way to the death. That they were not good enough at sharing the feelings of the deceased; that they had failed him/her as parents, wife or child, or had overlooked what with hindsight were obvious cries for help. These thoughts and feelings hinder the process of recovery. They have to be set aside and, despite the inner scars, a deliberate effort must be made to live life as positively and cheerfully as possible.

Attempts may be made to hide the facts from children in the family but this is likely to be misguided as they will learn of the event not from a close relative but from other children at school, where their loss is likely to be the subject of ridicule. Children orphaned by suicide have the greatest unfulfilled needs, and the increased incidence of mental ill health and delinquency that they display reflects the inability of adults to deal adequately with their turmoil. The situation is confounded by a lack of expertise among those who may wish to help these children. Few will have been involved with more than a handful of such cases and the children find that they are faced with problems that no one understands or is able to resolve.

The problem may be intensified if the suicide is a well-known person like Sylvia Plath, who died in 1963, and then became an icon of the feminist movement. Almost 40 years later, her daughter Frieda recalled her own anger as a child, the vilification that her father endured, his care for the children, her beloved stepmother and her subsequent happy childhood. A professional painter, thrice married and having recovered from chronic fatigue syndrome, she summarized her experiences thus: 'I could make a job out of being a victim, but then it wouldn't be my life. I would be living through the wrongs I perceive other people doing to me. You have to take responsibility for your own life.'[27]

Attempted Suicide

The term 'attempted suicide' implies a genuine, unsuccessful attempt to kill oneself. The exact incidence is not known as only a proportion of suicidal attempts are recorded and there is no official agency responsible for collecting them. The writers Graham Greene and Malcolm Muggeridge both tried to end their own lives. Greene played Russian roulette with a loaded revolver and Muggeridge made a deliberate attempt to drown himself in the Indian Ocean. Both men made these incidents public only in their later writings. Whilst such disclosures may make books of memoirs more honest and interesting, they also reveal something else about the authors. Having attempted suicide once, both men were at risk of making a subsequent, successful suicide attempt, for those who have attempted suicide, and failed, are particularly likely to kill themselves later in life.

This was the pattern followed by Bishop David Johnson, of Massachusetts, who died from a self-inflicted gunshot wound in January 1996. A bishop in the Episcopalian Church in the USA, his diocese later revealed that he had been involved in extramarital affairs over several years and had made at least one previous attempt to take his life. About 1 per cent of attempted suicides succeed in killing themselves within the following year and 3–10 per cent do so eventually. Judy Garland, the child actress who featured in the film *The Wizard of Oz* and later had a successful adult career in films, made repeated attempts to kill herself before dying from an overdose of sleeping tablets.

Emotionally charged festivals such as Christmas and St Valentine's day are occasions when vulnerable people are particularly likely to attempt suicide. Although the exact incidence is not known, a profile has emerged of those who are most at risk. In contrast with successful suicides, unsuccessful attempts are more common in women than in men, and among young adults than elderly people. The peak age for unsuccessful suicide attempts is between 25 and 45 whilst most suicides involve people aged between 55 and 65.

Most cases of attempted suicide are due to self-poisoning by an overdose of drugs.[28] The unemployed, students, nurses and young Asian women are particularly vulnerable. Those involved have often experienced an increase in stress and problems during the previous months. As with suicide, attempted suicide is often associated with a recent significant traumatic life event such as a breakdown in a relationship, a death in the family or a loss of status due to unemployment. People find themselves in a hopeless situation, which they cannot resolve except by attempting to flee from life and all its problems. They see death as the only escape route.

Feelings of frustration are common among young prisoners, and their ability to relieve this frustration and the associated anger is greatly restricted. Apart from the prison sentence itself, common trigger events are being bullied by other inmates, 'Dear John' letters from the girlfriend, and the unexpected death of family and friends. Such bereavements are surprisingly common, and some involve very young children as many of these youths are fathers. If they are allowed to go to the funeral, they must do so in handcuffs. The overwhelming grief experienced has no natural outlet for expression. The prison staff, especially the chaplains, are sensitive to the inmates' need to grieve, and do their best to be helpful but are restricted in what they can do. Sometimes the lads express their anger by smashing their cells or hitting other inmates, but this can lead to loss of remission and a spell in solitary confinement. Often they make suicidal gestures, usually by slashing their forearms and wrists with a razor blade. However slashing rarely causes death: and prisoners who are really intent on suicide are more likely to hang themselves. Inmates who are considered to be suicidal are closely monitored by the prison authorities but, despite the precautions taken, a large number of suicides are attempted in prisons and some are successful.

Most people who attempt suicide do so on their own. There was however a widely reported incident of 'multiple attempted suicide' in Labrador in 1993. Almost a year after six children had burned to death in a house fire at Davis Inlet, six 12–14-year-old Innu (Eskimo) children barricaded themselves in an unheated shack, at –40 °C, and tried to kill themselves by inhaling gasoline fumes. Their intention was discovered by the local Innu policemen who videotaped them as they were removed from the hut. The film was shown on television, and its impact was enormous as viewers in North America saw pictures of young children struggling and screaming 'Leave me alone: I want to die.' The underlying cause of their distress soon became apparent. Davis Inlet was rampant with alcoholism and solvent inhaling, with poverty and squalor, with sexual abuse and violence. Between 80–85 per cent of the residents over the age of 15 were alcoholic and the suicide rate, both real and attempted, was extremely high. Such problems are not confined to Davis Inlet but are common among native communities across Canada and elsewhere. They are closely associated with the loss of the traditional rights, belief systems and cultures of these communities. This was emphasized by the United Nation's Human Rights commission in April 1999, when it concluded that 'the most pressing issue facing Canadians' was the situation of its indigenous people.[9]

I visited Davis Inlet in 1959 when I worked in Labrador with the International Grenfell Association. It was a much smaller community then but still a bleak and impoverished place. I remember the Inuit (Eskimos) as a cheerful people but the Innu (North American Indians) always seemed depressed. Both communities were provided with wooden shacks but the Innu also used tepees. They spread branches of spruce trees on the floor of the tents so that the interior always smelt fresh and clean. Fifty years ago suicide was not a major problem in Labrador: tuberculosis was the big scourge but it was being dealt with successfully by Dr Tony Paddon using the new anti-tuberculosis drugs, and surgical excision when this was appropriate. Nor was alcoholism very evident, probably because access to alcohol was very limited in Labrador 50 years ago. This situation seems to have changed with disastrous consequences.

Chapter 20
Euthanasia and
Assisted Suicide

Be absolute for death: either death or life
Shall thereby be the sweeter. Reason thus with life;
If I do lose thee, I do lose a thing
That none but fools would keep: a breath thou art,
Servile to all the skyey influences

Measure for Measure

Euthanasia and physician-assisted suicide are controversial, emotive issues that have been at the forefront of public debate for many years. Although they are quite distinct issues, clearly separated by ethical considerations and legal principles, it is generally conceded that there is a close association between the two. As a consequence, pressure groups supporting voluntary euthanasia see the legalization of physician-assisted suicide as an important first stage to the eventual decriminalization of euthanasia. They are pursuing this goal with vigour and are achieving major breakthroughs in the judiciaries and legislative assemblies of a number of countries, notably in Australia, the Netherlands and the USA.

The practice of euthanasia has always been condemned by the major world religions – Christianity, Buddhism, Islam and Judaism, and that situation remains unchanged. Its practice has also been vigorously opposed, since the days of Hippocrates (c.400 BCE), by the medical profession. That opposition continues but is weakening. The views of the British Medical Association, which reflect those of other national medical associations, were outlined in a discussion paper published in April 1998. This said:

> While the BMA opposes euthanasia primarily on the grounds that it is alien to the traditional ethos and moral focus of medicine, some of the most convincing arguments have been purely practical. The difficulties of effectively monitoring euthanasia to ensure against abuse are acknowledged even in the Netherlands where experts estimated that, contrary to the

regulations, six out of ten cases of euthanasia were going unreported. From a practical perspective, the BMA considers that acceptance of euthanasia as an option could exercise a detrimental effect on societal attitudes and on the doctor–patient relationship, jeopardising in particular, the fate of vulnerable individuals. Some of these arguments apply equally to physician assisted suicide. Nevertheless, a 1996 nationwide survey of doctors appeared to indicate attitudinal differences to the two acts.[1]

What is Euthanasia?

The word euthanasia means 'a good or easy death'. It now tends to be regarded as synonymous with the term 'mercy killing' but this was not its original meaning. In fact, the idea that someone could legitimately kill another person for compassionate reasons is a relatively, recent concept. Euthanasia is derived from two Greek words *eu* meaning 'well', and *thanatos* meaning 'death'. In ancient Greece, euthanasia meant that a person had achieved a dignified death, at the proper time, with tranquillity and peace of mind. It was a natural and peaceful, even aesthetic, end to life.[2] More recently it has come to be understood as the deliberate termination of a patient's life by a doctor at the urgent request of the patient.[3] Such an act is contrary to medical ethics and statutory law, but despite these prohibitions some doctors do admit to practising euthanasia. This is most evident in the Netherlands where the practice has been permitted by the Dutch judiciary since 1970, even though it has not been sanctioned by the Dutch Parliament. More recently in Belgium, one of the arguments used by politicians seeking to legalize euthanasia is that while euthanasia remains murder under the law, it has become 'almost a daily practice in our country'.[4]

Types of Euthanasia

The act of euthanasia may be classified in various ways. It can be carried out with the consent of the individual (voluntary euthanasia) or without consent (non-voluntary euthanasia). It may involve active or passive means. In active euthanasia, drugs are given or procedures carried out with the intent of causing death. In passive euthanasia, life-sustaining treatments are withheld or withdrawn with the object of precipitating death. The outcome then is less certain than with active euthanasia. The case of Karen Quinlan is a well-known example of passive euthanasia not precipitating death. It was also a landmark in the field of medical jurisprudence.

Karen Quinlan was a young woman with severe and irreversible brain damage whose life was maintained by means of a mechanical respirator. Her parents asked her physicians to stop the artificial respiration so that Karen could die a natural death. This request was refused for ethical and legal reasons. In 1975, the parents petitioned the New Jersey Supreme Court for permission to have Karen's respirator disconnected on the grounds that patients had the right to refuse medical treatment that offered no chance for a cure. The Supreme Court ruled, on the basis of common law, that Karen's father could lawfully disconnnect the respirator as he was her appointed guardian. In order to reassure the physicians, it also decreed that if her father did exercise this right all the parties involved would be granted legal immunity from civil or criminal prosecution. The respirator was disconnected; when this was done Karen was able to breathe normally as the medical/nursing team had successfully weaned her off it. She survived another 10 years; during this time her parents felt unable to remove the nasogastric tube by which she was fed.

The boundary between passive euthanasia and allowing nature to take its course by withholding treatment is not always clear. Making this distinction can be particularly difficult when the treatment to be withheld includes nutrients. Sometimes the terms 'ordinary means' and 'extraordinary means' are used to clarify the uncertainty. The words 'extraordinary' and 'ordinary' have a different meaning in this context than when they are used in everyday speech. 'Ordinary' is understood as 'morally obligatory' whilst 'extraordinary' is 'morally optional'. So 'ordinary means' of maintaining life should be pursued at all times, but 'extraordinary means' are a matter of choice for the physician and relatives. The crucial factor is usually one of intent. If the intention is to precipitate death the act is one of passive euthanasia; if there is no such intention, the withholding of treatment may be looked upon as allowing nature to take its course.

When moral dilemmas cannot be resolved, and involve conflict between opposing parties, courts of law are often asked to resolve the dispute. In 1987, the Supreme Court of New Jersey was petitioned in the case of a mentally competent woman, Kathleen Farrell. She was an intelligent person who suffered from amyotrophic lateral sclerosis, a disease with a poor prognosis. Mrs Farrell developed respiratory distress and was admitted to hospital where she underwent a tracheotomy and was connected to a respirator. Whilst she was in hospital, she refused to allow the staff to insert a nasogastric feeding tube and when she returned home she informed her husband that she wanted to be taken off the respirator. Her husband sought legal authority to implement her wish, together with a judgement that disconnecting the respirator would not attract civil or criminal liability. In a unanimous judgement, the Supreme Court upheld Mrs Farrell's right to refuse medical treatment, even at the risk of her personal injury or death. It emphasized that the decision was based on the common law right of self-determination. The court also ruled that this right to refuse life-sustaining treatment is not absolute. It recognized that due weight should be given to four other principles. These are the duty to safeguard life, to prevent suicide, to safeguard the integrity of the medical profession, and to protect innocent parties. Despite the importance of these issues, the court found that in this particular case none of these concerns outweighed Mrs Farrell's right to self-determination.

Non-voluntary euthanasia

The accepted basis for voluntary euthanasia is the freely expressed wish of a mentally competent adult that their life should be terminated by medical means, either immediately or at some future date. If the person is not mentally competent and consent is given by the legal guardian, as happened with Karen Quinlan, the act is called surrogate euthanasia. Non-voluntary euthanasia is the medical termination of life for compassionate reasons, done without the individual's consent. Although potentially a moral minefield, it does not have a high profile in the present debate which is mainly concerned with active voluntary euthanasia. A special type of non-voluntary euthanasia is known as 'compulsory euthanasia'. This is rarely mentioned nowadays, though it was widely discussed in medical circles in the 1930s. It is carried out after those in authority have decided that a seriously ill or handicapped person, either against their will or without being able to give consent, should have his or her life terminated. This form of euthanasia is now universally condemned but it was practised extensively in Germany during the Third Reich and may still be practised covertly in other countries today.

Although never formally legalized, government sanction for euthanasia was given in Germany in 1939, when Hitler signed the 'Führer-order' authorizing Dr Kurt Brandt and Reich-leader Philip Bouhler to permit euthanasia in certain cases. This was intended to be a humanitarian act, and followed a direct plea to Hitler from the father of a severely disabled child that the child's life should be ended humanely. Subsequently, all state institutions were required to report on patients who had been ill for five years and who were unable to work. On the basis of these reports alone, and without seeing the people involved, expert consultants decided which patients should die. Most of these experts were professors of psychiatry in key universities. As a result of this policy an estimated 275,000 mentally defective, senile, epileptic and physically handicapped Germans – adults and children were killed in gas chambers disguised as shower baths.[5] The introduction of compulsory euthanasia in the Third Reich had one other important consequence. It is considered to have been the first step that led inevitably to the subsequent mass murders in the concentration camps.

Why Euthanasia?

Five principles are invoked by those who argue the case for euthanasia, of which the first two are considered paramount. These are:

- the right to make one's own decisions;
- the importance of the quality of life;
- compassion;
- economic need;
- social progress.

The ability to exercise the 'right to decide' varies between countries but it is normally protected either by common law or a written constitution. This right can be used both as an argument to support the legalization of euthanasia and as a means of by-passing the legislature and appealing to the judiciary. The argument has a firm legal base and also a strong emotional appeal. As one supporter of euthanasia stated: 'no-one has the right to decide for me how much I shall suffer or for how long'.

Everyone agrees that people should have a good quality of life. There is no conflict on this issue. Supporters of euthanasia also see it as a compassionate act that would enable those who desire it, to die in dignity and without fear of a prolonged vegetative existence or a painful death. It would for instance provide a graceful end for people with Alzheimer's disease. The journalist, Margaret Forster, described in a newspaper article the last years of her mother's life as a victim of the disease. Its progress was slow, starting with short-term memory loss and proceeding through incontinence and loss of mobility to loss of speech. For the last few years of her life she was unable to feed herself. She died in a mental hospital that Mrs Forster described as Dickensian. For five years the family had coped with her at home at a cost of £40,000 and much personal effort. Forster expressed her feelings unequivocally. 'We are faced with a plain choice: either we agree that those in the last irreversible stages of Alzheimer's disease should be helped to die, or we insist that they are kept alive in conditions that do not make a mockery of the sanctity of life school of thought'.[6] Here we are faced with economic reality. The alternatives are confronted bluntly: either the living conditions of demented people are improved to a satisfactory level or these people should be helped to die.

Economic necessity has a nasty habit of deflating high moral principles. Difficult choices have to be made as the resources for health care will never be sufficient to satisfy all demands. The first requirement is to ensure the wellbeing of people who can make a useful contribution to society. This does not mean that people who are severely disabled by incurable mental or physical diseases should automatically be viewed as suitable candidates for euthanasia but its general availability as an acceptable option would enable finite resources to be distributed more profitably. As the Secretary of the World Federation of Right to Die Societies stated so clearly: 'We do not agree that anyone should perform euthanasia on us without our consent, either out of pity or because we have become a burden, or because we have become too expensive. Neither do we accept that our lives be prolonged as decrepit relics without our consent, out of a supposed respect for life.'[7]

Opinion Polls

The contribution that euthanasia could make to social progress is now considered to be a peripheral issue, probably because the arguments were mainly based on eugenic principles. But public opinion polls show that people are finding the idea of legalized, voluntary euthanasia increasingly acceptable. National opinion polls in Australia, Britain, Canada and the USA have produced remarkably similar results. Three-quarters of the respondents voted 'yes' when asked the following, or a similar question. 'When a person has an incurable disease that causes great suffering or pain do you, or do you not, think that competent doctors should be allowed by law to end the patient's life through mercy killing if the patient has made a formal request in writing?' The proportion of Canadians supporting this idea increased from 45 per cent in 1968 to 78 per cent in 1990 and a similar trend has been recorded in Australia.

Doctors appear to be less keen on euthanasia than the general public. In the British survey of 1985 only 15 per cent of doctors agreed that euthanasia should be permitted by law, though the figure was higher in Australia when doctors were questioned there in 1988. The latter survey was carried out in Melbourne where nearly half the doctors said that they would practise euthanasia if it were a legal procedure.

Doctors still perceive a real difference between euthanasia and assisted suicide. A random survey in the UK of 1,000 health professionals (predominantly hospital doctors, but including general practitioners, nurses and pharmacists), found that 51 per cent of respondents said that they would be willing to assist a patient to commit suicide, and 37 per cent said that they would never do so. Most respondents found assisted suicide preferable to euthanasia (43:19 per cent) but a high proportion was undecided. One noteworthy finding was that a much higher percentage of pharmacists than doctors supported legal change (72:48 per cent), and pharmacists also expressed the greatest willingness to assist in suicide without any preconditions, for example evidence of a terminal illness or extreme suffering.[8]

Legislating for Euthanasia

The advocacy of euthanasia reached a landmark in 1931, when Dr Killick Millard made it the subject of his presidential address to the Society of Medical Officers of Health in Britain. He followed this up with a book, *Euthanasia: A Plea for Legislation*. His ideas gained enough support for the Voluntary Euthanasia Legislation Society to be formed in 1935. This provided a forum for supporters of euthanasia and was the first national society to be established to promote the cause of euthanasia. A similar society was formed in the USA in 1938, although the movement there is now led by the Hemlock Society, which was formed in 1980. Similar societies exist in many other countries.

Bills to legalize euthanasia in the UK were debated and rejected by Parliament in 1936, 1969 and 1976. In 1994, the House of Lords Select Committee on Medical Ethics published a report which concluded with two comments relevant to this section. The first concerns protection of vulnerable people. The Committee referred to the moving representations it had received from people who wanted euthanasia themselves or who had witnessed relatives dying in a distressing way. Whilst recognizing that every person hopes for an easy death, without suffering or dementia, or dependence, the Lords concluded:

> Ultimately we do not believe that the arguments are sufficient reason to weaken society's prohibition of intentional killing. That prohibition is the cornerstone of law and social relationships. It protects each one of us impartially, embodying the, belief that all are equal. We do not wish that protection to be diminished. We acknowledge that there are individual cases in which euthanasia may be seen by some as appropriate. But individual cases cannot reasonably establish the foundation of a policy which would have serious and widespread repercussions. Dying is not only a personal or individual affair. The death of a person affects the lives of others, often in ways and to an extent which cannot be foreseen. We believe that the issue of euthanasia is one in which the interest of the individual cannot be separated from the interest of society as a whole.[9]

Its second conclusion was based on practical considerations:

> We do not think it possible to set secure limits on voluntary euthanasia. Some witnesses told us that to legalise voluntary euthanasia was a discreet step which need have no other consequences. But issues of life and death do not lend themselves to clear definition, and without that it would not be possible to frame adequate safeguards against non-voluntary euthanasia if voluntary euthanasia were to be legalised. It would be next to impossible to ensure that all acts of voluntary euthanasia were truly voluntary and that any liberalisation of the law was not abused.[9]

Here the Lords were particularly concerned with the pressure that might be exerted on the elderly, lonely and the sick to request euthanasia.

Despite these caveats, the pressure to legalize euthanasia is increasing. So is its practice. In the Netherlands, it has been openly practised with the support of the judiciary since 1970, though euthanasia has never been sanctioned by the Dutch parliament. The practice has always been legal in Japan provided four conditions are met. These preconditions are:

- that the patient is close to death;
- the condition is untreatable;
- the patient is in great pain;
- the patient expresses a clear wish to die (this last clause is often ignored).

The first place to legislate for euthanasia was the Northern Territory of Australia. It did so in 1996, when The Rights of the Terminally Ill Act was passed, which legalized the practice of voluntary euthanasia in the Northern Territory from 1 July 1996. There was instant uproar throughout Australia. Some opinion polls showed a high level of support for the move but Church leaders, Liberal politicians and the medical establishment strongly opposed it. Their reaction was swift, and the Australian Parliament passed a private member's bill repealing the Act in March 1997.

Four people died under the Rights of the Terminally Ill Act before it was declared unconstitutional by the Federal Parliament. The first was Bob Dent, an elderly man with cancer of the prostate gland. He died from a self-administered lethal injection. He managed to do this by keying prearranged commands on to a computer that had been connected to a machine capable of injecting drugs into his arm. The pioneer doctor in the enterprise was Dr Philip Nitshke who said that over 60 patients had contacted him with a view to ending their lives.[10]

Belgium may be the first European country to legalize euthanasia. Its politicians have debated the subject since 1996 and there is considerable pressure to change the law early in the second millennium. Changes in legislation are opposed by the medical establishment which is of the opinion that altering the law will do nothing to prevent abuses of it, but only 'make the exception become the rule'.[4] The medical profession realizes that the care of the terminally ill has long been neglected and that more resources and training need to be directed towards this aspect of care.

A different approach to improving the care and autonomy of the terminally ill has been suggested by Helme.[11] He proposes the establishment of two bodies – a Euthanasia Tribunal and a Terminal Care Commission. The latter would promote the development of terminal care along the lines laid down by the hospice movement, thereby helping to ensure the practice of euthanasia in its original sense of being 'a good death'. It would also provide a consultancy service for doctors, patients and relatives to help them to make non-treatment decisions and to avoid the use of inappropriate aggressive therapies. The Euthanasia Tribunal would help people to exercise their existing right to die – as allowed in the UK by the Suicide Act of 1961 and by similar legislations in other countries – but only if and when it appears compassionate to do so. In exercising this function, the tribunal would seek to ensure that the 'right to die' was not acted upon inappropriately or capriciously. The establishment of such a tribunal would require some changes in the Suicide Act 1961, as under this Act it is illegal to aid or counsel a person to commit suicide.[11] An approach of this sort would perhaps be more acceptable to doctors, as there is evidence that they view physician-assisted suicide as less repugnant than euthanasia.[1]

Euthanasia in the Netherlands

Since 1970, there has been a unique and official tolerance of euthanasia in the Netherlands, which has made its open practice permissible. The Dutch approach developed, not through government approval or an Act of Parliament, but through a change of attitude in the judiciary. As a consequence, the Netherlands has a greater public and professional acceptance of euthanasia than any other country, and its practice is open, extensive and well documented. It is probably true to say also that its palliative care services are not well developed.

Under the present arrangements, Dutch doctors may certify that a patient has died from euthanasia or unnatural causes, and they are then required to provide the coroner with a written report. They do so knowing that the coroner will inform the public prosecutor and that the doctor involved may be asked to attend a judicial enquiry. If the case goes to court, the doctor will admit to a charge of euthanasia but will plead that he carried out the act under a conflict of duties. The court will accept the plea that, because of the conflict of duties, the doctor has acted under a *force majeure* caused by a merciful compulsion to relieve the patient of unmitigated suffering, and will acquit the physician. This open admission to the practice of euthanasia is becoming more common in other countries with Dr Leon Schwartzenberg, who was briefly the French Minister of Health, being the most prominent doctor to do so.[12] Dr Schwartzenberg has not been prosecuted, possibly because the patients involved could not be identified, but reports from America and the UK show that when legal action is taken against doctors or relatives who can make an effective plea of *force majeure*, the defendant is almost invariably acquitted.

Judicial approval of euthanasia was obtained in the Netherlands as a result of decisions taken in various courts of law, including the Dutch Supreme Court. Dutch doctors practising euthanasia are free from prosecution if they follow certain guidelines. These were laid down by the courts and endorsed by a state conunission in 1991. The guidelines, which apply only to doctors, require that the mental and physical suffering of the patient must be very severe and have no prospect of relief. There must be an explicit and repeated request by the patient for euthanasia, which leaves no room for doubt that the person wishes to die. The patient's decisions must be well informed, free and enduring, and all other options for care must have been exhausted or refused by the individual. The doctor must consult with another medical practitioner, and this colleague must agree with the decision. Dutch case law does not require relatives to be involved in the discussions, but although such consultations are common the final decision is taken by the doctor and patient alone.

After administering the lethal drug, the doctor is required to issue a death certificate. This should state that death was due to euthanasia or unnatural causes but this legal requirement is not always observed as it may result in a judicial enquiry with the unlikely possibility that the doctor might be found guilty of some criminal offence. Consequently, some doctors are likely to certify another cause of death such as the preceding illness. The Netherlands Association for Voluntary Euthanasia would like euthanasia to be made legal by a completely unambiguous Act of Parliament. The association believes that as long as euthanasia remains an offence, doctors will not report it.[13] On the other hand doctors have little to fear if they keep within the stated guidelines.

The Remmelink Commission

There has always been considerable uncertainty about the real incidence of euthanasia in the Netherlands. Estimates have ranged from 2,000 to 20,000 cases a year but the incidence of such deaths has never been properly estimated. In order to clarify the situation, the Minister of Justice and the State Secretary of Welfare and Health set up a body – the Remmelink Commission, with the brief to assess the medical decisions which are associated with the termination of life. The Commission published its findings in 1991.

According to its report,[14] 2,300 cases of active voluntary euthanasia and 400 cases of assisted suicide occur each year in the Netherlands. The Commission also found that about 1,000 cases of active euthanasia, mainly involving handicapped babies and comatose patients, take place annually without the patient's consent. A further 22,500 deaths result each year from the withholding or withdrawing of treatment from mainly elderly patients in nursing homes. These figures indicate that passive euthanasia has a role in 17.3 per cent of all deaths, active voluntary euthanasia in 1.8 per cent of deaths, active non-voluntary euthanasia in 0.8 per cent and assisted suicide in 0.3 per cent of all deaths in the Netherlands. Doctors, mainly general practitioners, are involved in all of these deaths. Not all are easy deaths. The Dutch admit that some have been 'horribly botched' but consider that 'with time and training their doctors have got better at administering death'.[15]

A follow-up study was undertaken between 1995 and 1996. This showed that the number of reported cases of euthanasia increased threefold, from 486 in 1990 to 1,466 in 1995. Explicit requests for euthanasia or physician assisted suicide were made by 9,700 individuals, a 9 per cent increase on the 1990 figures though this was offset by a 5 per cent increase in the overall mortality of the population. Most requests for euthanasia were not complied with. The report found no evidence that doctors were making end-of-life decisions less carefully and said that monitoring these decisions was possible.[16] But whether this is being achieved remains problematic. According to the British Medical Association[1], a co-author of the report – Professor van der Wal – when interviewed by the Voluntary Euthanasia Society in 1997 said that six out of 10 cases of euthanasia go unreported.

The physically ill are not the only people seeking euthanasia in the Netherlands. Each year hundreds of physically healthy people seek help from the Dutch Society for Voluntary Euthanasia. The most recent test case involved the Dutch Supreme Court, a psychiatrist, Dr Boudewijn Chabot, and a healthy woman who was not suffering from any mental illness but who had wanted to die since the death of her two sons. The Supreme Court found Dr Chabot guilty of deliberately aiding the woman's suicide but chose not to punish him as he had followed the guidelines that require him to establish that his patient was competent, was suffering unbearably, and had a voluntary, well-considered wish to die. It recognized the care he had taken to consult colleagues and his efforts to persuade his patient against suicide. Dutch doctors see this ruling as a considerable help in clarifying the law on euthanasia and assisted suicide. It is now clear that mental suffering, as opposed to mental illness, can be a sufficient reason for acceding to a request for euthanasia and assisted suicide, and that the patient does not have to be either physically or terminally ill.[17]

Assisted Suicide in Germany

The situation is different in Germany. There euthanasia is not countenanced possibly because most Germans associate the practice with the Third Reich, and the involuntary killing of people for political and racial as well as medical reasons. On the other hand assisted suicide is legal and openly practised though without the participation of doctors. Its legality is dependent upon the person committing it being *tatherrschaftsfähig*, that is capable of exercising control over his or her actions. The act must also be based on *freiverantwortliche Wille*, that is a freely responsible choice. It is illegal to assist the suicide of a mentally disturbed, demented or depressed person. The non-involvement of doctors may be partly due to the existence of a legal provision in German law that requires individuals who have a professional or personal relationship with suicidal victims to resuscitate them if this is possible.

Various factors may have made the idea of assisted suicide acceptable to the German people. Frederick the Great decriminalized suicide over two centuries ago in 1751, so probably the suicidal act does not carry the same intense obloquy in Germany as in some other Western countries. Linguistic niceties may also play a part. The German language has at least four words, all with different shades of meaning, which can be used for the act, in English only the word suicide is available. Germans may choose to use the word *Suizid* (suicide), *Selbstmord* (self-murder), *Selbsttötung* (self-killing) or *Freitod* (voluntary death). *Suizid* is the technical term used by clinicians and implies the presence of a psychiatric illness. Lawyers and bureaucrats tend to use the word *Selbsttötung*. Both *Suizid* and *Selbsttötung* tend to have a morally neutral tone though with slightly negative implications. The most commonly used word is *Selbstmord*. This carries all the negative connotations that are normally associated with the English word suicide. In contrast *Freitod*, the freely chosen death, carries the same positive heroic overtones as the Japanese term *seppuku*. The difference is apparent even in the grammatical construction used when speaking of *Selbstmord* and *Freitod*. One commits *Selbstmord* (*man begeht Selbstmord*) but chooses *Freitod* (*man wählt den Freitod*).

Provided the act is not one of despair or dementia, and is freely chosen, it is not against the law to help another person to end his or her life. The German people, however, do not want their doctors to be too closely involved in the affair. They see *Freitod* as a freely chosen act and the medical profession as too authoritarian for the latter to have any role other than as the signatories of prescriptions for drugs, which can be accumulated and eventually used for that purpose.

Those who have chosen to end their lives may seek help from the Deutsche Gesellschaft für Humanes Sterben (DGHS), the German Society for Humane Dying. The DGHS, which was founded in 1980 to help the terminally ill commit suicide, has no direct links with the medical profession or any government agency. In 1991, it had 50,000 members with 1,000 new members joining each month: but by the year 2000, partly because of internal problems, its member-ship numbered only 38,000 and the new intake was down to 200–400 per month. Anyone who had been a member of the DGHS for more than 12 months and had not received psychiatric treatment during the previous two years, could receive a copy of the DGHS's booklet *Menschenwürdiges und selbsverantwortliches Sterben (Dignified and Responsible Death)*. This booklet provided specific advice on commit-ting suicide and gave a list of drugs, which were available on prescription in Germany or without prescription in neighbouring countries, and the recommended dosages for producing an easy death. This booklet has now been withdrawn but members can obtain directly from the publisher in Scotland a new publication *Selbsterlösung durch Medikamente (Self-relief through Medication)*.

When asked to do so, the DGHS will arrange for someone to sit with a member during the hours preceding death but prefers to encourage friends and relatives to undertake this role. To assist these 'companions', it has established an Akademie der Sterbebegleitung (a School for Accompanying the Dying) where relatives can acquire the confidence to perform this final service in a meaningful way. Battin[18] reported that between 2,000–3,000 members of DGHS were committing suicide each year but the Society no longer wishes to confirm these figures and says numbers of suicides are not available.[19]

Members are asked to sign a pink form immediately before they kill themselves. This form is entitled *Freitod-Verfügung* (free death directive), and carries the statement *Ich habe heute meinen Freitod eingeleitet* (I have brought about my free death today).[18]

Physician-Assisted Suicide

Although assisted suicide is still illegal in most states in the USA, it probably does occur quite extensively. A survey of physicians in Washington has found that one-quarter of patients wishing to commit suicide who asked their doctors for help were given a prescription for that purpose. It found also that one quarter of patients requesting euthanasia received their doctor's help. The survey was based on a random sample of 25 per cent of primary care physicians in the state and all the physicians in selected subspecialties who were likely to treat severely and terminally ill patients. Twenty-six per cent of the physicians had received requests for euthanasia or help with suicide. They refused to give lethal prescriptions to 73 per cent of the patients seeking help with suicide and to 67 per cent requesting euthanasia. Forty per cent of those who received a prescription for the purpose of ending their lives did not use it.[20]

Immediately after the report was published, the American Medical Association reiterated its opposition to physician-assisted suicide. It pointed out that the report strengthened the Association's contention that physicians needed to be better educated in pain management. Once this was achieved and a greater use made of advance directives such as living wills, there would be virtually no need for physician-assisted suicide.[21]

The best known advocate of physician assisted suicide in the USA is the retired pathologist, Dr Jack Kevorkian. Once known as 'Dr Death' he began his campaign to bring about the legalization of euthanasia in 1990, by helping Janet Adkins, a patient with Alzheimer's disease, to die. By his own account he has helped over 100 people to die: many with terminal illnesses but some with severe chronic diseases such as amyolateral sclerosis. He was acquitted on three separate occasions of illegally assisting in the suicide of patients, and after his second acquittal a juror said that the issue had been more fundamental than just the point of law on which Kevorkian's lawyers had based their defence. Pointing out that suicide is not illegal in the state of Michigan where the trial was held, he asked, 'How could we convict someone for helping to do something that is legal.'[22] In 1998, the doctor forced the courts to charge him again by videotaping himself injecting a lethal dose of barbiturates into Thomas Youk. He gave the tape to a television company which broadcast it two months later. He was indicted and found guilty of second degree murder and sentenced to prison. He is now inmate No. 284797 in a remote gaol in Michigan and will not become eligible for parole until May 2007.

In 1996, the American Courts of Appeal ruled that Washington State's law against physician assisted suicide is illegal, and that New York statutes criminalizing assisted suicide for the terminally ill are unconstitutional. Both these judgements were later overturned by the Supreme Court of the United States in June 1997. It ruled that there was no fundamental right to assistance in committing suicide, and declared that people who are most vulnerable to abuse in assisted suicide, and those whose decisions would not be totally voluntary, would continue to need the protection of the court.

The Supreme Court also ruled that patients have the right to refuse treatments or interventions, even if to do so would hasten their death. It points out that differences exist between 'the long legal tradition protecting the decision to refuse unwanted medical treatment', and the right to assistance in ending one's life. Whilst recognizing the constitutionality of existing laws prohibiting physician assisted suicide, implicit in the Supreme Court's rulings is the idea that the states are free to experiment and to make physician assisted suicide legal if they so choose.[23]

The debate continues elsewhere. Oregon became the first American state to legalize physician assisted suicide when it passed a Death With Dignity Act in 1994. Opponents blocked its implementation until November 1997 but in the following 14 months 15 people used the act to obtain lethal prescriptions.[24] In July 1999, a new statute clarified the provisions of the act regarding psychiatric evaluation, residency requirements, pharmacist conscience clause, and the rights of health care organizations. Right-to-die legislation is pending in other states as well.

Living Wills

Some people equate the existence of a 'living will' directive with a request for euthanasia or assisted suicide. No such relationship exists and more importantly the ethical considerations are quite different. The purpose of a living will is to enable people to control the medical and nursing decisions that may be taken if they become terminally ill. The idea was introduced in the USA in 1967 and its importance was enhanced when Congress passed the Patient Self Determination Act in 1991. This Act gives people the right to complete a living will testament and direct medical attendants to withhold certain treatment. Similar legislation has been passed in other countries but not in the UK, where English law has always expected doctors to respect the previously expressed and clearly stated wishes of their patients, including how they wish to be treated if they become terminally ill or mentally incompetent.

However, in response to a request by the House of Lords Select Committee on Medical Ethics,[9] the British Medical Association has published a Code of Practice[25] on living wills/advance directives. This states that when drawing up an advance directive, individuals must ensure that the following information is included:

- full name and address;
- name and address of general practitioner;
- whether advice was sought from health professionals;

- signature;
- date drafted and reviewed;
- witness signature;
- a clear statement of the individual's wishes, either general or specific;
- the name, address and telephone number of their nominated person, if there is one.

Storage of an advance statement and notification of its existence are primarily the responsibility of the individual. A copy of any written advance statement should be given to the person's general practitioner. People close to the patient should be made aware of the existence of an advance statement and be told where it is. For chronically ill patients who are treated by a specialist team over a prolonged period of time, a copy of the advance statement should be in all relevant hospital files and the general practitioner's record. Some people carry a card, bracelet or other measure indicating the existence of an advance statement and where it is kept.

The basis of a living will is the statement: 'If I were in the following conditions . . . I would not want my life extended by artificial means.' Three types of conditions are usually mentioned: these are a terminal illness, severe and irreversible dementia, and a persistent vegetative state in which life can only be maintained by artificial means. A legal alternative to a living will, and one that is sometimes used in conjunction with it, is a durable power of attorney. This allows a mentally competent person to appoint an agent to act on his or her behalf, in specified matters of health care, if and when that patient becomes mentally incompetent. However, the effectiveness in law of these provisions is sometimes not as absolute as may appear to be the case, and there is considerable variation in the extent to which they are honoured in different countries.

Finally, in the absence of any indication to the contrary, there is a common-law duty to give appropriate treatment to incapacitated patients when the treatment is clearly in their best interests.

Values Histories

A precisely worded advance directive is legally binding, but as these directives become increasingly explicit they can also become less useful, particularly in intensive care units. When living wills were first introduced, a general directive about refusing say, cardiopulmonary resuscitation, could be regarded as a wise decision given the uncertain outcome of the treatment but the rapidly changing technology of these units may now lead to a situation where following such explicit instructions would fail to achieve the patient's wishes. Consequently, the 'values history' is becoming an increasingly favoured alternative, or adjunct, to the living will.

A 'values history' is goal based rather than instruction based. It gives guidance on the policy to be implemented rather than explicit instructions as to what should be done. It provides a record of the declarant's core values and beliefs to act as a basis for decisions on medical treatment. Values histories are not as legally binding as advance directives, but intensive-care doctors are finding them more useful to patients and doctors than a too precisely worded advance directive.[26]

Chapter 21
The Death of a Pet

Brothers and Sisters, I bid you beware
Of giving your heart to a dog to tear.

Kipling: The Power of the Dog

Introduction

The grief that follows the death of a loved relative can be very intense, yet it is similar in nature to that experienced by people who are deprived of other things that they hold dear. The loss of a job and the security it offers, eviction from one's home, the break-up of a close friendship, and the loss of hearing or mobility frequently give rise to feelings of deep sorrow.

Shakespeare realized how devastated people can be when they lose what they treasure and his plays are full of the tragedy that fate inflicts on the unwary. Such a person is Shylock, the Jew and widower, featured in *The Merchant of Venice*. Everything seems to be going well for him, then his daughter Jessica elopes with her lover, the Christian Lorenzo, taking with her Shylock's money and jewels. The most hurtful aspect of this desertion was that Jessica had taken his turquoise ring and exchanged it for a monkey. The ring was the most precious memento Shylock had of his wife Leah and when he learns, from his friend Tubal, that it has gone, his response is bitter

> Out upon her! Thou torturest me,
> Tubal. It was my turquoise: I had it of Leah
> when I was a batchelor: I would not have given
> it for a wilderness of monkeys.

But this is just the beginning of Shylock's downfall. Later, he is defeated in a lawsuit and is forced by the court to allow his daughter to marry Lorenzo, and he is also required to forfeit half his goods to the state. He is bereft and humiliated, and his request to the court,

> I pray you give me leave to go from hence;
> I am not well:

is totally understandable, and reminds us that people frequently fall ill after a bereavement or any other deeply felt loss. Foremost among the latter for many people, is the death of a pet

The relationship that exists between people and animals is variable and complex. Some animals are hunted for food or thrills, others are feared and avoided. Farmers rear cattle and sheep for food and profit. However, the most distinctive of interactions is that people are prepared to welcome them into their homes as pets. This can give rise to a particularly significant relationship, which is likely to be most close if the pet is also a working animal such as a guide dog.

A wide range of insects, birds, reptiles and mammals are kept as pets. The association is one of mutual support, for even the simple stick insect or pet mouse provides children with an opportunity to become responsible for the care of another creature and this enlarges their understanding of natural life. The death of a pet is often a child's first real encounter with death.

Having a pet stimulates elderly people and helps them to remain physically active and mentally alert. The care that ownership entails also enables them to view themselves as people who have responsibilities and not just as has-beens dependent on others. Most importantly, pets provide a constancy of companionship, affection and physical contact that friends and relatives so often fail to do. No wonder people sometimes say that they prefer their dogs, cats or horses to other people.

A Pets' Hierarchy

There is a noticeable hierarchy in the intensity of relationship that exists between people and their pets, and this is reflected in the severity of grief experienced when a pet dies. The closest relationship is usually formed between dogs and their owners and, not surprisingly, people tend to grieve more after the death of a dog than for other household pets. On the other hand, many people prefer cats to dogs and the death of a well-loved cat can be a severe blow to its owner. It is probable, however, that the death of a cat can be borne more philosophically and there are two reasons for supposing this to be so. First, cats tend to be more independent than dogs and are less interested in establishing a cosy relationship with their owner. Second, and particularly if the cat is a tom, they are likely to disappear for long periods of time and this enables the family to become accustomed to their periodical absence.

Apart from horses and donkeys, which are usually much cherished by their owners but which cannot be deemed household pets, rabbits probably occupy the next rung in the hierarchical relationship, and then other small animals and birds such as budgerigars. It is difficult to judge beforehand how people will react to the death of these small creatures, but one should not underestimate the amount of grief experienced by children, or even adults, when a well-loved pet hamster dies.

The Grief of Owners

People react in widely differing ways to the death of a pet, just as they do when a close relative or friend dies. Some will be scarcely affected by the loss, while others will pine, and a few may be so heart broken that they seem to die of grief soon afterwards. The following accounts are illustrative, some I have observed at first hand, the others have been told to me.

Barry was an 18-year-old youth who had 'lost loads of animals including dogs, cats, birds, rats, mice and a hamster'. His 'best bitch' was a three-year-old and she had died of distemper. He said: 'It never really affected me: just one of those things in life.'

Dave had had various pets including 12 budgerigars, two iguanas and a golden retriever. For the most part, he was able to accept their deaths with equanimity but he did admit: 'The iguanas upset me a bit because they cost me a bit (£170 for two). It wouldn't have been too bad, but they only lived 6 months.' It was not clear whether he grieved their death more than the financial loss, but both elements appeared to be present.

In contrast, Jean died in middle age quite suddenly and only six weeks after the death of her elderly corgi to whom she was devoted. A senior nurse and workaholic, the dog had been her most constant companion, even in the hospital, and her main source of affection. She had nursed him through various illnesses and was quietly distraught when he eventually died. Soon afterwards she went on holiday for the first time in many years, and died a few days later from a stroke.

Richard, a 17-year-old re-offender whom I met in prison, had this to say about the death of his dog, a nine-year-old Jack Russell. The dog had died the previous year, when Richard was serving a five-month sentence. He said: 'My father told me when I got home from prison. I didn't believe him at first; I thought it was a joke. I shouted for it but when it didn't come I realized. I was upset and cried. My father comforted me. He put his arm around me and said, he is with God now – and I believe him, he is with God. I hadn't cried for three years but I cried then. I still keep his basket and blanket, like one of the family. I couldn't accept it at the time, and I still can't accept it; it brings a lump to my throat when I think about it. He died of a broken heart because I was away for five months. I still think it was my fault because I was inside; I did a wicked thing and if I was out he would still be alive. My mate got killed on my motor bike, but I was more upset by the death of my dog than by the death of my mate. I prayed, the first time I ever done it. I prayed, I just said I'm sorry if it was me. I believe a dog has a soul.'

Disappearing Cats

Many sick animals are 'put down' by veterinary surgeons, usually with a lethal injection of a barbiturate. This occurs more frequently with dogs than cats, as cats tend to go off and disappear when they are terminally ill. When a pet leaves home and doesn't return, there is a lingering sense of uncertainty, which can act as a major block in the grieving process. In these cases, it may be helpful to say a belated goodbye to the pet in some ritual way, for instance, by planting some bulbs or a small bush in the garden. Children may find this a help in coming to terms with the loss.

Some cats do return home even though they are dying. Clausa was a young cat with her first litter. Whilst out foraging, she was severely injured, probably by a passing car. Despite her injuries, which were not immediately apparent, she crawled back to the house and fed her kittens. She was in great distress and had difficulty in breathing. I took her to the vet where an X-ray showed extensive damage to the thorax; there was nothing that could be done to save her. We were extremely sad to lose her but this was offset by the admiration we had for her courage, and strong maternal instinct at seeking to return to her kittens. She was buried in a special plot in the garden, whilst my son played the *Last Post* on his trumpet.

Euthanasia

Although it can be done at home, animals are most frequently 'put to sleep' in the vet's surgery. A consent form is signed beforehand and most owners are pleasantly surprised at how smooth and easy the death can be. Children are not usually present, but this is a decision that will have been made by the parents. It is not an unpleasant event for the pet, as sick animals are normally passive and without much fight, but when the owners are themselves distressed this tends to communicate itself to the animal. Veterinary surgeons and nurses are exceptionally good at understanding and sympathizing with their client's feelings, as many have lost pets of their own and realize that it is a traumatic experience.

The 'putting down' of an animal is often preceded by anticipatory grief. This was pointed out to me by a veterinary nurse who had grieved the loss of her elderly cat for 10 days before she took him to the surgery to be put to sleep. She said: 'I knew he hadn't much longer. For 10 days I found it almost harder than when he was put down.'

A common practice among veterinary surgeons is to send sympathy cards to their clients after a pet has died. This small gesture tends to be greatly appreciated.

Grieving Pets

Animals are likely to grieve the death of a close companion, and they make their feelings apparent in various ways. They may stop feeding, become restless, call repeatedly for the mate, or mutilate themselves. Self-mutilation is particularly common in cats, but sometimes birds will pluck out their feathers when a partner dies, but very few pets pine to death.

Loss of appetite, restlessness and calling are readily recognized signs of distress. So too are listlessness, withdrawal and despondency which may also be apparent in some bereaved animals. Less easy to discern, if present at all, are feelings of disbelief, anger and guilt which are such important features of grief in human beings. Nor is there any way of knowing whether animals have a sense of the presence of their dead companion though this is often experienced following a human bereavement.

Horses and donkeys are particularly likely to be upset by the death of a companion. I am told that it is generally considered beneficial to let them see the dead body, as this is likely to reduce the length and severity of the grief. Brandy, one of my elder daughter's two geldings, died suddenly in a field a few years ago; he was in his mid-twenties. His half-brother and life-long companion, Copper, was alone in the field with him the night he died. Hoof marks were evident on Brandy's face where Copper had pawed at him, presumably in an attempt to revive him. For days afterwards, Copper, normally a quiet horse whinnied repeatedly and moved restlessly within his field, and tended to avoid people whom he would otherwise have approached.

Brandy was not buried or cremated; he was taken to the knacker's yard. This was the most practical way of dealing with the corpse though it did nothing to ease my daughter's distress. There was really no alternative. She owned no land in which the horse could be buried and there was no animal crematorium nearby where Brandy could have been cremated and the ashes scattered.

Burial and Counselling

The death of a pet brings emotional distress and practical problems. An immediate concern is arranging for the disposal of the body. If the animal is not too big — and if local by-laws permit it, the pet may be buried within a suitable plot in the garden, maybe under a favourite bush or tree: cats are likely to be buried in this way. Urban dwellers who lack this facility can use the services offered by pet cemeteries and crematoria. The Hyde Park Pet Cemetery was among the first to be opened for public use in England but it is now of antiquarian interest only as it was closed in 1903 after all its plots had been utilized. It is worth noting that only dogs could be buried there and this is perhaps indicative of the special place that dogs tend to have in the affections of people. In the UK only a small proportion of animals are buried in pet cemeteries (about 2 per cent of dogs and 3 per cent of cats) but the proportion is much higher in the USA where many cities have local laws forbidding burial at home.[1]

Pet cemeteries are becoming increasingly popular and common, though they are usually the most expensive way of disposing of the pet's remains. The costs of interment vary considerably and depend on such factors as the type of casket used, the headstones and lettering selected and the dimensions of the grave. Sometimes an annual maintenance fee is required.

Some large animals have a particular place in the affections of their owners. This may be reflected in the type of burial accorded to them. The grave of Copenhagen, the horse that carried the Duke of Wellington at the Battle of Waterloo in 1814, can still be seen at Stratfield Saye, the Duke's country home, whilst the epitaph of Eugenie is clearly visible in the pet cemetery at Powerscourt near Dublin.[2] It reads:

Eugenie
Jersey Cow
Died 1967 aged 17 years
She had 17 calves and produced
Over 100,000 gallons of milk

Most pets that are disposed of by veterinary surgeons are cremated communally though it is always possible to arrange for individual cremation. Otherwise the bodies are collected and cremated by a local pet crematorium. Cambridge Pet Crematorium in Hertfordshire is said to be Europe's biggest, disposing of 35 tons of cats and dogs a week. This adds up to a lot of heartache and some people are so devastated – 10 per cent in one survey,[1] that they consult their family doctor about their feelings of grief and take time off from work. Other people seek support from voluntary agencies. The Society for Companion Animal Studies operates a helpline for grieving owners in the UK whilst in the Republic of Ireland similar support is obtainable from the Pet Bereavement Counselling Service.[2]

Memories

The death of a pet can trigger memories of other losses and thus intensify the grief. This may not be a bad thing if other significant losses have not been adequately mourned. I was surprised, for instance, at the extent of my distress when my toy poodle was suddenly killed. I grieved for him a great deal more than I had done, with a few exceptions, for any of my patients.

Similarly, young men may find it easier to cry when a well-loved dog dies than when a mate is killed, possibly because they feel the latter demands a macho response which is not expected of them after the loss of a pet. It is amazing how much anger, guilt and grief the death of a pet can unleash in an otherwise placid person. In general, the owner's reaction to such a death is very similar to that which occurs when a close relative dies. When the bonding has been close and prolonged, particularly with dogs, some people even admit to feeling the presence of the dead pet, an experience many widowed people have of their dead spouse.

It is helpful to retain some reminders of the dead pet. Photographs are particularly important in this respect, and so is a special place in the garden, or pet cemetery, where the remains or ashes have been placed. The significance of these special sites is enhanced if a short burial service is performed as the remains are scattered or placed in their final resting place.

For many people, fond memories are not a sufficient substitute for the dead animal, they need to replace it with a new pet. Usually it is best to wait a while before doing so, though some people prefer to get a replacement animal immediately. One of the problems arising on these occasions is that the new pet can never quite replace the old one. Each animal has its unique personality and needs to develop its own special relationship with its owner.

Chapter 22
The Bereaved and the Living Dead

I have heard, – but not believ'd, the spirits o' the dead
May walk again; if such things be, thy mother
Appeared to me last night; for ne'er was dream
So like a waking.

The Winter's Tale

Some words, such as table and chair, have specific meanings that cannot readily be misunderstood. Other words carry variable undertones and may be interpreted differently by writers and their readers. There will always be problems with words like ghosts, apparitions, hallucinations, after-death communications (ADCs),[1] illusions, pseudohallucinations and a sense of the presence (SOP) all of which have been used in reference to the subject matter of this chapter. I had hoped to circumvent this dilemma by not using any of these words but this I have been unable to do. In fact I have added to the confusion by introducing the term 'living dead' which Mbiti[2] says is the African way of referring to people who have died. This term has philosophical implications. It also has the merit of implying both the unreality of a hallucination and the true nature of the subjective encounters that many people seem to have with deceased relatives. People who have such experiences usually find them helpful and – this needs to be emphasized – do not seek them in a deliberate way. The incidents occur spontaneously in normal everday life almost as though a continuing relationship exists between the living and the dead.

Surprisingly little was known about the frequency and content of these experiences until quite recently. They were rarely openly discussed, and Western society's attitude to any personal disclosures was at best ambivalent, at worst condemnatory. Few people felt able to mention an apparent encounter with a dead relative even to their closest kin. They knew that their stories would have been simply dismissed as foolish fabrications or wish-fulfilling imaginations. Ghosts were an acceptable subject for jokes and people might feel sympathy for those seeking comfort at séances, but a personal encounter with the dead was not a subject to be discussed seriously in most circles. There was also the possibility that anyone who persisted in such claims might be locked up in a mental institution.

Enforced custodial care in a psychiatric hospital was fairly easily effected for inadequate reasons in the nineteenth and early part of the twentieth century. A senior psychiatrist used to illustrate this point with the story of a Dutch sailor who missed his ship after a drunken spree and was marooned in a Welsh seaport. The sailor was eventually committed to a psychiatric unit because he was agitated and talking gibberish. He was discharged from hospital only when it was discovered that he was speaking Dutch, not gibberish, and was frightened because he was far from home and could not communicate with those around him. Even more poignant are the occasional reports of women committed to mental hospitals many years ago because they had persisted in their claims that they had been raped by their employers. Within such a social climate, to speak openly about perceiving the presence of dead relatives would appear to court the risk of being certified insane. It may not have happened often, if at all, but it was a potential threat. Doctors could not be trusted with such revelations, and the clergy were no less suspect. Ministers of religion would be expected to denounce such talk as sinful and contrary to doctrinal belief, or accuse them of dabbling with spiritualism. Dramatists, novelists and poets were able, however, to portray the subject freely. The plays of Shakespeare, and lesser writers, are full of ghosts, and their ready acceptance by the public suggests that the authors were describing a manifestation that had a real, though perhaps unformulated, meaning for their audiences.

Lack of Data

Little was known about these perceptions of the bereaved until 1971 when I published a paper, entitled The Hallucinations of Widowhood, in the *British Medical Journal*. Since then the situation has changed greatly: the experiences are now recognized as a normal feature of bereavement and people talk about them much more readily. Before 1971, it was a taboo subject, never mentioned to doctors or clergy or family. Standard text-books on psychiatry did not mention them and *The Complete Psychological Works of Sigmund Freud* dismissed them in three lines as psychotic hallucinations. The overall situation was neatly summed up by a hospital consultant in 1972, when he informed a medical meeting that he had not encountered a single such case in over 30 years of psychiatric practice. However, some sociologists and psychiatrists had noted that certain of their patients/clients experienced a meaningful relationship with their dead partner. Lindemann[3] and Gorer[4] mentioned this briefly. Parkes[5] reported that 15 of the 22 widows he had interviewed had an SOP of their dead spouse, Marris[6] that 36 of the 72 widows he had met during a socio-economic survey in London had mentioned similar experiences to him. In Japan, Yamamoto[7] found that 18 out of 20 young widows had felt the presence of their dead husband and that none had actively cultivated the idea of his presence.

The first scientific report to mention an SOP was the *Census of Hallucinations*, published by the Society for Psychical Research in 1894.[8] This census, which has the distinction of being the forerunner of our modern opinion polls, was not specifically concerned with bereavement – its steering committee was particularly interested in telepathic communications. Its conclusions were based on information provided by 17,000 respondents of different nationalities. The census found that 2 per cent of all respondents had perceptions of dead relatives and that these were the most vivid of all the recorded experiences. Considerable differences were noted between different nationalities and between men and women. The overall incidence of hallucinations was greater in women than men, and it was twice as high in Brazilians (19.3 per cent) and Russians (18.6 per cent) than among English speaking respondents (7.8 per cent). The census did not ask respondents to record a sense of the presence of a dead person but 24 such instances were reported. This would now be considered a surprisingly small number but the report did say of them 'that the impression is so strong as to appear (to be) a very striking phenomenon and to produce a great effect on the mind'. The report concluded that while the respondents provided remarkable instances that suggested action on the part of the dead, the evidence did not provide a conclusive case for a post-mortem agency.

Learning from the Bereaved

My own interest in bereavement started after I joined a medical practice in 1960. It was a rural, dispensing practice centred on Llanidloes, a town in Wales near the source of the river Severn and about 35 miles from the English border. It was an old-fashioned practice and proved to be an excellent base for a young doctor with aspirations to undertake research work in general practice. There was an interesting diversity of cultures and occupations in the area, and an easily demarcated region in which all the residents were patients of the practice: this enabled any studies to be based on a defined community of over 5,000 people. I was fortunate to be able to publish papers in the medical journals on various topics including agricultural tractor accidents, road traffic accidents, depression in pregnancy and, with Sylvia Lutkins, a statistical appraisal of the increased mortality associated with bereavement.

I then designed a longitudinal survey of the effects of bereavement on the surviving partner: the intention was to look at and monitor 76 physiological/clinical variants such as the incidence of weight loss, headaches, insomnia, tearfulness, depression, anxiety and the obvious debilitating conditions that might be expected to follow such a loss. However, no provision was made for the possibility that people who had lost a close relative would refer to their continuing encounters with the deceased. But this is what happened. Most commonly, they spoke of feeling a presence – as if the dead person were there with them. Less frequently they spoke of seeing or hearing, or even being touched by them. Almost all of those who mentioned such incidents described them as being pleasant and helpful. I also learned that people did not talk about these experiences, which in retrospect makes it interesting that they spoke so easily to me. I suppose they knew me well, being the local doctor, and realized that I was interested in their stories.

When I consulted my general practitioner and hospital colleagues, and all had been qualified longer than I, they could not recall any patient mentioning such an experience to them. The same was true of the local clergy. For the most part they were completely unaware that members of their congregations were hearing, seeing or feeling the presence of dead relatives. Some clergy were obviously interested in learning about these occurrences but a few appeared to be slightly apprehensive in case I was luring them into the field of spiritualism. The local Catholic priest said his people would be very reluctant to inform him as they would expect him to react in a denunciatory way. A Free Church minister did recall one 'particularly cultured' widower who had calmly reported seeing his dead wife, and thought that during a ministry of over 30 years about 12 other people had described feeling that the deceased was still with them.

I found all this fascinating. Because so little was known about this aspect of bereavement, I felt that the subject needed to be studied properly and I decided to concentrate on this work. The University of London allowed me to register it for an MD thesis,[9] Sylvia Lutkins kindly agreed to do the statistical analyses, and four senior psychiatrists (Drs John Pollitt and Colin Murray Parkes; Professors Ken Rawnsley and John Hinton) and Dr R.J.F.H. Pinsent – a pioneer in general practitioner research, were generous with their help and advice.

Studying the Bereaved

The widowed people living in the survey area proved to be very helpful. Some people had to be excluded beforehand because of serious illness and a few could not be contacted. Of the remaining 295 widows and widowers only two refused to take part. Those who co-operated did so without knowing beforehand the purpose of the survey, other than that it was related to widowhood. During the interview, each person was encouraged to talk freely about the dead spouse but care was also taken to ensure that all the items listed on a standardized form were covered in the discussion. Dreams were noted, when mentioned, but these were carefully differentiated from any hallucinatory experience that occurred in full consciousness, and they were not included in the final analyses. Experiences that occurred at night, other than those occurring immediately after retiring to bed, were discounted as dreams. The interviewees were also asked to complete a Hysteroid-Obsessoid questionnaire to determine whether there was a relationship between hallucinatory experiences and basic personality type. A hysteroid person is more imaginative than an obsessoid one and approximates to the extrovert of Jungian psychology whilst the obsessoid conforms closely to the Jungian introvert.[10]

It was not only dreams that were discounted; particular care was taken in assessing the statements of those who said that they had had hallucinations of the dead spouse. Only those who did not rationalize the incidents were recorded as having had a hallucinatory experience. If, for instance, they said that they had seen the deceased 'in their mind's eye' or if there was any doubt about the reality of the experience, then a nil response was recorded.

The main finding of the survey was that a perception of the dead partner was a common and normal consequence of widowhood.[11] Almost 50 per cent of widowed people reported having had such an experience and, though the incidence declined over the years and some of the interviewees had been widowed for many years, 36 per cent of the people contacted were still having experiences of this type when I discussed it with them. The most commonly occurring one was the SOP, and this was reported by 39 per cent of widowed people.

Personal Statements

The nature of the experience is perhaps best described in the following statements that were made by the interviewees themselves. The duration of widowhood, when interviewed, is indicated in brackets after the verbatim report.

> I know she is with me, when I speak to her she goes away. (9 years)
>
> She did come last week. She was there in spirit. I was surprised. (2½ years)
>
> I know quite well that she is not here and yet I sometimes have the feeling that she is here sometimes. It gives me a feeling of sad comfort. (9 months)
>
> It is a sacred thing. I feel that there is some nearness; that he hasn't actually gone out of my life. I am never afraid. (3½ years)
>
> He seems so close. (7 years)
>
> Very often he is by my side. It is a funny thing, I've never dreamt of him. (4 years)
>
> I feel he is watching me. (2 years)
>
> He's there with me now; I am not a bit nervous or miserable. Whenever I am out, I want to go home because he is there. I slept from the first night he was buried. (8 years)
>
> I was very bad at the time. I really thought he was with me but I've got over that now. (20 years)
>
> There's nothing like it. It's worth more than all the money in the world to me. It's a lovely feeling. I'm very happy, I never feel alone. (10 years)
>
> I felt for one week about two years ago that he was with me all the time. I was not afraid of it. (10 years)
>
> It stops me doing things I might otherwise do – like drinking. (14 years)
>
> He's always with me. (2 years)

The impression created by an SOP can appear so real that whilst 26 people had remarried, four said they had declined opportunities to do so because they felt their dead spouse was opposed to it. One young widow had even broken off an engagement for this reason. Among those who did remarry, 11 had experienced the presence of their dead spouse and this sometimes continued well into the second marriage. One elderly widow felt that both her dead husbands were still with her. A few people had no hallucinatory experiences after the death of their partners, but did as a consequence of other personal tragedies such as the death of a son.

An SOP is often accompanied by a feeling of being protected and helped by the dead.

> I feel that no harm can come to me because he is always around me. (6 years)
>
> I feel many times that there is some guidance. (4 years)
>
> I feel that he is with me and looking after me. Before he died I was always terrified of going upstairs alone and wouldn't go up without a light. Since he's died, I don't mind going up one bit. (11 years)
>
> I feel he is guiding me. (15 years)
>
> He hasn't gone far away yet. He is very real now. Before he died, I was always afraid of the dark. That fear has now gone from me. (2 years)
>
> If something crops up, I feel him very close and am guided by him. (3 years)
>
> I don't feel a bit afraid; he is with me all the time. It's beautiful. (3½ years)
>
> I feel he is helping me still. (26 years)

Whilst an SOP is the perception most frequently reported by the bereaved, auditory and visual hallucinations are also common though tactile hallucinations are rare. Visual hallucinations occurred in 14 per cent of cases.

> I've shaken hands with her once or twice. I thought 'it's nice to see her'. (11 years)
>
> She's always wearing the same clothes. (20 years)
>
> He was very plain to me, I was about my work in the house. He disappeared when I was about to speak to him. (10 years and remarried)
>
> Once he came to the door when I was preparing lunch. It was an awful shock. (5 years)
>
> I have only seen him once. He was walking through the gate. He looked very happy. I didn't have a chance to speak to him. (4½ years)

Auditory hallucinations are slightly less common than visual ones: 13.3 per cent of widowed people reported hearing the deceased spouse.

> I think she got me my present house. I find hearing her breathing disturbing but I like the feeling that she is in the house. (16 years)
>
> Whenever I am troubled he seems to say 'keep a stiff upper lip'. (12 years) (This report is particularly interesting as her husband had absconded with another woman 10 years before his death. After his death, though never beforehand, she had visual and auditory hallucinations of him and also felt his presence quite frequently. These episodes occurred in Mid-Wales even though they had spent their married life together in Sussex.)
>
> I am not lonely because he is with me all the time. I hear him saying 'I'm alright Mary'. I am very happy. (2 months)
>
> I hear him saying 'Don't worry'. (6 months)
>
> I often hear him singing. Sometimes I tell my sister that I hear Dick singing and she just smiles. (8 years)

> I fancy if I left here, I would be running away from him. Lots of people wanted me to go but I just couldn't. I often hear him walking about. He speaks quite plainly. He looks younger, just as he was when he was alright, never as he was when he was ill. (9 months)
>
> I heard, how shall I put it, sounds of consolation for the first three months. (20 years)

Some people not only hear deceased spouses but converse with them.

> I talked to her once as I was going to bed. They were very appropriate words. Her voice was as plain as ever. (7 years)
>
> I often have a chat with him. That's why I've never bothered with anyone else. (27 years)

The most infrequently reported hallucination was of being touched by the dead spouse. Only 2.7 per cent of widowed people reported having such an experience.

> I felt on one occasion he touched me on the shoulder when I was standing at the sink. I have heard him breathing during the night and calling me during the day. He was ill for many years and had terrible nights. It was so hard for me and he used to accuse me of going with other men. When I die I want to be cremated and my ashes put in his grave. I feel closer to him than to Edmund. I married Edmund for company. There's no one like your first love. (Widowed 22 years and remarried.)
>
> I very often feel that he is with me in bed. I pull the clothes over me and think that's silly. (2 years)
>
> I have felt him touch my shoulder. (10 years)
>
> On one occasion in the afternoon, soon after he died, I definitely felt his presence and he kissed my face.

Most people (69 per cent) found their perceptions of the dead helpful and only a small proportion (6 per cent) found them unpleasant. But these negative impressions also need to be recorded.

> I felt him touch me. It frightened me. Made you think you were going up the wall. (8½ years)
>
> When I heard his voice I would think, why he's alive, and then I would think, no it can't be, he is dead. It upset me very much. It wasn't right. (5 years)
>
> He called 'mam, mam' from the bottom of the stairs. It frightened me. I didn't answer because they say you shouldn't answer the dead. (6 years)
>
> I was wondering whether I was going a little bit mental at the time. (20 years)
>
> I find it frightening. (8 years) (This man's wife had committed suicide.)
>
> It wasn't right. It upset me very much. (5 years) (This woman had recurrent auditory hallucinations.)

People talk about such things more easily nowadays but an important finding at the time of the survey was the reluctance of people to disclose their experiences, and the care with which they choose their confidants. Most people (72.3 per cent) had not mentioned the experience to anyone else, and those who had usually told a friend outside the family. Nobody had informed their doctor, and only one person had confided in a clergyman. Most people could not, or would not, say why they kept the experience a secret. The most commonly expressed reasons were fear of ridicule and that the experience was too personal.

> It's a thing between you and her; nothing to do with outsiders. (22 years)
> I have always heard that it is very unlucky to repeat what was said on those occasions, and I have never told anyone and I am not going to tell you. (7 years)
> It's not to be mentioned. (20 years)
> It's too personal; I hide many things especially the things most important to me. (13 years)
> I didn't want to worry anyone. (20 years)
> I've never told anyone. I'm keeping it to myself. (4 years)
> I'm frightened to tell anyone. I am so glad you asked me, I wouldn't have told you otherwise. (11 years)
> I still feel that I am a foreigner, although I have been here 50 years, so that I couldn't confide in anyone. (7½ years)
> I don't think people want to hear all that. You've got to hide that from the rest of the world. (19 years)
> I tell no one; not even the girls. I keep it to myself. They would think that I was soft. (11 years)
> People would laugh at you if I told them. (10 years)
> They'd think I was silly. It does seem silly after nine years. I don't want to upset them. (9 years)
> It's like this. People don't really believe you. (10 years)
> I don't know. I've only got my daughter. It might upset her if I tell her things like that. (15 years)
> They would think that I was silly; that I was imagining them. (3½ years)
> Perhaps they would laugh at me, saying I am dreaming, but I don't think I am. (35 years)
> It's no use telling the young ones. They wouldn't believe you. (10 years)
> No one else has asked me. (3½ years)

Social Patterns

The survey was designed to uncover any social and clinical factors that might influence the incidence of these experiences. The results were subjected to a detailed statistical analysis and, for the most part, showed that the frequency of hallucinations did not differ between social groups. They occurred with equal frequency in men and women and, usually, irrespective of age, though young widows were less likely to hallucinate than women widowed after the age of 40.

Social isolation was not a factor and the incidence was unaffected by whether or not people felt lonely, lived alone, had relatives nearby or were in regular employment. Change of residence did not affect the incidence, nor did the site of the dwelling place whether this was in a town, village or isolated farmhouse. Known religious practices had no bearing on the frequency of hallucinations. The incidence was the same in monoglot English and bilingual (Welsh and English speaking) families. One important finding was that the results were not just applicable to Mid-Wales. The statistical analysis showed that people who had been living in other parts of England and Wales when they were widowed were just as likely to experience hallucinations as those widowed in the survey area.

The hallucinations often continued long into widowhood though the incidence did decline with increasing years. A few people felt that the dead spouse was always with them, but in most cases the hallucinations were intermittent affairs occurring at variable times throughout the day. People whose marriages were unhappy were unlikely to have such experiences. They were most commonly reported by individuals whose marriages had been happy, and especially those who had reared children. The likelihood of hallucinations occurring also increased with increasing duration of marriage. One suprising finding was that the incidence was highest among members of the professional and managerial classes. No variation was found between other occupational groups tested. This unlikely finding receives some support from a study undertaken by David Hay.[12] By means of a national opinion poll, he found that members of the middle class were more likely to say that they had 'been aware of or influenced by a presence or power' than people belonging to lower social classes. A second survey questioned a random group of people in Nottingham. Quite unexpectedly, they found that 23 of the 107 people interviewed said that they had experienced the presence of a dead person – not always a spouse – and that half of these people looked upon it as a religious experience. The possibility that the bereaved would describe their hallucinatory experiences in such clearly numinous terms had not been considered in the Llanidloes survey.

The incidence of hallucinations was associated with some positive clinical findings. People experiencing them were less likely to have had sleep disturbances, loss of appetite and loss of weight. On the other hand, they did think about and miss the deceased more than those who had not hallucinated. There was, with one exception, no evidence to suggest that anyone had deliberately cultivated the image of the deceased or sought an encounter with the dead person. The one exception was a woman who, because she had wanted to feel close to her husband, had attended a spiritualist meeting. The study also showed that there was no association between the incidence of hallucinations and post-bereavement depression. Neither did the incidence vary with the suddenness of death, cause of death or place of death.

A relationship was found between the incidence of hallucinations and the basic personality of the surviving spouse as determined by the Hysteroid/Obsessoid questionnaire. The incidence was higher among the hysteroid (extrovert) type than among obsessoid (introvert) people. This is contrary to what one might expect as introverts are normally considered to be more concerned with their own thoughts and feelings than extroverts. Within this context, it is worth noting that Freud and Jung differed both in their basic personalities and in their experience of such phenomena. Carl Jung, an introvert, recorded many personal encounters with the dead in his memoirs. Sigmund Freud, an extrovert, appears to have had no such experiences.

The main conclusion to be drawn from the survey is that a perception of the dead is a normal feature of widowhood.[11] Almost half of all widowed people have such experiences, and they can occur for many years after the individual has been bereaved. Whilst affirming the normality of these experiences, it is, of course, just as normal not to have them. To have such hallucinations can be considered normal because they are both common and helpful. They do not affect overt behaviour, and most people are able to integrate the experience and keep it secret. They are not associated with any mental derangement or depressive illness, and people who have these experiences are less likely to have sleep disturbances, or loss of appetite and weight, than those who have not been affected in this way.

Confirmatory Reports

The Llanidloes survey showed that 46.7 per cent of widowed people had an experience of the dead spouse that they considered to be significant and real. This conclusion, whilst interesting, has general validity only if it is substantiated, or at least not seriously questioned, by parallel studies. Other reports do indeed appear to confirm the validity of this assessment. Some variations are to be expected especially when surveys are, as is sometimes the case, based on self-selected or atypical samples, but all the studies seem to agree that these phenomena are a common accompaniment of bereavement. The earlier reports by Parkes,[5] Marris[6] and particularly Yamamoto[7] showed a higher incidence of hallucinations among young widows than was found in Llanidloes. Kalish and Reynolds[13] recorded an incidence of almost 60 per cent in a small group of widows in Los Angeles.

Surveys in the USA and Iceland have also confirmed the prevalence of hallucinations among widowed people. Greeley[14] and Haraldsson[15] found that about half of all the widows and widowers they contacted reported hallucinatory experiences of their deceased spouses. Similar results were obtained by Glick and his colleagues[16] in Boston. Although Glick and his co-workers had not expected to encounter the phenomenon, they found that 47 per cent of the young widows they interviewed had the feeling that 'my husband watches over me', even though the women knew quite well that their husbands were dead. Also, many of the widows, even 13 months after bereavement, had a fairly steady sense of their husband's presence. Rogo[17] says that: 'When the Rees findings were made known, research workers at Wayne State University were so intrigued that they decided to replicate the study. They obtained very similar data.'

A more recent study was undertaken in North Carolina by Olson and his colleagues.[18] They interviewed 46 widows who were living in nursing homes and found that 61 per cent reported having had hallucinatory experiences of their dead spouse, either in terms of a sensory perception or of an SOP. Most of the widows found the experience good or helpful, and most had not mentioned them to anyone previously. Forty-six per cent of the women continued to have perceptions of their dead spouse. The authors said that the results were surprisingly similar to those of the Llanidloes survey and showed that these experiences are more common in the United States than had been generally recognized. They also pointed out that the studies so far published had shown a remarkable agreement in the percentage of the bereaved who have a perception of their dead loved ones. They considered that these facts were not widely known to the medical community, or to the population at large, and suggested that a new nomenclature was needed to remove from these phenomena the stigma associated with the word 'hallucination'. The most recent report is provided by Schuchter and Zisook.[19] They state that in California 63 per cent of widowed people feel the presence of their deceased spouse 13 months after being bereaved.

Their Social Significance

It is one thing to establish the existence and normality of a subjective experience but quite a different matter to determine its significance. Yet, as Kalish and Reynolds[20] pointed out, these experiences have important philosophical and psychological implications both for the person concerned and for the community as a whole. However, the people involved, and the society to which they belong, may have very different views about the reality of the incidents and may interpret them quite differently. When such a discrepancy exists, it is not surprising if the individual decides to keep the information a secret.

Sometimes the personal and cultural interpretations coalesce to form a unified belief system. The Japanese and traditional African religions have a ritual of ancestor veneration that presumes that the dead have a continuing role to play in earthly affairs. In such societies, the bereaved are unlikely to feel restrained from mentioning an encounter with their deceased loved ones. The same official sanction was once apparent in other countries, but the cult of the ancestor has been greatly weakened in communist China and in many other communities that have been influenced by Western ideas and educational systems. This was no doubt looked upon as a rational development by the political leaders of these countries, but a possible outcome has been that, in a figurative sense, these subjective experiences have been forced underground. They will persist in the everyday life of the people, but their natural outlet of expression in social discourse and traditional customs has been severely curtailed.

A sense of the presence of the dead is not an experience that society should encourage people to conceal. It is a perfectly normal occurrence and compatible with a favourable outcome to the process of mourning. Although an SOP may take a few weeks to become established, it often persists at its original intensity for a prolonged period of time instead of slowly waning, as happens with the other components of the early phases of mourning. The people involved usually find the experience comforting and helpful, and some feel guided and protected by it. Its occurrence is often associated with a reduction in yearning and restlessness, and Glick et al.[16] found that a widow's progress towards recovery is often facilitated by conversations with her husband's presence. It is also not incompatible with an increasing capacity for independent action. Bowlby[21] suggests that this is because the widowed allow their feelings of attachment to the deceased to persist. As a consequence, their own sense of identity is preserved and this enables them to reorganize their lives in a meaningful way. He also pointed out that 'the high prevalence of a continuing sense of the presence of the dead and its compatibility with a favourable outcome' gives no support to Freud's well-known dictum that 'mourning has a quite precise psychical task to perform: its function is to detach the survivor's memories and hopes from the dead'.

Possible Explanations

The various explanations given for these phenomena are usually based on one of two general suppositions. The first is that they represent a direct contact between the living and the dead. This is the traditional belief in many societies and one that the experients themselves often hold. The opposing view rejects this proposition and seeks an answer that does not involve supernatural concepts. These two mutually exclusive interpretations should not be looked upon as representing a clash of views between religion and science – religious leaders can be as apprehensive of supernatural phenomena as sceptical scientists, and may have more difficulty in integrating such ideas into their philosophical systems. All the explanations put forward are, of course, merely theories that cannot be substantiated by any objective evidence, nor can their validity be tested in a scientifically acceptable manner. The phenomena do not provide any objective proof of life after death, neither can their significance in pointing to that possibility be disproved. The only certainties are that whilst the experiences sometimes provide individuals with the assurance that their partner has survived death, many people consider this assurance to be ill founded.

Explanations that are based on a natural causation are usually derived from two sources. The first is provided by loosely analogous phenomena that have a rational and demonstrable scientific explanation. The second source is the pool of ideas originally advanced by Freud and later developed by other depth psychologists. Some investigators, for instance, have likened the experiences of the bereaved to those of people who have lost a limb or breast. Many people with such a loss experience tingling, or even painful, sensations in the region of the amputated part and, when this occurs, they are said to have a phantom breast or limb. An explanation of these sensations is very simple. When a part of the body has been amputated, the ends of the severed nerves may still be stimulated by the surrounding tissues and continue to transmit electrical impulses to the brain. There they are interpreted in the usual way as originating from the region previously occupied by the breast or limb. But while the part of the brain which deals with these messages can be precisely located by neurosurgeons, there is no known site that can be held responsible for the hallucinations of bereaved people. Nevertheless, it may be argued that the two processes are similar, it is just that the stimuli and neuronal pathways producing the hallucinatory experiences of widowed people have yet to be uncovered. One important point needs to be made. The perception of a phantom limb is due to physiological processes only, there is no psychological component. The sensations are not the result of an inner 'search' or 'pining' for the lost part. This must be emphasized as some psychiatrists attribute perceptions of the dead to the pining (or yearning) of the bereaved and their need to search for and find the deceased.

The visual hallucinations have also been explained on the basis that they are illusions, similar to the mirages people sometimes see in the desert. The two phenomena are not really comparable however. Mirages are misapprehensions of actual objects with the objects being mislocated by the observer because the light rays coming from them are refracted through various layers of air at different temperatures. Mirages are interesting because the discerned objects are not only located in the wrong place: they also appear upside down. Sometimes a mirage is seen as a double object with an upright image above the inverted one. This is not a close parallel to the experiences of the bereaved, but it does remind us that people are capable of misinterpreting what they see. It is reasonable to assume that the widowed may occasionally mistake inaccurately perceived people or objects for their dead spouse, but to use this assumption as a general theory overlooks some important facts. Errors in identification are most frequently made in unfamiliar places, but the bereaved are most likely to perceive their dead partners in and around their own homes where such errors are less likely to occur. There is also no reason to suppose that widowed people are more likely to misinterpret data than other folk. If the pain of loss is considered to be the triggering factor, there should be as high an incidence of such hallucinations among people who have been deserted by their spouses and among the wives of prisoners of war. Yet there is no evidence to suggest that people who have lost their partners in these ways have hallucinatory experiences similar to those described in this chapter.

The idea that bereaved people may be misinterpreting perceived data has been incorporated into a more complex psychological explanation for these strange experiences. This explanation embraces the concepts of yearning and searching, and may have had its origin in a remark of Freud's when he referred to 'the insatiable and persistent yearning for the lost object' experienced by bereaved people. Many psychiatrists consider this yearning (or pining) to be of central importance in the mourning process, and that the function of mourning is to liberate the individual from such intense longings or, to use Freud's famous phrase, 'to detach the survivor's memories and hopes from the dead'.[21] Bowlby[22] and Parkes[23] went one stage further. They suggested that the pining is so painful that the bereaved are forced to search for the dead partner and that this search, which is of necessity unrewarding, is an essential preliminary to their accepting their loss.

The characteristic features of the search are not displayed when people inadvertently lay an extra place at the table or purchase something for the dead spouse. These are lapses of memory. The search proper has five distinct components and these do not include forgetfulness. The components of the search are: a state of restlessness in which the individual moves around and scans the environment in an effort to find the lost person; preoccupation with memories of the deceased, in which the bereaved thinks intensely about the dead partner; the development of a perceptual 'set' for the absent partner, so that attention is given only to stimuli which suggest his or her presence; focussing the attention on those parts of the environment that are associated with the deceased, and calling for the dead person by name.

According to this theory, the bereaved pay particular attention to stimuli that suggest the presence of the deceased and ignore those that do not. If ambiguous perceptions happen to fit the image of the deceased, attention is focused on this data and further evidence is sought to confirm the initial impression. As a consequence, the bereaved person is particularly open to the illusion that the dead person has been perceived. If the deceased is rediscovered in this way, the reunion provides a source of comfort to the widowed person; this reunion is often associated with a reduction in restless-ness and pining, which indicates that there has been a reduction in searching. Consequently, the bereaved no longer attempt to detach themselves from the deceased but cling to them. This enables the individual to retain, albeit in an unsatisfactory manner, the spouse that has been lost. The theory is an interesting one but it leaves some questions unanswered. One problem is that it fails to explain why the bereaved should be so prone to misinterpret data when looking so intently for the deceased. People who are intent on finding a very familiar object tend to be highly discriminatory. They know exactly what they are seeking and will reject everything else. Even if there is a momentary misunderstanding, they will check the evidence and discover their mistake.

In his carefully considered advocacy of the search theory, Parkes[24] pointed out that although the bereaved may think about the deceased a great deal, these are bitter-sweet memories that bring pain as well as consolation. Mourners naturally wish to be free from their distress, and common ways of mitigating the pain are to concentrate on other thoughts and avoid situations that revive painful memories. These attempts to mitigate the pain oscillate or alternate with the search, with its exposure to painful stimuli. There are therefore two opposing tendencies: an inhibitory tendency that seeks to avoid disturbing stimuli, and what Parkes calls a facilitative or reality-testing tendency, which enhances perception and thought about disturbing stimuli. Both these tendencies decrease with time as the intensity of grief diminishes. Eventually people who have been mainly preoccupied with thoughts of the deceased find it easier to think of other things, whereas those who have avoided such thoughts find it easier to accept situations which might revive painful memories. Implicit, though not stated explicitly, in the search theory, is the supposition that perceptions of the dead occur only, or mainly, during the searching phase. If so, there is nothing to support such an assumption. The available evidence indicates that these events occur unexpectedly and spontaneously. As C.S. Lewis wrote: 'Something quite unexpected has happened . . . suddenly, at the very moment when, so far, I mourned H. least, I remembered her best. Indeed, it was something better than a memory; an instantaneous unanswerable impression . . . I said, several notebooks ago, that if I got what seemed like an assurance of H's presence, I wouldn't believe it. Easier said than done.'[2]

Parkes[24] also compares the hallucinations of the bereaved with the 'vacuum activities' that are sometimes displayed by birds and fish. He points out that captive starlings continue to perform the movements of fly catching even when there are no flies present, and that the male stickleback has been seen to perform its characteristic zig-zag courting dance in the absence of an ovigerous female stickleback. But there is no reason to believe that these creatures pursue these activities because they feel the presence of, or perceive, the absent food or mate. It is a well-known fact that birds and fish have genetically set patterns of behaviour that determine the time of day, or year, when certain biological functions are best carried out. The annual timing of reproduction and migration are two such examples. Young birds prepare for migration by completing the development of their plumage and by storing fat, and normally day-active birds migrate at night probably for thermoregulatory reasons. These patterns have obvious adaptive functions, but the perception of the dead has no evolutionary function and cannot be explained in Darwinian terms.

It has been suggested that discerning the presence of the dead may mitigate the pain of bereavement, and this appears to be true. But nature is 'red in tooth and claw' and is concerned with the survival of the species, not with easing the distress of older members of society whose capacity for reproduction has diminished or ended. Why then has this most subtle of consolations been evolved and enabled to persist? It has no place in a philosophy that confines mankind to a material world, but it does make sense if a spiritual dimension to life is also accepted. Bowlby[21] suggested that a perception of the dead may be the preferred solution of the bereaved to the agony of their loss. This may be partly true, but it is not an outcome they anticipate or consciously choose, nor one that the ethos of Western society encourages.

The explanation based on the search theory is interesting, but it does not really explain how the search leads to the discovery of a phantom nor the evolutionary significance of the latter. It is not entirely compatible with the descriptions given by the widowed, as their experiences happen quite unexpectedly and involuntarily, and are occasionally disagreeable. Neither does it explain the reluctance of people to talk about their perceptions for fear of mockery and disbelief. The theory does accept the reality of the subjective experiences reported by the bereaved, but explains away the significance that they themselves may wish to attribute to it. In that sense the bereaved are deprived of their own interpretation of what is happening. This occurs even if they have made a reasonable adjustment to widowhood by changing residence, remarriage and resuming a normal role in society. The psychological theory also carries the implication that if the bereaved have hallucinations of the dead, they have not completed the mourning process and, in that sense, are still emotionally disabled. It does not accept the possibility that the widowed may have been enlarged by the experience and their lives thereby enhanced. A spiritual explanation opens up a new perspective for the bereaved as it implies a continued existence after death which, though it cannot be actually proved, is affirmed by the near presence of the deceased.

Their Theological Significance

So far we have considered the psychological approach to the hallucinations. The phenomena also have a theological significance, especially for Christians. The psychological explanation, though inadequate, may be sufficient for secular humanists and those who share their belief that life ends at death. But for those who postulate a spiritual dimension to life, to accept the psychological theory in its entirety means failing to take account of all the implications of the available data. Judaism is justified in doing so, as it has always turned its face resolutely from the possibility of any contact with the dead. Christianity is not so justified even though it has little liking for anything that may seem to be connected with spiritualism.

The Christian belief in the resurrection of Christ is based on the reports of the disciples who met Jesus after his crucifixion. Similar phenomena are experienced in a lesser way by millions of people today. If the resurrection of Jesus is true then the perceptions of the dead by widowed people living today must be accorded their own, albeit less significant, reality. It is illogical to accept the one and deny the other, especially as the bereaved report, just like the disciples, that they have heard, spoken to and been touched by the deceased. This is obviously a difficult issue for the Church to resolve and one can understand the reluctance Christian leaders may have in approaching it. Nevertheless it is a subject that needs to be widely discussed.

As Kalish and Reynolds[20] have pointed out, these phenomena have important philosophical as well as psychological implications both for the individual and society as a whole. A theology of the Resurrection must remain incomplete if the current experiences of the widowed are not somehow incorporated into it. One cannot say that Christ lives, and that this fact was proven by his reappearance 2,000 years ago, but that the perceptions of the dead experienced by many people today have no reality. If Christian theology wishes to explain these experiences in psychological terms, then it must do the same for the disciples' meetings with the resurrected Christ, or clearly state why one phenomenon is a reality and the others illusory. Psychiatrists are trying to explain these experiences in terms that are acceptable to their discipline; theologians also need to address this problem from their own distinctive perspective. That ordinary churchgoers regard this as necessary is apparent from the letters quoted in the appendix to this book.

Chapter 23
Near-death
Experiences

A man can die but once.

King Henry IV, Part 2

People who have had a close encounter with death usually have an interesting story to tell. This applies even when their accounts are limited to a brief description of what actually happened. A natural reticence affects many people about such matters and they are quite likely to say nothing at all unless they are encouraged to talk about the event. Their stories are likely to be most fascinating if they contain unusual elements like the out-of-the-body states and mystical visions/encounters, which form the subject-matter of the many articles and books that have been written about near-death experiences (NDEs). This term was used first by Dr Raymond Moody,[1] in 1975, and refers to the cluster of subjective experiences that are sometimes reported by people who have been confronted by imminent death.

Deathbed Visions

Articles dealing with near-death experiences sometimes fail to draw a clear distinction between NDEs and deathbed visions. Yet the two phenomena are quite distinct and need to be clearly differentiated. Of the two, NDEs are much the more common. The term 'deathbed vision' is self explanatory. It is a vision seen by someone who is dying. Rarely, some indication of the vision is noted by an attendant in the sick room but, usually, its presence is made apparent only by a few brief words spoken by the dying person. Deathbed visions are uncommon events, they are not mentioned in publications dealing with palliative medicine or psychiatry, and their incidence appears to be reduced when terminally ill people are given analgesic and sedative drugs. They need to be clearly distinguished from confusional and hallucinatory states, from NDEs and from the sense of peacefulness that can precede death. They may be attributed to pathological causes, but the nature of these events makes such a diagnosis questionable. The characteristic feature of a deathbed vision is that a dying patient perceives the presence of a non-physical entity whom he/she may identify as someone who has died or as a spiritual being. Moreover, the sick person knows that the individual has come to 'take them away' and usually accepts the summons gladly.

The nature of the visions can best be described by two personal experiences. The first involved my mother, who had been ill with terminal cancer for 15 months and comatose during the previous 24 hours. We were alone in her bedroom when she suddenly sat up and extended her arms as if she was welcoming an unseen presence. The most remarkable change was in the liveliness of her gaze and the radiance that appeared in her face. My immediate reaction was that she was welcoming a dearly loved person, possibly my father who had died a few weeks previously. She then lay back in her bed, said goodbye to me and relapsed into an apparent coma. I was so overwhelmed by the incident that I left the room to regain my composure. When I returned a few minutes later she was dead. It may be reasonably argued that I was in a distraught state and read too much into the experience. This cannot be gainsaid, one merely remains aware of the deep impression it made. I understand also that a clinical cause can be postulated for the sudden movement – that it might have been due to the occlusion, by an embolus, of the spinal artery. This would not explain, however, the return to a conscious state, the radiance and liveliness of gaze, or the farewell. I have seen many people die but I have never experienced anything quite like this. Many years later, when speaking at a conference in London for hospice workers, I asked those present if they had encountered anything similar. No one replied even though they had been responsive to previous questions. After the meeting, an elderly nursing sister came to me and said that she knew exactly what I meant as she had witnessed such a change many years previously in a dying child. She added that she was not alone at the time and that another nurse had also seen and been impressed by the transformation.

The second incident involved a lady who was about 60 years old. She was one of those people who always appear to be fit and rarely consult a doctor, but I was asked to visit her urgently late one night. When I arrived in the house she was lying on the sitting room couch and was obviously dead. She had gone to bed apparently perfectly well but had got up during the night and gone downstairs. Soon afterwards she had called out to her husband, 'Come down quickly, I am dying, I can see Jesus.' Her husband hurried downstairs, but by the time he reached her she had lost consciousness and could not be roused.

The relative infrequency of deathbed visions makes a detailed study of the phenomenon difficult and few reports have been published on this subject. One of the first was published in 1926 by Sir William Barrett, a professor of physics.[2] In collaboration with his wife, a consultant gynaecologist, he collected some 50 accounts of deathbed visions, including some from as far back as the eighteenth century. Barrett was particularly interested in the descriptions of visions that would not have conformed to the patients' normal expectations. He recorded instances of dying children who reported seeing angels without wings, and those of eight other people who described the presence of people who were dead without knowing that these people had actually died.

An interesting attempt to compare the deathbed visions of people of different cultures was undertaken by Osis and Haraldsson, using India and the USA as the centres for their study.[3] The conclusions drawn from the survey may be questioned on methodological grounds but some interesting patterns were demonstrated. The analysis was based on 471 deathbed visions reported by doctors and nurses in the two countries, mainly involving patients who had not received drugs that could affect their level of consciousness or produce hallucinations. They found a remarkable similarity between the deathbed visions of Hindus and Americans. Most occurred within 24 hours of death and were of brief duration – 47 per cent lasted for 5 minutes or less, and only 17 per cent for more than 1 hour. The patients usually realized that the apparitions had come to 'take them away' to another realm of life, and most responded with serenity, peace or elation. A few were fearful, and this was a more common finding among the Indians than among the American patients.

Osis and Haraldsson considered that the visions were mainly 'survival related apparitions' as they were predominantly perceptions of dead relatives or spiritual beings. The most clear cultural difference was apparent in the type of vision seen. The Indian patients usually reported seeing religious figures, whilst the Americans were more likely to see dead relatives. Not surprisingly, the type of religious figure seen was culturally related. Hindu deities, including the God of Death, were seen by the Indian patients, whilst Americans reported the presence of Jesus, the Blessed Virgin Mary and other Christian saints. Female figures were rarely perceived by the Hindus but were commonly seen by the Americans. The main findings of the survey were that deathbed visions are of short duration and occur shortly before death. The visions are mainly of 'survival-related apparitions', who have a 'take-away' purpose and usually induce feelings of peace, serenity and elation. The incidence appears to be reduced if the patients have been given drugs. The experience is not dependent on sex, age, education, socio-economic status or religious beliefs, though the latter is likely to give a cultural orientation to the vision.

Deathbed Vision or NDE?

Deathbed visions always involve a dying patient, but this is not invariably the case with NDEs. The latter have been reported by many people who believed that their life was at risk but who were not terminally ill. They include people who were involved in accidents from which they emerged unscathed, individuals who were planning to commit suicide and others who were just hyperventilating.[1,4,5] Other features help to distinguish deathbed visions from NDEs. The former are reported by the patient as they occur, and some inkling of what is happening may be apparent to an outside observer. In contrast, NDEs are reported at a later date by the percipient and were not apparent to anyone else. People who have deathbed visions know that the apparition has come to take them away, but beings encountered in NDEs do not have such a function. Finally, out-of-the-body states – a situation in which people find themselves so completely separated from the body that they can observe themselves from an outside vantage point – are common occurrences in NDEs but are not mentioned in accounts of deathbed visions.

Cardiac Arrests

Near-death experiences can occur in various fraught situations but they are particularly well-documented in people who have had a cardiac arrest. The fact that these patients were so close to death gives the 'other-world' experiences reported by some of the survivors their special medical and philosophical interest. However, some experts wish to separate NDEs from a medical assessment of the imminence of death. Zaleski adopts this attitude in her excellent book *Other World Journeys – Accounts of Near-Death Experience in Medieval and Modern Times*.[6] She suggests that a looser interpretation of the concept of death than that provided by medical criteria is appropriate in the case of NDEs. This wider interpretation would not be restricted by physical signs; it would recognize that a profound, imaginative rehearsal for death can be triggered by people just feeling themself to be *in extremis*. Zaleski would also prefer NDEs to be classified as part of the dissociative or out-of-the-body states. This seems sensible as an out-of-the-body state is one of the distinguishing features of an NDE. It would also be consistent with a belief, shared by many cultures, that the spirit can leave the body in sleep, illness and ecstasy, and that death is just a more persistent form of separation. Whilst accepting the logic of these arguments, there is a general view that an NDE has a particular significance if it is clearly related to a clinical diagnosis of death. Such a diagnosis would not be based on brain death criteria, which are irreversible, but on the cessation of cardiac or respiratory function and the subsequent need for immediate resuscitation. It is with this aspect of NDE that we shall be mainly concerned.

Core Experiences

The present wide interest in NDEs is remarkable. They have been reported since early times, and more recently in autobiographies. Carl Jung gave a clear account of his own NDE, following a heart attack in 1944, in which he describes travelling in outer space, being surrounded by light and in contact with angels. Everything was 'glorious' and there were 'ineffable states of joy', and later he felt 'a violent resistance to my doctor because he brought me back to life'.[7] But despite these reports NDEs were not considered to merit much objective study before 1975, the year in which Dr Raymond Moody published his book, *Life after Life*.[1] In it he described the unusual subjective experiences of people who had been close to death, including some whose hearts had stopped beating and who had been resuscitated. He outlined a sequence of events that was based on the 14 most commonly reported experiences. These included descriptions of being outside the body, travelling along a tunnel, meeting dead relatives or spiritual beings – especially a 'being of light', approaching a borderline of no return and coming back to Earth. He reported that the survivors' attitude to life and death was usually changed by the experience. In general, they lost any previous fear of death, considered life to be more precious than formerly, emphasized the importance of love in personal relationships and the need to learn throughout life as 'the acquisition of knowledge continues even in the after-life'.

Dr Moody's book was soon a bestseller, with many people assuming that it provided conclusive evidence of survival after death. It also stimulated considerable academic interest. New, and better, research studies were undertaken, books and articles were written on the subject and various individuals, including Dr Kenneth Ring, a professor of psychology at the University of Connecticut, reported reaching the same general conclusions as Dr Moody. A further development was the establishment in 1981, of the International Association for Near-Death Studies (IANDS) with offices at the University of Connecticut. IANDS organizes conferences, encourages discussion and research on NDEs and publishes the *Journal of Near-Death Studies*, formerly *Anabiosis*. It enables people with similar, or conflicting views to share their ideas and argue about the significance that should be ascribed to NDEs. Some of its members support Dr Moody's belief that NDEs provide evidence of life after death.[8] Other people with an interest in NDEs are more sceptical and advance alternative theories to explain their occurrence.

The significance that can be attributed to NDEs is disputed, but most researchers agree that the pattern of events described by survivors tends to be similar, though remaining highly personal in content. One unresolved puzzle is why the same pattern of events occurs in so many dissimilar circumstances. Another problem that remains unanswered is why some people have an NDE after a cardiac arrest whilst the majority of victims have no recollection of anything that could be classified in such terms.

Near-death experiences are said to have five distinct stages, which unfold in a characteristic sequence, the last stage being the least frequently reported. These five stages, known as the 'core experience' consist of 1) a sense of peace and well-being, 2) separation from the body, 3) entering the darkness – travelling along a tunnel and having flashes of panoramic memory, 4) seeing the light – an experience of light which is bright, warm and attractive, 5) entering the light – and perhaps meeting other people. The most commonly reported feature of an NDE is a sense of peace and well-being in a moment of physical danger. However, its most significant feature is probably the out-of-the-body state as this is the precursor of any subsequent visionary experiences.

Incidence

Near-death experiences occur irrespective of religious convictions,[9] race, sex and age, though children tend to be more concise in describing their experiences than adults.[10] Their exact incidence has yet to be determined. The reported frequency among people who have had a cardiac arrest is highly variable ranging from 0–60 per cent.[6,11,12] There are a number of possible reasons why this should be so. Most people are reluctant to mention the experiences to other people, unless directly questioned, and few people working in intensive care units are likely to enquire about such possibilities. Those who do so consistently will record the highest number of incidents among their patients. One must also allow for the fact that patients have varying degrees of amnesia after a cardiac arrest. Dobson and her colleagues[11] found that 80 per cent of patients had some memory loss, and that 24 per cent had no recollection of the events which occurred in the 2–14 days that followed the heart attack.

Although the figures are so variable, it seems that a large number of people can claim to have had an NDE, if the first stage of the core experience is considered sufficient evidence of an NDE. A survey undertaken in the USA by Gallup[13] found that 15 per cent of the population reported having had a close brush with death, though not necessarily a cardiac arrest. Thirty-three per cent of these people remembered feelings of peace and painlessness, separation from the body, a sense of being in another world or having a life review. On the basis of this survey it has been calculated that 5 per cent of American citizens have had some form of NDE, that is about 8,000,000 people. This assessment is based on the premise that a feeling of peace and painlessness is, by itself, sufficient evidence of an NDE.

Some experts say that stricter criteria must be fulfilled before an experience can be classified as an NDE, and that the minimum requirement should be the awareness of an out-of-the body state. They recognize that a feeling of 'peace and painlessness' has its own significance, but it lacks the 'other-world' nature that characterizes the later stages of an NDE, which provide NDEs with their most distinctive features. Not to include it as an essential aspect of an NDE would not dimininish the significance of this peaceful experience in any way. It has its own validity, as David Livingstone discovered when he was attacked by a lion. Moreover, Livingstone thought that the experience was not peculiar to man but one shared by all animals when they are caught by a predator.

Attack by a Predator

Death is not a unique experience of mankind, all forms of life die. Despite recent advances in our understanding of people's experiences of dying we have little conception of how it affects animals, especially those which die suddenly and violently. Cat owners are often dismayed when their pet catches a small animal or bird, and plays with it while it is still alive. Instinctively they feel that the captured animal must be suffering pain and fear, and they may wonder at the docility with which it lies under the claws. It is only rarely that predators kill human beings, but there are instances when people have found themselves caught by a large cat and lived to tell the tale. This happened to the explorer David Livingstone.[14]

In his *African Journals,* Livingstone recorded an incident when he was standing with some companions and was suddenly attacked by a large lion. The beast caught him by the shoulder, dragged him to the ground and shook him like a terrier does a rat. The shock and shaking produced a stupor in which there was no terror or pain, but just a dreamy state in which Livingstone remained aware of what was happening. He experienced no sense of horror, even when he looked at the beast, as the shaking had removed all sense of fear. Livingstone suggested that a similar reaction occurs in all animals that are killed by a carnivore and, being a religious man, ascribed it to the 'merciful provision of our benevolent Creator for lessening the pain of death'. Livingstone may not have been correct in saying that animals that are killed by a carnivore feel a sense of peace before they die. If, however, he was right, then the first stage of the 'core experience' is common to both animals and man. We have, of course, no way of determining whether animals can experience anything that remotely resembles the later stages of an NDE and it seems reasonable to assume that these later phenomena are peculiar to man.

Not Quite an NDE

Livingstone experienced the initial phase of an NDE, a sense of peace that was devoid of pain. Unfortunately, the terminally ill often suffer some degree of pain, though the perception of pain does appear to decrease with increasing age.[15] A good account of the physical distress a young adult experienced, when she was suddenly confronted with a life threatening illness, was reported in the *British Medical Journal* by Dr Barbara Young.[16] She also described clearly her state of mind at the time. The incident occurred in the hospital ward where Dr Young worked. She had taken an antibiotic for a mild sinusitis – a seemingly harmless thing to do, but within 30 minutes she had collapsed from anaphylactic shock and was close to death.

She reported having two levels of awareness when conscious. Most of her mind was absorbed by the intense physical distress, the difficulty she had in breathing, the numbness of her mouth and extremities, and the feeling that she had been struck on the chest with a hammer. She could not speak, or move, and her head kept spinning and buzzing. She wanted to vomit and empty her bowels simultaneously. At a different level, she was observing the activities of those around her in a detached, unemotional way; watching her attendants rushing around her looking terrified. She knew that she might die but did not feel distressed by the thought. She was admitted to an intensive care unit and was lucky to survive the illness. Her account is of interest because of the two levels of awareness she described and the lack of mental distress she experienced when confronted by imminent, sudden death. Another feature of the report was that it lacked any of the typical elements of an NDE. It reminds us that dying is not always easy and that a close encounter with death does not of necessity produce an NDE.

Some NDEs

Dr Moody's book, *Life after Life*, contains many verbatim reports of NDEs. This format has the advantage of allowing people to tell their stories in their own words and recount both the emotional and intellectual contents of their experiences. It is the most effective way of helping the reader to share the experience more fully with the narrator. A similar method is used in the following accounts of NDEs which have been related to me, though these are not given exactly word for word.

> *Case 1.* An elderly priest, who was involved in a car accident whilst working in South Africa, was admitted to hospital with multiple injuries. His injuries were severe and to these were added the complication of a cardiac arrest. He remembered floating out of his body and looking down at the doctors and nurses who were trying to resuscitate him. Then he moved upwards towards an area of light, which he entered, and there he was told to return to his body. On doing so he became conscious again of the physical pain caused by his injuries. He would have liked to have stayed in the light, and believed that the reason he did not do so was that his parishioners, on hearing of the accident, had immediately prayed for his survival and recovery.
>
> *Case 2.* A 59-year-old woman, who was suffering from terminal cancer and chronic heart disease, had difficulty in accepting the fact that she would soon die and be separated from her family. Then, surprisingly, she

mentioned that she had been close to death once before and that it had been a wonderful experience. The incident occurred after she had been admitted to hospital with palpitations and chest pain. She could remember the anxiety displayed by the doctors and nurses as they gave her an intravenous injection, and then she felt she was travelling along a tunnel. Movement along the tunnel was downwards not upwards. It was a wonderful feeling; there was a sense of lightness in the air and of moving towards a light at the end of the tunnel. She was not floating but travelling at speed, so that she could feel the wind in her face and her hair being blown backwards. All she could think of was of this wonderful feeling. Then an acquaintance, who was still alive but whom she had not seen for years, came behind her and placed his hands on her shoulders; she heard him say 'Not yet Shep', and then he pulled her back so that instead of falling she was drawn upwards. When she came out of the tunnel there was a lot of joy in the intensive care unit. She was pleased, not so much for herself as for her family whom she had observed, whilst in her disembodied state, gazing anxiously through a window at the attempts that were being made to resuscitate her. Apart from telephoning the acquaintance who had pulled her back, she had not mentioned this episode to anyone previously. She was not sure whether there was another life after death but said that if it should happen again she would just have to put herself in God's hands.

This report mentions four features commonly found in an NDE – the 'wonderful feeling' it produced, the out-of the-bodystate, travelling at speed along a tunnel and the light. It also reveals the tendency, commonly reported, for people to keep the experience a secret. The most unusual aspect of this NDE is that the person who was credited with bringing the woman back to life was not the doctors or nurses, or a celestial spirit, but a distant acquaintance who had not even been informed of her critical condition. More usually people say that they were sent back by dead friends or relatives, or by a spiritual being.

Case 3. This experience was related by an elderly man with advanced motor neurone disease. His terminal illness had not impaired his intellect but he was very weak and had difficulty in speaking. The NDE had occurred some years previously. It had not changed his attitude to life and he did not consider it the most significant event in his life. He considered that the experiences he had undergone during World War II were far more important. He regarded that period with a certain nostalgia, as a time when people seemed to think more of one another and to be more helpful to each other. Despite the good memories, his war-time experiences must have been quite harrowing. He recalled seeing people blown to bits, helping to patch some of them up, and kneeling to say a prayer beside the bodies of others. During part of the war he had the unpleasant task of getting dead airmen out of crashed aircraft. These bodies were often burnt and shattered, and some had to be removed piecemeal. When he was doing this he had the strange feeling that he was not extricating just an arm, or leg, but that he was removing the whole person.

He was unwilling, or unable, to say a great deal about his NDE. The incident took place when he was a patient on the operating table. Suddenly he was looking down at his body and at a rather stout surgeon and two nurses. Then he was rushing along a dark tunnel at a terrific speed. He had flown jet aircraft and said that this movement was faster than flying in such planes. It was a pitch black tunnel with no light at all. He slowed down before reaching the end of the tunnel, stopped and then went backwards, but not so quickly. Whilst this was happening the essential part of himself was outside the tunnel, watching him travelling along the inside. He was not frightened – it was a new and peaceful experience. He knew that he was going somewhere but did not know where.

Case 4. This incident was told to me by the nursing sister in charge of an acute medical ward. A 45-year-old woman, who had been admitted with acute chest pain, suddenly collapsed and died. The sister pressed the buzzer to summon the resuscitation team, passed a Brook's airway and commenced cardiac massage. The emergency team replaced the airway with an endotracheal tube, set up an ECG recording which showed asystole, and established intravenous lines with N-Saline and bicarbonate. The patient was defibrillated twice and irregular contractions commenced, which were supported by external cardiac massage. Normal respiration and heartbeat were re-established and the now partially conscious patient was transferred to the coronary care unit. The sister was away on leave for the following two days but when she returned she found that the patient had been transferred back to her ward. When she started her ward round the woman called her over and greeted her with great warmth and affection, hugging and thanking her for the care she had given. The patient did not thank the sister for the prompt care she had provided immediately following the collapse but for what she had done after the resuscitation team had arrived. Then she had covered the patient's exposed pelvis and thighs with a sheet, held her hand and spoken reassuringly to her. At first, the sister could not believe that a comatose woman could have been aware of these actions at the time. But the woman explained that whilst she was being resuscitated, she had left her body and floated to the ceiling where she was able to observe everything that was happening. She had a clear view of the actions taken by the emergency team, and saw herself being covered and comforted. In her disembodied state, everything was light and warm. An outside voice eventually instructed her to return to her body, whereupon she floated down and awoke in the coronary care unit.

The NDE Analysed

Apart from the 'core experience', other perceptual and cognitive changes can occur in the disembodied state. These include an enlargement of consciousness with clearer and sharper mental activity, a diminished sense of taste and smell, and enhanced sight and hearing. There may be a very rapid life review, similar to the *Kamma Nimmitta* of Buddhist teaching, in which the individual recollects, in part or completely, his or her past life, or has a prophetic vision of the future.

Some people say that their NDE was not a good experience but hellish. In a minority of instances the overwhelming feeling is of fear and panic, of being surrounded by evil and of descending into hell.[17] These unpleasant encounters are usually referred to as negative NDEs whilst the good experiences are designated positive NDEs.[4] It is possible for people to have more than one NDE if they find themselves in life threatening situations on more than one occasion, and in that event the two experiences can be quite different. A passing acquaintance once gave me photographs of the pictures she had drawn of two NDEs she had experienced. Both depicted tunnel-like, almost vaginal structures; the first had the dark and lurid colours of a negative NDE whilst a subsequent NDE was painted in bright and joyful colours. This progression is quite normal. Some people who have had a negative NDE say that they have had a positive NDE at a later date, but the opposite appears not to have been reported.

It has been suggested that different types of NDE may be associated with different precipitating causes. To test this hypothesis, Greyson classified the components of the NDE into three separate groups, which he called the cognitive, affective and transcendental components.[18] The cognitive component includes the life review, heightened intellectual activity and a new perception of space and time that makes normal concepts of space-time less meaningful. The affective component consists of feelings, such as peace, joy, cosmic unity and the presence of a brilliant light. He included in the transcendental component an awareness of a heavenly realm, angelic beings, visible spirits and a border, which if crossed would preclude any possibility of returning to the physical body.

Greyson found that all three components occur with equal frequency in the NDEs of people who were close to a sudden unexpected death, whether this was due to an accident, a cardiac arrest, or an anaphylactic reaction in a previously healthy person. When the death may have been anticipated, for example by a person attempting suicide or undergoing a surgical operation, the cognitive component is rarely present. This finding may be of little consequence but it does place a question mark against a theory, accepted by some NDE researchers, known as the 'invariance hypothesis'. According to this theory, the components of NDEs are essentially the same whatever the cause of the experience may have been. It does not allow for any difference in the NDEs that follow a cardiac arrest and those that occur when a person has not been harmed but merely extremely frightened.

It was not possible to establish exactly why the four people whose case histories were presented earlier had been close to death, but they were all medical emergencies, probably involving a cardiac arrest. Their stories had a common pattern and the experiences were viewed positively by the people involved. It is possible that some aspects of the NDEs were not disclosed, as the length of each discussion was determined by the suitability of the occasion and the health of the patient. Nevertheless, their accounts illustrate most features of the 'core experience' and, in particular, describe out-of-the-body states in which each patient, although comatose, was clearly aware of the therapeutic measures that were being taken by their medical and nursing attendants. None of the patients encountered a friend or relative who had died; nor was there anything suggestive of a life review, though both these events are said to be common in NDEs.

Life reviews appear to be components only of the adult experience. They are not mentioned in the NDEs reported by children.[10] Those who have a life review describe it in terms of a three-dimensional reconstruction of the events of their life, seen from the perspective of a third person. During it they relive the experiences, both loving and unloving, of the people with whom they have interreacted. They experience, empathetically, the effects they have had on other people, particularly the emotional impact, with the most significant factor being the quality of human love they displayed. In some NDEs people find they reach a borderline, of no return, where they are given the choice of going forward or returning to their physical life. Parental responsibility and the needs of young children are said to be decisive factors in helping people to decide to return to their bodies. Some people who choose to return do not really wish to do so, and can harbour feelings of anger towards the physician who resuscitated them.

Character Changes

Survivors of NDEs often report noticing a change in their character and attitude to life as a consequence. Some deterioration in personality might be expected from the hypoxia associated with a cardiac arrest but this is not the normal observation reported. Usually the survivors say that they have a greater zest for life, a greater delight in the natural world, a new sense of purpose and meaning in life, and a greater tolerance, compassion and understanding towards others. Less frequently people claim to have developed a greater spiritual awareness, the ability to heal, and an increased extra-sensory ability particularly in the field of telepathy. These changes are not dependent on having a positive NDE, they also occur after negative ones.[4]

The validity of these claims was tested by Dr Melvin Morse in association with Paul Perry. They interviewed 100 adults who had had an NDE in childhood and 250 controls who had had no such experience. Those who had childhood NDEs generally scored better than the controls in all categories, including psychosomatic complaints, drug use and income management. They were less anxious about death, had more psychic experiences, a greater zest for life and radiated a greater sense of wellbeing.[19]

Some people who have had an NDE take a very pragmatic, even cynical, view towards such experiences and the claims made for them. The humanist philosopher, A.J. Ayer, described his response to an NDE that followed a cardiac arrest in sceptical terms.[20] His first remark on regaining consciousness was 'you are all mad'. He was not sure subsequently how this statement should be interpreted. It was possible that he had mistaken his visitors for Christians and was informing them that he had discovered nothing 'on the other side'. It was equally possible that he had assumed they were sceptics and was suggesting that he had discovered something of interest there. He decided that the first was the more likely explanation as in the latter case he would probably have exclaimed 'we are all mad'. The earliest remark he could remember making, apart from the initial exclamation, was in French which he spoke fluently. 'Did you know that I was dead?' he asked, 'it was most extraordinary, my thoughts became persons.' He had only one vivid memory of the experience. He was confronted by an extremely bright, and painful, red light which was responsible for governing the universe. Among the light's ministers were two creatures who were in charge of space. They had failed to carry out their duties correctly and, as a result, space had become slightly disjointed and the laws of nature had ceased to function properly. He felt he had to escape from the red light and correct the anomalies in space. It occurred to him that, because modern physicists consider space-time to be a single entity, he could reorder space by operating on time. Consequently, he walked around, waving his watch in the air, and shouting to attract the attention of the ministers but without any success. He became increasingly despondent until suddenly the experience ended. Professor Ayer admitted that the NDE had slightly weakened his conviction that death would be the end of him. Later he modified this original statement and said that the experience 'had weakened, not my belief that there is no life after death, but my inflexible attitude towards that belief.' He remained quite sure that the event had not shaken his conviction that there is no God.

Possible Explanations

In *Life after Life*, Dr Moody divided the possible explanations for NDEs into two main categories, the supernatural and the natural. At its simplest level, the supernatural explanation sees NDEs as normal occurrences that are clearly related to a person's transit from life in this world to life in the next. This is not a new idea, it has been taught by Buddhism in terms of a *Kamma Nimmitta* for many centuries, but it is a concept that has not been developed within Western cultures. At a more complex level, the supernatural explanation has a special significance for people who espouse New Age doctrines.

The New Age philosophy is based on the belief that the world is passing out of the Christian, Piscean Age into the new 'Age of Aquarius', an idea that was advanced in the early part of the twentieth century by C.G. Jung. New Age teachings take this idea further and affirm that the Age of Aquarius, which will last about 2,000 years, will be a time of enhanced spiritual development for mankind. Two intertwining lines of thought about NDEs are discernible in the New Age conceptual theory. These may be called the numerical and spiritual strands. The numerical strand points to the increasing number of people who have survived close encounters with death as a result of advances in medical technology. Consequently more people who have had NDEs are living today than could have been possible in any previous era.

The spiritual strand is based on the claim that an NDE enhances the spiritual development and psychic sensitivity of the survivor. Consequently, these people can bring to their life on earth the new spirituality they acquired, when on the threshhold of death, and thereby benefit the rest of mankind. It is suggested that the increasing number of people with a heightened spirituality as a result of having had NDEs represents an evolutionary thrust towards a higher level of consciousness for mankind as a whole. Moreover, the theory holds that the evolutionary advance will not be restricted to mankind; it will also enhance the spiritual development of the planet Earth, which, according to some New Age teachings, is not just an inert mass of material but the embodiment of a highly developed spiritual entity. Although this idea may appear nonsensical, a surprisingly similar concept has been formulated by the Jesuit priest and palaeontologist, Teilhard de Chardin.

In his erudite, but somewhat obscure, book *The Phenomenon of Man*, Pierre Teilhard de Chardin suggested that consciousness, by which he meant 'every kind of psychism from the most rudimentary form of interior perception imaginable to the human phenomenon of reflective thought', is present in inert matter throughout the universe.[21] This innate consciousness has evolved throughout many millions of years to produce the reflective mind of man. But, according to Teilhard de Chardin, the evolutionary process has gone even further and produced a noosphere – a layer of thought – that surrounds the world, just like the biosphere – the world of plants and animals – but outside and around the biosphere. During the course of its evolution, the noosphere has increased in size and complexity and become a closed system with its own centre. Teilhard de Chardin called this centre the 'Omega point'. The centre has four attributes; it is autonomous, real, irreversible and transcendent, and it is also both loving and loveable. The Omega point is not obviously part of the Trinitarian God-head of Christianity; if it were Teilhard de Chardin would have said so, but this he failed to do. In fact he goes further. He says that God unifies the universe by 'uniting it organically with himself. How does he unify it? By partially immersing himself in things, and by becoming "element", and then from this point of vantage in the heart of matter assuming the control and leadership of what we call evolution.'

Before considering the natural explanations that have been suggested for NDEs, a distinction needs to be drawn between the types of question the two main theories are trying to answer. In general, the supernatural theory is mainly concerned with the question 'why?' and seeks to give some sort of existential meaning to the experience. Natural explanations are more concerned with the underlying mechanism, with answering the question 'how?' Both these questions are relevant but they approach the subject from different perspectives. The natural explanations usually begin with the premise that NDEs are complex hallucinatory phenomena, and these are accounted for by various psychological and scientific hypotheses. No single natural explanation has the merit of being generally accepted, but this lack of consensus is itself interesting and, perhaps, illustrates most clearly the conflict of opinions that surround NDEs.

It has been suggested that NDEs may be the result of sensory deprivation. This is an interesting idea as hallucinations can be readily induced in people who are deprived of auditory, visual and some tactile stimuli in laboratory experiments. The rationale for this theory is that terminally ill people live a sort of cocooned existence in hospitals and are therefore likely to be subject to some degree of sensory deprivation.[22] This may be so in certain cases, but it fails to take into account the physical distress experienced by many terminally ill patients and the intense physical stimulation to which those with cardiac arrest are subjected by their medical attendants.

Another suggestion is that the anxiety caused by the imminence of death is, by itself, sufficient to produce the complex hallucinatory response, which constitutes an NDE. This proposal lacks any objective evidence to support it and provides no explanation for the NDEs experienced by comatose patients. It does, however, offer a possible explanation for the NDEs reported by people who have been literally 'frightened out of their life'.

A more interesting theory links NDEs to the scientific observation that an out-of-the-body state can be induced by stimulating the temporal lobe of the brain with an electric probe. The experimental and experiential situations are dissimilar, but it has been suggested that the temporal lobe of a patient, suffering from a cardiac arrest, may be stimulated by the hypercapnia or anoxia induced by his critical state, thus producing a near-death experience. This theory would also account for NDEs caused by hyperventilation or drowning. Other ideas that have been advanced include the suggestions that a near-death experience is a reactivated birth memory, or the manifestation of an archetype, in a critical life situation.

The possibility that an NDE may be caused by drugs prescribed for the patient has been carefully studied. Psychedelic drugs can produce ineffable feelings, out-of-the-body states and hallucinations. Ketamine, an anaesthetic drug, can produce all the aspects of an NDE, including the feeling of rapid movement through a tunnel and emergence into light. On the other hand, drugs cannot be implicated in all, or even most, of the NDEs reported and access to ketamine is usually limited to anaesthetists in hospitals.[23]

The close association that exists between the states that can be induced by certain drugs and the experiences of near-death survivors points to the possibility that a specific, physiological cause could be found for such experiences. Experiments with animals show that ketamine and phencyclidine (PCP) are two of the drugs that can bind to a site on the N-methyl-D-aspartate (NMDA) receptors, situated at the neuronal synapses in the brain.[24] This site, which is known as the PCP site, is involved in memory, learning, epilepsy and possibly psychosis. The activity of the NMDA receptors is reduced by ketamine and PCP but increased by the amino acid L-glutamate, which is a major neurotransmitter. There is evidence that the level of L-glutamate rises during the anoxic state and that an excess of L-glutamate can kill the neurone. By binding preferentially to the NMDA sites, drugs like ketamine counteract the lethal effects of the increased L-glutamate concentrations. There is also in-vitro evidence that the body produces its own ketamine-like drug, α endopsychosin. It is suggested that, during a cardiac arrest, there is a massive release of an endogenous NMDA blocker, such as α endopsychosin, which reduces the risk of L-glutamate mediated brain damage following hypoxia. If this was so, a consequent effect would be the dissociated, hallucinogenic state associated with NDEs.[25]

An alternative physiological explanation for NDEs is based on the supposition that, in a critical situation, there is a sudden release of endorphins, the endogenous opioids that have receptor sites close to the NMDA receptors. Endorphins are not, however, powerful hallucinogens and do not produce a state comparable to the NDE. Despite this caveat, it is possible that they have a role in producing the pain-free state associated with NDEs.

Whilst many of the suggestions put forward to account for NDEs have an intrinsic interest, none provides a completely satisfactory explanation. Some alternative theory or possibly a combination of those already advanced may produce the correct answer. Whilst research workers accept that both life-threatening and less critical situations can cause NDEs, it remains to be determined whether these are caused by the same internal processes. The likelihood is that they are, but the physiological explanation that would be generally acceptable to clinicians and scientists remains to be formulated and proven. Such an explanation need not affect the beliefs of those who see NDEs as evidence of the spiritual journey between this world and the next. In the last analysis all human perceptions, whether objective or subjective, are determined by biochemical activities within the brain.

Chapter 24
The Significance of Death

Men must endure
Their going hence, even as their coming hither:

King Lear

Death has two attributes that make it uniquely important to every individual. These are its inevitability and its finality. There is also an uncertainty, even mystery, about death that enhances its uniqueness. Every sane adult realizes that he or she will die, but no one knows when – or what, if anything – happens afterwards. Two possibilities arise. Death may simply be the end of life, with the individual ceasing to exist as a conscious being; or it may be what the Buddhists call a *bvanga* state, a transition phase that leads to a new mode of consciousness or being. The most rational explanation is that death is the end of life, full stop, and this was the opinion held by Sigmund Freud. The origins of this belief can be traced back to the fifth century BC and to the teachings of the Greek philosopher Protagoras (c.480–410 BC) but it has always been a minority viewpoint, for most people hold or have held to a belief in some form of life after death.

The more traditional viewpoint was the one favoured by Carl Jung. He was careful not to conjecture about the nature of any possible afterlife, but he was quite explicit in his belief that the human psyche, or some aspect of it, has the capacity to survive death. This certainty arose from his understanding of the nature of the psyche, which he considered to be a much vaster and more complex structure than did Freud and which, most importantly, he considered was not restricted by space or time.

Belief in an afterlife is one of the most universally held concepts, though descriptions of its possible nature are subject to many regional and cultural variations. There are considerable differences, for instance, in the afterlife as depicted in African, Chinese, Hindu, Japanese and Jewish cultures. Wide variations can occur even within these separate traditions. Secular Jews will deny the possibility of an afterlife, liberal Jews see it as having a spiritual dimension, whereas the ultra-orthodox look forward to the physical resurrection of the Jewish dead in the Messianic era.

The prospects offered by the hereafter are not always seen as being happy and desirable. For tribal Africans, life on earth is a much more joyous and warm experience than the life they can expect in the land of the spirits. The Chinese believe that their welfare in the afterlife is dependent on a continuous line of male descendants, as only sons can make the sacrifices that will ensure their wellbeing in the spirit world. Indian religions offer the burden of *karma* and the continuous cycle of reincarnation from which the individual must strive to escape, whilst Christianity and Islam provide the uncertainties of Heaven and Hell. As Jung pointed out, the hereafter has its dark and difficult aspects, just like life. Against these formidable prospects Freud's belief that death is the end, full stop, provides the enduring comfort of eternal sleep. Nevertheless, humanity persists in holding to the idea of life after death. Why should this be so?

The concept of an afterlife does offer prospects that the individual may consider desirable. According to his beliefs, a person may hope to become one of God's chosen elite in heaven – or on earth at the coming of the Messiah – enjoy an honoured existence as a spiritual ancestor or *kami*, or evolve as a spiritual being in a realm of wisdom, light and love. Children do not formulate these ideas for themselves; they absorb them from the society in which they live, and particularly from religious rituals and teachings.

Human societies almost invariably develop cultures that affirm the existence of a hereafter, but this does not explain how the belief arose or why it should persist. Christianity, for instance, did not introduce such an idea into the Western world, it already existed in Judaism and prior to that amongst other religions in the Middle East and Europe. Moreover, the belief arose despite the lack of objective evidence to support it and, in the case of the Jews, whilst the traditional viewpoint opposed it. Nor is it enough to say that people believe in an afterlife because they are frightened of death. Too many people seek to escape life by suicide, or risk their lives in dangerous enterprises, for this argument to carry much weight.

The only evidence that supports the idea of an afterlife is provided by the subjective experiences of mankind. The evidence these experiences provide is usually considered to be less substantial than that provided by sense perception, by seeing and hearing, but the subjective or inner life has its own validity and reality. Anger and love, for instance, are two subjective states that are very real to the person experiencing them but which others can only perceive from the effects they produce. No one has found an eternal soul when dissecting a corpse, but neither has any anatomist found evidence of anger or love.

Subjective feelings, such as fear and hunger, exist and have to be accepted as real. There are also less common experiences, which cannot be readily discerned objectively, such as out-of-the-body experiences and perceptions of the dead. These experiences have their own reality and are likely to have contributed to the significance people ascribe to life and death. Also, they enable a traditional belief in a soul and an afterlife to retain some experiential validity. Beliefs that are based on intellectual conviction and religious traditions alone are likely to falter and disappear. In order to be retained with any vigour within society, they have to touch a chord within humanity's collective psyche as well as appeal to the conscious mind. If a belief in the afterlife does satisfy some deep-rooted human need, its validity receives its confirmation by the subjective experiences mentioned in previous chapters and by ideas that arise from the unconscious mind, often in the form of symbols.

Carl Jung defined symbols as the expression of intuitive ideas that cannot be formulated in any other, or in any better way. They are the best expression of something unknown – bridges thrown out from a far shore.[1] The works of artists provide many symbols that point to life after death, but we can look in vain for symbols that display the inner psyche's assurance of utter destruction. Art galleries are full of pictures depicting angelic presences, the afterlife and the ascent to heaven – symbols that Jungian psychologists say appear typically in the dreams of people who are approaching death. All are rebirth symbols; the ascent to heaven representing a journey, the haloes of the saints one of the many light motifs symbolizing the world of the spirits, whereas the resurrection from the tomb, which was often portrayed in Egyptian art, is a powerful symbol of rebirth. Perhaps we have become so used to these symbolic representations that we see them only as just another object on a canvas, but they represent something deeper, the intuitive response of the artists who first conceived them to the psyche's understanding of death. Whilst most great artists have dealt with the subject of death, none depict it unequivocally as the end of life. Some do portray death in realistic terms but they never provide symbols which indicate the complete extinction of life. Freud described the situation most clearly when he wrote, 'the unconscious does not believe in its own death; it behaves as if it were immortal'.[2]

Besides using symbols that are universally meaningful, every race and tribe explains the significance of death in terms which are particularly relevant to its own culture. In Christian countries this interpretation is based on the death and resurrection of Christ. Its rendering in art has produced some of the most powerful of visual and musical images, and modern artists continue to use this theme. Contrary to possible expectations, Jewish artists have shown a remarkable interest in Christian motifs. Marc Chagal, Epstein, Zadkine and Benno Schotz are among the many artists of different Jewish traditions who have included the figure of Jesus in their works. Most see him as a coherent part of ancient Jewry and usually depict him as an ordinary man, even on the cross.[3]

In the *White Crucifixion* (1938), Chagal used both Jewish and Christian symbols to portray the fears, experiences and expectations of European Jewry as they approached the Holocaust. The crucified Jesus, wearing a Jewish prayer shawl as a loin cloth, is suspended in a shaft of light, whilst a menorah with lighted candles stands upright at the foot of the cross. All else is chaotic, tilted or obscured by smoke. Terrified people flee in all directions, houses and a synagogue are burning, books and a blazing Torah lie scattered on the ground. Only in the heavens is there security, and there four figures, representing simultaneously ordinary Jewish people and angelic presences, fly above the cross.

Music also explores the mystery of death. A bagpiper's lament needs no words to evoke a sense of grief. A state funeral without such music as Chopin's *Marche Funèbre* would lose some of its mood of deep solemnity. The world would be a poorer place if Bach had not written the *St Matthew Passion* or Beethoven his *Missa Solemnis*. Hymns sung in unison touch hearts and minds more deeply than a funeral oration. The subject of death often inspires composers to produce some of their best works, especially as settings for a requiem mass. Verdi composed his *Requiem* as a tribute to the poet, Manzoni. Fauré did so soon after the death of his mother. Both requiems reflect the musical style and attitude to death of the composer. Verdi's *Requiem* is sometimes described as his greatest opera and, as many of his operas deal with tragic death, we should not be surprised that his *Requiem* is scored in a dramatic way. The pleas for mercy are most powerfully expressed in *Lacrymosa*, but this is overwhelmed by the thunderous *Dies Irae*, as if death is dominated by the inevitability of judgement and the fear of hell. Fauré's approach is quite different. The terrors of the afterlife are scarcely touched upon; the untroubled mood of *In Paradisum* evokes a comforting sense of eternal peace, and the entire work is one of serenity and hopeful expectancy.

Elgar's work, *The Dream of Gerontius*, for choir, orchestra and soloists is quite different. Based on Cardinal Newman's poem it depicts the journey of a soul from the moment of death to its judgement and experience of God, and thence its sojourn in Purgatory. The title is slightly misleading, as we are not presented with a dream but with the reality of Gerontius's death. Various themes are portrayed in the work, and among these we can identify Fear, Prayer, Sleep, Despair, Committal and Judgement. The principal soloists are Gerontius and his Guardian Angel, whilst the chorus represents friends, demons, angels and souls in purgatory. The work begins with Gerontius at the point of death, surrounded by friends in prayer; it moves into a bass solo 'Go Forth Upon Thy Journey Christian Soul' and Part 1 ends with the Committal March. Part 2 recounts Gerontius's conversation with his Guardian Angel as they journey to the Heavenly Throne, accompanied by the dissonant voices of demons, the prayers of friends and the rapturous songs of angels. The work ends with Gerontius making his way to Purgatory and the angels singing Newman's famous hymn 'Praise to the Holiest in the Height'.

Benjamin Britten depicts both the horrors of war and the reality of the afterlife in his *War Requiem*. This oratorio welds together the funeral mass of the Roman Catholic Church with the poetry of Wilfred Owen.[4] Much of the music is martial, angry and grieving but this is interspersed with quiet passages and the clear sounds of children's voices. The solo tenor begins with the line, 'what passing-bells for these who die as cattle?' Two dead soldiers, one British and the other a German, meet above the battlefield. They reminisce, the one reminding the other that 'I am the enemy you killed my friend'. They are concerned not with the future but with the past and their present weariness; and remain unaware of what lies ahead as the final chorus, *In Paradisum deducant te Angeli* – may the angels lead you into paradise, is gently sung.

Britten's *War Requiem* was first performed in Coventry Cathedral in 1962. The architectural theme of this modern cathedral is not the crucifixion but the Majesty, Eternity and Glory of God. Light streams on the central altar from three sides, most notably from John Hutton's massive, glass screen, engraved with angels. But the most dominant feature is Graham Sutherland's huge tapestry, *Christ in*

Glory in the Tetramorph. At the base of the tapestry is the crucified Jesus, fixed to the cross like a bolt on a crossbow that is aimed towards the heavens and his ultimate glorification.

In the ruins of the old cathedral stands Sir Jacob Epstein's sculpture, *Ecce Homo*, a massive almost primitive carving of Jesus. On the outer wall of the new cathedral is Epstein's last great work of art, the bronze sculpture of *St Michael and the Devil*; it was a theme Epstein said he had wanted to portray all his life. When asked how he managed to reconcile accepting such commissions with his Jewishness, he replied quite simply, 'my beliefs can be clearly seen through my works'. Epstein died some months after the bronze sculpture was completed but before it was unveiled. In his account of the building of Coventry Cathedral, the architect Sir Basil Spence records, 'Two years before the consecration we placed St Michael on the Cathedral. Lady Epstein unveiled it, for Sir Jacob did not live to see the finished sculpture in place. During the ceremony I felt his presence.'[5] This last statement is made so simply that it is easily overlooked, yet Sir Basil Spence obviously thought it merited a place in the history of the cathedral that he designed and helped to build.

Experiences such as the one recorded by Sir Basil Spence are likely to reinforce a person's belief in an afterlife. It seems reasonable to suggest that mankind developed its concept of a hereafter as a direct consequence of many such experiences. Some may be more vivid than others and this seems to have been singularly true of those that followed Jesus's crucifixion, when he appeared so clearly to his friends on the first Easter Sunday and in the following weeks.

But it is not only Christians who have perceptions of the dead; these experiences are part of a universal phenomenon that is found in all races and creeds. Widowed people are probably more likely to have such experiences than celibate priests and nuns but the Trappist monk, Thomas Merton, records such an encounter with his dead father. In his autobiography *The Seven Storey Mountain*, Merton relates how he was in his room alone one night, with the light on, when he suddenly had the feeling that his dead father was in the room with him. He says: 'The sense of his presence was as vivid and as real and as startling as if he had touched my arm or spoken to me.' Merton goes on to question how he can be certain that this perception of his father was not just imagination, or something that could be traced to a purely natural, psychological cause, and he has to admit that it is impossible to say and that he is not trying to offer an explanation. Then he continues: 'But whether it was imagination or nerves or whatever else it may have been, I can truly say that I did feel most vividly, as if my Father was present there, and the consequences I have described followed from this, as though he had communicated without words an interior light from God, and about the condition of my soul – although I wasn't sure I had a soul.'[6]

Schopenhauer has said that the problem of death stands at the onset of every philosophy.[7] This is true whether the philosophy is a religious or a secular one. Religious philosophy is concerned with belief in, secular philosophy with a denial of, life after death. The latter philosophy has the merit of simplicity, the former is overlaid with many considerations of ethics, ritual and dogma. The philosophy of belief is based on the traditional teachings and historical records of different religions, but underlying this belief are the countless experiences of individuals which uphold the central tenet of a hereafter. The philosophy of disbelief has nothing to sustain it except an unswerving faith in the overriding importance of sense perception.

Those who dismiss the subjective experiences of people as irrelevant are likely to be found in both philosophical camps. Secularists simply reject the claims on the basis that there is no objective evidence to support them. The religious teacher is likely to find them unacceptable as being contrary to faith and established doctrine. Faith does not require proof, it relies on trust; it is not concerned with the subjective evidence provided by personal experience even when this confirms faith's validity and points to its origins; neither is it concerned with the fact that similar beliefs and experiences exist in societies that lack the sacred texts that are so important to Western religions.

Does it really matter whether people believe in an afterlife or not? The answer must be yes, because people's responses have importance not only for themselves but for society as a whole. Whilst religious groups can be rightly criticized for their intolerance of other faiths, the wars they appear to have engendered and the human failings of their adherents, the positive role they have played in human affairs must also be acknowledged. Religious principles have furnished society with codes of behaviour that enable people to co-operate together, and they have also provided a basis for the various legal systems in common use. Religious beliefs cannot suppress the hatreds and enmities inherent in the human condition, but they do act as dampeners on the more aggressive and selfish tendencies in mankind. Above all they provide a meaning and significance to life, which pure rationalism fails to do.

For the person who is uncertain about the existence of an afterlife, the subjective experiences mentioned point to its reality. For young people making their way in life, this may be of passing interest. On the other hand, a concept of a hereafter will enable them to conduct their lives within a wider perspective than that offered by a purely materialistic outlook. If Jung was correct in saying that from middle age the primary purpose in life is an inner preparation for death, then each individual has an important task during his or her declining years and this is made more meaningful if they have a concept of a life to come. The evidence for either viewpoint is inconclusive, but the words an elderly lady spoke to me a few days before her death may be relevant. 'Doctor' she said, 'the veil is thinner than people realize?'

Appendix

Thirty years have passed since the verbatim reports listed in Chapter 22 were collected and people now speak more openly about their encounters with the dead but, despite this greater openness, the topic is still a taboo in ecclesiastical circles. A letter I wrote on the subject, which was printed in the *Church Times* of 3 March 2000, produced an interesting correspondence, which merits inclusion here. Two of the letters I received are not included as they were mainly concerned with other topics. Not one letter was antipathetic.

From Mr C

I was interested, and greatly encouraged by your letter in the *Church Times* of 3rd March this year, re 'presence of the deceased'.

Shortly before Christmas, I lost my beloved wife. I had known her for some 56 years and we were very close. Some little while ago, I had gone up to our bedroom. preparing to lie down when she was there, so real I could reach out to her: she said 'I love you dear'. In a few moments she had gone but I felt wonderful. It happened just as you said, spontaneously and unexpectedly. I had not been thinking of anything in particular. It was not simply a dream. I was still holding my little cat who was with me at the time.

I spoke of this, in confidence, to one of our clergy who received it sympathetically but I felt that perhaps I was being regarded as a potential candidate for the 'funny farm', I am after all 75 years old, and at that age, well!

The event spoken of was not at night but late on a sunny afternoon. More recently, I was in the dining room; She was there, I put my arms around her, She was as real and warm as I knew her, She smiled and was gone. I have not mentioned this later experience to anyone. Again it was in the daytime. I have never before experienced any paranormal events.

I am a Reader, now in my 20th year and have conducted hundreds of funerals, and no! I am not into necrophilia! some years ago I was asked to take funerals by my previous vicar.

When my wife died there was this awful feeling; was there really life after death? I have just finished a sermon based on John 20: 19–31. It seems to me that Christ appearing among the disciples even though the doors were locked against intruders is not such a fanciful thought at all.

There is still this awful gap in my life and the grief still hurts, but somehow there is something else too.

From Mrs W

I have just read your letter in the *Church Times* and having lost a dear husband a few years ago, your observations are very interesting.

For a long time now and before my husband's death I have been concerned about the attitude of the clergy to death and the question of the afterlife. We are taught about the resurrection of Christ in detail, but when it comes to serious discussion, and asking how that teaching affects, as you say, the common experiences of humanity, the questions are 'skirted around' and in doing so are no comfort to those who grieve the loss of a loved one.

My friend's husband who is a sacristan in my church had the wonderful experience of having my husband, who died two months earlier, *sit by him* all during a funeral service. I was nearby – as I was playing the organ for the service. He described my husband who had been churchwarden for many years, in detail.

My friend's husband is not a 'fanciful' man, he is very 'down to earth' and it was a tremendous emotional experience for him. He is a man of 78 years and has never had any kind of spiritual experience before. He was very moved by this, and after being reassured by his wife that I would not be upset he told me what had happened. I was overwhelmed and so happy to know that my husband is still with me.

It is a shame that this, and countless other experiences you speak of are not taken seriously by the clergy in general. Christ's resurrection is preached but it seems that to bring it down to our level is ignored. We are indeed separated; and our transformation beyond this life, confirmed by so many encounters, by so many people, is never mentioned.

I trust that your wish that this subject will be considered and discussed in theological colleges will come about and be acted upon.

From Ms S

I read your letter in the *Church Times* with interest. May I make two brief points. 1) I am sure that you did not mean to imply that such experiences happen only to widows and widowers. I can assure you it is not so and I am writing to prove it. 2) You did not mention the work of the Alister Hardy Research Centre in Oxford, which is so important in this field. They keep archives of such experiences, and I was grateful to be able to send them a full account of mine, and know that it will be retained.

From Revd S

Thankyou for your letter to *Church Times*, 3.3.00 regarding reported contacts from dead loved ones. This is the first time I have read or heard anything on the subject.

I have been ordained nearly five years in parish ministry and I have visited and spoken with probably 100–150 people about their deceased relative. I have heard a very large number of consistent accounts of contact as described in your letter. I find it hard to dismiss these reports as simple emotionalism or folk religion, but I struggle to understand any way of accepting the reports as true or having a context against the teaching of the Bible.

I trained at XY College and my beliefs are consistent with evangelical theology. My initial responses to these reports was that these people were expressing a wish based on the folk religion or pursuing relief through practices which might be similar to those used by mediums and the like. An alternative explanation might be that it was the Lord revealing his love to them in some way which they mistook for comfort from the dead loved one. I am uncomfortable with both these theories.

Today I am to conduct the funeral of a 15-month-old child. The young mother's only expressed wish was that she might hear from her son, that he would tell her he was now well and did not blame her for his death. I was unable to offer her such a hope. I can only pray that Jesus might speak into her life and release her from some of her pain.

If there is a 'healthy' theology to support after death contact I might at least allow a hope that her wish was met or even intercede on her behalf.

Perhaps you can suggest some reading on the subject which will allow me to integrate and reaffirm the value of such experiences under our understanding of the resurrection of Christ.

From Revd K

Your *Church Times* letter on the frequency of contact by loved ones from the grave brought great reassurance to me. I'm a retired priest from the Church in Wales, but when I was chaplain to the XY university I was privileged to meet a certain wise woman who knew about these things. She was safely 'earthed', and although the ex-wife of an MP looked for all the world like a Lancashire barmaid!

I've never looked back, and the knowledge that this life is but a chapter of something much more has encouraged me, and I hope my congregations, over the years – 'filling out' the Faith once delivered to the Saints.

There is indeed a growing interest and awareness of these realms, though not I regret to say amongst the clergy, according to my (admittedly limited) experience. However I wasn't hounded out of XY diocese when I shared stories with curates doing post-ordination training.

Do you have a copy of your 1971 *BMJ* article please? I have read certain material from the Religious Experience Research Unit founded by Sir Alister Hardy, and your own research sounds parallel, so I should be fascinated to read it.

I've also been a member for many years of the Churches' Fellowship for Psychical and Spiritual Studies, whose most famous member is the Revd Dr Martin Israel – this society has beavered away since the late 1940s to provide reassurance and discernment in this area.

From Mrs S

I am writing to thank you for your recent letter to the *Church Times* under the heading 'contact from beyond the grave' and tell you of my experiences.

My husband died in 1980. About 3 months after his death as I was waking after a restless night, worrying about something that had to be done the following day I had a very strong feeling of his presence and felt his hands upon my shoulders. This was not a dream – it was a very real experience.

My mother died 5 years ago and some time after her death I was aware of her presence, but this time 1 did not feel any physical touch. I have never related these experiences before not even to my family. Partially because I thought they would not be understood, but mainly because they were extremely personal, spiritual and precious moments which were mine and I did not need or want to share them. Until I read your letter I was not aware how common an experience this is. Maybe others, like me, do not want to talk about them – but perhaps we should, especially in the context of resurrection.

You are probably right when you say that theology of the resurrection has generally become too intellectualized, but we are very fortunate here in having a parish priest who very much places it in the present and within common experience.

From Mr T

I was most interested in your letter (*Church Times*) 'Contact from Beyond the Grave'. I am not a member of the clergy, just an ordinary member of the Anglican Church, so I hope you won't mind me writing to you. I had an experience one Christmas in recent years which has always stayed in (or at the back of!) my mind. In January 1985 my dog of those years died, 'Penny' died after a long life and in October 1986 my mother died.

That Christmas already mentioned I went to dinner with an old friend in London. It was a happy evening with much chatter about the coming Christmas, and the exchange of gifts. When I arrived back at my cottage here in Essex, I knew at once that mother was 'there'. Her perfume Yardley's Freesia was on the staircase and just a slight smell of incontinence (mother due to age had been slightly incontinent before she passed away). Penny's successor, 'Emma' was jumping about with excitement, when normally when I arrived home late she would be happily asleep, then wake up for a late night walk!

I thought 'what do I say or do?' So, calming Emma, and assuring her that 'walkies' was coming very soon, I said in the direction of the perfume, 'Hello Mum, a lovely Christmas visit with 'Penny', you will both be in all our minds especially during Christmas here at the cottage, and I'm sure you will have a lovely time too.' Immediately the perfume and slight smell left the staircase, and 'Emma' calmed down.

Now, Dr Rees an interesting point, do animals 'see' what we only sense at times? It's my definite opinion that mother came on a Christmas visit that December just to see that all was well, and brought 'Penny' with her.

I didn't find the 'visit' frightening, but I'm not normally into that sort of thing. I quite agree with you though when you say that we hear little from our clergy or church leaders on the subject. I should be most interested to hear any further comments you have on this neglected subject, and I enclose a stamped addressed envelope.

From Mrs H

My brother Tony wrote to you on 8th March. His letter was sparked off by a letter that you wrote to the *Church Times*. I wonder if you would like to hear of the experiences my husband and I had regarding our mother.

As Tony probably told you our mother died in 1986, a year after Penny the dog died. My husband Eric and I live in Dagenham and since mother's death we too often sense a smell or scent, partly the perfume she used Yardley's Freesia and partly slight incontinence. As Tony probably told you mother was a little incontinent in the years before her death. We notice these things if we have been out and come home later, just as Tony did on mother's Christmas visit, and I often turn to Eric and say that Mum has either been here or is still here.

There is also another experience that Eric has had several times. Sadly a boyfriend of my oldest daughter committed suicide a few years ago, and Eric has 'seen' him in our house several times always coming down the stairs. This raises an interesting point. Are we maybe a family Eric, Tony and myself who tend to pick up these things fairly easily, or is it that lots of people have these after death experiences but just do not talk about it?

Tony is the only regular church goer in the family but like him Eric and I feel that things of this nature should be discussed far more openly in church circles. I should be very interested to hear your comments.

From Mr J

I slipped into the local library the other day and glanced over the *Church Times* and saw your letter 'Contact from Beyond the Grave'. I do not belong to any denomination anymore but I used to attend the Welsh Anglican church in Cardiff during the seventies – Eglwys Dewi Sant. Since the sixties I have had an interest in the Quakers and I attend the local meeting as I have for the past 7 years, but not a member.

Three weeks ago there was an advert in the *Friend* for a booklet of 64 pages *Continuing Life* by Angela Howard. She had conversations with her deceased father. I must admit that I have been rather sceptical myself. The interest that I have is due to the fact that my mother died aged 25 with TB in 1941 when I was about $3^1/2$. I have never been aware of a presence but as you know, losing a mother at that age is quite traumatic for any child at that age.

You inention the 'Harvard Child Bereavement Study' I was brought up by my great aunt and her husband but any mention of my mother was taboo. I have had this behind my mind all my life but not in an obsessive way either. I do not know where I could get hold of the Harvard report, perhaps you could advise me and on the after life as well.

From Mr L

As a result of your letter in the *Church Times* dated 3 March 2000, I wish to inform you of the personal relief and reassurance I received from it. If it had not been printed I doubt if I could have spoken to anyone about the experience I had 3 weeks ago. Just let me give you a few personal details. I am a 70 year old widower (my wife died on 10th Dec 1999) and consider myself a rational, level headed, unemotional, highly sceptical, and often critical person.

If I may I would like to relate to you the experience I encountered about 3 weeks ago. It happened during the night. I had retired to bed at approximately 10 pm. I had not taken any stimulants whatsoever, unable to sleep I lay in bed thinking of what I would do the following day. I heard the Grandmother clock in the hall strike 11 pm and shortly afterwards I sensed someone in bed beside me. I knew immediately that it was my wife. She put her arm about me as she did in life, I sensed a tender warm feeling that was so natural. I then turned to face her but her face was just a blur. I then spoke to her and said. 'You shouldn't be here you know' and she replied 'I know' and then she left me with a feeling of intense pleasure and comfort. I then heard the clock strike quarter past 11. The whole experience I judge to have taken between 2–3 minutes and I was wide awake the whole time.

As I said previously it was the result of your letter that I was able to approach my local Rector, the Revd GSR and told him of what had occurred, he was very understanding and sympathetic. He told me many people had related similar experiences to him during his ministry which I found very reassuring as I was beginning to wonder if I was a one off freak.

Only last night I showed your letter to two ladies who had recently been bereaved. I know one of them a Mrs S of G had a similar experience in broad daylight. The other lady Mrs D of T told me that her husband had touched her face and that she was constantly in contact with him asking for help and instructions and receiving them. May I conclude with the following information – the two ladies and myself are fully committed and practising Christians. We have a great faith that has sustained us through our sad times but we have sure and certain knowledge that we will meet our loved ones once again in The Good Lord's own and not our time.

This has not been an easy letter to write, please excuse its length.

References

Preface

1   Huxley A (1959) The Perennial Philosophy. London: Collins. (Fontana Books). p 123.

Chapter 1. What is Death?

1   Taylor NB (Ed) (1950) Stedman's Medical Dictionary. (17th rev. ed.). London: Bailliére, Tindall & Cox.
2   Snowdon DA, Kane RL, Beeson WL (1989) Early natural menopause. A biological marker of health and aging. American Journal of Public Health. 79: 709–14.
3   Swain J (1990) Executed Chinese used as organ donors. The Sunday Times. June 24th: p 24.
4   Parry, J (1991) Organ donation after execution in Taiwan. British Medical Journal 303: 1420.
5   Yamauchi M (1990) Transplantation in Japan. British Medical Journal 301: 507.
6   The Danish Council of Ethics (1989) Death Criteria, First Annual Report 1988. Copenhagen; Danish Council of Ethics.
7   Pallis C (1990) Return to Elsinore. Journal of Medical Ethics 16: 10–13.

Chapter 2. Western Attitudes to Death

1   Gay P (1988) Freud. A life for our time. London: PAPERMAC. pp 650–1.
2   Budge EAW (1985) Translation of 'The Book Of The Dead'. London: Arkana Paperbacks. p 21.
3   Smart N (1989) The World's Religions. Cambridge: Cambridge University Press. pp 214–19.
4   Zaehner RC (1959) Zoroastrianism. In RC Zaehner (ed.) The Concise Encyclopaedia of Living Faiths. London: Hutchinson. p 222.
5   Shaw P (1980) Judaism. In J Prickett (ed.) Living Faiths. Death. Guildford: Lutterworth Educational. pp 102–9.
6   Werblowsky RJ Z (1959) Judaism, or the Religion of Israel. In RC Zaehner (ed.) The Concise Encyclopaedia of Living Faiths. London: Hutchinson. p 47.
7   Good News Bible (1976) 1 Samuel ch. 28: v 3–23. London: The Bible Societies/Collins.

8   Toynbee A (1968) Traditional attitudes towards death. In A Toynbee et al. Man's Concern With Death. London: Hodder & Stoughton. p 92.

9   Singer S (1962) The Authorised Daily Prayer Book of the United Hebrew Congregation of the British Commonwealth of Nations. London: Eyre & Spottiswoode. p 95.

10 Good News Bible (1976) Acts ch.9: vv 2–7. London: The Bible Societies/Collins.

11 Brandon SGF (1973) Religion in Ancient History. London: Allen & Unwin. pp 82–4.

12 The Holy Qur'ān. Text, Translation and Commentary by Abdullah Yūsuf Alī (1989) Maryland: Amana Corporation. Sūrah 4. pp157–8, and notes 663 and 664.

13 Good News Bible (1976) 1 Corinthians ch. 15: vv 42–44. London: The Bible Societies/Collins.

14 Smart N (1989) The World's Religions. Cambridge: Cambridge University Press. p 281.

15 Anon (1989) Why Islam. Islam International Publications. pp11–12.

16 Gibb HAR (1959) Islam. In RC Zaehner (ed.) The Concise Encyclopaedia of Living Faiths. London: Hutchinson. p 200.

17 Smart N (1968) Attitudes towards death in Eastern religions. In A Toynbee et al. Man's Concern With Death. London: Hodder & Stoughton. p108.

18 Smoker B (1984) Humanism. London: National Secular Society. pp11–12.

19 Jupp R (1997) Unsatisfactory services for the dead. Church Times. 23 May. p 8.

20 Moseley C (1995) Debrett's Guide to Bereavement. London: Headline Book Publishing. pp 245–8.

Chapter 3. Reincarnation and Rebirth

1   Guirdham Arthur (1982) We Are One Another. A Record of Group Reincarnation. Wellingborough: Turnstone Press.

2   James W (1960) The Varieties of Religious Experience. London: Fontana. p146.

3   Smart N (1989) The World's Religions. Cambridge: Cambridge University Press. p 43.

4   Sivanada S (1977) All About Hinduism. Himalayas: Divine Life Society. pp166–8.

5   Basham AL (1964) Hinduism. In RC Zaehner (ed.) The Concise Encyclopaedia of Living Faiths. London: Hutchinson. p 226.

6   Basham AL (1964) Hinduism. In RC Zaehner (ed.) The Concise Encyclopaedia of Living Faiths. London: Hutchinson. pp 227–8.

7   Sharma D (1984) Hindu Belief and Practice. London: Edward Arnold.

8   Basham AL (1964) Hinduism. In RC Zaehner (Ed) The Concise Encyclopaedia of Living Faiths. London: Hutchinson. pp 243–53.

9   Thomas P (1975) Hindu Religions, Customs and Manners. Bombay: DB Taraporevala. pp 83–5.

10 Thomas P (1975) Hindu Religions, Customs and Manners. Bombay: DB Taraporevala. p 78.

11 Singh G (1964) On the Philosophy of Sikh Religion. In his introduction to and translation of 'Sri Guru Granth Sahib'. Delhi: Gus Das Kapur. pp 20–7.

12 Freemantle F, Trungpa C (1987) The Tibetan Book of the Dead. Boston and London: Shambhala. pp 1–10.

13 Levine S (1989) Letting Go. Raft, the Journal of the Buddhist Hospice Trust. 1: 6–8.

14 Hookham M (1989) Reflections on the Death of Chögyam Trungpa Rinpoche. Raft, the Journal of the Buddhist Hospice Trust. 1: 5–6.

15 The Dalai Lama (1979) Foreword, in L Rinbochay, J Hopkins Death, Intermediate State and Rebirth in Tibetan Buddhism. London: Rider. pp 7–8.

16 Basham AL (1964) Jainism. In RC Zaehner (Ed) The Concise Encyclopaedia of Living Faiths. London: Hutchinson. p 264.

Chapter 4. The Cult of the Ancestors

1 Saunders E Dale (1964) Buddhism in Japan. Philadelphia: University of Pennsylvania Press. pp 264–8.

2 Oguchi I (1955) The Religions of Japan. Past Traditions and Present Tendencies. New York: Intercultural Publications.

3 Picken DB (1980) Shinto. Japan's Spiritual Roots. Tokyo: Kodansha International. p 10–13.

4 Spae J J (1972) Shinto Man. Tokyo: Oriens Institute for Religious Research. p 36.

5 Spae J J (1972) Shinto Man. Tokyo: Oriens Institute for Religious Research. pp 36–9.

6 Yamamoto J, Orongi K, Iswaki T, Kartunnen M (1969) Mourning in Japan. American Journal of Psychiatry 125: 1660–5.

7 Ono S (1962) The Kami Way. Tokyo: Charles E Turtle. pp 56–61.

8 Picken DB (1980) Shinto. Japan's Spiritual Roots. Tokyo: Kodansha. p 32.

9 Baker HDR (1981) Ancestral Images Again. Hong Kong: South China Morning Post Publications Division. p 86.

10 Graham AC (1964) Confucianism. In RC Zaehner (ed.) The Concise Encyclopaedia of Living Faiths. London: Hutchinson. pp 365–6.

11 Baker HDR (1979) Chinese Family and Kinship. London: Macmillan. pp 71–9.

12 Eichhorn W (1964) Taoism. In RC Zaehner (ed.) The Concise Encyclopaedia of Living Faiths. London: Hutchinson. pp 387–8.

13 Sen A (1992) Missing women. British Medical Journal 304: 587–8.

14 Baker HDR (1981) Ancestral Images Again. Hong Kong: South China Morning Post Publications Division. p 86.

15 Baker HDR (1979) Chinese Family and Kinship. London: Macmillan. pp 71–9.

16 August O (2000) Bereaved are all at sea in Shanghai. The Times. 21 April. p 17.

Chapter 5. African and Afro-Caribbean Beliefs and Customs

1 Kirby Reverend E. Personal communication.

2 Smart N (1989) The World's Religions. Cambridge: Cambridge University Press. p 524.

3   Parrinder EG (1954) African Traditional Religion. London: Hutchinson's University Library. p 98.
4   Parrinder EG (1954) African Traditional Religion. London: Hutchinson's University Library. p 67.
5   Mbiti JS (1969) African Religions and Philosophy. London: Heinemann. pp164–65.
6   Creider J T (1986) Two Lives: My Spirit and I. London: The Women's Press. pp 2–7.
7   Mbiti JS (1969) African Religions and Philosophy. London: Heinemann. p 91.
8   Mbiti JS (1969) African Religions and Philosophy. London: Heinemann. pp 82–4.
9   Mbiti JS (1969) African Religions and Philosophy. London: Heinemann. p 155.
10 Mbiti JS (1969) African Religions and Philosophy. London: Heinemann. p 200.
11 Mbiti JS (1969) African Religions and Philosophy. London: Heinemann. pp149–55.
12 Krige EJ (1936) The Social Systems of the Zulus. London: Longmans, Green & Co. pp 159–75.
13 Mbiti JS (1969) African Religions and Philosophy. London: Heinemann. pp 158–9.
14 Mbiti JS (1969) African Religions and Philosophy. London: Heinemann. pp 25–6.
15 Parrinder EG (1974) African Traditional Religions. (3rd ed.). London: Sheldon Press. p 100.
16 Mbiti JS (1969) African Religions and Philosophy. London: Heinemann. pp 144–5.
17 Mbiti JS (1969) African Religions and Philosophy. London: Heinemann. pp 149–65.

Chapter 6. Jewish and Muslim Funeral and Mourning Customs

1   Rabbinowicz Rabbi H (1969) A Guide to Life. Jewish Laws and Customs of Mourning. London: Jewish Chronicle Publications. p 85.
2   Kolatch AJ (1981) The Jewish Book of Why. New York: Jonathan David. pp 70–1.
3   Kolatch AJ (1981) The Jewish Book of Why. New York: Jonathan David. p 55.
4   Goldberg D (1988) The Jewish Way of Death. Jewish Chronicle. 5 February. p 24.
5   Henley A (1982) Asians in Britain: Caring for Muslims and their Families; Religious Aspects of Care. Cambridge: National Extension College. p 67.
6   El Droubie R (1980) Islam. In J Prickett (ed.) Living Faiths. Death. London: Lutterworth Educational. pp 93–4.
7   Lamb C (1985) Belief in a Mixed Society. Tring: Lion Publishing. p 86.

Chapter 7. The Funeral Rites of Christians

1   National Association of Funeral Directing (1981) Manual of Funeral Directing. London: NAFD.
2   Gauld RS (1982) The role of the funeral director. Update. 1st January: pp 85–8.

3   Ottossom K (1980) The Eastern Orthodox Tradition. In J Prickett (ed.) Living Faiths. Death. Guildford: Lutterworth Educational. pp 71–2.
4   Lazor P (1972) Eastern Orthodoxy. In JC Davies (ed.) A Dictionary of Liturgy and Worship. London: SCM Press. p 98.
5   Welbers T (1984) The Rituals of Christian Dying. Modern Liturgy. 11: 2.
6   Cieslak W (1990) Console One Another. Commentary on the Order of Christian Funerals. Washington DC: Pastoral Press. p 28.
7   Jupp P (1997) Unsatisfactory services for the deceased. Church Times. 23 May. p 8.

Chapter 8. New Religions and New Sects

1   Bahá'í Publishing Trust (1992) Becoming a Bahá'í. An Introduction to the Bahá'í Faith and its Teachings. London. pp 38–9.
2   Bahá'u'lláh (1983) Gleanings from the Writings of Bahá'u'lláh. Translated by Shoghi Effendi. Illinois: Bahá'í Publishing Trust. pp 151–71.
3   Hellaby J (2000) Personal communication.
4   Vickers A (1993) Personal communication.
5   Wilkinson P (2000) Personal communication.
6   Main J (1987) The Joy of Being. Daily Readings with John Main. Selected by C Hallward with an introduction by L Freeman. Darton: Longman & Todd. p 11.
7   The Church of Jesus Christ of Latter-day Saints (1998) Brochure provided for visitors to the Preston England Temple.
8   Barrett DV (1996) Sects, Cults and Alternative Religions. London: Cassell. p 85.
9   Harris AD (1992) Mourn Us Not. J Harris (ed.). Surrey: Friends Fellowship of Healing. p 13.
10 Parker PL (1905) George Fox's Journal. First edited by T Ellwood in 1694. Abridged version by PL Parker. London: Pitman pp 494–6.
11 Moseley C (1995) Debrett's Guide to Bereavement. London: Headline. pp 189–91.
12 Larner C (1984) Witchcraft and Religions. London. Basil Blackwell.
13 Corbett PE (1977) On Wings of Spirit. London: The Research Publishing Co. p 34.
14 Pole WT (1960) The Silent Road. London: Neville Spearman. pp 46–56.
15 Greaves H (1969) Testimony of Light. Saffron Walden: Neville Spearman. p 34.

Chapter 9. The Reburial Issue

1   Hubert J (1989) A Proper Place for the Dead: A Critical Review of the Reburial Issue. In R Layton (ed.) Conflict in the Archaeology of Living Traditions. London: Unwin Hyman. pp 131–65.
2   Delamothe T (1991) Aboriginal skeletons in the closet. British Medical Journal 303: 1564.

Chapter 10. Freud, Mourning and Death

1   Bettelheim B (1991) Freud and Man's Soul. London: Penguin. p 37.
2   Freud S (1957) Thoughts for the Times on War and Death. Vol 14 of the Standard Edition of the Complete Psychological Works of Sigmund Freud. Toronto: Hogarth. p 293.
3   Freud S (1983) Totem and Taboo. London: Routledge & Kegan Paul. Ark Paperbacks. pp 51–74.
4   Freud S (1957) Mourning and Melancholia. Vol 14 of The Standard Edition of the Complete Psychological Works of Sigmund Freud. Toronto: Hogarth. pp 237–58
5   Freud S (1957) Thoughts for the Times on War and Death. Vol 14 of The Standard Edition of the Complete Psychological Works of Sigmund Freud. Toronto: Hogarth. pp 292–6.
6   Freud S (1964) The Future of an Illusion. Vol 21 of The Standard Edition of the Complete Psychological Works of Sigmund Freud. Toronto: Hogarth. pp 18–44.
7   Freud S (1964) Civilization and its Discontents. Vol 21 of The Standard Edition of the Complete Psychological Works of Sigmund Freud. Toronto: Hogarth. pp 106–33.
8   Freud S (1964) Theory of the Instincts. Vol 23 of The Standard Edition of the Complete Psychological Works of Sigmund Freud. Toronto: Hogarth. pp 148–150.

Chapter 11. Jung and Self-realization

1   Jung CG (1963) Memories, Dreams and Reflections. London: Routledge & Kegan Paul. pp 270–6.
2   Jung CG (1985) On the Relation of Analytical Psychology to Poetry. In Vol 15 of The Collected Works of CG Jung. London: Routledge & Kegan Paul. p 65.
3   Jung CG (1981) Introduction to Kransfeldt's Secret Ways of the Mind. In Vol 4 of The Collected Works of CG Jung. London: Routledge & Kegan Paul. p 327.
4   McGuire W, Hull RFC (1980) CG Jung Speaking. Interviews and Encounters. London: Pan Books. p 84.
5   Jung CG (1969) Instinct and the Unconscious. In Vol 8 of The Collected Works of CG Jung. London: Routledge & Kegan Paul. pp 133–4.
6   Jung CG (1969) The Soul and Death. In Vol 8 of The Collected Works of CG Jung. London: Routledge & Kegan Paul. pp 404–15.
7   Jacobi J (1967) The Way of Individuation. London: Hodder & Stoughton. p 42.
8   Bennett EA (1966) What Jung Really Said. London: MacDonald. pp 171–4.
9   Jung CG (1981) The Psychology of the Transference. In Vol 16 of The Collected Works of CG Jung. London: Routledge & Kegan Paul. p 184.
10 Jung CG (1981) Answer to Job. In Vol 11 of The Collected Works of CG Jung. London: Routledge & Kegan Paul. p 469.

11 von Franz ML (1987) On Dreams and Death. A Jungian Interpretation. Boston
    and London: Shambhala. pp 24–40.
12 Jung CG (1981) Psychological Commentary on The Tibetan Book of the Great
    Liberation. In Vol 11 of The Collected Works of CG Jung. London: Routledge
    & Kegan Paul. pp 488–91.
13 Jung CG (1963) Memories, Dreams and Reflections. London: Routledge &
    Kegan Paul. pp 290–1.
14 Jung CG (1963) Memories, Dreams and Reflections. London: Routledge &
    Kegan Paul. p 287.
15 Jung CG (1963) Memories, Dreams and Reflections. London: Routledge &
    Kegan Paul. pp 296–7.

Chapter 12. Shakespeare, Death and Grief

1   Steiner Ricardo (1993) Introduction. In R A Paskauskas (Ed). *The Complete
    Correspondence of Sigmund Freud and Ernest Jones 1908–1939*. Cambridge, MA:
    Harvard University Press. p xxiii.
2   Huxley A (1959). *The Perennial Philosophy*. London: Collins. p 123.
3   Davis DR (1968) Personal View. *British Medical Journal*. 555.
4   Jung, C.G. (1985). Psychology and literature. In Vol 15 *The Collected Works of
    C.G. Jung* London: Routledge & Kegan Paul. pp 89–105.
5   Jonson B (17th century) *To the Memory of Shakespeare*.
6   Trelease ML (1957) Dying among Alaskan Indians: A matter of choice. In E
    Kübler-Ross (ed.) *Death, The Final Stage of Growth*. Englewood Cliffs, NJ; Pren-
    tice–Hall. pp 33–7.

Chapter 13. Dying: the Last Months

1   Rees WD (1990) Opioid needs of terminal care patients; variations with age and
    primary site. Clinical Oncology 2: 79–83.
2   Kübler-Ross E (1990) On Death and Dying. London: Tavistock Publications.
3   Kübler-Ross E (1990) To Live Until We Say Goodbye. Englewood Cliffs, NJ.
    Prentice-Hall. pp 18–19.
4   Frankl V (1987) Man's Search for Meaning. An Introduction to Logotherapy.
    London: Hodder & Stoughton.
5   Phillips DP, King EW (1988) Death takes a holiday: mortality surrounding
    major social occasions. The Lancet 11: 728–32.
6   Phillips DP, Smith DG (1990) Postponement of death until symbolically mean-
    ingful occasions. Journal of the American Medical Association 14: 1947–51.
7   Imara M (1978) Dying as the last stage of growth. In E Kübler-Ross (ed.) Death
    The Final Stage of Growth. Englewood Cliffs, NJ: Prentice-Hall. pp 160–2.
8   Rees WD (1972) The distress of dying. British Medical Journal 3: 105–7.
9   Hinton JM (1963) The physical and mental distress of dying. Quarterly Journal
    of Medicine 32: 1.
10 Burton SW (1987) The psychiatry of HIV infection. British Medical Journal
    295: 228–9.
11 Carne CA (1987) ABC of AIDS. Neurological manifestations. British Medical
    Journal 294: 1399–401.

12 Christakis NA, Lamont EB (2000) Extent and determinants of error in doctors' prognoses in terminally ill patients: prospective cohort study. British Medical Journal 320: 469–72.
13 Smith J (2000) Commentary: Why do doctors overestimate. British Medical Journal 320: 472–3.
14 Parkes CM (2000) Commentary: Prognoses should be based on proved indices not intuition. British Medical Journal 320: 473.

Chapter 14. Caring for the Dying

1   Stedeford A (1984) Facing Death. Patients and Professionals. London: William Heinemann Medical. p 25.
2   Hinton J (1994) Which patients with terminal cancer are admitted from home care? Palliative Medicine 8: 197–210.
3   Crispell KR (1987) Proper care for the dying: a critical public health issue. Journal of Medical Ethics 13: 74–80.
4   Dover SB (1987) Syringe driver in terminal care. British Medical Journal 294: 553–5.
5   Age Health and Care Study Group (1999) The Future of Health and Care of Older People: The Best is Yet to Come. London. Age Concern.
6   Grogono J (2000) A good death. British Medical Journal 320: 1205.
7   Bosch X (2000) Spain launches national plan for palliative care. British Medical Journal 320: 1162.
8   Fowell A, Finlay 1 (2000) A good death. British Medical Journal 320: 1206.

Chapter 15. Bereavement: The Basics

1   Holy Bible (King James Version) Exodus 22:22. London: Eyre & Spottiswoode.
2   Holy Bible (King James Version) Deuteronomy 14:29. London: Eyre & Spottiswoode.
3   Frazer JG (1922) The Golden Bough (abridged version). London: Macmillan. p 207.
4   Lindemann E (1944) The symptomatology and management of acute grief. American Journal of Psychiatry 101:141.
5   Bowlby J (1961) Processes of mourning. International Journal of Psychoanalysis 44: 317–40.
6   Bowlby J (1985) Attachment and Loss: Vol 3. Loss: Sadness and Depression. London: Penguin. p 85.
7   Parkes CM (1970) The first year of bereavement. A longitudinal study of the reaction of London widows to the death of their husbands. Psychiatry 444–67.
8   Parkes CM (1986) Bereavement. Studies of Grief in Adult Life. London: Penguin. pp 60–4.
9   Parkes CM (1970) Seeking and finding a lost object. Evidence from recent studies of the reaction to bereavement. Social Science and Medicine 4: 187–201.
10 Bowlby J (1961) Process of mourning. International Journal of Psychoanalysis 42: 317.

11 Bowlby J (1985) Attachment and Loss. Vol 3. Loss: Sadness and Depression. London: Penguin. pp 98–100.

12 Freud EL (1961) Letters of Sigmund Freud (ed.). New York: Basic Books. p 386.

13 Gay P (1988) Freud. A Life for Our Time. London: PAPERMAC. p 422.

14 Worden JW (1991) Grief Counselling and Grief Therapy. (2nd ed.). London: Routledge. p 35.

15 Freud S (1983) Totem and Taboo. London: Ark Paperbacks. pp 51–74.

16 Worden JW (1991) Grief Counselling and Grief Therapy. (2nd ed.). London: Routledge. pp 10–18.

17 Rees WD (1984) Making contact with the recently bereaved. The Practitioner 228: 309–12.

18 John A (1964) Finishing Touches. London: Jonathan Cape.

19 Birtchnell N (1975) Psychiatric breakdown following recent parent death. British Journal of Mental Psychology 48: 379–90.

20 Parkes CM (1986) Bereavement. Studies of Grief in Adult Life. London: Penguin Books. p 129.

21 Ironson G et al. (1997) Post-traumatic stress symptoms, intrusive thoughts, loss, and immune function after Hurricane Andrew. Psychosomatic Medicine 59: 128–41.

22 Schleifer SJ, Keller SE, Camerino M (1983) Suppression of lymphocyte stimulation following bereavement. Journal of the American Medical Association 250: 374–77.

23 Irwin M, Weiner H (1987) Depressive symptoms and immune function during bereavement. In S Zisook (ed.) Biopsychosocial Aspects of Bereavement. Washington DC: American Psychiatric Association Press. pp 157–74.

24 Jacobs SC (1987) Psychoendocrine aspects of bereavement. In S Zisook (ed.) Biopsychosocial Aspects of Bereavement. Washington DC: American Psychiatric Association Press. pp 139–55.

25 Kim K, Jacobs S (1993) Bereavement and neuroendocrines. In MS Stroebe, W Stroebe, RO Hansson (eds) Handbook of Bereavement. Theory, Research and Innovation. New York: Cambridge University Press. pp 143–58.

Chapter 16. Bereavement: Medical and Social Issues

1   Engel GL (1961) Grief as a disease process. Psychosomatic Medicine 23: 18.

2   Gay P (1988) Freud. A Life for Our Time. London: PAPERMAC. p 422.

3   Malcolm JA, Dobson AJ (1989) Marriage is associated with a low risk of ischaemic heart disease in men. Medical Journal of Australia 151: 185–8.

4   Maddison D (1969) The consequences of conjugal bereavement. Nursing Times 65: 50–2.

5   Marris P (1958) Widows and Their Families. London: Routledge & Kegan Paul. pp 14 and 22.

6   Parkes CM (1964) The effects of bereavement on physical and mental health. British Medical Journal 2: 274.

7   Stroebe W, Stroebe MS (1993) Determinants of adjustment to bereavement. In MS Stroebe, W Stroebe, RO Hansson (eds) Handbook of Bereavement. Theory, Research and Intervention. New York: Cambridge University Press. pp 208–26.

8   Gallagher-Thompson D et al. (1993) The impact of spousal bereavement on older widows and widowers. In MS Stroebe, W Stroebe RO Hansson (eds) Handbook of Bereavement. Theory, Research and Intervention. New York: Carabridge University Press. pp 227–39.

9   Zisook S, Schucter SR, Lyons LE, (1987) Adjustment to widowhood. In S Zisook (ed.) Biopsychosocial Aspects of Bereavement. Washington DC: American Psychiatric Association Press. pp 51–74.

10 Rees WD, Lutkins SG (1967) Mortality of bereavement. British Medical Journal 4: 13–16.

11 Clayton P (1974) Mortality in the first year of widowhood. Archives of General Psychiatry 30: 747–50.

12 Stroebe MS, Stroebe W (1993) The mortality of bereavement. In MS Stroebe W Stroebe, RO Hansson (eds) Handbook of Bereavement. Theory, Research and Intervention. New York: Cambridge University Press. pp 175–95.

13 Helsing KJ, Szklo M (1981) Mortality after bereavement. American Journal of Epidemiology 114: 41–52.

14 World Health Organization (1998) World Health Statistics Annual. Geneva: WHO.

15 Wortman CB, Silver RC, Kessler R (1993) The meaning of loss and adjustment to bereavement. In MS Stroebe, W Stroebe, RO Hansson (eds) Handbook of Bereavement. Theory, Research and Intervention. New York: Cambridge University Press. pp 349–66.

16 Lopata HZ (1993) The support systems of American widows. In MS Stroebe, W Stroebe, RO Hansson (eds) Handbook of Bereavement. Theory, Research and Intervention. New York: Cambridge University Press. pp 381–96.

17 Charlton R, Dolman E (1995) Bereavement: a protocol for primary care. British Journal of General Practice 45: 427–30.

18 Rees WD (1984) Making contact with the recently bereaved. The Practitioner 228: 309–11.

19 Garb R, Bleich A, Lever B (1987) Bereavement in combat. In Zisook S (ed.) the Psychiatric Clinics of North America, Vol 10, No 3, Grief and Bereavement. Philadelphia. WB Saunders. pp 421–36.

20 Penman I (1989) Track of Truth. A Report on Return from Vietnam: Everyman, BBC1 TV. The Independent. 3 April.

21 Goldstein RD, Wampler NS, Wise PH (1997) War experiences and distress symptoms of Bosnian children. Pediatrics. 100: 873–7.

22 Kaminer H, Lavie P (1993) Sleep and dreams in well-adjusted and less-adjusted Holocaust survivors. In MS Stroebe, W Stroebe, RO Hansson (eds) Handbook of Bereavement. Theory, Research and Intervention. New York: Cambridge University Press. pp 331–45.

23 Osterweiss M, Solomon F, Green M (1984) Bereavement: Reactions, Consequences and Care. A Report of the Institute of Medicine, National Academy of Sciences. Washington. DC: National Academy Press. pp 99–141.

24 Shapiro F (1995) Eye Movement Desensitisation and Reprocessing. Basic Principles, Protocols and Procedures. New York: The Guildford Press.

25 Botkin AL (2000) The induction of after-death communications using eye-movement desensitization and reprocessing: a new discovery. Journal of Near-Death Studies 18: 181–209.

Chapter 17. The Death of a Child

1   Hall RCW, Beresford TP, Quinones JE (1987) Grief following spontaneous abortion. In Zisook S (ed.) The Psychiatric Clinics of North America, Vol 10, No 3 Grief and Bereavement. Philadelphia: WB Saunders. pp 405–20.

2   McAll K, Wilson WP (1987) Ritual mourning for unresolved grief. Southern Medical Journal 80: 817–21.

3   Seller MJ (1982) Ethical aspects of genetic counselling. Journal of Medical Ethics 8: 185–8.

4   Shepperdson B (1983) Abortion and euthanasia of Downs syndrome children. Journal of Medical Ethics 9: 152–7.

5   Lewis E, Bourne S (1989) Perinatal Death. In MR Oates (ed.) Baillière's Clinical Obstetrics and Gynaecology, Vol 3, No 4. London: Baillière-Tindall. pp 935–53.

6   Wolf JR, Nielson PE, Schiller P (1970) The emotional reactions to a stillbirth. American Journal of Obstetrics and Gynaecology 108(1): 73–7.

7   Forrest GC, Claridge RS, Baum JD (1981) Practical management of perinatal death. British Medical Journal 282: 31–2.

8   Royal College of Obstetricians and Gynaecologists (1985) Report of the Working Party on the Management of Perinatal Deaths. London.

9   Armstrong H. (1995) There is now a place to grieve. British Medical Journal 311: 1098–99.

10 Mitchell E (1999) Commentary: Cot deaths – the story so far. British Medical Journal 319: 1461–2.

11 Blair PS et al. (1999) Babies sleeping with parents: Case control study of factors influencing the risk of sudden infant death syndrome. British Medical Journal 319: 1457–61.

12 Harman W (1981) Death of my baby. British Medical Journal 282: 35–7.

13 Emery JL (1985) Infanticide, filicide and cot deaths. Archives of Disease in Childhood 60: 505–7.

14 Reder P, Duncan S (2000) In 1994, 29% of suspicious deaths were officially recorded as due to sudden infant death syndrome. British Medical Journal 320: 311.

15 Emery JL, Waites AJ (2000) These deaths must be prevented without victimizing parents. British Medical Journal 320: 310.

16 Foundation for the Study of Infant Deaths (1998) Report on 5000 babies using CONI (Care Of Next Infant programme). London: FSID.

17 Rubin SS (1993) The death of a child is for ever: The life course impact of child loss. In MS Stroebe, W Stroebe, RO Hansson (eds) Handbook of Bereavement. Theory, Research and Intervention. New York: Cambridge University Press. pp 285–99.

18 Baldock I (1995) Stephen. In E Mirren (ed.) Our Children. London: Hodder & Stoughton. pp 55–63.

19 Cooke MH, Cooke HM, Glucksman EE (1992) Management of sudden bereavement in the accident and emergency department. British Medical Journal 304: 1207–9.

20 Yates DW, Ellison G, McGuiness S (1990) Care of the suddenly bereaved. British Medical Journal 301: 29–31.

Chapter 18. A Child's Response to Death

1   Lansdowne R (1985) The development of the concept of death in bereaved children. Bereavement Care. Published by Cruse, the National Organization for the Widowed and their Children. 4: 15–17.
2   Goodall J (1980) Suffering in Childhood. The 1979 Barnardo Lecture. London: Christian Medical Fellowship Publications. p 14.
3   Goodall J (1980) Suffering in Childhood. The 1979 Barnardo Lecture. London: Christian Medical Fellowship Publications. p 18.
4   Stickney D (1982) Waterbugs and Dragonflies – Explaining Death to Children. London: Mowbray.
5   Silverman PR, Worden J W (1993) Children's reactions to the death of a parent. In MS Stroebe, W Stroebe, RO Hansson (eds) Handbook of Bereavement. Theory, Research and Intervention. New York: Cambridge University Press. p 309.
6   Osterweis M, Solomon F, Green M (1984) Bereavement: Reactions, Consequence and Care. A Report of the Institute of Medicine, National Academy of Science. Washington DC: National Academy Press. p116.
7   Silverman PR, Worden JW (1993) Children's reactions to the death of a parent. In MS Stroebe, W Stroebe, RO Hansson (eds) Handbook of Bereavement. Theory, Research and Intervention. New York: Cambridge University Press. p 315.
8   Pettle MSA, Lansdowne RG (1986) Adjustment to the death of a sibling. Archives of Disease in Childhood 61: 278–83.
9   Elizur E, Kaffman M (1982) Factors affecting the severity of childhood bereavement reactions following the death of a father. Journal of the American Academy of Child Psychiatry 21: 474–80.
10 Kaffman M, Elizur E (1983) Bereavement response of kibbutz and non-kibbutz children following the death of a father. Journal of Child Psychology and Child Psychiatry 24: 435–42.
11 Rutter M (1986) Bereaved Children. In Children of Sick Parents. Maudsley Monograph XV1. London: Oxford University Press. pp 66–75.
12 Van Eerdewegh M, Bieri M, Parilla R, Clayton P (1982) The bereaved child. British Journal of Psychiatry 140: 23–9.
13 Cain A, Fast I, Erickson M (1964) Children's disturbed reactions to the death of a sibling. American Journal of Orthopsychiatry 34: 741–52.
14 Osterweiss M, Solomon F, Green M (1984) Bereavement: Reactions, Consequence and Care. Washington DC: National Academy Press. p 116.
15 Black D (1983) Children may benefit from help in mourning. Modern Medicine. February: 13.
16 Kitchener S, Pennells MA (1990) A bereavement group for children. Bereavement Care. Published by Cruse the National Organization for the Widowed and their Children 19(3): 30–1.
17 Pennells M, Smith S, Poppleton R (1992) Bereavement and adolescents – groupwork approach. Newsletter. Association of Child Psychology and Psychiatry 14(2): 173–8.
18 Kmietowicz Z (2000) More services needed for bereaved children. British Medical Journal 320: 893.

19 Chaudhuri A (2000) Studies in mortality. The Times. 2 February.
20 Dyregrov A (1991) Grief in Children. A Handbook for Adults. London: Jessica Kingsley Publishers. pp 52–4.
21 Sedgwick M (2000) Personal communication.
22 Mearns MB (1986) Special problems for teenagers with cystic fibrosis. Journal of the Royal Society of Medicine. Supplement No 12 79: 51–4.
23 Martinson IM, Enos M (1985) The dying child at home. In Corr CA, Corr DM (eds) Hospice approaches to paediatric care. New York: Springer. pp 65–86.

Chapter 19. Suicide

1   Roy A, Segal NL, Centerwall BS, Robinette CD (1991) Suicide in twins. Archives of General Psychiatry 48: 29–32.
2   Durkheim E (1952) Suicide: a study in sociology. London: Routledge & Kegan Paul.
3   Orr D (2000) Suicide bomb kills 12 in Columbo. The Times. 6 January: p 16.
4   Zinn C (1995) South Pacific leads the world in rates of youth suicide. British Medical Journal 311: 830.
5   Smith R (1991) Taken from this place and hanged by the neck. British Medical Journal 302: 64–5.
6   Fairbairn GJ (1995) Contemplating Suicide. London: Routledge. pp 125–37.
7   O'Donnell I, Farmer R (1995) The limitations of official suicide statistics. British Journal of Psychiatry 166: 458–61.
8   World Health Organization (1998) World health statistics annual. Geneva: WHO.
9   Samson C, Wilson J, Mazower J (1999) Canada's Tibet the killing of the Innu. *Survival*. England. Survival International. pp 5–7
10 Yamey G (2000) Suicide rate is decreasing in England and Wales. British Medical Journal 320: 75.
11 McClure GMG (2000) Changes in suicide in England and Wales 1960–1997. British Journal of Psychiatry 176: 64–7.
12 (1996) Health Line 38:14–16.
13 Allebeck P, Allgulander C, Fisher LD (1988) Predictors of completed suicide in a cohort of 50,465 young men. British Medical Journal 279: 176–9.
14 Platt S (1984) Unemployment and suicidal behaviour – a review of the literature. Social Science Medicine 19: 93–115.
15 Lewis G, Sloggett A (1998) Suicide, deprivation and unemployment: record linkage study. British Medical Journal 317:1283–6.
16 Kendall RE (1991) Suicide in pregnancy and the puerperium. British Medical Journal 302: 126–7.
17 Jacobson B, Bygdeman M (1998) Obstetric care and proneness of offspring to suicide as adults: case control study. British Medical Journal 317:1346–49.
18 Salk L, Lipsitt LP, Sturner WQ, Reilly BM, Levat RH (1985) Relationship of maternal and perinatal conditions to eventual adolescent suicide. Lancet i: 624–7.
19 Appleby L (1998) Violent suicide and obstetric complications. British Medical Journal 317: 1333–4.
20 Brown M, Barraclough B (1997) Epidemiology of suicide pacts in England and Wales, 1988–92. British Medical Journal 315:

21 Gunnell D, Frankel S (1994) Prevention of suicide: aspirations and evidence. British Medical Journal 308: 1227–33.
22 Stroebe MS, W Stroebe (1993) The mortality of bereavement: A review. In MS Stroebe, W Stroebe, RO Hansson (eds) Handbook of Bereavement. Theory, Research and Intervention. New York: Cambridge University Press. p187.
23 Stengel E (1973) Suicide and Attempted Suicide. London: Penguin. p103.
24 Baker H (1981) Ancestral Images Again. Hong Kong: South China Morning Post Publications. p150.
25 Fusé T (1980) Suicide and culture in Japan. Social Psychiatry 15: 57–63.
26 Gallagher-Thompson D *et al.* (1993) The impact of spousal bereavement on older widows and widowers. In MS Stroebe, W Stroebe, RO Hansson (eds) Handbook of Bereavement. Theory, Research and Intervention. New York: Cambridge University Press. pp 233–5.
27 Hughes F (1999) Interview with Libby Purves. *The Times*. 28 December. pp 28, 30.
28 Merrill J, Edwards S (1989) Attempted suicide in the elderly. Update, September: 373–5.

Chapter 20. Euthanasia and Assisted Suicide

1   British Medical Association (1998) Euthanasia and physician assisted-suicide: Do the moral arguments differ. A discussion paper from the BMA's Medical Ethics Department.
2   Goldberg RT (1987) 'The Right to Die': the case for and against voluntary passive euthanasia. Disability, Handicap and Society 2: 21–38.
3   Rigter H, Borst EE, Leemen HJ (1988) Euthanasia across the North Sea. British Medical Journal 297: 1593–5.
4   Sheldon T (2000) Belgium considers legalising euthanasia. British Medical Journal 320: 137.
5   Leo A (1949) Medical science under dictatorship. New England Journal of Medicine 241: 39–47.
6   Forster M (1989) Alzheimer's: slow death in Dickensian squalor. Sunday Times. 19 November.
7   Caucanas-Pisier P (1986) Speech given at the Sheraton Crystal City Hotel, Washington DC. 26 September.
8   McLean S, Britton A (1986) Sometimes A Small Victory. Glasgow University (commissioned by the Scottish Voluntary Euthanasia Society but carried out by an independent Agency).
9   House of Lords (1994) Report of the Select Committee on Medical Ethics. London: HMSO.
10 Zinn C (1997) Australian voluntary euthanasia law is overturned. British Medical Journal 314: 994.
11 Helme T (1991) The Voluntary Euthanasia (Legislation) Bill (1936) revisited. Journal of Medical Ethics 17: 25–9.
12 Dorozinski A (1992) Euthanasia around the world – France. British Medical Journal 304: 7–10.
13 Hellema H (1992) Euthanasia around the world – Netherlands. British Medical Journal 304: 7–10.
14 Remmelink Commission (1991) English precis of the Remmelink Commission's Report. London: The Royal Netherlands Embassy.

15 Leading article (2000) Where the 'right to die' is open, and disturbing. The Times. 26 February.

16 Sheldon T (1995) Judges make historic ruling on euthanasia. British Medical Journal 309: 7–8.

17 Van der Wal (1996) Euthanasia, physician assisted-suicide and other medical practices involving the end of life in the Netherlands, 1990–1995. New England Journal of Medicine 335: 1699–705.

18 Battin MP (1992) Assisted Suicide: can we learn from Germany? Hastings Center Reports 22(2): 44–51.

19 von Koelichen J (2000) personal communication.

20 Back AL, Wallace JI, Starks HE, Pearlman RA (1996) Physician assisted suicide and euthanasia in Washington state. Journal of the American Medical Association 275: 919–25.

21 McDaniel C-G (1996) US patients seek doctors help in suicides. British Medical Journal 312: 865–6.

22 Roberts J (1996) Kevorkian cleared again. British Medical Journal 312: 656.

23 Churchill LR, King NP (1997) Physician assisted suicide, euthanasia, or withdrawal of treatment. British Medical Journal, 315: 137–8.

24 Wineburg H (2000) Oregon's death with dignity act: 14 months and counting. Archives of Internal Medicine 160: 21–3.

25 British Medical Association (1995) Advance Statements About Medical Treatments. London: BMJ Publishing Group.

26 Docker C (2000) Decisions to withdraw treatment. British Medical Journal 320: 54.

Chapter 21. The Death of a Pet

1   Lee L, Lee M (1992) Absent Friend. Coping with the Loss of a Treasured Pet. High Wycombe: Henston. pp 134–5.

2   Moseley C (1995) Debrett's Guide to Bereavement. London: Headline Book Publishing Company. pp 298–300.

Chapter 22. The Bereaved and the Living-Dead

1   Botkin AL (2000) The induction of after-death communication utilizing eye-movement desensitization and reprocessing: a new discovery. Journal of Near-Death Studies 18: 181–209.

2   Mbiti JS (1969) African Religions and Philosophy. London: Heinemann. pp 82–91.

3   Lindemann E (1944) The symptomatology and management of acute grief. American Journal of Psychiatry 101: 141.

4   Gorer G (1965) Death, Grief and Mourning. London: The Cresset Press.

5   Parkes CM (1970) The first year of bereavement. Psychiatry 33: 444–67.

6   Marris P (1958) Widows and Their Families. London: Routledge & Kegan Paul. p 22.

7   Yamamoto J, Okonogi K, Inasak T, Yoshimura S (1969) Mourning in Japan. American Journal of Psychiatry 125: 1660–5.

8   Society for Psychical Research (1894) Report on the Census of Hallucinations by Professor Sidgwick's Committee. Proceedings of the Society for Psychical Research. London: Kegan Paul, Trench, Trübner & Co.

9 Rees WD (1971) The Hallucinatory Reactions of Bereavement. MD thesis. University of London Library.

10. Caine TM, Hope K (1967) Manual of the Hysteroid-Obsessoid Questionnaire. London: University of London Press.

11 Rees WD (1971) The hallucinations of widowhood. British Medical Journal 4: 37–41.

12 Hay D (1987) Exploring Inner Space. London: Mowbray. pp 123–55.

13 Kalish RA, Reynolds DK (1974) Widows view death: A brief research note. Omega 5(2): 187–92.

14 Greeley A M (1975) The Sociology of the Paranormal: A Reconnaissance. Beverley Hills: Sage Publications. p 29.

15 Haraldsson E (1988) Survey of claimed encounters with the dead. Omega 19(2): 103–13.

16 Glick IO, Weiss RS, Parkes CM (1974) The First Year of Bereavement. New York: John Wiley/Interscience.

17 Rogo D S (1986) Life After Death. Wellingborough: The Aquarian Press. p 81.

18 Olson PR, Suddeth JA, Peterson PA, Egelhoff C (1985) Hallucinations of widowhood. Journal of the American Geriatric Society 33: 543–7.

19 Schucter SR, Zisook S (1993) The course of normal grief. In MS Stroebe, W Stroebe, RO Hansson (eds) Handbook of Bereavement. Theory, Research and Intervention. New York: Cambridge University Press. pp 23–43.

20 Kalish RA, Reynolds DK (1983) Phenomenological reality and post-death contact. Journal for the Scientific Study of Religions 12: 209–21.

21 Bowlby J (1985) Attachment and Loss: Vol 3: Sadness and Depression. London: Penguin. pp 96–100.

22 Bowlby J (1985) Attachment and Loss: Vol 3: Sadness and Depression. London: Penguin. p 87.

23 Parkes CM (1969). Separation anxiety: an aspect of the search for a lost object. The British Journal of Psychiatry Special Publication No 3. pp 87–92.

24 Parkes CM (1986). Bereavement. Studies of Grief in Adult Life. London: Penguin. pp 77–96.

25 Lewis CS (1961) A Grief Observed. London: Faber.

Chapter 23. Near-death Experiences

1 Moody RA (1975) Life after Life. New York: Bantam. pp 71–73.

2 Barrett Sir W (1926) Death-Bed Visions. Wellingborough: The Aquarian Press.

3 Osis K, Haraldsson E (1977) Deathbed observations by physicians and nurses: a cross-cultural survey. The Journal of the American Society for Psychical Research 71: 238–59.

4 Grey M (1985) Return from the Dead. London: Arkana.

5 Roberts G, Owen J (1988) The near-death experience. British Journal of Psychiatry 153: 607–17.

6 Zaleski C (1987) Otherworld Journeys. Accounts of Near-Death Experiences in Medieval and Modern Times. New York: Oxford University Press. pp 163–4.

7 Jung CG (1963) Memories, Dreams, Reflections. Recorded and edited by Aniela Jaffe. London: Collins/Routledge & Kegan Paul. pp 270–7.

8 Moody RA (1989) The Light Beyond. London: Pan. p 154.

9 Appleby L (1989) Near-death experiences. British Medical Journal 298: 976–7.
10 Morse M, Castillo P, Venetia D, Milstein J, Tyler TC (1986) Childhood near-death experiences. American Journal of the Diseases of Childhood 140: 1110–14.
11 Dobson M (1971) Attitudes and long-term adjustment of patients surviving cardiac arrest. British Medical Journal 3: 207–12.
12 Duss RG, Kornfeld DS (1967) The survivors of cardiac arrest. Journal of the American Medical Association 201: 291–6.
13 Gallup G Jr, Proctor W (1982) Adventures in Immortality: A Look Beyond the Threshold of Death. New York: McGraw-Hill.
14 Livingstone D (1872) Adventures and Discoveries in the Interior of Africa. Philadelphia: Hubbard.
15 Rees WD (1990) Opioid needs of terminal care patients: variations with age and primary site. Clinical Oncology 2: 79–83.
16 Young B (1985) Personal view. British Medical Journal 290: 1975.
17 Rawlings M (1979) Beyond Death's Door. London: Sheldon Press. pp 102–20.
18 Greyson B (1985) A typology of near-death experiences. American Journal of Psychiatry 142: 967–8.
19 Morse M, Perry P (1992) Transformed by Light. London: Piatkus. pp 58, 220–4.
20 Ayer AJ (1989) That undiscovered country. New Humanist May: 10–13.
21 Teilhard de Chardin P (1959) The Phenomenon of Man. London: Collins. p 57.
22 Siegel RK (1980) The psychology of life after death. American Psychologist 10: 911–31.
23 Soners M, Keena J FW, Eckard W (1988) Phencyclidine and psychotimetic sigma opiates: recent insights into their biochemical and physiological sites of action. TINS 1: 37–40.
24 Foster AC, Fagg GE (1987) Taking apart NMDA receptors. Nature 329: 395–6.
25 Jansen K (1989) Near-death experiences and the NMDA receptor. British Medical Journal 298: 1708.

Chapter 24. The Significance of Death

1 Jung CG (1985) The Spirit in Man, Art and Literature. Vol 15 in The Collected Works of CG Jung. London: Routledge & Kegan Paul. pp 70–6.
2 Freud S (1957) Thoughts for the Times on War and Death. Vol 14 of The Standard Edition of the Complete Psychological Works of Sigmund Freud. London: Hogarth. p 296.
3 Merchant M (1990) Fragments of a Life. Dyfed: Gomer. p 236.
4 Owen W (1974) War Poems and Others. London: Chatto & Windus. p 76.
5 Spence Sir B (1962) Phoenix at Coventry. The Building of a Cathedral. London: Geoffrey Bless. p 72.
6 Merton T (1975) The Seven Storey Mountain. London: Sheldon. pp 111–12.
7 Schopenhauer A (1983) In Sigmund Freud Totem and Taboo. London: Ark Paperbacks. p 87.

Index